Entrepreneurship

CREATING A VENTURE

About the cover

Entrepreneurs see opportunities where most people see problems; patterns where others see only pieces of a puzzle. Entrepreneurs envision the shape of the enterprise, then focus on success and take action.

Each jigsaw puzzle piece on the cover contains the picture of an entrepreneur you will discuss or read about during your course work. Very few of you will be able to identify any of these people. That is not surprising. Most entrepreneurs work behind the scenes; making things happen their way; getting the various parts of their enterprises organized; putting the pieces of their ventures together.

Each entrepreneur on the cover is also pictured in the text. As you work through the text, you will come across them and learn about their particular entrepreneurial efforts. Create a chart like this one. Fill it in as you work through the course. When your chart is completed, you will have a clearer picture of how entrepreneurs solve the puzzles that most of us struggle with.

NAME	VENTURE	OUTCOME
name of the entrepreneur	description of the venture	What were the results of the venture? Was anyone helped? Were our lives changed in any way? Was the entrepreneur successful in terms of money? personal satisfaction? helping others become successful?

Entrepreneurship
CREATING A VENTURE

M. LILY KRETCHMAN
Peel Board of Education
Mississauga, Ontario

LORI CRANSON
David & Mary Thomson Collegiate
Scarborough, Ontario

BILL JENNINGS
Frontenac Secondary School
Kingston, Ontario

JOHN WILEY & SONS

Toronto New York Chichester Brisbane Singapore

While every effort has been taken to include accurate and up-to-date **information** about the creation of a venture, the authors and the publisher recommend that members of the legal, financial, and business fields be consulted for professional advice before any major venture is launched.

Canadian Cataloguing in Publication Data

Kretchman, M. Lily, 1932-
Entrepreneurship : creating a venture

ISBN 0-471-79565-8

1. Entrepreneurship. 2. New business enterprises.
1. Cranson, Lori. 11.Jennings, William E.,
1945- . 111. Title.

HD62.5.K74 1990 658.1'1 C89-090638-6

PRODUCTION CREDITS

ACQUISITIONS EDITOR: Joseph Gladstone
MANAGING EDITOR: Lee Makos
DEVELOPMENTAL EDITOR: Vivien Young
PRODUCTION EDITOR: Linda Scott
EDITORIAL ASSISTANT: Elizabeth McCurdy
DESIGN: Brant Cowie/ArtPlus Limited
PAGE MAKE UP: Dale Bateman/ArtPlus Limited
TYPE OUTPUT: TypeLine Express Limited
ILLUSTRATOR: David Shaw

Printed and bound in Canada by John Deyell Company
10 9 8 7 6 5 4 3

Text and Photo Credits

Text Credits (Venture Profiles)

Chapter 1: pp. 4-5, 6-7: The *Toronto Star* Syndicate; p. 14: *The Globe and Mail*; **Chapter 2:** pp. 34-35: Rod McQueen, *Canadian Business*; pp. 37-38: The *Toronto Star* Syndicate; pp. 54-55: David Silburt, *Canadian Business*; **Chapter 4:** p. 120: Youth Employment Skills Canada; **Chapter 5:** pp. 128-129: The *Toronto Star* Syndicate; pp. 132-133: *The Chicago Tribune*; **Chapter 6:** p. 154: Paul Lebel, *The Globe and Mail*; pp. 176-177: Robert Hough, *The Financial Post*, "Moneywise Magazine"; pp. 177-178: Arnold Edinborough, *The Financial Post*; **Chapter 7:** pp. 184-185: Paul McLaughlin, *Canadian Business*; **Chapter 8:** pp. 222-225: Larry Krotz, *Canadian Business*; pp. 233-234: Cathy Hilborn, *Small Business Magazine*; **Chapter 9:** pp. 258-259: The *Toronto Star* Syndicate; pp. 280-282: Nathan Rudyk, *Small Business Magazine*; pp. 284-285: The *Toronto Star* Syndicate; **Chapter 11:** pp. 322-324: Marie Mendenhall, *Saskatchewan Business*; pp. 331-332: Mary Ann Prychoda, *Small Business Magazine*; pp. 341-342: *The Globe and Mail*, "Report on Business"; pp. 350-351: Brenda Spiering, *The Financial Post*, "Moneywise Magazine"; **Chapter 13:** p. 394: Tim Falconer, *Canadian Business*; **Chapter 14:** pp. 434-435: Philip Mathias, *The Financial Post*; pp. 436-437: Steve Kruegber, *The Globe and Mail*.

Photo Credits

Chapter 1: pp. 4, 6: The *Toronto Star* Syndicate; p. 8: Canapress; p. 14: E.D. Smith & Sons; **Chapter 2:** p. 34: Canapress; p. 37: The *Toronto Star* Syndicate; p. 42: Universal Press Syndicate; p. 47: Ashleigh Brilliant; p. 54: David Lawrence; **Chapter 3:** p. 60: Ron Foxcroft; p. 60: Proshred Security; p. 64: Musée J.A. Bombardier; p. 78: Lily Kretchman; **Chapter 4:** p. 98: Sony of Canada Ltd.; p. 101: The Famous People Players; p. 118: Statistics Canada; p. 120: Youth Employment Skills Canada; **Chapter 5:** p. 128: The *Toronto Star* Syndicate; p. 132: The Chicago Tribune; **Chapter 6:** p. 174: John Wiley and Sons Canada Ltd.; p. 176: The *Toronto Star* Syndicate; **Chapter 7:** p. 201: Ford Motor Company of Canada Ltd.; **Chapter 8:** p. 222: Alan McTavish; p. 231: John Wiley and Sons Canada Ltd.; p. 242: Mountain Equipment Co-op; p. 252: Robert Karpa; **Chapter 9:** p. 258: The *Toronto Star* Syndicate; p. 265: The British Tourist Authority; p. 272: Canapress; p. 278: John Wiley & Spns Canada Ltd.; p. 284: The *Toronto Star* Syndicate; p. 286: Marg Stewart; The Great Atlantic and Pacific Company of Canada; Lever Brothers Inc.; **Chapter 10:** p. 292: The Whig Standard; **Chapter 11:** p. 322: Marie Mendenhall, *Saskatchewan Business*; p. 331: Canapress; p. 338: The Canadian Imperial Bank of Commerce; p. 339: DUCA Community Credit Union; p. 341: Alex Meyboom; p. 350: Robin Wong; **Chapter 12:** p. 365: Canapress; p. 381; Patricia Barry Levy; **Chapter 13:** p. 394: John Douglas Kenny; **Chapter 14:** p. 423: Northern Telecom Canada Ltd.; p. 436: *The Citizen* (Kipling, Sask.)

Acknowledgements

We wish to thank the entrepreneurs who, through their adventures, provided a great deal of the direction for this book. Our thanks also go to the students at David and Mary Thomson Collegiate and at Frontenac Secondary School, who tested the ideas and material in the text and who became enthusiastic entrepreneurs.

We acknowledge the special efforts of our editors, Vivien Young and Linda Scott. The successful publication of this text owes much to the important contribution made by the people at John Wiley & Sons Canada Limited: Joseph Gladstone, Lee Makos, Elizabeth McCurdy, Jeffrey Aberle, Zane Kaneps, and Deborah Starks.

In addition, we thank the following reviewers for their professional evaluations and thoughtful suggestions:

Wayne Trail, *Vice-Principal, Moncton High School, New Brunswick*

Kris Munt, *Red River Community College, Winnipeg, Manitoba*

William Liabotis, *Mohawk College, Hamilton, Ontario*

Carmella D'Elia, *Co-ordinator of Business Studies, Dufferin-Peel R.C.S.S.B., Ontario*

Hartley Loraas, *Templeton Secondary School, Vancouver, British Columbia*

Marilyn Ball, *Supervisor of Instructional Services, Oromocto District School Office, Oromocto, New Brunswick*

John Danson, *Continuing Education, Peel Board of Education, Ontario*
Terry Murphy, *Frontenac Secondary School, Kingston, Ontario*

Finally, we acknowledge the Canadian Foundation for Economic Education and Tier 1 Communications, who provided us with some of the information for the Agents of Change. We would also like to thank John McKirdy, Queen's University, and Peter Huxtable of the Federal Business Development Bank for the valuable information they provided. Our thanks also to the Innovation Centre, Waterloo, for the use of resource materials adapted for this text.

We dedicate this book to the youth of Canada — May they catch the entrepreneurial spirit! — and to our families, who gave up so much of their time with us while we worked to complete this book:

Alex, Janice, Julie, and David (LK)
Steve, Brett, Devon, and Dayna (LC)
Ted and Jake (BJ)

Preface

We live in a world of accelerating change. The need for young people to learn how to respond to this change in new and innovative ways grows ever more critical. Confident self-expression, positive personal development, and the ability to create and launch solutions—the hallmarks of the entrepreneur—become increasingly important. *Entrepreneurship: Creating a Venture* leads students through this changing, exciting world. The text provides a basis for students to discover opportunities for innovation and to use their creative energies to launch out with new and worthwhile ventures.

Entrepreneurs are in demand today. They are needed on our farms, in our science labs, in businesses, hospitals, schools, government, and social agencies. Entrepreneurship could become one of Canada's highest priorities. This text addresses the questions: "What can we do to develop more entrepreneurs?" and "What can we do to help young entrepreneurs create and launch successful ventures?"

Entrepreneurial attributes can be acquired and improved in a school setting. They can be polished and applied in school activities, in local community service initiatives, and in startup business ventures. Young people in entrepreneurship classrooms across the country have developed the ability to seek out new opportunities, to develop creative and innovative ideas, and to plan for and launch exciting new ventures to address opportunities and challenges. These students of entrepreneurship are preparing today for tomorrow's world.

Entrepreneurs are explorers, searchers, and adventurers who thrive on excitement and challenge. *Entrepreneurship: Creating a Venture* provides opportunities for students to learn about and experience that excitement and challenge.

To the Student

Entrepreneurs make things happen! This book is about how *you* can make things happen. From the very first Venture Profile to the last Venturing Out, you will be actively involved in the dynamic process of entrepreneurship. You will learn to view problems as opportunities. You will generate and test out your own ideas to meet these opportunities. You will organize and plan a launch of an entrepreneurial venture of your own undertaking. You will become an entrepreneur!

The Venture Profiles contained in each chapter, together with the Agents of Change in the margins, illustrate a huge array of Canadian and international accomplishments. As you explore these accomplishments, you will see how entrepreneurs identify and then achieve their goals. You will recognize that success to entrepreneurs means more than money. You will be tempted, by their enthusiasm, to reach out to catch the spirit of entrepreneurship. We encourage you to do this. The rewards can, both monetarily and personally, be great. Jump on board the entrepreneurial adventure and use our model of the Venture Creation Wheel to drive your success.

The Your Turn questions throughout each chapter give you practice in some of the more important entrepreneurial attributes and skills. You will have opportunities to identify successful entrepreneurs in your own community who might be able to help and advise you. You will have opportunities to practise and apply the ideas and procedures covered in each chapter. By the end of Chapter 14, your entrepreneurial venture will have been created, planned, and organized, and will be ready to launch.

The Venturing Out section at the end of each chapter provides an opportunity for you to apply what you have learned to your own special venture. When you have finished the Venturing Out assignments in Chapters 7-11, you will have completed the major components of your venture plan. Chapter 13 helps you put each of these components into a complete, polished, and well-prepared venture plan. Chapter 14 helps you to examine what you have learned and to consider how you can apply your knowledge to many areas of your life.

Creating, planning, and preparing to launch your very own venture provides opportunities for you to explore a variety of business principles related to marketing, retailing, finance, communications, economics, human relations, management, production, and business planning. Whether your venture is for profit or not for profit, these business principles serve as useful models against which you can test the components of your plan.

We hope you enjoy using *Entrepreneurship: Creating a Venture*. Entrepreneurship is the way of the future. We wish you a happy and sucessful journey.

THE AUTHORS

To the Teacher

Entrepreneurs embody the spirit of innovation. This text is designed to nurture the development of entrepreneurs and that spirit of innovation. Your students will learn that entrepreneurship requires a high degree of vision, initative, and skill. They will become comfortable in taking initiatives of varying size and intent. They will learn that they can seek out new opportunities, develop innovative and creative ideas, and plan and launch ventures to address the needs, wants, and/or problems of their local communities or of society as a whole. Your students will develop the skills and attributes required to help them contribute in a meaningful way to our economic and social future. They will learn how to make meaning out of the process of change and to be challenged, rather than daunted, by it. They will have the opportunity to learn about themselves, set personal goals, and develop entrepreneurial skills.

Entrepreneurship: Creating a Venture is divided into three sections. Section One, Entrepreneurs—Made Not Born, is designed to foster and develop entrepreneurial skills and attitudes. Section Two, Looking at the Big Picture—The Plan-ning Process, will help students understand how they can plan for success. Chapter assignments provide students with opportunities to learn about their community and the particular field of interest in which they might want to apply their innovative talents. Section Three, Managing Resources, offers students a framework for managing their ventures. Management skills in such key areas as finance, marketing, personnel management, and technological adaptation are explored in this section.

Entrepreneurship: Creating a Venture uses a variety of techniques to help students develop entrepreneurial skills and attributes and apply them to personal, school, business, and community service endeavours. Since entrepreneurs are action-oriented, the text emphasizes activity and application. It involves students in co-operative, small group learning situations, simulations, investigations, research, evaluation, and planning.

Each chapter begins with a Venture Profile, followed by Exploring questions. These questions encourage students to think critically and creatively and to apply their newly acquired knowledge, skills, and attitudes. Students can answer Exploring questions individually, in pairs, or in small groups. In order to help students understand the entrepreneurial process and to see that the same process is applied in all ventures, Exploring questions sometimes refer to Venture Profiles from previous chapters. Each chapter contains between two to seven Venture Profiles. The Student Workbook that accompanies this text has additional Venture Profiles for each chapter.

Your Turns are interspersed throughout each chapter. These activity-based learning experiences allow students to practise their newly acquired entrepreneurial skills in both classroom and community settings and to feel the fun, creativity, and excitement of the entrepreneurial process.

Important words that appear in the text are listed, in the order in which they appear, in the Entrepreneurial Language section at the beginning of each chapter. These words are explained in context when they first appear in the text and are more formally defined in the Glossary at the end of the text.

Key information is highlighted within each chapter. Interesting quotations, questions, and trivia appear in the margins throughout the text. These are designed to stimulate thought and can be used to create small group discussions, debates, or written assignments. The Agents of Change that appear in the margins throughout each chapter provide snippets of information about entrepreneurs. These can be used as starting points for discussions, research, or role playing.

The What Did You Learn? reading review questions at the end of each chapter can be used by the students as a self-test of their understanding of the facts in the chapter.

The Venturing Out section that ends each chapter extends the knowledge, skills, and attitudes accumulated thus far. It provides students with the opportunity to pursue their entrepreneurial initiatives and to use the entrepreneurial process to plan and achieve their goals.

All of the chapter activities and applications have been designed to encourage students to scan a wide range of alternatives, think creatively and critically, assess priorities, and be creative in posing solutions to problems.

The Venture Creation Wheel, introduced in Chapter 2, is designed to help students focus on the content of each chapter. The material covered in each chapter refers to one of the spokes in this wheel. Each spoke is essential to the success of a venture.

The study of entrepreneurship is fun and exciting. Celebrate your students' successes with them, encourage them to learn from their mistakes, support their efforts to gain a better understanding of the entrepreneurial process, and watch them flourish.

THE AUTHORS

Contents

SECTION ONE Entrepreneurs — Made Not Born

Chapter 1

Chapter 2

SECTION TWO Looking at the Big Picture — The Planning Process

Chapter 6 Moving into Action: The Venture Plan 153

Chapter 7 Analyzing Your Market 183

Chapter 8 Rolling up Your Sleeves: Team Building and Structuring Your Venture 221

Chapter 9

Chapter 10

Chapter 11

SECTION THREE Managing Resources

"Entrepreneurship makes a difference." It is a driving force in our economy and in our communities. Entrepreneurship is like a wheel that generates creative energy, innovation, and improved standards of living.

CHAPTER 1

What Is Entrepreneurship?

LEARNING OUTCOMES

By the end of this chapter, you should be able to:

- understand the meaning and role of entrepreneurship
- define the term "intrapreneurship"
- determine the entrepreneurial characteristics that play a role in successful entrepreneurial ventures
- determine which factors are most likely to motivate an entrepreneur

ENTREPRENEURIAL LANGUAGE

ventures
profile
need
want
entrepreneurship
innovation
profit
not-for-profit
service
good
intrapreneurship
entrepreneur
agents of change
chains
franchises
capital
franchisor
franchisee

Venture PROFILE

Calendars that have no dates allow you to wipe out the past

TIME MASTERS: David Opie, left, Katherine Trebilcock, and Kevin Burrows show off their timeposters. They expect to sell $2.9 million worth over the next 12 months.

By Pat Brennan, *Toronto Star*

If he hoped to survive law school, David Opie knew he had to become better organized.

And to do that he needed a big calendar to keep track of such things as his next exam or an upcoming social event.

He either had too many exams scheduled or too many social events booked — he won't say which — because he couldn't find a calendar big enough to map out his month.

So he made his own.

It worked. He graduated with flying colours from Osgoode and, by day, began articling with a large firm in downtown Toronto.

At night, however, he returned to his real job — making calendars. Opie, 25, expects to sell $2.9 million worth of them over the next 12 months and projects sales to leap 300 per cent a year in the following two years.

Don't call them calendars in front of Opie. To him they're timeposters, which seems appropriate.

A calendar loses its value as the year progresses and most don't function well after December 31.

But timeposters, Opie points out, are infinite. They're good to your last day and then you can bequeath them to your heirs.

START AGAIN

A timeposter is simply a stiff, laminated piece of cardboard about the size of your average wall poster. The seven days of the week run across the top of the timeposter and marked off below are 35 spacious boxes without dates.

You write those in yourself with the grease pencil attached to each poster.

Plenty of space remains within the box to note any daily plans you dare reveal.

Down one side of the timeposter are 31 lines to preview the big things visiting your life next month. Across the bottom is an area for writing important little reminders, like take a bath or write to your mother.

At the end of the month, you merely use a damp cloth to wipe out your past and start again.

Soon after Opie hung his own personal timeposter on the wall, fellow students tried to steal it, switching on a light in Opie's head. There appeared to be a demand for timeposters.

He customized timeposters for various Ontario universities, blazing the name and school colours across the top. He first approached Ryerson Polytechnical Institute and was told, "No Thanks." But the

University of Western Ontario in London loved it, and business started booming.

Ryerson is now among the dozens of schools throughout North America where timeposters are hot items.

Katherine Trebilcock, 24, a languages graduate of the University of Toronto and a friend of Opie, shared his vision for Timeposters Inc. and joined as a partner.

Along with her marketing experience, Trebilcock also contributed a basement to the fledgling company.

Before it got too big, Timeposters Inc. worked out of her family's basement in the Annex area of Toronto. The company then moved into a refurbished warehouse on Dupont Street.

Opie quit articling to work full time on timeposters while still studying for his Ontario bar exams. He persuaded fellow law graduate Kevin Burrows, 27, his undergraduate roommate at Queen's University, to join Timeposters Inc. as a partner.

Now the three partners are going full time, along with eight employee sales agents, trying to keep up with the demand for timeposters.

More than 50 schools from McGill to Harvard to the University of Florida sell their own specialized timeposters in campus stores. There are only 4000 students at Brock University in St.Catharines, but more than 1000 Brock timeposters have been sold on campus.

Opie says there are 250 universities in Canada and the United States and his company aims to put timeposters on every campus.

But the partners are aware there are a lot more kitchens and bedrooms and recreation rooms and business offices in North America than there are campuses. So Timeposters Inc. has expanded into generic themes as well for their timeposters.

Fitness, baby's room, foods, sailing, and polo are among the non-school themes on timeposters being sold by major retailers.

The Royal Bank of Canada has ordered 1000 timeposters bearing the bank's name, colours, and corporate logo, and Timeposters has been licensed to put Batman and other characters owned by D.C.Comics on calendars — oops — timeposters.

Successful Ventures

Throughout this text, you will read about a number of **ventures**, or undertakings, that have changed the way we live. Opie, in the **profile**, or case study, you have just read, identified a personal need — a calendar large enough to allow him to list everything that he had to do on every day for a month at a time. He needed this extra large calendar to help him manage his time more efficiently. He soon discovered, however, that a number of people needed and, indeed, even wanted to become better organized — more efficient. He identified a **need** and then generated Timeposters to satisfy it.

Shirley McNaughton and Rick Hansen, the subjects of the next two Venture Profiles, also determined specific needs. Their ventures may have been different from Opie's, but in many ways they were very similar. Each venture, each different undertaking, provides an answer to a particular need or **want**.

Venture PROFILE

Symbols that speak for those who can't

By Walter Stefaniuk, *Toronto Star*

Symbols that speak for those who can't.

SPECIAL LANGUAGE: Shirley McNaughton opened a new world for people such as John Dowling, who has cerebral palsy, with the Blissymbolics system of communication. McNaughton received the Order of Canada for her work.

Sue Odell, emaciated from the cerebral palsy that has left her without speech, is pointing to symbols on her Blissboard to tell the story of how, at 17, she learned to communicate with the world.

"I was the first adult to learn Blissymbolics," the symbols say as she struggles, but rapidly, to direct her hand movements through the pages of the board. "In two weeks, I learned 400 symbols."

That was in the early 1970s. Before that, the thoughts, hopes and dreams, needs and desires and intelligence of non-speaking people such as Odell were trapped inside helpless bodies. They couldn't hold a pencil to write. They couldn't do hand signs. People who didn't know better wrote them off from humanity.

But the world for thousands of people such as Odell was changed in 1971 by Shirley McNaughton, a Metro teacher of children with special needs, and a team at what is now the Hugh MacMillan Medical Centre. McNaughton developed the symbols through which non-speaking people could communicate.

Odell best expressed the importance of that breakthrough to thousands of people like her. She was asked what she felt that first moment she found she could express her mind and be understood by others at last.

Odell shook her head and moaned. A hand swept over the Blissboard on her wheelchair as if dismissing it. The hand disdainfully waved away the computer in her living room and the telephone with a modem for symbol communication. She shook her head again, indicating "No."

"She is saying there are no symbols to express her feelings," says Odell's friend, June Wiancko of the Easter Seal Communications Institute, who is acting as facilitator. "Try 'like' words," she tells Odell.

The woman bends over the Blissboard and finds symbols to indicate, however inadequately, something of what she felt a decade and a half ago the moment her spirit became unfettered: "Excited. Free. Proud. Lucky. Happy. Not lonely anymore because I was able to communicate."

She spells the name Shirley McNaughton on the board. "She is very special," Odell's symbols say.

McNaughton built a communications bridge for non-speaking people through symbols invented by Austrian Charles K. Bliss. A World War II concentration camp survivor, Bliss held the altruistic hope that the symbols could bring world peace by surmounting language barriers. That didn't happen, but McNaughton's use for the symbols delighted him.

McNaughton has helped thousands of non-speaking and disabled people through a career that ranges from instructor to those with special needs, to innovator, administrator, lecturer, writer, and, lately, even computer programmer.

For her work on behalf of non-speaking people, McNaughton was invested as a Member of the Order of Canada by the Governor-General at a formal ceremony on April 12, 1989, at Rideau Hall. Investiture in the order is the highest civilian honour the country can bestow.

"Beyond the personal recognition, the thing for me is the area that I work in is being recognized as worthy of this kind of honour...working with non-speaking people is a worthy thing to do. I guess that's what the award says to me," says McNaughton.

John Dowling, 25, who has cerebral palsy and learned to communicate through Blissymbolics before developing functional speech, recalls the hours fundraising and teaching took: "She [McNaughton] was there from 6 in the morning till 11 at night. That was her workday."

And wherever she goes, at least a half-dozen plastic shopping bags go with her, each full of current projects she's working on, sort of like moveable filing cabinets. "We lovingly call her the Bag Lady," Dowling explains. "And she knows what and where everything is in every one of them."

The nickname amuses McNaughton, a strong teacher figure — easy authority, patience, dignity, all lightened by humour flickering through blue eyes.

Dowling's admiration for McNaughton is unlimited. "I want to see more people like Shirley and her family in the world. Her whole family helped me."

"REAL RESPONSIBILITY"

He recalls the "happiness" the day he first learned to express his feelings through Blissymbolics. "I was a bottle in a box. Shirley took me out of that bottle and I burst out like champagne."

Without McNaughton's work, "I would be in that box. No one would be able to understand me," he says.

But McNaughton sees new challenges ahead.

"We've created a new adult, adults that were non-speaking in the 1970s," McNaughton says. "We've given these young people a feeling about themselves, that they now shall have the same opportunities as you and me.

"That's a real responsibility...helping them find vocations, helping them find the meaning in their lives, and there's nothing out there waiting for them because they're so new. They don't even know how to serve as their own advocates yet."

She says this is the area where she's focusing her time now.

"Our young people, being the first generation, just aren't into that kind of assertiveness yet; we have to do it for them at this time. But I truly believe that the next generation will help themselves, not only to communicate, but also to take their place in the world."

Venture PROFILE

RICK HANSEN Man in Motion World Tour

Rick Hansen—a man in motion

The Rick Hansen Man in Motion World Tour spanned 2 years, 4 continents, 33 countries, over 700 hotel rooms, and 40 000 km...and its dreams and goals continue.

Rick Hansen was 14 years old when he was involved in a tragic car accident in which his spinal cord was damaged and he lost the use of his legs. After fighting many frustrations and fears, Rick Hansen declared war on himself — maybe he couldn't walk but he could live, and a dream began to evolve. He fought to rebuild his body to be the best it could be — and drive it as far and as high as it could go. Sports played a very important part in Rick's youth and adult years — his accomplishments serve to underline his determination and perseverance. Rick won many athletic awards, beginning in high school with "Most Inspirational Athlete", going on to win 19 wheelchair marathons on three continents setting record times. A champion in numerous other awards, Rick Hansen was voted National Disabled Athlete of the Year in 1979, 1980, and 1982, and in 1983 shared the Lou Marsh trophy as Canada's Outstanding Athlete of the Year. Rick's perseverance was not limited to athletics, for he realized the importance of being the best person he could be by setting goals and striving to reach them. In 1986, he became the first disabled person to graduate from the Physical Education program at the University of British Columbia. Sometime during these years, Rick established a new personal goal: to wheel around the world in order to "deliver a message to the world. To challenge people to have positive attitudes about disabled people and take actions to break down barriers standing in the way of reaching their potential," emphasizing the importance of sports and rehabilitation, and to raise funds for spinal cord research and rehabilitation.

On March 21, 1985, Rick Hansen and his crew rolled out of Vancouver and began the historic journey. Initially setting a pace of 70 km per day, the Tour commenced by travelling down the U.S. west coast and across the southern states to Miami. On June 26, the Tour headed for London, England, via Toronto, and on July 3, Rick resumed wheeling through much of England, Ireland, Scotland, and Northern France. Rick then went on to travel through the Netherlands, West Germany, Denmark, Sweden, and Norway. Two days out of Norway, Rick clocked into Helsinki, Finland, at 11 300 km, completing one third of the journey. From Helsinki, the Tour flew to Lenningrad on September 5 where he was given a very warm welcome and allowed to wheel 5 km — the first of many political barriers the Tour was to break. From Russia, Rick went on to win over the people of Poland, Czechoslovakia, Austria, and Switzerland. Some of the highlights included the exhausting 16 hour, 116 km wheeling up to St. Anton's Summit in the Swiss Alps. The 16 000 km point of the trip was broken in Pisa and, shortly thereafter, Rick was greeted by the Pope in Rome. After going through Greece, Rick reached Jordan, where he made a very significant crossing of the Husein/Allenby bridge, which was reopened specifically for him to cross from Jordan to Israel, after receiving special permission from both countries for the crossing. Rick and his crew arrived in New Zealand in mid-December and went on to Australia, where Rick reached his halfway point in Melbourne. From there, Rick went on to conquer the Far East: to conquer "the steepest hill of his whole life" and become a hero with "a heart of a dragon" on the Great Wall of China.

After wheeling through Korea, Japan, the United States, and Canada's prairie winter, Rick noted that everywhere he had travelled he had seen the barriers that exist for disabled people and their continued attempts to enter the mainstream of life — and this, he believes, underlines the importance of maintaining a public perspective on the importance of educational awareness to promote the attitudes of disabled and able-bodied people alike to pursue their potential.

Rick Hansen once again achieved his goals. Belief in a dream and the perseverance to work to make it happen kept Rick on the road for two years, wheeling 40 000 km.

In each of the 34 countries he passed through, he changed attitudes towards disabled persons and helped associated groups raise funds for their programs.

Rick always maintains that it was a team effort which reached the goals of the Man in Motion World Tour. People working together to help other people. People working together to ensure rehabilitation and vocational retraining for disabled people; to realize the potential we each have; to research the possibilities of recovering fully from spinal cord injuries. By using education and example as the keys to promoting his dreams, Rick Hansen has surpassed his goals, and in creating awareness of them has shown us that all people have setbacks and barriers standing in the way of their potential but that with a positive attitude and perseverance those obstacles can become a challenge and goal to overcome.

The Rick Hansen Man in Motion Tour has finished but its dreams and goals continue.

EXPLORING • VENTURE PROFILES

1. What needs or wants were addressed in each of these three ventures?
2. Briefly state the vision, or dream, of each of David Opie, Shirley McNaughton, and Rick Hansen.
3. What risks or chances did they each take?
4. What compensation or benefit was received in each case?
5. Where did the motivation come from for each venture?
6. How are these three profiles similar? How are they different?
7. What innovation or new creation was involved in each?
8. Outline the process that David, Shirley, and Rick took to accomplish their individual ventures.
9. Describe these three individuals. What kind of people are they?
10. Identify statements in each of these three Venture Profiles that suggest that David, Shirley, and Rick are self-confident, motivated, hard-working, and determined to achieve.

The Meaning of Entrepreneurship

Entrepreneurship is a way of looking at things, a way of thinking and a way of doing. It is not an art or a science. It is a practice and as a practice it is sometimes difficult to describe in certain terms.

Entrepreneurship involves bringing about change to achieve some benefit. This benefit may be financial but it also involves the satisfaction of knowing you have changed something for the better.

The word *entrepreneurship* comes from the French word *entreprendre,* which means to undertake, to pursue opportunities, to satisfy needs and wants through **innovation** or new creation.

Characteristics of Entrepreneurial Ventures

AGENTS OF CHANGE

Terry Fox put together a team of advisors and assistants and organized a fund-raising effort for cancer research. With only one good leg and a serious cancerous condition, he started his run from coast to coast across Canada. Even though he could not complete it, his venture brought in millions of dollars for cancer research and taught us all how the strength of one person can change the lives of many.

Entrepreneurial ventures can have one or more of the following characteristics. They may be:

▪ for profit or not-for-profit

Business entrepreneurship is undertaken for profit, in other words, to make money. However, a number of entrepreneurial ventures are for social or community service purposes. Not-for-profit organizations, such as Amnesty International, The Red Cross, Big Brothers, Big Sisters, The Heart and Stroke Foundation, may be involved in fund-raising initiatives. Their goal, however, is not to make a profit but rather to raise the money they need to deliver a special **service** or satisfy a specific need in society.

▪ large scale/small scale

Entrepreneurship is not dependent on size. Large business corporations or large not-for-profit organizations are involved in satisfying needs or wants on a large scale, usually at a national or an international level. Smaller companies or not-for-profit organizations work at satisfying a need or a want on a smaller, more local level. The Cancer Society, for example, annually mounts an international appeal for funds and then directs money raised to large-scale research initiatives. A smaller community service organization in your own neighbourhood might, on the other hand, initiate a smaller fund-raising campaign to help a local family with a special need.

AGENTS OF CHANGE

Legal actions, such as divorce, are often more expensive than many people can really afford and can be taken without a lawyer. Jack James, an articling lawyer in British Columbia, started Self-Counsel Press to provide practical legal information in a straightforward manner. His attempts to simplify the law have made it more user-friendly and accessible to many more people.

- **service production/goods production**

Entrepreneurial ventures can be organized to produce either a **good** (a product) or to provide a service. Both can be entrepreneurial. The *good* might be something that eventually will be sold for profit at a local store, or it might be something that a not-for-profit organization will produce and distribute free to those in need. The *service* can be anything from the work that an electrician would perform for a price to the advice provided free of charge for people looking for work.

- **local/national/international in scope**

Entrepreneurship exists in your school, in your local community, in larger urban centres nearby, throughout your province, on a national scale across the country, and internationally around the world. Often it is local entrepreneurship that gives a town or city its personality and its strength. These pockets of entrepreneurship become the foundation for a strong and creative national environment.

Entrepreneurship in Society

Since entrepreneurship is undertaken to satisfy a need or want or to solve a problem, it is important to society's well-being. Opportunities for innovation, designed to improve our performance, our living conditions, or the living conditions of others, call out to us every day. Community daycare centres are set up in areas where children need to be cared for while their parents are at work. Cleaning services have sprung up to meet the needs of busy, two-career families. Senior citizens' activity centres are created to help an older generation spend their time creatively. Special fund-raising drives are launched to help care for someone in need or to finance a special project. Business ventures are started to provide a product or service to satisfy a special need or a want.

Entrepreneurship generates new processes or ways of doing things. It creates a wider variety of goods and services than would otherwise exist, improves our standard of living, and lowers prices. Entrepreneurship stimulates new business ventures and provides opportunities for employment. Entrepreneurship encourages women, youth, the elderly, as well as members of minority groups to participate wholeheartedly in venture creation.

Entrepreneurship causes more wealth to be distributed throughout a community and eventually benefits society as a whole. The success of one new business venture can produce a variety of additional entrepreneurial and investment opportunities. For example, the successful introduction of the personal microcomputer opened up a number of opportunities for new software, hardware, training programs, repair services, computer magazines, trade journals, newsletters, cartoons, movies, and even literature. It also provided opportunities for new causes and campaigns to advocate appropriate personal, social, and ergonomic (the relationship between human beings and technology) conditions.

Entrepreneurship flourishes in a supportive environment. It is strong in countries where the financial and legal institutions provide a strong foundation; where money for starting new ventures is easily accessible; where education and training are widely available; where laws and regulations do not deter new venture creation; and where free or open trade exists. Entrepreneurship is strong where support groups in government, business, and education are available to collaborate, advise, and encourage entrepreneurship. In countries where these strong foundations and supportive conditions do not exist, entrepreneurship is likely operating "underground", or not openly for all to see.

AGENTS OF CHANGE

Replacing stained ceiling tiles was expensive. Kaaydah Schatten, a Native woman who bought and renovated properties in Toronto, wanted a quick, easy way to clean them. She experimented until she discovered the perfect cleaning mix, which she called The Ceiling Doctor. Her invention proved so successful, Kaaydah had time and money to spend promoting Native rights. Success in one field created the opportunity to build in another.

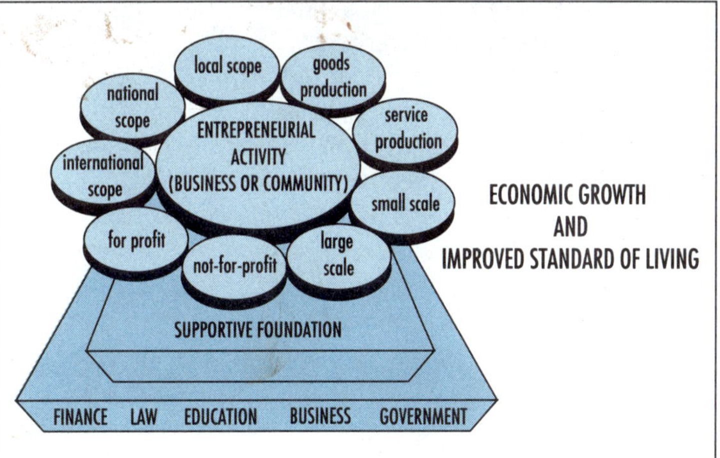

Figure 1.1 Model of Entrepreneurship in a Supportive Society

Intrapreneurship

Intrapreneurship is entrepreneurship operating within a corporation. More and more corporations are encouraging intrapreneurial activity in order to become more competitive, improve their productivity, or keep pace with changing markets, technology, and new opportunities.

These corporations use a variety of methods to stimulate intrapreneurship within their organizations. Some have restructured their organizations into smaller, more innovative teams and then challenged each team to turn a particular idea into a new product, service, or process. Others are inviting customers to give them ideas about needed changes in product or service. Still others are devising ways to reward innovation and recognize the intrapreneurs within their organizations.

Venture PROFILE

E.D. Smith promotes intrapreneurship.

E.D. Smith rewards employees with bonus

By Margot Gibb-Clark, *The Globe and Mail*

E. D. Smith & Sons Ltd., the jam and sauce company, is holding a party Wednesday to hand back to employees half of the $1.5 million savings they helped generate last year.

Each worker will get at least $1850 for the year, the first slice received last July. Some will get more than $3500. Cheques are to be presented by Dave Andreychuk and John Tucker, Buffalo Sabres hockey players.

For the past three years, employees have been encouraged to build teams to think of money-saving ideas. Team players are allowed to set aside an hour a week to work on these ideas.

Just over half the company's 260 workers have taken part in the teams, even those who don't share in the savings. Teams which submitted ideas get extra money, company spokesman Mary Siemiesz explained.

Last year, one idea, which saved a quarter of a million dollars, was to ship all products directly from the company's Winona headquarters in southern Ontario, instead of using warehouses around the country. Winona is near Hamilton. Employees get different payouts for three different kinds of ideas, Ms. Siemiesz explained. Type A ideas, which save money right away, bring the most. Type B might increase sales, but do not clearly introduce savings.

Type C ideas are initially rejected, but even they bring money because the company has, on several occasions, found they can be re-jigged into something that does bring savings.

The family-owned company manufactures jams, pie fillings, and vegetable juice, as well as manufacturing sauces under licence.

EXPLORING • E.D. SMITH REWARDS EMPLOYEES

1. What did E. D. Smith do to encourage intrapreneurship?
2. Why do you suppose the company supports this kind of activity?
3. What kind of environment should corporations provide if they want to encourage intrapreneurship?
4. What can companies do to encourage their employees to generate new ideas or make suggestions for improved productivity?

YOUR TURN

1. In pairs, identify an entrepreneurial venture operating in your local community. Is the venture a for-profit or a not-for-profit initiative? Does it operate on a large or a small scale? Identify the product or service provided and determine if the organization is local, national, or international in scope.
2. As a class, share the information you have gathered about local entrepreneurial ventures and prepare a chart describing entrepreneurship in your community.
3. In small groups, prepare a map, collage, report, or oral presentation to describe the variety of entrepreneurial ventures operating in your community.
4. Prepare a brief written report on the need for intrapreneurship in Canada today.
5. In small groups, identify a part-time job that you have had. Determine how the company you worked for could encourage its employees to become intrapreneurs. Identify any procedures that could have been introduced to improve the service or product provided and describe them to the class.

Entrepreneurs

AGENTS OF CHANGE

Variety Village, a recreational facility for children who are physically challenged, is continually seeking to expand its services. Vicki Keith, a marathon swimmer, wanted to use her skills to help Variety Village raise money to build an aquatic wing. She swam the five Great Lakes to inspire people to donate. Vicki's amazing feat drew attention to the needs and goals of others and gave us all a way to help.

To understand the personality of an **entrepreneur,** we can examine the individuals we have met so far in this chapter.

What did they do to initiate a change or respond to a perceived need or want? They all saw opportunities to satisfy a need or want and they brought together the expertise, labour, materials, financial or other resources needed to introduce a special venture.

David Opie created a calendar or timeposter that worked for him. Then he customized it to meet the needs of students in various universities. He took in a partner with marketing experience, and eventually added another partner and eight employee sales agents to keep up with the demand for his timeposters.

Shirley McNaughton took an invention designed by someone else and used it for a different purpose to build a communications bridge for people who cannot speak.

Rick Hansen identified what he felt society needed, set a goal for himself, decided what he wanted to accomplish, and brought together the people he needed to help him achieve his dream.

Entrepreneurs are able to see what others have not seen and have the courage and skill to act on the opportunities they perceive.

When David Opie saw that students needed something to help them plan their daily activities, it did not take him long to identify an opportunity.

Shirley McNaughton saw the symbols, invented by Charles Bliss, and identified an opportunity to help non-speaking people communicate.

Rick Hansen saw that he could show society something about the physically challenged and worked out a plan to achieve his goal.

All the entrepreneurs in these three Venture Profiles brought about or effected a change. Students at a number of universities are now recording their daily plans on large, reusable timeposters. Non-speaking people are communicating with speaking people as well as with each other. People around

AGENTS OF CHANGE

Hearing-impaired people had no fast and simple means to communicate. Charles Michel de L'Epée invented a language using movements of the hands and arms to "speak". Millions of hearing-impaired people could enjoy easier conversation because of this man's idea.

the world have a new understanding of what physically challenged individuals can be expected to accomplish.

Figure 1.2 When entrepreneurs see an opportunity, they have the courage to act.

Figure 1.3 Entrepreneurs are agents of change who make things happen.

Entrepreneurs are **agents of change** who are continually challenging the status quo. Each of our entrepreneurs, or agents of change, identified, measured, and then minimized the risks they saw in their ventures. They took controlled and calculated risks and created viable ventures.

Figure 1.4 Entrepreneurs carefully weigh opportunities against risks before acting.

Our entrepreneurs set goals to help themselves stay on track. David Opie's goal was to adapt his timeposters for other markets. Shirley McNaughton's goal was to help non-speaking people express their thoughts, hopes, dreams, and needs. Rick Hansen's goals were to challenge people around the world to develop a more positive attitude toward disabled people; to promote opportunities for their rehabilitation and vocational retraining; and to help them realize their potential.

"Would you tell me, please, which way I ought to go from here?"
"That depends a good deal on where you want to get to," said the Cat.
"I don't much care where—" said Alice.
"Then it doesn't matter which way you go," said the Cat.
Alice's Adventures in Wonderland

Entrepreneurs have a vision. They work towards clearly defined goals.

Entrepreneurs look for something unique that will meet a need, satisfy a want, or solve a problem. They spend a lot of time asking "What if?" and "Why not?" They question and

Figure 1.5 Entrepreneurs question everything in order to assess the potential of an idea.

explore everything around an idea until they can see its potential. They develop a vision and work diligently asking questions until they have reached their goal.

AGENTS OF CHANGE

Looking for a fun evening in Toronto? Paul Schiffner and Rod Bell saw an opportunity in the video rental market and set up a company that would deliver videos and popcorn right to your door. They began franchising in June of 1988 and are enjoying a huge success. They saw a new use for a new technology and took advantage of it.

Modifying an Entrepreneurial Concept

Entrepreneurs, like David, Shirley, and Rick, can generate their own ideas and start up new ventures. Alternatively, they can take a concept that someone else has used and modify it in a way that will improve it. There is an element of risk in either case. Ray Kroc, the former owner of McDonald's, did not invent the hamburger nor the first McDonald's restaurant, which he bought from the McDonald brothers in the mid-1950s. He certainly took a risk though. He applied a new concept for fast-food service to the lowly hamburger and gave birth to a gigantic McDonald's fast-food network. He modified an existing concept and became a famous entrepreneur.

Figure 1.6 Taking a concept and modifying it for improvement is one means of creating a successful venture.

Ray Kroc developed a network of McDonald's restaurant **chains** under central management and then branched out into **franchises**. Franchises are a system of ownership that allows the originators of a successful business to expand without having to raise additional **capital** (or money). A franchise purchase is a continuing agreement between the **franchisor** (or seller), the company that originated the venture, and the **franchisee** (or buyer), the individual(s) purchasing the right to operate a copy of the venture. The franchisor's knowledge, image, success, and his or her manufacturing, marketing, and management techniques are part of the agreement.

Generally speaking, franchisees are not free to run the business exactly as they wish. They are not really encouraged to be entrepreneurial. They must, under contract, follow the franchisor's policies, standards, and operating procedures. Each individually owned franchise is expected to operate as though it were part of a large chain. Each franchise uses the same trademark, equipment design, and operating procedures. Each franchise produces a standardized product or service. It does not matter how many McDonald's restaurants you eat in, a Big Mac will taste the same in every one of them.

Rick Hession, in Kingston, Ontario, owns and operates a McDonald's franchise. He follows the McDonald's operating procedures in the way he manages his franchise. However, Rick Hession is also an entrepreneur, not in the way he operates his McDonald's franchise, but in what he does with it. He uses his store and his goodwill with the community to raise money for local charities. He shares the same philosophy as Ray Kroc: "Put something back into the community that gives you business." As a proponent of that philosophy, he has raised over $1 million for local community needs.

YOUR TURN

6. In pairs, visit an older person in your community to hear about the changes experienced in his or her lifetime. Bring these experiences back to share with the class.
7. As a class, categorize these changes into groups such as work, leisure, technology, family life, and any others you learn about from your visit.
8. Select one of the following individuals' names and determine whether or not the person you selected was an entrepreneur: Amelia Erhardt, Nellie McClung, Thomas Edison, Coco Chanel, Alexander Graham Bell, Frederick Banting, Norman Bethune, Mother Theresa, or Laura Secord. Give reasons and specific examples to justify your stand.

Entrepreneurs: Born or Made?

Studies of entrepreneurs indicate that individuals born into families in which their parents or grandparents were self-employed are more likely to start their own business than individuals born into other families. This leads some people to the conclusion that entrepreneurs are born not made. This inevitably results in the following set of questions: Were these entrepreneurs influenced by the environment in their family home? Did they get caught up in the excitement of a venture from the talk around the dinner table? Did they share the satisfaction of success with a parent or a grandparent? Were they simply born with entrepreneurial traits? Whether entrepreneurs are born or made is likely still to be an issue many years from now. Even though heredity is important in establishing basic entrepreneurial traits, the environment is a major influence on prospective entrepreneurs. The two often work together in shaping a future entrepreneur.

Entrepreneurs: Pushed or Pulled?

Entrepreneurs are explorers, adventurers, and conquerors who are always analyzing and conceptualizing. They are observant of their surroundings, always being pulled in the direction of a new opportunity. They can also be pushed into entrepreneurship. If, when working for someone else, they realize that they do not have a great deal of influence over the direction that the organization is taking, they are pushed into finding something of their own to direct.

AGENTS OF CHANGE

Women were not accepted into engineering in Karachi, Pakistan, before Dr. Safia Wasi. She fought to become the first female student in Karachi's pre-engineering school. She earned a Fulbright Scholarship to study in the U.S.A. Today, she directs the Immuno-chemistry Section of the Canadian Red Cross Reference Library. One woman's strength changed a whole school of thought!

The New Entrepreneur

The typical profile of an entrepreneur, that is, one who is a married male, born in Canada, university educated, and between the ages of 25-45, is changing rapidly. Recent studies have shown that women, senior citizens, immigrants, and youth are creating their own jobs at a much faster rate than males in the 25-45 year age bracket. These new entrepreneurs may be your friends or relatives. They may be male or female. They may be experienced business managers or high school students. They may be moms or dads. They may be 14 or 75 years of age. They will all have in common, regardless of their age, sex, or background, a strong desire to satisfy a need or want in an innovative way.

There are three kinds of people in this world: those who are in the parade, those who are watching the parade, and those who don't know that a parade is going on.

Figure 1.7 Entrepreneurs come from many varied backgrounds.

Preparing To Visit Community Entrepreneurs

A number of student activities found in the Your Turns in this text will require you to examine entrepreneurial initiatives in your local community. One of the best ways to do this is to visit entrepreneurs and conduct detailed interviews.

When interviewing entrepreneurs, it is important to do your homework. Be prepared, punctual, and professional. The following strategies will assist in this:

- Arrange, at the convenience of the entrepreneur, a time when you might meet with him or her.
- Be on time. An entrepreneur's time is very valuable. Do not waste it.

- Prepare your questions ahead of time and, if possible, practise asking them by roleplaying your interview with another student in the class.
- After the interview is completed, write a thank-you note to show your appreciation for the time you were given.
- Review the responses to each question and prepare a summary of what was said.
- Identify the name of the entrepreneur, the venture, the location, and the date of your visit. File this information for future reference.

YOUR TURN

9. In pairs, prepare for a visit to a local entrepreneur by developing a list of questions about a particular entrepreneurial venture. Use the following list of questions to get started:
   - What is the name of the venture?
   - Does it provide a good (product) or service?
   - How many people are presently employed?
   - What need or want did you identify when you started this venture?
   - What change or changes occurred as a result of your innovation?
10. In pairs, visit a local entrepreneur and ask the questions you developed in Question 9. When you have completed your visit, prepare an outline of what you learned to share with the rest of your class.
11. In small groups, using one of the outlines prepared in Question 10, write a short Venture Profile.
12. Exchange the Venture Profiles you wrote in Question 11 with another group and prepare a set of questions for someone reading your Venture Profile to explore.
13. In pairs, identify a particular business owner or someone who is providing a local community service. Arrange to meet with this entrepreneur and ask the following questions. (If no such person is available, base your answers on case studies of entrepreneurs from current issues of business or entrepreneurship magazines.)
    - Were either of your parents entrepreneurs?
    - What work and/or educational experiences did you have prior to starting your venture?

- How did you identify an opportunity for your venture?
- What were your goals when you started your venture?
- How are your goals different now?
- What kind of planning did you do before you got started?
- What outside help did you receive?
- What do you perceive to be your own strengths and weaknesses?
- What things do you find personally rewarding and satisfying as an entrepreneur?
- What advice would you give an aspiring entrepreneur?

Prepare an oral class presentation of your findings.

14. Prepare a brief written argument on why you feel that entrepreneurs are either born or made, or some combination of the two.

Venture PROFILE

Former figure-skater embarks upon new career

Olga Kubinec has devoted much of her life so far to the pursuit of a figure-skating career. For the past 12 years, she has taken daily figure-skating lessons near her home in Winnipeg. She was a silver medalist in a recent Olympic competition. Two years ago, Olga became a professional instructor: but her career was cut short by a severe knee injury. Olga has spent the last six months recovering from her injuries.

To keep herself busy, she learned how to knit. Knitting from a predesigned pattern did not keep her interest, so she began to create patterns of her own. Olga is able to knit quickly with the help of a knitting machine, and soon she began selling her original designs to friends. Her friends and family are now urging her to start a formal business designing and manufacturing hand-knitted sweaters.

EXPLORING • NEW CAREER FOR SKATER

1. What personal characteristics were required for Olga to succeed as an Olympic competitor?
2. Will the characteristics Olga displayed as an Olympic athlete help her to succeed as an entrepreneur? How?
3. What motivated Olga to start her knitting designs?
4. Does Olga appear to be self-confident? What evidence can you find to support your answer?
5. How is this profile different from the Shirley McNaughton profile at the beginning of this chapter?
6. Are there any similarities between David Opie, Rick Hansen, and Olga Kubinec? If so, what are they?
7. How would your community respond to the knitwear that Olga might produce?

Entrepreneurial Characteristics

Entrepreneurs march to the beat of their own drums.

Figure 1.8 No two entrepreneurs are alike; however, they may share many of the same qualities.

Most of the characteristics identified in the diagram on page 25 can be learned and developed by individuals who want to become entrepreneurs.

Entrepreneurs are:

- **Self-confident**

They are realistic about what they can accomplish. They believe in themselves and in their ability to succeed. Their goals are clear and they make a direct attempt to accomplish them.

Whatever your goal, you should know that effort always repays you in the future.

- **Perceptive**

Entrepreneurs are intuitive. They know what is going on. They are able to identify problems and find creative solutions.

- **Hardworking**

Entrepreneurs work long and hard to achieve success.

Entrepreneurial endeavours are a "labour of love" for which entrepreneurs always have the necessary energy and stamina.

- **Motivated**

Entrepreneurs are motivated to work long hours because of their determination to succeed.

- **Resourceful**

Entrepreneurs explore, ask questions, and generally use all their resources to find ways to achieve their goals. They are able to find solutions.

- **Able To Manage Risk**

Entrepreneurs view risk as a challenge, not as a chance. They calculate and measure it and then find ways to minimize it. They like to have control over an outcome. Entrepreneurs will take a risk if it is a calculated one — where the chances for success are greater than the chances for failure.

AGENTS OF CHANGE

Everyone, as a child, probably spent some time blowing bubbles. A computer company has now developed a printer that uses this "bubble" concept to provide precise inking quality for everything from computer-generated text to graphics. Sometimes even the most advanced technology starts with a simple idea.

▪ Creative

Entrepreneurs look at things in new and different ways. They like challenges and feel comfortable with ambiguity. They do not sit and wait for things to happen. Entrepreneurs create ideas and then make them happen.

▪ Achievement Oriented

Entrepreneurs thrive on results. They set goals for themselves. Once these goals are reached, they set new goals. Personal satisfaction and accomplishment push them forward.

▪ Optimistic

Entrepreneurs have a positive mental attitude. They are not daunted by minor setbacks or roadblocks. They believe they can touch the future and are enthusiastic about what it holds.

▪ Flexible

Entrepreneurs are able to adjust to changing technology, competition, and the environment.

▪ Independent

Entrepreneurs need the freedom to make their own decisions and their own mistakes. They do not respond well to being managed by others. It is often for this reason that they will move out on their own. They need to have control over their own destiny.

Figure 1.9 Entrepreneurs identify the cup as half full, not half empty.

▪ Visionary

Entrepreneurs have a vision of how things should be. That vision stays with them until they have completed each step along the way to their goal.

▪ Able To Get Along with Others

Entrepreneurs cannot work in a vacuum. They gather experts around them for advice on various aspects of their venture.

What Makes an Entrepreneur Tick?

Entrepreneurs are linked by the need for personal achievement. They are motivated by a number of different factors. The following list indicates those motivating factors that entrepreneurs consider to be most important and those they consider to be least important.

Most Important

- To achieve a personal sense of accomplishment
- To be my own boss
- To have an element of variety and adventure
- To have better use of my training and skills
- To have considerable freedom to adapt to my own approach to work
- To be challenged by the problems and opportunities of starting and growing a new business venture

Least Important

- To continue a family tradition
- To do the only thing I could
- To contribute to the welfare of my ethnic group
- To escape unsafe working conditions
- To follow the example of a person I admire

Although the individual characteristics and motivations of each entrepreneur contribute to the success of his or her venture, additional influences — such as education, family background, values and attitudes, political structure, and competition — also play an important role. The more supportive the family, society, and the prevailing political structure, the greater the likelihood that the venture will flourish. The higher the level of formal education and the stronger the moral attitudes and values, the greater the likelihood of success. Finally, if there is no competition, or if it is only minimally present, chances are that the venture will do well.

Figure 1.10 The personality of an entrepreneur is shaped by a variety of influencing factors.

P·O·I·N·T·S TO R·E·M·E·M·B·E·R

- Entrepreneurship is the act of bringing about change for a benefit.
- Entrepreneurship is important for the well-being of society.
- Entrepreneurship satisfies a need or a want through innovation.
- Entrepreneurship flourishes in a supportive environment.
- Intrapreneurship is entrepreneurship within a large organization.
- Intrapreneurship helps companies remain competitive and productive in today's changing society.
- Entrepreneurs bring together the resources needed to initiate change in response to an identified need or want.
- Entrepreneurs see what others have not seen and have the courage and skill to act.
- Entrepreneurs take controllable risks.
- Entrepreneurs are realistic, goal-directed, and self-confident.
- Entrepreneurs come from a variety of backgrounds.
- Entrepreneurs are born and made.

- Entrepreneurs exhibit one or more of the following characteristics:
  - self-confident
  - perceptive
  - hardworking
  - motivated
  - resourceful
  - able to manage risk
  - creative
  - achievement oriented
  - optimistic
  - flexible
  - independent
  - visionary
  - able to get along with others

W·H·A·T H·A·V·E Y·O·U L·E·A·R·N·E·D?

1. What is entrepreneurship?
2. What characteristics do entrepreneurial ventures demonstrate?
3. How does entrepreneurship benefit society?
4. Identify the supportive conditions that are necessary for entrepreneurship to flourish.
5. What is intrapreneurship?
6. Why is intrapreneurship important in Canada today?
7. Are entrepreneurs born or made?
8. Identify the characteristics that entrepreneurs share.
9. What is the most important motivating factor for entrepreneurs?
10. Give two examples of those factors that are considered least motivating to entrepreneurs.

V·E·N·T·U·R·I·N·G O·U·T

1. Refer to the entrepreneurial characteristics identified in Figure 1.8 (page 25). Identify activities in your own life where you would have benefited from applying any five of these.

2. In small groups, prepare a written description or illustration of a typical entrepreneur.
3. Write a brief "personal biography" of 50 words or less for your bulletin board. Be realistic. You can either write a short paragraph or use a format that often appears in yearbooks, like the following:

   Name:
   Nickname:
   Ambition:
   Probable Future:
   Favourite Saying:
   Pet Peeve:
   Biggest Regret:

   When you have completed your biography, post it on your bulletin board for other members in your class to read. Attach a small picture of yourself to the bottom of the page.
4. In small groups, respond to the following questions and discuss your answers:
   - How did you feel about writing your own biography?
   - Did you feel that you were taking a risk describing yourself to others?
   - What is a risk?
   - How do you feel when you take one?
5. Write a paragraph that describes how being an entrepreneur would affect your lifestyle.
6. As a class, prepare a list of ten achievers from fields such as athletics, art, music, community service, and business. Identify the personal characteristics of each individual and compare these to the attributes of a typical entrepreneur.
7. Select one of the following industries and suggest a number of ways in which a company within that industry could encourage and benefit from intrapreneurship: fast-food, music, technology, health, and recreation.

"You, too, can become an entrepreneur." The SELF spoke of the Venture Creation Wheel is highlighted to help you focus on your entrepreneurial skills and characteristics. Identify your strengths and areas that may need to be improved. Set personal goals and plan to achieve them.

CHAPTER 2

Focus on You: The Soon-to-be Entrepreneur

LEARNING OUTCOMES

By the end of this chapter, you should be able to:

- understand the Venture Creation Model and the components of the Venture Creation Wheel
- recognize that entrepreneurial success involves a wide range of variables
- understand the importance of goal setting and planning to a successful entrepreneurial activity
- identify and classify your own goals
- assess the three major types of skills required in entrepreneurship
- recognize the importance of the entrepreneur to the venture creation process

ENTREPRENEURIAL LANGUAGE

Venture Creation Model
Venture Creation Wheel
Self Spoke
Ideas Spoke
Opportunities Spoke
Resources Spoke
Operations Spoke
Finance Spoke
Management Spoke
goal
stepping stone
milestone
target date
interpersonal skills
critical and creative thinking skills
practical skills

Venture
PROFILE

Bryan Adams

SUPERSTAR BRYAN ADAMS Rock 'n Roll Inc.

Canadian Business

Bryan Adams plants his right foot on the stage near the microphone, the left heel bumps to the beat of his opening guitar chords, and his raspy voice comes rolling through 56 giant speakers toward 14 000 fans. Currently, he is by far the most successful all-round songwriter, artist, and merchandiser in a Canadian music industry that is just now coming of age.

Adams has managed to succeed in both the U.S. and in his contract negotiations with A&M Records Inc. like no other Canadian. Adams's rise has been greatly aided by his own innate business sense. He understands all the elements of the business. He could have made it in any business. He's intelligent, he's worked hard, and he's paid his dues.

Adams was born in Kingston, Ontario, but because his father was a mid-level diplomat with External Affairs, the family moved several times during his childhood. When he was 12, he announced he was going to be a rock star. His parents' marriage broke up at about the same time and his mother, Jane Clark, has since remarried and serves as a director for her son's company, Adams Communications Inc.

He left school in Vancouver after Grade 12, took the $2000 his parents had set aside for his education, and bought a piano. Adams played with a local band called Shock, then joined another B.C. rock group, Sweeney Todd. When that band broke up in 1978, he began collaborating with songwriter Jim Vallance.

In the early stages, it looked as if Adams would never be signed by any record company. In 1978, after being turned down by a dozen firms, he finally signed with Irving-Almo of Canada Inc., which at that time was the Canadian publishing arm of A&M Records. Adams was so desperate to be signed with someone that he agreed to the payment of a paltry $1. By contrast, his success in the 1980s has meant that his contract, now with the parent company, A&M Records in the U.S., has been renegotiated three times and on increasingly favourable terms.

To make ends meet, Adams sang radio commercials for such firms as Thrifty's, Eaton's, and the Bay until 1983. He succeeded because he worked his tail off. He stayed out on the road incessantly. He played every little joint.

In 1983, when Adams came out with hit singles "Cuts like a Knife" and "Straight from the Heart", he performed more than 100 U.S. dates in five months followed by a six-week, 11-country tour of Europe. That December, he won the Juno Award as the top male vocalist in Canada.

Adams has the aura of a successful businessman running a medium-sized enterprise. He has gathered almost six dozen people around him. In addition to the four band members, there are five or six staff working in manager Bruce Allen's office, there are fan club and mail order administrators working for Allen, and there are eight people whose company handles the sale of Adams's merchandise; and then there are 38 people involved in the concert tour, including the road crew and drivers.

Apparently, Adams is a good employer. He's had the same crew, the same band, the same people around him for a long time. A lot of people depend on him for their livelihood and he's very responsible in that regard.

As president of Adams Communications, Bryan Adams receives income from a variety of sources. In addition to concert profits and merchandising, there's also revenue from record sales. In total, he has sold about 10 million albums for earnings of $12.5 million.

Despite his success, Adams has donated his time for social causes and charitable events. He performed at the Philadelphia portion of the Live Aid concert for famine relief; participated in the 1986 Conspiracy of Hope Tour, a benefit for Amnesty International; and twice appeared at London's Wembley Arena for the Prince's Trust, a benefit to raise funds for charities picked by Prince Charles. In 1986, when he played Vancouver's Expo 86 for an audience that included the Prince and Princess of Wales, Adams donated his $100 000 fee to three charities.

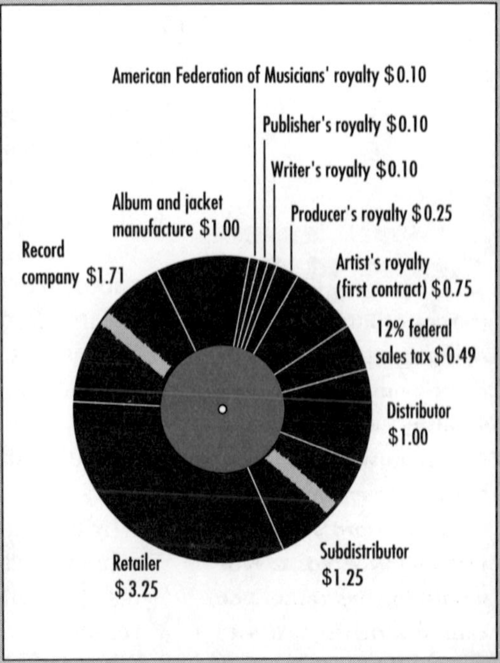

Who Gets What When You Put Out $10 for an Album

EXPLORING • SUPERSTAR BRYAN ADAMS

1. What was Bryan Adams's goal?
2. How did he go about achieving his goal?
3. What personal characteristics does Bryan have that have helped him become successful?
4. If Bryan Adams had decided to open a chain of restaurants, how well do you think he would have succeeded? Explain your answer.
5. Bryan Adams is considered to be a very good employer. Why is this important to his success?
6. Why do you think Bryan Adams agreed to a $1 payment for his first contract?
7. How did Adams manage to support himself in the early years?
8. Why do you think Bryan Adams donates his time and money to charities and social causes? Do you agree or disagree with his actions in this regard? Give your reasons.
9. What do you feel is the motivating factor for Bryan Adams?
10. Find information on a rock group of your own choice. Are there any similarities between Bryan Adams and this group?

AGENTS OF CHANGE

Millions of Ethiopians were dying of starvation. The music industry is extremely wealthy. Bob Geldof, a British musician, brought together other famous musicians to record songs and perform in concerts to raise money for this cause. Bob caused a rich industry to make a difference for millions of poor people.

Venture PROFILE

Successful Restauranteur and Racehorse Owner, George Bigliardi

George Bigliardi is proof that it pays to dream big

By Leslie Scrivener, *Toronto Star*

Thirty years ago when he stepped off the boat, a skinny, lonely kid without a word of English, Bigliardi wanted to go back home to Parma, Italy.

He arrived in Toronto on a Tuesday, by Wednesday, he was working as a bus boy at the Club One-Two. He didn't know a bacon and tomato sandwich from a crème caramel. Sometimes he'd substitute one for the other.

Today, Bigliardi wears a tuxedo every working night. He owns a restaurant with trademark wood panelling, brass rails, and five-centimetre thick steaks; he owns the Church Street building that houses the restaurant; he owns racehorses; he owns a Cadillac El Dorado.

Ingenious and playful as he seems, he runs his restaurant and staff of pokerfaced waiters with a discipline worthy of a Prussian general. Service is discreet, reliable; most waiters have been with him for years.

Those in the know order *potato à la Gordon*, named after the singer Gordon Lightfoot, a friend and regular customer.

Carol Padmore is a long-time friend of Bigliardi's; they met at Harry's Steak House, where she did the books and he was manager. "I remember when I first met him, he was giving and warm and sensitive. That doesn't come across in the day-to-day running of his business. You see the boisterous, outgoing side. That sensitive, quiet side doesn't come out very often."

When Padmore's husband died several years ago, Bigliardi quietly paid for the grave marker. "That's just the kind of friend he is," she says.

When it is time for the Variety Village Bike-a-thon fundraising, Bigliardi isn't shy to ask his prominent and, more often than not, wealthy customers for a donation. Last year he raised $8000 for Variety Village.

He's been working since he was eight years old. He quit school when he was eleven—his parents didn't have much money and he wasn't crazy about education himself.

He was a grocery salesman, and one day he met a salesman who'd been in the business 12 years and was at the top of his profession. Bigliardi knew immediately that the man wasn't earning enough or accomplishing enough to fulfil his own dreams.

His parents were so upset by his departure, they couldn't bear to see him off from the docks at Genoa.

When the Club One-Two folded, he went to work at the King Edward Hotel as a bus boy earning $40 a week. He was hired as manager at Harry's. "From a waiter who takes orders to a manager who gives them, it was a whole different ball game," says Bigliardi.

Ten years ago when the Seagull restaurant went up for sale across the street, he bought it with two silent partners, whom he bought out within a year.

Now, he has a system of house accounts where customers sign rather than pay by cash or credit card. One regular customer accumulated $1700 in bills, then wasn't seen in the restaurant for eight months. Bigliardi called him and said, "Come back, why spend your money some place else? Come back and pay cash and pay off the bill when you can."

"Without realizing it, I built a restaurant around myself," he says.

EXPLORING • BIGLIARDI'S BIG DREAM

1. Refer to the list of characteristics common to successful entrepreneurs given in Chapter 1 (pages 26-27). Identify those that Bigliardi has. Give reasons for your answer.
2. What was Bigliardi's goal?
3. How did Bigliardi go about achieving his goal?
4. In what ways did Bigliardi's plans to achieve his goals differ from those of Bryan Adams?
5. "Without realizing it, I built a restaurant around myself." Do you think this is an accurate statement? Why or why not?

The Venture Creation Model

The process of entrepreneurship, using entrepreneurial skills to create a new venture, involves ability, a set of values, and an overall plan or procedure for action. Venture creation needs more than knowledge: it requires appropriate skills and attitudes to bring about positive results. The **Venture Creation Model** helps explain the entrepreneurial process.

This model may be consulted when undertaking a new entrepreneurial venture.

The model itself should not be followed in a linear pattern. The process of venture creation involves a great many variables. It combines seemingly chaotic, creative thinking and behaviour with highly disciplined, critical thinking and decision making. For these reasons, venture creation cannot be described as a set of step-by-step instructions such as exists in an instruction manual for a product.

The process of venture creation looks more like a bicycle wheel, known as the **Venture Creation Wheel**. In a bicycle wheel, there is a hub with many spokes. Each spoke is connected to and supports the rim. The rim gives the wheel its shape and stability. It forms the foundation to which the wheel is attached.

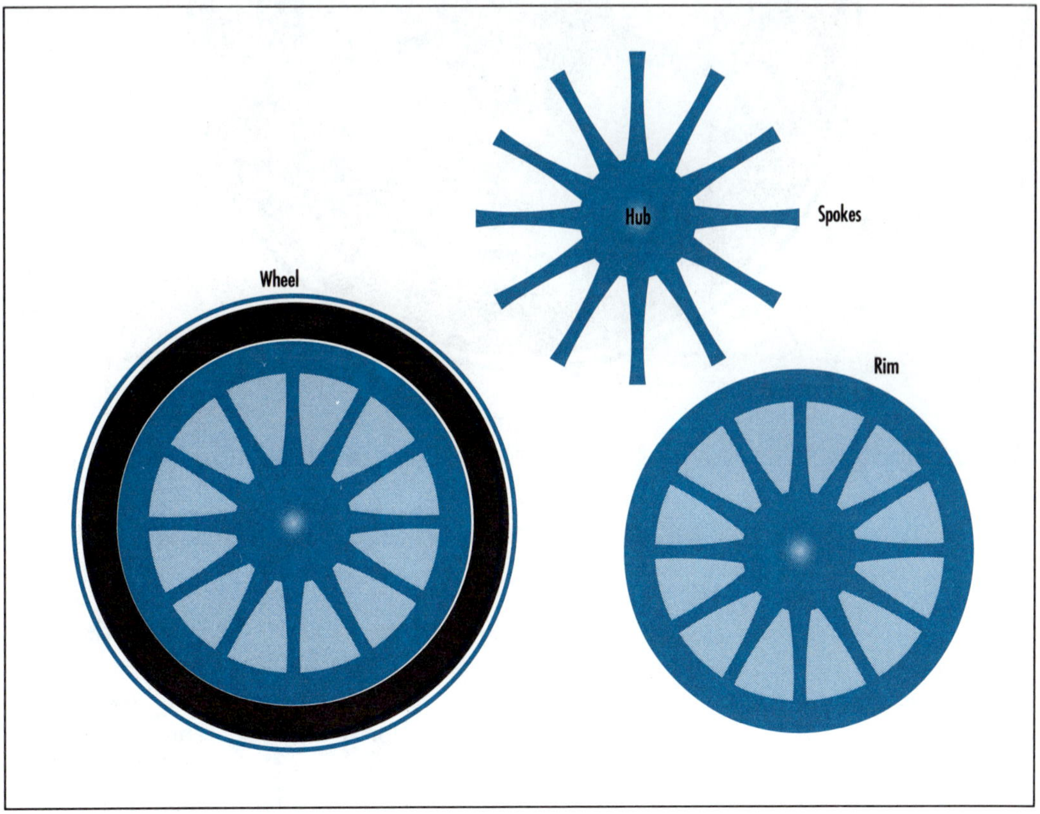

Figure 2.1 The Venture Creation Process is similar to the bicycle wheel.

The process of venture creation helps the world go around.

Figure 2.2 The Venture Creation Wheel. With the Venture Creation Wheel, all the elements support the venture creation process.

Spokes in the Venture Creation Wheel

The foundation of the venture is created by the hub and the spokes. Just as it takes many spokes to give a bicycle wheel strength and stability, so it is with the Venture Creation Wheel. The success or failure of the venture depends on how well the entrepreneur at the hub performs the tasks represented by the spokes. There are seven spokes in the wheel: Self, Ideas, Opportunities, Resources, Operations, Finance, and Management.

The **Self Spoke** looks at you, the entrepreneur, at the hub or centre of the venture creation process. Starting a venture requires effort and skill. It entails commitment and persistence. For these reasons, it is important for aspiring entrepreneurs to question themselves continually. What are my needs? My strengths? My interests? What do I enjoy doing? What are my goals? What do I know? What can I do? Asking such questions begins the process of self-assessment which will help determine what an individual is trying to achieve and what kind of venture he or she is best suited to. This chapter focuses on the self, or you, the prospective entrepreneur.

The **Ideas Spoke** generates and evaluates ideas for a venture. Generating ideas requires the entrepreneur to use the right side of the brain—the creative side. Learning to be a creative thinker takes practice. In Chapter 3, you will learn some techniques to help unlock the right side of the brain.

AGENTS OF CHANGE

Business and government in Toronto always need documents translated from French into English. Louise Piller-Thay is bilingual and recognized that her skill could be used to start a translation business. Today, her firm translates more than two million words per year. Toronto's need translated into big business for Louise.

The **Opportunities Spoke** identifies entrepreneurial opportunities by examining and tracing trends and changes in society that give rise to opportunity. In Chapters 4, 5, and 7 you will discover how to identify and evaluate opportunities.

Chapter 6 offers an overview of the components of a venture plan. All the spokes on the wheel are required to create a successful venture.

Mobilizing resources is an entrepreneurial activity that leads to the successful venture. The **Resources Spoke** is described in Chapter 8.

The **Operations Spoke** of the Venture Creation Wheel deals with organizing resources and using them on a day-to-day basis. Details of how to do this are included in Chapter 9.

Raising capital and planning the finances of the venture over the short and long term are essential to the success of the venture. The **Finance Spoke** demonstrates how to organize a financial strategy for the venture. This is described in Chapters 10 and 11.

Chapter 12 deals with the **Management Spoke** of the venture. Once the venture is started, it is crucial that the entrepreneur develops management strategies for the survival of the venture.

The venture plan is essential to the startup of any entrepreneurial endeavour. Chapter 13 illustrates how to pull all of the components of the venture plan together.

You, the entrepreneur, are the most important element of any venture. Chapter 14 focuses on you and your entrepreneurial future.

Goal Setting and Planning

A **goal** can be defined as a process or direction that you work towards. Achieving a goal is measureable. Along the way, you will encounter **stepping stones**—smaller objectives towards the goal that can be achieved in a shorter time frame. Specific events that mark progress towards the goal are termed **milestones.** For example, if your goal is to graduate from high school, stepping stones might be passing your assignments and tests; and a milestone would be earning an additional credit toward your diploma.

CATHY **by Cathy Guisewite**

Figure 2.3 Set realistic, challenging, and worthwhile goals.

Goals should always be written down. This helps to ensure that you understand exactly your commitment to yourself. The written list of goals serves as a reminder as you work through the goal-setting process.

Goals should also be realistic. If you set an impossible goal for yourself, and you do not have the resources to help make it happen, frustration and failure will be the result. However, goals should be challenging and should require some degree of effort. You should set a **target date** for achieving your goals. If progress towards your goal is not on target, you should be flexible enough either to increase your resources to meet the target date or to alter the target date.

AGENTS OF CHANGE

Opportunities to succeed in society were few if you were a woman; especially if your skin was black. Mary Ann Shadd, a gifted woman, worked selflessly and tirelessly to improve conditions for African-Canadians in Canada's West, devoting years to developing a school for African-Canadian children. One woman's strength helped change the lives of countless generations.

Your goals should be worthwhile. Only you can determine this. If you do not take the time to plan your own goals, you may wind up adopting those of someone else. The question to be answered is: "Is this important to me?" If the answer is "yes", pursue it wholeheartedly. If the answer is "no", it is time to reflect on what is important to you.

It is likely that you will have more than one goal. You may have financial goals, entrepreneurial goals, family goals, social goals, or any combination of these.

Goals are not just something you think about, goals are something you achieve.

It is easier to talk about goal setting than it is to actually set goals. Many obstacles prevent us from taking the time to sit down and set our goals. Being too busy is a typical excuse for not focusing on our goals. We rarely have enough time to determine what we are doing in the present, so how are we supposed to find time to determine what we will do in the immediate and distant future?

It is important to recognize that goal setting may have a wide variety of results. It can lead to happiness, lifestyle changes, wide-ranging risks, frustration, no change at all, or any combination. Goal setting does, however, help us look into the future and select the best path. It can make all of us more effective and efficient in our personal and business lives. Establishing goals and organizing a way of achieving them is the first step in achieving them.

Where there is a way, there is a goal.

YOUR TURN

1. Prepare a wish list for yourself. Write down as many things as you can think of that you would like to have and that you would like to do. You might want to buy a Porsche, to retire at 50, to find a cure for AIDS, or to develop a new method of transportation. Do not worry if your wishes are not realistic. Rank the wishes in order of priority. Set a target date for the achievement of each. Now go through the list and cross out the ones that you think are impossible for you to achieve. You may be left

with one realistic wish, or you may have harvested a large crop. Take the wishes remaining on your list and rewrite each one in terms of a goal.

2. List your strengths, weaknesses, and areas in which you can improve. Formulate a plan to make use of your strengths and to improve areas in which you are lacking. Be sure to be completely honest with yourself.
3. Below is a lifeline. Picture your life as a series of events. Make your own lifeline, listing the milestones that will help shape your life.

____

Now   Death

4. Write a letter to yourself indicating your goal(s). Include the stepping stones and milestones that you will encounter along the way. Write down a plan for achieving your goal(s). You might want to first answer some of the following questions to help you determine your personal goals.
   a) How do you see your daily activities evolving over the next ten years?
   b) What kind of work do you have in mind for yourself?
   c) Do you see yourself working with others in a team environment?
   d) Are you thinking about a family? How will this affect your career plans?
   e) What hobbies or sports do you want to spend time on?
   f) Do you want to travel? Should travel be part of your work activities or part of your leisure time?
   g) How much formal education would you like?
   h) What do you want to learn on your own?
   i) What do you think you need to learn to achieve your goals?
   j) Are any of your goals in conflict?

   Put the letter in a sealed envelope with your name on the outside. Give the envelope to your teacher. In Chapter 14, you will be asked to open your envelope to help you plan for an entrepreneurial life. Your teacher will return it to you at that time.
5. Are your goals similar to any of those of the entrepreneurs you have already met?

Flexibility Is the Key

"Minds are like parachutes — they don't function unless they are open."
Elwood Chapman

People who are entrepreneurial need to believe in themselves if they are to realize the goals they set. It is important to keep an open mind when setting goals and preparing a plan to achieve them. There is a greater chance of success in achieving goals if you remain flexible in your attitude and change the plan of action if the need arises. Flexibility does not diminish the importance or worth of a goal. Rather, it increases its importance because it increases the likelihood that the goal will be attained.

Your Turn

6. Suggest several reasons why people might have to revise or change some of their goals as they get older and acquire more education.
7. Why is flexibility important in goal setting?
8. Some goals are impossible to achieve. Why? What can be done about this? What are the dangers in consistently setting these types of goals?
9. Should career goals relate to personal goals? Explain.

Goal Setting and Commitment

Achieving goals requires commitment. The following story is an example:

> The chicken and the pig were walking down the street one day when they came upon a restaurant with a sign: "Ham and Eggs 79¢." The chicken was really proud about those eggs and she began strutting back and forth claiming, "What would breakfast be without eggs? Eggs and breakfast are synonymous," and she was going on and on until finally the pig interrupted her and said, "Yes, you are absolutely right. But with me, it is a total commitment."

If an individual makes a total commitment to a goal and believes in success, he or she greatly increases the chances of success. Vicki Keith and Carolyn Waldo are athletes who

Figure 2.4 Commitment can take a variety of forms.

> "The three great essentials to achieve anything worthwhile are first, hard work; second, stick-to-itiveness; third, common sense."
> *Thomas Alva Edison*

achieved their goals through their commitment to practise several hours every day. k.d. lang is a performing artist who rehearses to achieve her goals. Greig Clarke, founder of College Pro Painters, has a plan to help him achieve his entrepreneurial goals.

When an obstacle is encountered while carrying out a plan to achieve a goal, it should be turned into a new challenge. This new challenge provides motivation to develop new strengths and abilities that will eventually lead to future successes.

Achieving a goal is hard work. Entrepreneurs need to develop strategies to help achieve the goal.

YOUR TURN

10. Learning to know yourself is a life-long process. Just when you begin to feel comfortable, circumstances change, your reactions change, and you need to learn something new about yourself. It is important to continue the quest to know yourself, particularly if you want to be successful as an entrepreneur.

    Getting To Know ______________________ (your name)

    Activity

    a) Divide a large piece of paper (11" x 14") into four parts. In part one, write your name and three facts about yourself. In part two, list 10 questions another person should ask you to get to know you better. In part three, list five people you admire (it could be from afar), and in part four, write three of your pastimes.
    b) When you have completed your page, select a partner in the class. Exchange pages with your partner. Ask each other the questions you have written. Explain to each other why you selected the five people you admire.
    c) Join another set of partners so that you now have four people in your group.
    d) Describe your original partner to the group.
11. Upon reflection, what did you learn from this activity? Do you feel you understand yourself a little better?
12. How can the opinions of others help you to know yourself?

Figure 2.5

Venture PROFILE

Learning by experience

It is a good idea to gain experience in a field before you enter it as a career.

Gina daSilva has played the guitar since she was ten and has been a member of an informal band throughout her high school career. Her dream is to become a rock star, but everyone tells her she would be unlikely to make a living at it. As she nears graduation, she realizes she has no clear goals for her future. Gina's Entrepreneurial Studies teacher suggests she selects Co-operative Education for a semester so that she can work in a music-related field to gain some experience and see if she would like music as a career.

Her co-op placement involves four months in a music specialty store. Gina discovers that she enjoys the business but feels she would be unhappy working for someone else. Gina decides to examine the possibilities of starting her own music-related business. She begins with a look at herself.

EXPLORING • LEARNING BY EXPERIENCE

1. In what way is Gina working to establish goals for herself?
2. What plan should Gina begin to develop to achieve her goals?
3. How has a co-operative education placement helped Gina to focus on her goals?
4. What options do you think are open to Gina? Brainstorm these with some of your classmates.
5. In what ways, if any, are you similar to Gina?

Understanding Yourself

> "The most difficult thing in life is to know yourself."
> *Thales*

It is important for a prospective entrepreneur to understand himself or herself, and to understand the skills, traits, and values that he or she could bring to a new venture. Without this self-knowledge, the entrepreneur could begin a venture unequipped to handle the demands of the venture.

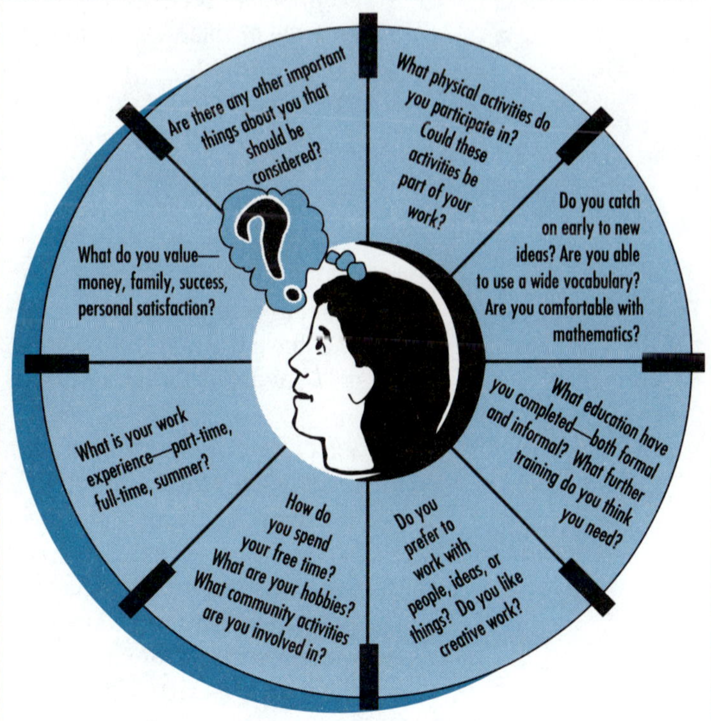

Figure 2.6 The Wheel of Fortune. By questioning yourself, you learn more about your skills, traits, and values.

Answering the questions contained in the Wheel of Fortune will help the entrepreneur determine what his or her personal fortune is in relation to the venture. Once strengths and weaknesses are sorted out, the entrepreneur can begin to implement a plan of action.

YOUR TURN

13. In your notebook, write the heading: "DO I HAVE WHAT IT TAKES? CHECKLIST". Respond to each of the following statements according to the following continuum:

Most of the time	Sometimes	Hardly ever

a) I have a great deal of energy.
b) I am confident I can do what I set out to do.
c) I can plan for the future.
d) Money is important to me.
e) I take responsibility for my own actions.
f) Achieving my goals is more important to me than financial security.
g) I see problems as challenges that make daily life interesting.
h) I am able to set goals for myself.
i) I am comfortable with risk.
j) I am able to learn from my mistakes.
k) I am willing to seek help when I need it.
l) I strive for excellence in everything that I do.
m) I am flexible.
n) I am reliable.
o) I have the ability to be creative and innovative.
p) I am able to interact well with others.

14. Select four of the above statements to which you responded "Most of the time". Write a brief paragraph outlining an example from your background or experience to illustrate these personal characteristics.
15. On a separate sheet of paper, draw a circle similar to the one in Figure 2.6 (page 49). Inside each section of your new circle, answer the questions from the original Figure 2.6 circle. When you have completed your answers, turn to the person next to you and discuss your answers.
16. What did you learn from completing the chart?
17. In what ways did sharing your answers with another person enhance what you learned about yourself?
18. Select one thing about yourself that you would like to change. Write it down in your notebook so that you can refer to it later.

Figure 2.7 Take stock of yourself.

Assessing Your Skills

To succeed as an entrepreneur, you must develop skills that will help you to achieve clearly defined goals.

> As an entrepreneur you will be required to transfer your specific skills into more general ones.

For example, going to the library to look up information for a school research project has given you a valuable research skill. How can this specific skill of knowing how to use the library for a school research project be transferred into a general research skill?

Interpersonal skills, **critical and creative thinking skills**, and **practical skills** are all essential in varying degrees for an entrepreneur to be successful. What are these skills and which ones do you have?

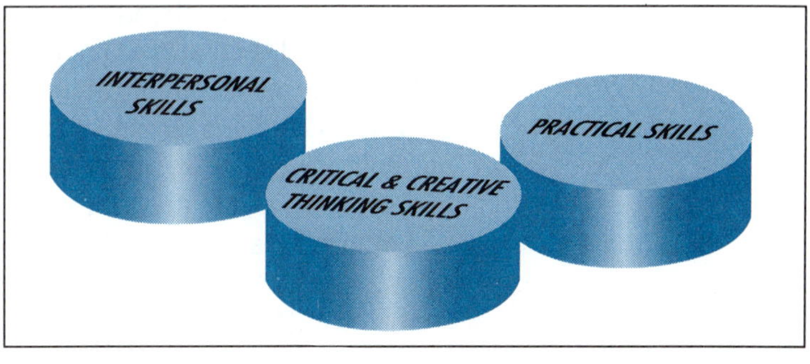

Figure 2.8 Successful entrepreneurs require these three types of skills.

AGENTS OF CHANGE

Europeans did not understand the Inuit people, and so the two sides were often at war. Mikak, the daughter of an Inuit Chief, was taken prisoner while fighting the Europeans. Freed from an English jail, she worked hard to help the English understand the Inuit and raised money to build a mission in Labrador. One person's wisdom brought a nation to understanding.

Interpersonal Skills

These skills involve the following:

- willingness and ability to talk to others, especially those different from ourselves
- ability to listen to and understand what others are saying
- motivating others
- encouraging others
- negotiating and resolving conflicts
- caring

Critical and Creative Thinking Skills

- ability to solve problems by evaluating a variety of solutions
- confidence to make a decision and act upon it
- ability to set goals, plan how to achieve them, and carry out the plan
- keeping records and being accountable for all actions undertaken
- ability to generate ideas and identify opportunities

Practical Skills

- ability to follow instructions
- knowledge of specific tools in the entrepreneurial venture, for example, computer literacy, manual dexterity, the ability to work with very small objects

Most of us will never attain the fortune and fame of Bryan Adams; however, with clear, attainable goals and a solid skill base, each of us should be able to reach our own personal level of satisfaction. It is up to each individual to determine the skills he or she already has and the skills that need to be acquired, and then devise a plan for acquiring them.

Rick Hansen demonstrated interpersonal skills when he communicated his dream and won the support of a large number of people for his Man in Motion Tour. Hansen used his critical and creative thinking skills in setting his goals and preparing a plan of action to achieve them. His practical skills were demonstrated throughout his tour and were a contributing factor to his success.

Figure 2.9 Your present skills can be projected into the future.

Strategies for Entrepreneurial Success

A number of strategies exist to increase the chances of entrepreneurial success. It is important for entrepreneurs to think before acting and to consider a problem from different perspectives. Reflective rather than impulsive decisions are typically better decisions.

Entrepreneurs should resist the pressure to conform. They should be confident in their own abilities and only compete with themselves to improve. Constant comparison and pressure to conform can often lead to stress and unhappiness for the entrepreneur.

When creating a venture, an entrepreneur should thoroughly consider his or her abilities, personality traits, skills, and goals. To experience the full effect of the entrepreneurial spirit, the venture should challenge the entrepreneur's abilities, allow for the use of creativity, suit the entrepreneur's personality, and be compatible with the entrepreneur's vision of him or herself.

YOUR TURN

19. Reread the Venture Profiles of David Opie and Shirley McNaughton in Chapter 1. Write a paragraph similar to the one on page 52 on Rick Hansen illustrating the skills these entrepreneurs have demonstrated.
20. Make a list of those skills which you feel you need to improve in yourself. Then briefly list the strategies you would use for self-improvement. Set it up in chart form as follows:

SKILL	STRATEGY FOR IMPROVEMENT

21. Give three strategies that a prospective entrepreneur should use to help increase his or her chances of entrepreneurial success.

> "I am a great believer in luck and I find the harder I work, the more I have of it."
> *Stephen Leacock*

Venture PROFILE

Success in small doses

By David Silburt, *Canadian Business*

Lukas struck gold in capsules by letting other firms in on the action.

In the early 1950s, young pharmaceutical salesman Stephen Lukas toured his employer's production facility and saw his future unfold. "The dream started the first time I walked into the plant," he recalls. "I saw 16 machines in one room and just a couple of operators. Millions of capsules were coming out of those machines."

Impressed by that kind of production efficiency, Lukas began to think about starting his own company to manufacture gelatin capsules, the digestible shells that encase individual doses of drugs. More than three decades later, his dream has come true, but not the way he originally imagined.

Today, 62-year-old Lukas heads up Capsule Technology Group Inc. The Windsor, Ontario-based company does manufacture and market capsules. But it has made its real reputation and found a unique niche for itself in manufacturing and selling capsule-making machinery to other companies around the world. By thinking internationally and marketing aggressively, Lukas has built a small Canadian company into a significant player in the global market.

A native of Austria, Lukas emigrated to Canada in 1950 after the communist takeover of Czechoslovakia caused him to end his medical studies there. His first job in the pharmaceutical industry was in sales with the Toronto office of Parke-Davis. At the time, the worldwide capsule-manufacturing business was controlled entirely by two companies: Parke-Davis and Eli Lilly. In 1964, Lukas left the firm to realize his long-time dream of starting a new firm to compete against the giants.

He founded Gelatine Capsules Ltd. in Windsor to sell hard capsules directly to drug manufacturers. He invested $80 000 and a partner put in $140 000. The company's sales were $500 000 in its first year and $16 million by 1974. Then, feeling he'd taken the firm as far as it could go, Lukas sold it to R.P. Scherer Corp. for $1.3 million and remained with Scherer as president of capsule operations.

While working there, he proposed to his colleagues that the company should move into the business of turnkey capsule-making plants: selling overseas customers as many self-contained, automatic capsule-making machines as each needed to set up an efficient manufacturing facility. The other Scherer people weren't interested, but Lukas was sure that developing countries would jump at the chance to save money and gain independence by making their own capsules.

Lukas left Scherer in 1978 and, while waiting out a five-year, non-competition agreement he signed before leaving, he lived on savings and organized his plans for Capsule Technology International. In 1988, he projected total sales of $54 million.

Lukas relies heavily on foreign markets to meet his ambitious sales goals. "If you think world, that's the important thing," he says. "To think just Canada or the United States is an old story. You've got to think Indonesia, Brazil—all those other places."

EXPLORING • SUCCESS IN SMALL DOSES

1. What was Lukas's goal?
2. How did the goal change over time?
3. How did Lukas's attitude contribute to his success?
4. What personal characteristics does Lukas have that have been identified as entrepreneurial?
5. Lukas has many skills. What are these skills?
6. Are Lukas's skills transferable to other entrepreneurial endeavours?

7. Did Capsule Technology International challenge Lukas's ability and encourage him to be creative? Provide a brief explanation with your answer.
8. Were Lukas's entrepreneurial activities compatible with his vision of himself?
9. Read this case study over again. What underlying message might exist here that could help you focus on achieving your entrepreneurial goals?

P·O·I·N·T·S T·O R·E·M·E·M·B·E·R

AGENTS OF CHANGE

In 1909, Canadian born Elizabeth Arden opened a beauty salon on New York's Fifth Avenue. A pioneer in advertising of cosmetics, she was soon marketing up to 300 different beauty aids in pharmacies and department stores throughout the world.

- The process of venture creation is like a wheel with the seven spokes of Self, Ideas, Opportunities, Resources, Operations, Finance, and Management.
- Entrepreneurial activity begins with a dream which must be translated into goals, stepping stones, and milestones.
- Thorough self-examination and self-knowledge are important both before starting a new venture and as an on-going activity.
- A firm belief in oneself and a commitment to that belief is the key to success for any entrepreneurial venture.
- Interpersonal skills, critical and creative thinking skills, and practical skills are all important to entrepreneurs.
- A positive, confident, and creative attitude helps the entrepreneur overcome barriers in achieving goals.

W·H·A·T H·A·V·E Y·O·U L·E·A·R·N·E·D?

1. What do Bryan Adams and George Bigliardi have in common?
2. List the skills that each of these two entrepreneurs has shown.
3. In what way does the Venture Creation Wheel relate to the venture creation process?
4. Differentiate between a goal, a stepping stone, and a milestone.
5. What characteristics should a goal have before you adopt it as your own?
6. Why is it easier to talk about goal setting than it is to practise goal setting?

7. In what ways are flexibility and commitment important in the goal-setting process?
8. What do entrepreneurs need to know about themselves to increase their ability to organize their ventures?
9. What is meant by transferring your skills from the specific to the general? Give an example.
10. Explain how interpersonal skills, critical and creative thinking skills, and practical skills are important for the entrepreneur.

V·E·N·T·U·R·I·N·G O·U·T

1. a) List two goals that you could take action on in the next month.
   b) How do you plan to achieve these goals?
   c) What obstacles stand in your way? How can you bypass them?
2. Reread the case studies of Bryan Adams and George Bigliardi. Write down obstacles which each of them had to overcome to achieve their goals.
3. "Creating a venture is more art than science." With two or three other students in your class, discuss what this means. Consider a number of examples of ventures that demonstrate this statement. Share your ideas with the class.
4. Interview three entrepreneurs in your community and ask them the following question: "How does the process of venture creation help the world go around?" Bring your answers back to class and discuss them with the rest of the class.
5. In pairs, create a poster incorporating some of the answers you received in Question 4.
6. Briefly explain, in written form, how interpersonal skills, critical and creative thinking skills, and practical skills are linked together in a successful venture.
7. Contact an entrepreneur in your community and ask him or her what skills were needed to achieve success in his or her venture. Provide an oral report on your findings.

"Think before you act." Chapter 3 introduces the four roles played by the successful entrepreneur and the six thinking hats the entrepreneur must wear while playing these roles. It is an exercise in "whole brain" thinking.

CHAPTER 3

The Creative Edge

LEARNING OUTCOMES

By the end of this chapter, you should be able to:

- identify each stage in the creative problem-solving process
- distinguish between the four problem-solving roles identified by Roger von Oech
- understand and apply Edward de Bono's concept of the six thinking hats
- generate ideas using the techniques of word clustering, mind mapping, brainstorming, and visualizing
- distinguish between an inventor and an entrepreneur
- describe the course of an idea from invention to entrepreneurial venture

ENTREPRENEURIAL LANGUAGE

prototype
problem-finding stage
fact-finding stage
idea-finding stage
solution-finding stage
criteria
The Explorer
The Artist
The Judge
The Warrior
lateral thinking
white hat
red hat
green hat
black hat
yellow hat
blue hat
inventors
right brain
left brain
word clustering
mind mapping
brainstorming
visualizing
innovation

Venture PROFILE

The Fox 40 Whistle

RON FOXCROFT
The Fox 40

The design of the pea-whistle hadn't changed in a hundred years, that is, until Ron Foxcroft, a part-time professional referee from Hamilton, had some embarrassing moments at the Summer Olympics in Montreal. He blew his whistle to stop the play, but his old pea-whistle wasn't equal to the task. The harder you blow a pea-whistle the louder it gets — up to a point. Then no matter how hard you blow, no noise results because the pea sticks in the barrel and silences the whistle. So Foxcroft decided to redesign the whistle. He sought the help of Chuck Sheppard, a design consultant. His new whistle works without a pea at all. Three chambers replace the one chamber, and the movement in and out of phase that the three different sounds make gives the impression of the vibrato of the old pea-whistle. The harder one blows, the louder it gets. The Fox 40 was an instant success. It sells in 17 countries, and 1988 sales were $3 million. The whistle costs $1 to manufacture and wholesales at $3-4.

Venture PROFILE

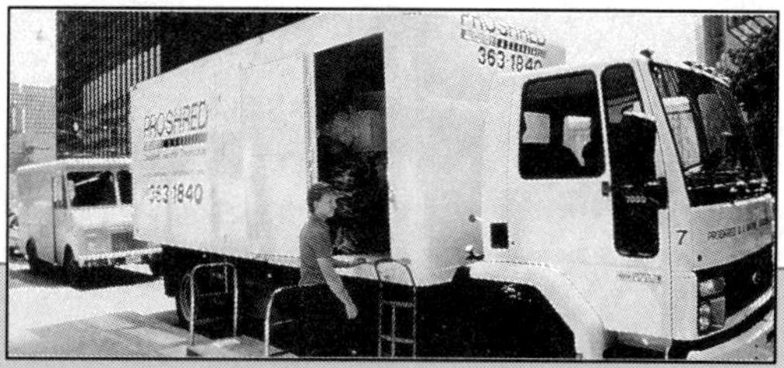

Proshred Truck

SCOTT SMITH
Proshred

Scott Smith, a Mohawk from the Six Nations Reserve, knew large corporations needed a paper document shredding service. Company budgets set aside a total of millions of dollars for shredding documents. Smith was determined to claim a share of this market. He began in December, 1985, with little more than a simple van loaded with the first **prototype**, or model, of a shredder and the promise of secure document disposal. Within three years, the company's revenues totalled more than $2.3 million. Today, Smith operates a fleet of 12 large shredder-equipped trucks and has more than 1500 clients. Future plans include a recycling plant and eventually the company intends to recycle 95 per cent of its paper.

EXPLORING • THE FOX 40 AND PROSHRED

1. What motivated Foxcroft to redesign the pea-whistle?
2. How did he go about redesigning the whistle?
3. What personal characteristics are shown in these two mini-profiles that could be considered entrepreneurial?
4. What similarities do you see between the personalities of Foxcroft and Smith?
5. What similarities are there in their ventures?
6. In each case, where did the idea for the venture come from?
7. What incident or situation helped each entrepreneur identify a need for a venture?

The Problem-Solving Process

The profiles you have just read provide examples of two inventive entrepreneurs. Each one had an idea, and then organized the resources needed to create first a prototype and then a venture. How are needs identified? From where do ideas come? How is an idea transformed into a venture? These are all part of a creative problem-solving process illustrated in Figure 3.1 on page 62.

AGENTS OF CHANGE

Peggie Pelosi, a mother of five, felt parents should choose educational and creative toys for their children. She used the shop-at-home parties, popular for selling everything from lingerie to kitchenware, to reach parents. She built Toy Workshop Inc. into a million dollar business. Peggie used an old idea to change the buying habits of millions of parents!

Stages and Skills in the Problem-Solving Process

The problem-solving process involves three stages: the problem-finding stage, the idea-finding stage, and the solution-finding stage. It also requires both creative thinking skills and critical thinking skills.

This chapter will describe the complete problem-solving process and highlight the creative thinking skills that can help to generate new ideas. The next two chapters will outline how to identify opportunities and use critical thinking skills to evaluate ideas.

Learning to become a critical and creative thinker is essential for all entrepreneurs.

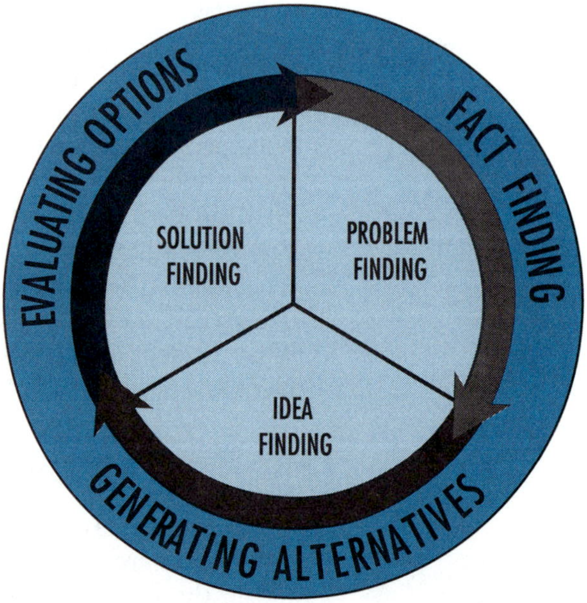

Figure 3.1 The Creative Problem-Solving Process

Problem Finding

In the **problem-finding stage**, the entrepreneur tries to define the problem by gathering all the facts, observations, feelings, and impressions about the situation. Attitudes are very important for they influence how the problem is perceived. The inventive or entrepreneurial individual will see a problem as a challenge or an opportunity. This problem can then be transformed into the creation of a venture to satisfy needs or wants.

Once the problem or opportunity has been identified, the entrepreneur has to investigate information that will support the idea that this is, in fact, a problem. This is called the **fact-finding stage**. If the entrepreneur had identified the 1989 California earthquake as a problem/opportunity, for example, the fact-finding step would have been to list the facts that support this notion. These might include:

- There are many homeless people.
- New technology is required to protect buildings and highways from giving way in the event of another earthquake.
- The 1989 world series baseball game had to be delayed.
- Many businesses in the area were closed for several days.
- Hydro-electric power was out for several days.

Idea Finding

The **idea-finding stage** is the second step in the problem-solving process. At this stage, the entrepreneur tries to come up with different alternatives or different ways of solving the problem.

> The quantity of ideas is more important than the quality of the ideas.

Some ideas may turn out to be useless or stupid, but no alternative should be dismissed at this stage. All ideas should be evaluated. Sometimes the craziest ideas lead to the best ventures, so every alternative generated should be recorded.

Solution Finding

The final step in the process is the **solution-finding stage**. During this stage, the quality of the ideas generated is evaluated. This involves first establishing the **criteria** that will be used to evaluate each option. Criteria are the standards, measures, or tests which will be used to evaluate the strengths and weaknesses of each idea. Those ideas that do not meet the criteria are put aside. The remaining ideas are considered to solve the problem.

Did you know that people who use their imagination and inventiveness change the world?

In 1935, in Valcourt, Quebec, Joseph Armand Bombardier got an idea that created a whole new industry. It also changed a season of the year for the entire world. The Bombardier profile introduced in this chapter and continued in Chapter 5 illustrates how the creative problem-solving process can result in the development of a new venture.

Venture PROFILE

JOSEPH ARMAND BOMBARDIER
The Inventor

Some of Bombardier's Early Designs

Eighty years ago, Valcourt was a small rural community in the Eastern Townships of Quebec. Life proceeded at a regular slow pace as dictated by the needs of the crops and the climate. When winter arrived, life seemed to grind to a halt. It is difficult for us today to appreciate the isolation and loneliness of a rural winter almost a century ago. Today, ploughs clear the roads. Salt and sand keep them clear. We get around. Even if we are stuck for a day, we can keep in touch with the world by phone, radio, and television. Eighty years ago, there were no ploughs or salt and sand for the roads. It didn't really matter much for there were no cars — only sleighs drawn by horses. There were no phones or radios or television. There was only snow and isolation which could last for days, even weeks. This was the setting into which Joseph Armand Bombardier was born in 1907. He was the eldest of eight children.

Most people accepted the isolation for there was little choice. Bombardier filled his time making and playing with toys of his own design. He had a fascination for things mechanical and, from an early age, he dreamed of inventing a machine that would shatter the isolation and boredom of winter. His interests and abilities were supported to an extent by his family. At 16, he went to Montreal for one and a half years to study mechanical and electrical engineering. In 1926, when Bombardier was 19, he returned back to Valcourt to run a garage his father had purchased for him. It was in that garage that his idea was born.

Twenty-five years after Bombardier's birth, the horse-drawn sleigh remained the usual method of transportation in Valcourt during the winter. There were better roads and cars, but the cars were stored away once the snow arrived. Bombardier's garage was not very busy during the winter months, which meant he had the time he needed to work on his dream. He had built his first prototype in 1922 at the age of 15. His father had given him an automobile. He removed the engine. He attached an airplane propeller to the place where the radiator fan would normally go. It was a dangerous contraption and his father, horrified at the danger of the bulky, propeller-driven machine, ordered it dismantled.

One day as he was looking at the tracks of a sleigh in the snow, Bombardier wondered what would happen if he changed the front wheels of a car for skis and put them closer together so they would run in the sleigh tracks. He also added extra wheels in the back with chains strapped to them. It worked, but not very well. He tried to adapt other mechanical devices, such as the propeller, to his own creation. His various models at times were part car, part airplane, and part sleigh. Each adaptation led him to a new idea of how he might improve his design. Using wheels on his machine meant that it must stay on the roads. To improve the machine's performance in deep snow and during off-road travel, he experimented with various types of belts. Eventually, he replaced the large wheels with many smaller ones and substituted a rubber track for the metal one.

In 1934, Bombardier's dream to build a machine which would travel quickly and safely over the snow was reinforced by a personal tragedy. One day at the garage, he received an urgent message to return home. His two-year-old son was suffering terrible pain. The doctor arrived and diagnosed it as appendicitis. The child had to be rushed to the hospital immediately. Unfortunately, the closest hospital was in Sherbrooke, and there was no way of getting there. The road was completely blocked by snowdrifts. All of Bombardier's prototypes were in pieces on his garage floor. His son died. At first, the tragedy emotionally drained Bombardier. He had little interest and less desire to continue his work. Later, after he recovered from the shock of his son's death, he returned to his dream with renewed energy.

In 1935, he discovered the key which would unlock the problem of providing power and traction in deep snow. He reinvented the wheel. He designed a wooden sprocket wheel with 12 cogs, and covered it with a track made of rubber belting and crosslinks. The cogs on the wheel fit neatly into the spaces between the steel bars along the tread. It proved to be *the* solution which provided both speed and traction in deep snow at reasonable cost. From that point on, everything Bombardier did was an extension of this simple but beautiful principle.

EXPLORING • BOMBARDIER: THE INVENTOR

1. What motivated Bombardier to venture out?
2. What was Bombardier's dream?
3. What problems and needs did Bombardier see his dream satisfying? (Think of both his own problems and needs and those of the community.)
4. "Necessity is the mother of invention."
   a) What does this well-known phrase mean?
   b) How is it illustrated in Bombardier's case?
5. Dreams spring most often from the individual's own experience, knowledge, and interests. How does this apply in the Bombardier case?
6. List the ideas Bombardier tried before he came up with the sprocket wheel and rubberized track.
7. What rewards do you think were important to Bombardier?

Roles and Thinking Skills in the Problem-Solving Process

Creative problem solving may be compared to a movie in which the actor or actress must play four different roles or characters. To make it even more challenging, two of these characters think creatively and two of them think critically. Roger von Oech in his book, *A Kick in the Seat of the Pants*, has defined these four characters as the **Explorer**, **Artist**, **Judge,** and **Warrior**.

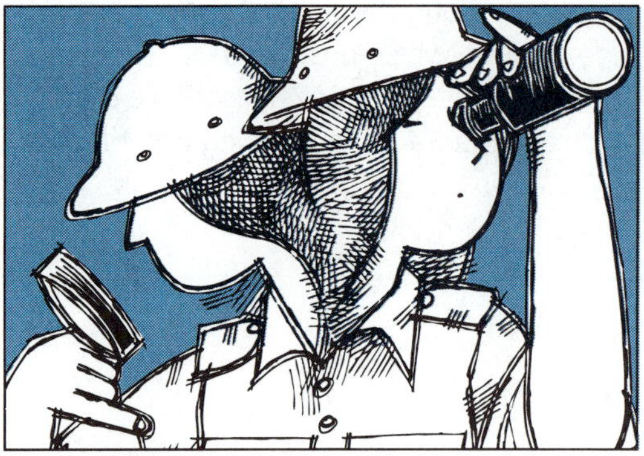

Figure 3.2 The Explorer is aware of both details and the big picture

Figure 3.3 The Artist is the creator of new ideas

Figure 3.4 The Judge evaluates different alternatives

Figure 3.5 The Warrior fights the battles that create ventures out of ideas

Larry Reynolds, in an article entitled "Making Creativity Pay", has explained von Oech's stages as follows:

> Each role requires different skills and serves a different purpose. The Explorer has the curiosity and willingness to look for ideas in out-of-the-way places and apply principles learned from other, seemingly unrelated topics.
>
> The Artist then takes this material and experiments with it in a variety of ways. The Judge helps determine if an idea is any good — if it's what the market really wants and needs. And the Warrior takes the offensive and devises strategies to overcome barriers to make the idea a reality.
>
> Using a role at the wrong time — such as employing your Judge to explore for information, or your Artist to implement an idea — is counter-productive. It's like driving down the highway in reverse. For best results, you have to pay attention to the type of role you should be playing for each situation and then shift into it.

These four characters and their roles in the problem-solving process will be carefully examined in this chapter and again in Chapter 5.

The Thinking Hats

Like von Oech, Edward de Bono is also an expert on creative thinking. From de Bono's point of view, creativity, or the generating of new ideas, is part of a lateral-thinking process.

Lateral thinking involves being flexible and creative in the thinking process. Lateral thinkers break away from standard solutions and solve problems in unique and different ways.

According to de Bono, there are six modes of thinking. To help individuals focus their thinking in each of the modes, de Bono has developed the concept of "thinking hats", one hat for each mode of thinking.

Figure 3.6 White Hat

The White Hat

White hat thinking is concerned with gathering facts, figures, and objective information. It does not allow opinions to interfere with factual information. The white hat thinker should imitate a computer when asked a question, using only the facts when providing output or reaction.

White hat thinking sounds like:
"Give me the facts and figures, please!"
"What is the problem?"
"What are the needs?"

Figure 3.7 Red Hat

AGENTS OF CHANGE

What else can you do with plastic? Well, Martha Sturdy, of Vancouver, decided that you could hang it from your ears and dangle it around your wrists and neck. She has produced "wearable plastic art" that has been featured on the covers of the top fashion magazines and is worn by some of the most fashionable women.

The Red Hat

The **red hat** recognizes that emotions and feelings influence thinking. The red hat thinker uses hunches and feelings to generate information.

Red hat thinking sounds like:
"I have a hunch..."
"This is how I feel about..."

Figure 3.8 Green Hat

The Green Hat

The **green hat** indicates a form of lateral thinking which includes creativity. The colour green is selected because it represents nature and things that grow from seeds. Creativity is also generated from seeds. These seeds are ideas.

Green hat thinking sounds like:
"Aha!"
"I've got an idea!"
"How else can this be done?"

Figure 3.9 Black Hat

The Black Hat

The **black hat** thinker must be logical when arguing against an idea. The black hat always has negative feedback which is objective and free from emotions.

Black hat thinking sounds like:
"It won't work."
"This could pose a problem."
"Yes, but...."

Figure 3.10 Yellow Hat

The Yellow Hat

The **yellow hat** is the opposite of the black hat. It is also logical, but in a very positive, constructive way. The yellow hat is always looking for the positive outcome from every thought and activity.

Yellow hat thinking sounds like:
"This fits together well."
"I want to explore this further."
"This idea has some value."

Figure 3.11 Blue Hat

The Blue Hat

The **blue hat** organizes and controls the thinking of the other hats, leading them and marshalling them into action. The blue hat thinker is the one who makes things happen.

Blue hat thinking sounds like:
"Focus!"
"Let's get started."
"It's your turn!"

It is interesting to note that in the three stages of problem solving, von Oech's four characters, and de Bono's thinking hats all interact and collaborate in the search for solutions. Carefully examine Figure 3.12.

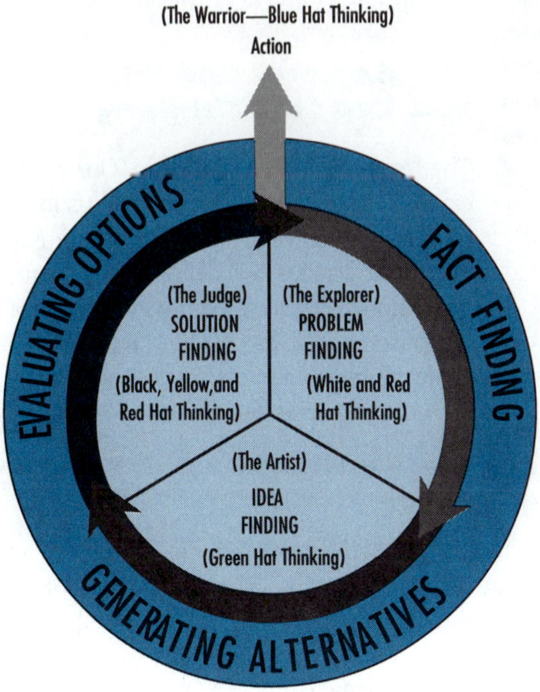

Figure 3.12 Problem Solving with von Oech and de Bono

YOUR TURN

1. What two types of skills are involved in problem solving?
2. Briefly outline what happens in each of the three stages of problem solving.

AGENTS OF CHANGE

Dr. Tuzo Wilson, former Director of the Ontario Science Centre, was once part of a rapidly growing number of scientists studying how a moving planet operates. Eventually, enough evidence was prepared to prove the planet was once a single, vast continent which broke up and drifted apart. These important insights have opened up new ways of looking at earthquakes and volcanoes.

3. List the similarities between von Oech's four characters and de Bono's six thinking hats.
4. Which hats will be worn most often by the Explorer, the Artist, the Judge, and the Warrior?
5. Which of the thinking hats might have uttered each of these comments?
   a) "I really like your idea."
   b) "I've thought of something simply wonderful."
   c) "I need all the information before I can make my decision."
   d) "Let's assemble this material and get started this afternoon."
   e) "I feel it in my heart that this is a good move for me."
   f) "The chances of this actually working are low."

The Explorer and White and Red Hat Thinking

The Explorer is like a detective. Our Explorer is at work when we carefully search the world around us for information. In terms of the problem-solving process, it is the Explorer who is needed to identify and accurately define the problem, challenge, opportunity, or need. Our Explorer has different ways of gathering information. To get some idea about how you prefer to gather information, read Table 3.1 below. For each statement, select either column A or B, for what you believe describes you best.

Table 3.1 How do I gather information?

A		B
I enjoy looking at details and proof that things are really as they appear to be.	Or	I tend to skim over details and look for hidden meanings in things.
I enjoy checking, inspecting, reading the fine print, finding out all the information I can.	Or	I become impatient with routine and repetition and slow, precise activities.
I enjoy things as they are, recall past events, and learn from the combination of these two in a "common sense" sort of way.	Or	In a flash of insight, I go with my hunches on many things.

It would be fairly accurate to describe me as realistic and practical.	Or	It would be fairly accurate to describe me as imaginative and inventive.
I rarely rely on inspiration to keep me going.	Or	I have many bursts of energy with slack periods in between.

(Source: C.M. Mamchur, *Insights: Understanding Yourself and Others*)

We may rely on our senses to gather information. Most of what we know depends on what we have seen, heard, touched, tasted, and smelled. If most of your choices were from Column A, you prefer the white hat approach of collecting information. If you selected more choices from Column B, you prefer to rely on your intuition, or hunches, as a source of information, the red hat approach. This is often thought to be a less accurate way of gathering information than relying on the senses and careful observation. Psychologists, however, have learned that people may interpret the same thing or event in many different ways. To examine how you interpret information, try these exercises.

YOUR TURN

Figure 3.13 How many squares do you see?

6. How many squares do you see in Figure 3.13 on page 73?
7. Show this Figure to others and find out how many squares they can see.
8. Read the following sentence. How many "fs" does it contain?

FINISHED FILES ARE THE RESULT OF SCIENTIFIC STUDY COMBINED WITH THE EXPERIENCE OF MANY YEARS.

9. Check with others to see how many they saw.
10. The same sentence appears below, but the words have been written backwards. How many "fs" do you see now?

DEHSINIF SELIF ERA EHT TLUSER FO CIFITNEICS YDUTS DENIBMOC HTIW EHT ECNEIREPXE FO YNAM SRAEY.

(Source: B. W. Goodspeed, *The Tao Jones Averages*)

Searching for Information

Most people do not see all the "fs" in the above exercise. Psychologists tell us that many factors influence human perception. In this exercise, the "fs" are often missed because when we learn to read we learn that the "f" in the word "of" is pronounced "v". We see what we are taught to hear — a "v" instead of an "f". In learning to acquire some skills, we tend to neglect or forget how to use others. An adult has much greater knowledge and experience than a child, but often the child is more interested in, and better at, exploring.

> As we accumulate knowledge of the world, we need to give our Explorer lots of practice.

We need to develop the Explorer's powers of both observation and intuition, for they work together. If we do not, we greatly limit our ability to solve problems creatively because we are unable to clearly define the problem, opportunity, challenge, or need.

The white and red hats can be associated with von Oech's Explorer. Both of these thinkers, like the Explorer, are seekers of information. The white hat is neutral: it is searching for ideas to make things better. The red hat helps us collect information at an emotional or intuitive level. It makes us aware of how we and others are feeling. This type of thinking encourages changes in perception, that is, seeing something differently than it was seen previously. This gives rise to creativity.

YOUR TURN

11. Exercise your Explorer with the following problem. There are four volumes of Shakespeare's collected works on the shelf. The pages of each volume are exactly 5 cm thick. The covers are each 0.4 cm thick. The bookworm started eating at page 1 of Volume I and ate through to the last page of Volume IV. What distance did the bookworm cover?

Figure 3.14 The Bookworm Problem (Source: B.W. Goodspeed, *The Tao Jones Averages*)

12. Look at the five different shapes on page 76 and select one which is different from all the others.

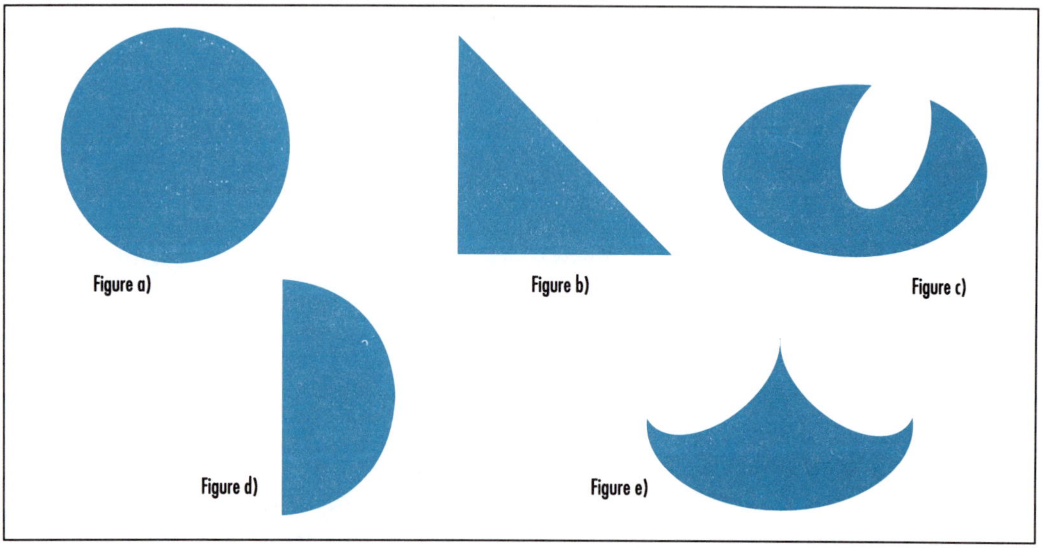

Figure 3.15 The Five Shapes (Source: R. von Oech, *A Whack in the Side of the Head*)

> "Nothing is more dangerous than an idea when it's the only one you have."
> *Emile Chartier*

Arriving at the Solution

Many problems like the Bookworm Problem in Question 11 have a specific solution. When trying to find that one correct solution, however, we should not stop at our first solution. There might be a better one. The Bookworm Problem in Question 11 is actually quite tricky: only one person in ten is able to solve it on the first try.

Some problems can have several correct solutions. In Question 12, for example, each of the answers is correct. Figure A is right because it is the only shape that is made from a continuous line. Figure B is right because it is the only shape made from all straight lines. Figure C is right because it is the only shape that is asymmetrical. Figure D is right because it is the only shape that is made from a curved line and a straight line. Figure E is right because it is the only shape that is a curved triangle. There is, in fact, something unique about each drawing. Developing our Explorer will help us see more than just one answer. It will help us suspend our judgment and encourage us to go beyond the first and most obvious answer, option, or alternative to find other possibilities, other solutions which may be better. In this way, the Explorer can help the Artist develop a whole range of creative options to a particular problem.

The best way to get a good idea is to have a lot of ideas.

The more ideas you have, the more options you have. Many options lead to many choices. The more choices you have, the better your opportunity to identify a good idea. Explorers never stop after finding one right answer. They look around for many right answers. The Explorer should always be curious. It should be constantly searching, looking, and probing. It should pay attention to a wide variety of different kinds of information. It should notice details without losing the perspective of the bigger picture. It should search both familiar and unfamiliar territory and not stop searching when it finds one solution to a problem.

How To Improve Your Explorer

Some strategies to improve the ability of your Explorer are given below:

- Change your routines.
- Talk and listen to people.
- Make lists and change them.
- Daydream.
- Look at things from different perspectives.
- Search for new information.
- Try something you have never tried before.
- Consider the ideas of others and think of ways to improve them or combine them.
- Write down all your new ideas before you forget them.
- Listen! Look! Observe!

Figure 3.16 The Explorer is both short- and long-sighted.

YOUR TURN

13. The first ten letters of the alphabet have been divided into the following two groups:
    Group # 1: A E F H I
    Group # 2: B C D G J
    a) What pattern differentiates the two groups?
    b) Into which group would you put K or R or M?
14. You can problem solve by yourself or with others who share the same concerns. Exercise your Explorer with the following activities:
    a) Examine your life as it is right now. List all the problems and challenges that are facing you and all the things you would like to change.
    b) Join with others in your class to form groups of three to five. Focus your Explorer on your school and identify problems and things you would like to see changed. (This is the time to bring out all those pet beefs!)
    c) As a class, list problems or things that you would like to see changed in your own neighbourhood and community.
    d) Have half the class wear white hats and the other half red hats. Determine the difference in the ideas that are generated.

Figure 3.17 Try putting on different hats yourself.

15. Bombardier's Explorer was alive and well. What proof of this is found in the Venture Profile about him?

The Artist and Green Hat Thinking

The green hat is representative of the Artist. The green hat thinker focuses on changing the perceptions and patterns that shape the idea.

> The green hat thinker is a creative thinker.

AGENTS OF CHANGE

The art world of Canada was dominated almost exclusively by white artists. With his colourful pictograph style of painting, Norval Morisseau, an Ojibway artist, broke into that seemingly private club and made an impression on an entire generation of Native Canadian painters. The domination of one world was broken by Morriseau's unique style.

After the Explorer has generated raw material for ideas, the Artist considers what would happen if ideas were added, taken away, or considered from a totally different viewpoint.

The second stage in the problem-solving process, idea finding, involves adopting the role of the Artist. The Artist takes the information the Explorer has discovered and transforms it into something new by generating a variety of creative possibilities. The Artist may adapt something to another use, look at an idea backwards, upside down, or inside out. He or she will form unlikely combinations, continually experimenting with the "what if" approach and breaking all the rules and conventions to come up with a new idea. The tools the Artist uses are imagination, creative thinking, and experimentation.

Figure 3.18 The Artist creating.

Creativity is the generation of new ideas. Sometimes creativity comes from a single individual; however, creative ideas can also come from the combined effort of a group. This effort involves individuals working together.

Individuals who create new ideas may not put the time and effort into developing those ideas.

New ideas often stay with their originator.

"Einstein was original. Yet he never described himself as creative. Nor did da Vinci, or Picasso, or John Lennon, or Woody Allen, or Ingmar Bergman, or Bryan Adams. None of these incredibly creative folks went around saying, "Hey! Look at me! I'm creative!" Instead, they said things like, I'm Albert or I'm Leonardo or I'm Pablo, and they just did their work."
Martin Myers

Sometimes creative individuals do not want to risk sharing the idea with others. They do not realize that other individuals may be able to take the idea and develop it into a concrete process or product.

Generating new ideas can become a career for some people. Many creative people get excited over the new ideas that they generate, but do not have the persistence to follow through with the idea to see it transformed into a valuable commodity. These individuals are motivated by the problem solving that occurs as a result of the new idea rather than by money. They are **inventors** but they may not necessarily be entrepreneurs.

The Left and Right Brain and Problem Solving

Some research indicates that the human brain is divided into two parts: the **right brain** and the **left brain.**

The right brain is the portion that is creative, imaginative, emotional, and intuitive. This creative side of our brain often gets forgotten in the details of everyday life. However, with the right brain, we often get sudden insight into something, and everything falls magically into place. The story of Archimedes displays the classic "EUREKA!" — "I have found it!" As the story goes, Archimedes developed the scientific principle that the volume of displaced water could be used to determine the volume of a solid object in a flash of insight that came to him while he was taking a bath.

Figure 3.19 Eureka! I think I've got it!

The left side of the brain is logical, analytical, and rational. It contains the function of language and all language-related activities.

Figure 3.20 Two brains are better than one.

Just as two heads are better than one, so also two brains are better than one. When the creative potential of the right brain is combined with the linear thinking of the left brain, the power of an individual's creativity can increase dramatically. Most education systems cater to left-brain thinking. In most of your classes at school, your left brain is called upon to work.

Your Turn

16. Make a list of the ways in which your school has developed the left side of your brain. How has it taught you to think critically?

17. a) Which side of the brain do you feel most comfortable using?
    b) How do you learn to play a game? Do you read the directions or do you learn as you go along from your friends?

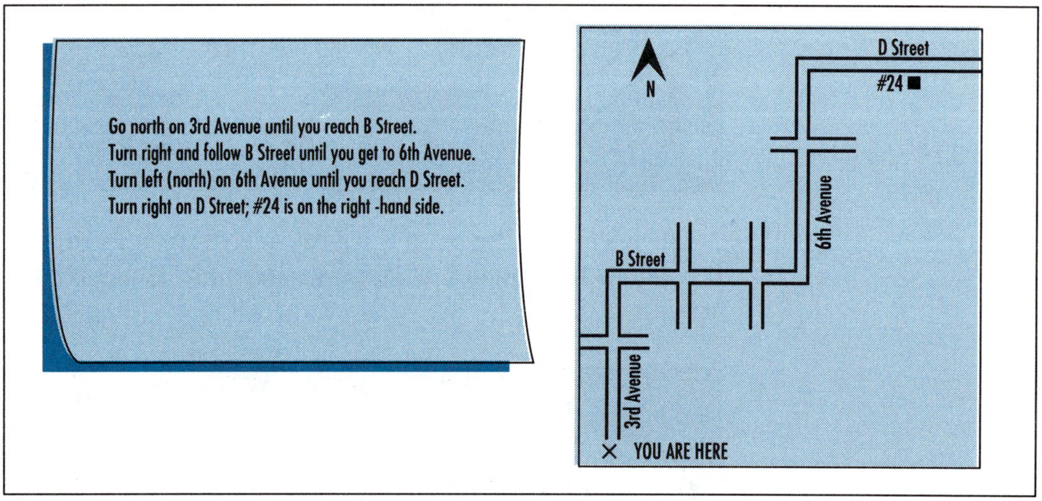

Figure 3.21 Which side of the brain do you feel most comfortable using?

18. Examine the map in the illustration above. Assume you were on Third Avenue and wanted to get to #24 on D Street. Would you prefer to follow the map or use the printed directions to guide you?

Techniques for Exercising Creativity

Those who prefer to learn a game by playing it and feel frustrated by reading the rules and those who prefer a map to printed directions are relying on their right brain. In your Entrepreneurial Studies class, you are encouraged to use intuitive and creative thought — a function of your right brain. This will help balance the development of your powers of critical analysis and evaluation.

Luckily, we can teach ourselves to become creative.

Exercising the right brain will bring it back into use, making us creative.

How do we exercise the right brain? Reading out loud helps gain the attention of the right brain. The sound stimulates the right side of the brain into action — creative action. The next time you have homework to do or a problem to solve, try reading it aloud — it will help.

Word clustering helps to stimulate the right brain into action.

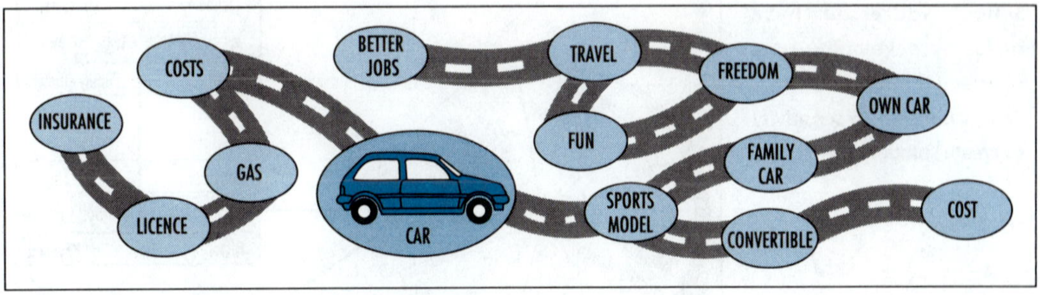

Figure 3.22 Word clusters help reach the Eureka!

Word Clustering

Word clustering is the free association of ideas and words. It helps to stimulate the right brain into action. You begin with a word, picture, or action which you write down in the centre of the page and circle. Then write down other words or pictures that come to mind. Circle each of them. Draw lines between the circles that are connected in your mind. Continue to work through the process of word or picture, circle or line. This activity is a right-brain exercise that will generate many ideas and will help you focus on the one idea that you will recognize as Eureka!

Mind Mapping

Drawing circles and lines that connect to and from circles is a form of **mind mapping** that is often used to chart the direction of our thinking process. For example, if you wanted to identify some of the needs in the educational field, you would draw a large circle to represent education in general. Divide that circle up into segments such as elementary school education, high school education, college and

AGENTS OF CHANGE

Some Canadian medical students are afraid of disease, of seeing their first cadaver, and of death. June Penney, associate professor of anatomy at Dalhousie Medical School, addressed these needs by developing new courses for these students. Fear was met with sensitivity to create solutions.

university education, specialized education and training provided by industry, and community group educational services. You would then select one segment and identify the existing services provided within that segment. You could then draw another line and direct your thinking to the other kinds of needs that segment might have that are not apparently being provided.

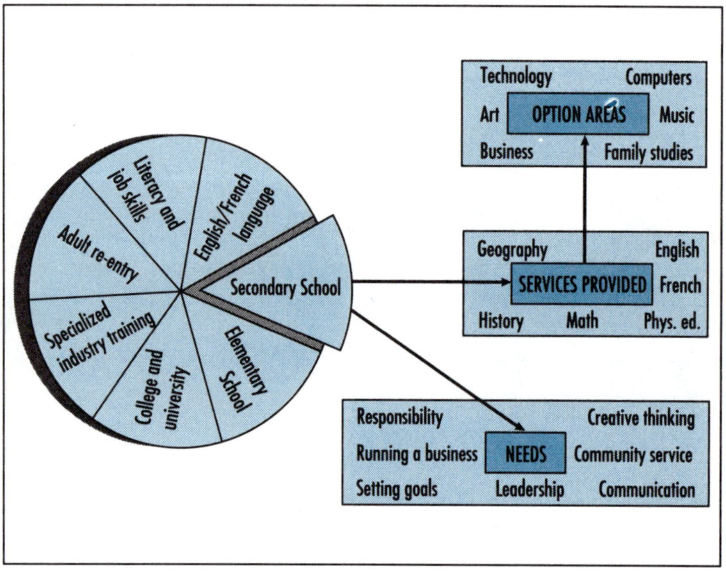

Figure 3.23 Mind mapping helps identify needs or opportunities.

By using mind maps and diagrams like the one in Figure 3.23, you will begin to get a feel for any gaps or missing services in a particular marketplace where innovation could occur. Working with mind maps may result in some messy areas of the map. Ignore the mess and keep the ideas flowing. You can always go back and regroup or cluster your ideas to prepare a more organized mind map later on.

Brainstorming

Completing a word cluster or a mind mapping exercise with other people is a form of **brainstorming**. Brainstorming, or productive thinking, as it is sometimes called, generates a large number of new and unusual ideas. There are certain rules associated with this creative activity.

Brainstorming joins together previously unconnected observation in an intuitive way to create something new.

Figure 3.24 Combining these two great tastes gives me an Idea for a new product: Pizza Butter.

It is the kind of thinking which can occur when we are not concerned about finding the "solution" or the "right answer". Judgment must be suspended, that is, every idea is a good idea and should be recorded for evaluation later on. Can you imagine what would happen if the Artist always had to answer to the Judge? How many new ideas would ever be developed? You never know when an idea that on the surface seems implausible can lead to another idea that is sensational.

New ideas can be generated by starting with something familiar. Existing ideas can then be modified in a variety of ways. They can be reorganized, combined, substituted, or modified to make them more attractive and appealing.

YOUR TURN

19. Do a word cluster for each of the following: ice cube, dome stadium, pizza.
20. Exchange word clusters with the person sitting beside you. Talk about the ideas generated by each of you. What are the similarities? What are the differences?
21. In groups of three, complete a word cluster for the following:
    a) entrepreneur
    b) the Explorer
22. Draw a circle or pie chart to indicate a particular field or industry that interests you. Divide the pie into the different segments of the industry of which you are aware. Choose one piece of the pie, or segment, draw out a line to help you direct your thinking, and map out circles that identify areas that are being well serviced. Then draw out another line, from the segment you selected, and map out circles that identify areas where

there still are some apparent needs. These represent opportunities in the field of your interest.

23. In small groups, brainstorm a list of items under the following heading: The best things in life are free! After five minutes have passed, exchange your list with that of another group in the class, and add on to this group's list. Use some of the other group's ideas as stepping stones to some new ideas of your own. When everyone is finished, share your list with the rest of the class.
24. In the same groups, use paper, scissors, and markers to develop a model of a new product idea. Write a brief description of your product idea indicating what it will be used for and how it will look.

Further Techniques To Stimulate Creativity

Changing routines and looking at things from different viewpoints will also help to stimulate creativity and generate new ideas. Asking yourself questions such as, "What if?" or "What might happen if?" will force the right side of the brain into action.

Closing your eyes and **visualizing** different scenarios in your mind can help you practise identifying new routines that generate new ideas. Most professional athletes visualize their new routines before they actually try them. Elizabeth Manley, Canada's Silver Medalist in the 1988 Olympics for Figure-Skating, does not try any new steps or routines on the ice until she has visualized them perfectly in her mind. Visualizing helps her practise and focus on patterns so that when she puts on her skates and goes out onto the ice, she is prepared. Visualizing can help you change patterns and identify new ideas.

The Idea Generation Spoke of the Venture Creation Wheel indicates that every successful venture is based on an idea. Thought precedes action. Creative thinking is the source of new ideas. This is the kind of thinking that sees possibilities and generates alternatives.

AGENTS OF CHANGE

The 6- to 13-year-old children who lived on the streets of Khartoum, in the Sudan, had no other way but stealing to get food for themselves and their families. Peter Dalglish taught them to be bicycle couriers, delivering mail and messages to offices, so they could earn money. By providing steady work, Peter helped many children to find an honest way to make a living.

Figure 3.25 Every successful venture starts with an idea.

YOUR TURN

25. In pairs, brainstorm answers to the following question: What if it snowed popcorn last night?
26. Get together with another pair in your class. Share your answers.
27. Select one of your answers and, using that answer as your starting point, do a word cluster. When your word cluster is complete, exchange with another group of four.
28. Select one of the circles on the new word cluster you have in front of you and do a mind map.
29. How many new ideas did you come up with while completing Questions 25 to 28?
30. Close your eyes and visualize what might happen if everything in the world were green. Once you have a clear pattern in your mind, open your eyes and draw a picture of the world you have just visualized.

Creative thinking can be learned even if it isn't logical.

By Herve De Jordy, *Toronto Star*

Why are entrepreneurs constantly spotting business opportunities and solving what seem to be insurmountable problems?

The answer: Entrepreneurs think differently from most people. The term commonly used to describe them is "creative thinkers". Walter Derzko, an entrepreneur inventor with a chemistry degree, helped to explain just what creative thinking is. "Most people concentrate on what they perceive to be true (facts and data). Creative thinkers go one stage beyond and challenge the underlying assumptions behind the facts and data.

"A classic example of a breakthrough in perception was the Wright brothers. Why were they the first to fly? They had no new information or technology that wasn't available to others. They simply challenged a notion that was taken for granted.

"Conventional wisdom at the time told us that you had to build a stable aircraft as you scale up from a hand-held model to actual size. Each technical advance took you closer to your design goal of a stable aircraft. This approach seemed logical, reasonable, and rational, yet, as we all know, was wrong.

"The breakthrough came when the Wright brothers changed their design focus, from a stable to an unstable aircraft. With this new design, you must include the notion of controls to keep the plane in steady flight. Curved wings, moving flaps, and new blade designs were added to give the pilot control. As we see, a simple change in perception led to the breakthrough."

How is that applied to recognizing business opportunities?

"Always remember to challenge your own perception of things," he [Derzko] replied."Most individuals head to the most obvious solution to any problem. They should examine the entire spectrum of options open to them, even if the first solution looks obvious. Everyone recognizes high-profile trends, for example, and you can hop on and ride the bandwagon, but the creative approach to recognizing small business opportunities would be to look at what is left behind, overlooked, or missed in that trend."

Most people associate thinking with decision making: "It's a logical process, so I must be thinking."

"Creative thinking is not logical; it is imaginative, intuitive, conceptual and, contrary to public opinion, it can be learned. It's just that we are not taught the operating skills to do so. Imagine teaching math without first exposing students to the basic tools of it: +, -, x, ÷. I doubt that it could be done."

"Then, why does it seem that entrepreneurs use creative thinking instinctively?" I asked.

"They don't," he replied.

"It's not an instinctive trait, it's a learned skill that they have been practising longer than others. It's usually brought forward from a feeling of frustration, maybe even desperation, from not feeling comfortable in an environment. People can be a success at something and still hate it. It can start with simple daydreaming, as in 'What else could I be doing?', to simply challenging the common definition for security. Creative thinking is examining alternatives and choices."

Derzko argues that the Western world's idea of an educated person is someone who has the right answer on cue — and that there is only one answer. But he maintains there never is just one answer to solving business problems. There are too many variables.

A seasoned entrepreneur has been practising creative thinking for a long time — granted, often unconsciously — but, nevertheless, for a long time. Some can even come up with creative answers on cue. Actually, it is an essential yet basic skill necessary to succeed in the creation of any venture.

YOUR TURN

31. Return to the list your Explorer identified as problems, challenges, or things you would like to change in your life (Your Turn, Question 14 a, page 78). Using the technique of word clustering, generate ideas about what you might do to bring about the change you want.
32. Re-form your class group that explored the school to find things which you believed needed to be changed (Your Turn, Question 14 b). Using the technique of brainstorming, generate a wide variety of ideas about what could be done.
33. As a class, go back to the community concerns you identified (Your Turn, Question 14 c) and, using brainstorming techniques, generate a list of possible solutions.

Roles of the Judge and the Warrior

After the Artist has examined the idea from a creative angle, it is time for the Judge to take a closer, more critical look at the concept and to consider whether it will work for the problem it was designed to address. If the solution is not right for that particular situation, the Judge will help determine if it can be used in other areas.

The Judge plays the third role in the problem-solving process — the solution-finding stage. Unlike the creative Artist, the Judge is a critical thinker. Its strength is the ability to carefully analyze every alternative to determine which one is best. You will learn more about critical thinking and the role of the Judge and the Warrior in creating a venture in Chapter 5. The Judge, however, is also important in the problem-finding and idea-finding stages of the creative problem-solving process. Not every concern is a real problem. Not every idea represents an opportunity. Not every solution is a good solution. The Judge helps us sort out and evaluate all the material our Explorer has discovered and all the ideas our Artist has created.

YOUR TURN

34. Briefly discuss the role of the Judge in the problem-solving process.
35. Bombardier's Judge rejected most of the prototypes his Artist developed. What did his Judge find wrong with the prototypes it rejected?

Inventors and Entrepreneurs

Finding a solution completes one cycle in the problem-solving process. It is not, however, the end of the process. The original problem and its solution must be continually evaluated. Should the problem disappear or change, the solution should be abandoned or altered. The Explorer may also find new information or the Artist may create new possibilities to make a better solution possible. Bombardier did this time and time again before he finally found the sprocket wheel and rubber track combination. Inventors are continually refining their prototypes to make them just a bit better.

Finding a solution to a problem also does not mean that a new venture has been created.

> The inventor must be able to move beyond inventive genius to innovation and entrepreneurial action.

Inventors tend to find this a difficult shift to make. The inventor's interest is to improve upon the idea, to build an *even better* mousetrap. Some inventors have little experience or interest in the entrepreneurial process of creating a venture from an idea. As a result, a good idea or a good solution may come to nothing. No change results. No **innovation** occurs because the idea fails to attract the attention of an entrepreneur.

"Thinking is the hardest work there is, which is the probable reason why so few people want to engage in it."
Henry Ford

Entrepreneurs develop and apply the new idea to satisfy a real need or problem. They organize the resources to produce the innovation. They know how to get it to those who need it. They may not be particularly good at designing a new improved product or technology. Yet idea finding remains an important spoke in the Venture Creation Wheel. The inventor's solution may represent the entrepreneur's idea.

The inventor and the entrepreneur make good partners in the process of creating a venture.

AGENTS OF CHANGE

Soon after she arrived in Prince Edward Island from Holland, Martina Trebeek discovered that all the Dutch cheese sold on the island was imported. Martina had always made Dutch cheese for her family, so she decided to make a little extra to sell. Today, she produces 240 kg of cheese a week and her company has become a special tourist attraction. An exported family tradition became a local institution.

Entrepreneurial ventures which grow from the invention of a new or improved good, service, or technology may result in revolutionary change. Bombardier's new sprocket wheel and track system led to the development of a whole new industry and changed winter around the world. The rate of change and innovation seems to be increasing all the time. Futurist Alvin Toffler, in his book *Future Shock,* studied the effects that the increasingly rapid rate of change have on our lives. He noted that rapid change produces stress even when it is a change for the better. If the stress becomes great enough, it can threaten your physical, mental, and emotional well-being.

Not all changes are revolutionary in nature, however. Most inventions and most entrepreneurial ventures bring about minor changes in the lives of just a few people and often seem to pass unnoticed. They become part of the evolutionary change that goes on around us every day. Few innovations involve the invention or application of sophisticated new technology. The impact is small scale rather than large scale. All entrepreneurial activity involves individuals who take the initiative, apply the creative problem-solving process, and create a venture to satisfy needs.

YOUR TURN

36. The following is a list of Canadian inventions: Pablum, Insulin, the radio, Canadarm, the telephone. Find out:
    a) who invented each
    b) who or what company(ies) used the invention to create a new or improved good or service
    c) to what extent the inventor was involved in, and gained from, the production and use of the new invention
37. Make a list of new inventions, technologies, goods, and services that have changed our way of life:
    a) since you were born
    b) since your parents were born
38. Make a "bug list", a list of all the things which bother you. Do a mind map of each "bug" to see if you can come up with a solution. Could this solution be the basis of a venture?

Venture PROFILE

SONIA JONES
Peninsula Farm Ltd.

For Sonia Jones, it began when her husband bought a farm near Lunenburg, Nova Scotia. The couple also bought a cow to keep the vegetation down. The cow produced too much milk for their needs, and government regulations prohibited its sale. So Sonia decided to use the milk to make yogurt. Her yogurt proved so popular with friends and neighbours that she began her own business, which last year sold $700 000 worth of yogurt.

Venture PROFILE

"MICKEY" AND MICHAEL MURPHY

The countryside around Delhi, Ontario, is some of the best tobacco-growing land in Canada. Due to decreasing demand for tobacco, more and more tobacco farmers are leaving the land. "Mickey" Murphy and her son Michael decided to stay on the farm but use the land in a different way. They have become trout farmers! Greenhouses which were once used to start the tobacco plants now house fish tanks. The old kilns used to cure tobacco are now used to smoke the fish. Each of their crops consists of 125 000 trout. The waste produced when preparing the fish is put back on the land as a natural fertilizer to grow a second crop of organic vegetables.

Venture PROFILE

CATERINE WHITE
Cat-Catering

Caterine White of Montreal has turned her love of cats into a business. She caters to the cats of her 400 clients. When the owners are away, she diligently changes the cat litter and provides food, toys, and water for the lucky felines so that they may stay in their own homes. So far she has no competition and has been able to make the cat-catering business a full-time job for the last two years.

EXPLORING • JONES, MURPHY, AND WHITE

1. Compare these Venture Profiles with the two at the beginning of the chapter. What are the differences? What are the similarities?
2. The creative problem-solving process involves identifying a problem, challenge, or opportunity and finding a solution. For each of the above three cases:
   a) identify the problem
   b) describe the solution
   c) explain the need or needs that were satisfied

P·O·I·N·T·S T·O R·E·M·E·M·B·E·R

- The problem-solving process involves problem finding, idea finding, and solution finding.
- Creative problem solving uses both creative and critical thinking.
- There are four roles in problem solving: the Explorer, Artist, Judge, and Warrior.
- The Explorer uses white and red hat thinking to identify problems, needs, and opportunities.
- The Artist uses green hat thinking to generate ideas and possibilities for consideration.
- The Judge uses black, red, and yellow hat thinking to evaluate possibilities and find the best solution.
- The Warrior uses blue hat thinking to transform thoughts and ideas into realities.
- The human brain is divided into two parts: the right creative brain and the left logical, rational brain.
- Inventors need entrepreneurs to bring their inventions to the world's attention.

W·H·A·T H·A·V·E Y·O·U L·E·A·R·N·E·D·?

1. Identify and describe each of the three stages in the problem-solving process.
2. List the four problem-solving roles identified by Roger von Oech and identify the main skills used in each stage.

3. Describe how the skills of each of von Oech's problem-solving roles can be applied to a problem-solving situation.
4. Describe the function of each of de Bono's six thinking hats.
5. How would wearing de Bono's white and red hats help you in the Explorer's role?
6. How would wearing de Bono's green hat help you in the Artist's role?
7. How would wearing de Bono's black and yellow hats help you in the Judge's role?
8. How would wearing de Bono's blue hat help you in the Warrior's role?
9. Identify three techniques used in creativity exercises and describe how each is conducted.
10. Trace the course of an idea from inventor to entrepreneurial venture.

V·E·N·T·U·R·I·N·G O·U·T

1. Use your Explorer to collect some magazines and find goods and services which are advertised as being "new" or "improved". Use your Artist to create an interesting and representative collage of all the ads you have found. Use your Judge to determine what, if anything, is new or improved about each product.
2. Use your research to write a report in which you:
   a) Identify five examples of claims that you believe are unsupported. Explain why each claim is not likely to be true.
   b) Find two examples of ads which do tell of something that is most likely really new or improved. Explain what is new or improved about the good or service being advertised.
   c) Bearing in mind that not all ideas are good ideas, find two examples of new ideas you believe will fail. Describe each idea and explain why you believe it will not catch on.

"Without opportunities, ideas are a dime a dozen." Both opportunities and ideas are needed for success in any new venture. This chapter will help you learn how to monitor change, watch trends, and identify opportunities.

CHAPTER 4

Where Are the Opportunities?

LEARNING OUTCOMES

By the end of this chapter, you should be able to:

- identify the relationship between opportunities and ideas
- distinguish between "market-pulled" and "product-" or "service-driven" entrepreneurship
- distinguish between fads and trends
- forecast and use a variety of trends to identify changes and find opportunities
- use research techniques to determine trends, identify opportunities, and evaluate ideas
- understand the concept of the "new wave" entrepreneur

ENTREPRENEURIAL LANGUAGE

market-pulled entrepreneurship
product- or service-driven entrepreneurship
trends
Agricultural Age
Industrial Age
Information Age
standardization
specialization
synchronization
centralization
concentration
downsizing
fads
megashifts
forecast
time-series forecast
growth trend
declining trend
stable situation
linear
irregular
cyclical
primary research
secondary research
new wave entrepreneur

Venture PROFILE

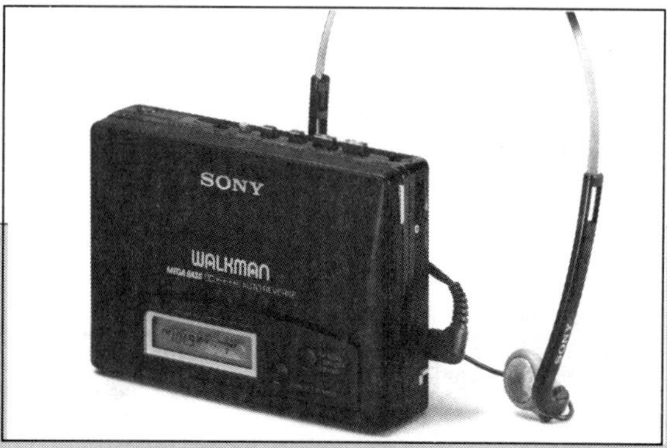

Sony has changed the way we live.

AKIO MORITA
The Rise of Sony Corporation

When Akio Morita, co-founder of Sony Corporation, was growing up in Nagoya, Japan, he was fascinated by electronics and sound reproduction. His mother was very fond of Western classical music, and the house was always filled with the sounds of phonograph recordings played on an old Victrola. Akio spent most of his free time, as a child, reading about, and experimenting with, sound reproduction and wire-recording devices.

In 1946, as a young man, he and a friend, Masaru Ibuka, opened a new company, Tokyo Tsushin Kogyo (Tokyo Telecommunications Engineering Company). They saw their company as an innovator that would make high-technology products in ingenious ways. They experimented with wire recorders but were unable to come up with a product that really worked. One day, after examining an American-made Wilcox-Gay tape recorder and recognizing that the fidelity of the recording was better with tape than with wire, they decided to redirect their efforts, forget the work with wire, and develop a recording device that used tape instead.

They didn't want to just build a recording machine. They knew that if they could also produce a high fidelity tape for their recorders they could count on a continuing market for many years. Their main problem was that they had no idea how to produce such a recording tape. They spent several years experimenting with and finally perfecting a tape that would give them high-quality sound reproduction. In 1950, they had a product — a tape-recording machine. It was somewhat bulky and heavy, but it had a quality tape. It worked. They knew that they were on their way to great success.

Akio and Masaru demonstrated their new recorder every day — to businesspeople, universities, and to friends. Everyone who saw it thought it was just a toy — great fun, but too expensive to purchase. Their invention was a failure. They could not sell a single recorder. It might have been a wonderful idea. It was certainly a well-built piece of equipment. It included a high-quality recording tape. It just did not have a market. There was no apparent need or want for this kind of device.

One day, a former cabinet minister, Tamon Maeda, talked to them about a shortage of stenographers in the Japanese court system. They wondered if their machine could be used to record court proceedings. With Tamon's help, they were able to demonstrate their recorders to the Japanese Supreme Court. What an opportunity! Here was a need. They immediately sold 20 recorders.

Realizing that success depended on finding people who had a need for their product, they were able to turn things around. They went on to look for other opportunities — other people who would need or want their new invention. The school system was their next direction. They showed teachers how tape recorders could be used to play prerecorded language tapes. They went on to sell their recorders to schools across the country. Our two entrepreneurs had found another market for their invention.

In 1955, Akio and Masaru produced their first transistor radio. Just about this time, they changed the company name from Tokyo Telecommunications Engineering Company, or Tokyo Tsushin Kogyo, to SONY (from "sonus", the Latin word for sound, and "sonny", a familiar English word). Following the new trend for smaller radios, in 1957 Sony brought their radio down in size so that it would fit into a shirt pocket. A number of years later, they attached small, lightweight, comfortable headphones that pumped hypnotically vivid sound directly into the human brain. The Sony Walkman was born. Today, this Walkman has reduced boredom on an international scale — and turned joggers around the world into traffic hazards!

Sony advises its managers to "keep looking for what the consumer will need during the next 10 to 20 years, and then make it!"

EXPLORING • THE RISE OF SONY

1. Where did Akio get his idea for a sound-recording device?
2. What else did he need to make his venture a success?
3. What need or want did his inventions fill?
4. What event seemed to turn things around for these two entrepreneurs?
5. Why do you suppose they went on to manufacture a transistor radio?
6. Why did they then reduce it in size to fit into a shirt pocket?
7. Why does Sony seem to be on the watch for electronic trends?
8. What effect should the advice of Sony management have on the success of the company over the next 20 to 30 years?

AGENTS OF CHANGE

Izzy Steen bought a Saskatchewan sunflower seed company and started looking for new markets. Several famous major league baseball players and coaches are now chewing sunflower seeds instead of tobacco. Izzy's company has expanded its market by combining a need (ball players' chewing) and a product.

Ideas need opportunities in order to succeed.

Ideas and Opportunities

Ideas are only a small part of entrepreneurial success. Customers did not come running to Akio for one of his new tape recorders just because they thought tape recorders were a clever idea. It might have been a brilliant idea. It was certainly an idea that had fascinated Akio for several years and consumed a great deal of his time and effort. However, with no want, no need, no market, no perceived opportunity, Akio's invention might still be sitting on the shelf. Once he had identified an opportunity — a market — his company had made a major breakthrough. The Sony Corporation and its technological innovations have reshaped the very way we live.

People frequently confuse entrepreneurial opportunities with ideas. When asked to give an example of an entrepreneurial opportunity, they will begin to offer suggestions or entrepreneurial ideas. It is relatively easy to come up with an idea for which there might very well be no opportunity. A new and different kind of restaurant in a particular area of town might be a great idea, but if no one wants a restaurant in that community, if there is no need or opportunity, the idea will fail. Ideas that are pursued when opportunities clearly do not exist are doomed to failure.

Venture PROFILE

The Famous People Players

DIANE DUPUY

The Famous People Players

For three generations, Diane Dupuy's family had been involved with the arts: painting, music, design, and theatre. So, one might say, she came by it naturally. Not so. It was a lot of hard work. Right from early childhood, she was somewhat of an outcast among her peers. They called her "retard!" and "weirdo!" She was skinny, with big eyes. She had a great deal of difficulty with schoolwork. She just didn't fit.

To escape the ridicule of her schoolmates, and the questioning and cajoling of her parents about her studies, she "escaped" to her cardboard puppet theatre and let her imagination run wild. She remembers:

> I could make people cry at the sight of Punch hitting Judy; I could make them laugh at Elsie the Cow dancing to the Sleeping Beauty music from my Walt Disney record; I could make them cheer and applaud. As awful as it was to be different in the eyes of the kids at school, it was wonderful to be different in the eyes of an audience. They loved it. They loved me.

Diane never lost her love of puppets and, when she grew up, she found herself doing puppet-theatre work for a living. She was full of imagination and creative energy. Her loudest applause came for puppet work that involved puppets of famous people. These puppets would act out fantasies based on their personal style, but fantasies that would be impossible for them to perform in real life.

Was it the ridicule she was subjected to as a child that made her relate to the needs of the mentally challenged? Or was it because she spent some time working in the offices of an organization that looked after them? Whatever it was, she knew she had found the opportunity of a lifetime.

> [I] imagined bringing other famous people on stage in much the same way, as puppets of themselves, acting out fantasies based on their personal style but impossible for them to perform in real life. But this time I would use the black-light technique so the characters could achieve even more magic. Liberace, in a magnificent rhinestone-encrusted suit, would swoop from the piano. And he wouldn't just play that piano. He would dance down in mid-

air, tickling the ivories with his toes while standing on his head. As the music built into the dazzling chords, scales, and arpeggios of the typical Liberace performance, dozens of dancing, cartwheeling, somersaulting musical notes would soar out of the piano, his own notes literally coming to life.

The notes, the piano, the piano bench, and the candelabra — as well as Liberace himself — would be puppets that seemed to dance and fly on their own. But the puppeteers, dressed in black and invisible under the fluorescent light, would be the ones making all this magic happen. And these performers would be people who are retarded. But no one in the audience would know this until the performers removed their black hoods and took their bows at the end of the show.

The Famous People Players would be like nothing that has ever been imagined in the theatre: a unique form of entertainment created by a unique group of performers. It would be more than a puppet show; it would be a black-light extravaganza of colour, movement, and music. The company would be a way to bring these people out of the shadows, to change the world's perception of the mentally retarded.

In her book, *Dare To Dream*, Diane describes the difficult journey with her friends, from a little church basement to a thunderous ovation on Broadway.

EXPLORING • FAMOUS PEOPLE PLAYERS

1. How is this Venture Profile different from the Sony story you just read?
2. What opportunity did Diane identify?
3. What was her vision?
4. How is this profile similar to the Rick Hansen one in Chapter 1? How is it different?
5. What problems do you think Diane would have encountered on her way to her dream?

What Comes First — An Idea or an Opportunity?

This question is a little like, "Which came first, the chicken or the egg?"

Sometimes, like Diane Dupuy, entrepreneurs will identify a problem, see an opportunity, and then develop an idea to resolve the problem. This process is referred to as **market-pulled entrepreneurship**. The opportunity actually encourages (or pulls) the development of ideas. Diane Dupuy saw an opportunity for mentally challenged people to show the world they could accomplish something and went about helping them change the way society perceived them. She discovered that the market had an enthusiastic response to her idea.

AGENTS OF CHANGE

By 1950, the poor and the lepers of India were all but abandoned. Seeing this, Mother Theresa founded the Order of Missionaries of Charity to serve those in need. The Order has grown into a world-wide movement of 1800 Sisters, while Mother Theresa herself has become a symbol of charity and love. One person's compassion helped millions of people around the world.

Figure 4.1 Market-Pulled Entrepreneurship

At other times, entrepreneurs, like Akio Morita, will first get an idea for a product or a service and then look for a marketing opportunity. This process or pattern of entrepreneurship can be referred to as **product-** or **service-driven entrepreneurship**. The idea is developed first and then the opportunity is found. The inventor of 3M's Post-it Notes knew that he was on to a great invention, he just had to find the right application for it. When he did, Post-it Notes changed the way people in business communicated. These little notes are on everything from manuscripts to files to business memos and reports. They even turn up on telephones to remind people to do something right away.

Figure 4.2 Product- or Service-Driven Entrepreneurship

Venture PROFILE

Entrepreneur sees problems as opportunities

The weather forecaster was gloomy and definite. "There will be heavy rains for 40 days and 40 nights," he announced.

The people of the town heard the weather forecaster's prediction and became very frightened. "If it rains that much, there will be considerable flooding," they cried. "We will lose everything." One man didn't cry, however. Instead, he invested in moving trucks, hired some labourers, and went into business moving the town's valuables to higher ground. He set up tents on a hill so that there would be dry places for people to stay during the flood. And, when the flood did come, there was no great loss to the town. The townspeople remained safe and dry on the top of the hill. Everyone was happy. And the man with foresight received a comfortable profit, which everyone agreed he had earned.

For he's a jolly good fellow!

The following year, the weather forecaster had more bad news. There would be a lengthy drought. Naturally, the townspeople were upset again. "Our crops will wither and we will all go thirsty," they moaned. But the man who had saved them from the flood merely smiled and went back to work. He imported bottled water for the town. He rented huge water trucks which would water the dry fields. And he planted crops which would thrive in dry soil on his own land. At the end of the drought, the town discovered, once again, that it had escaped disaster because of this man. Everyone was happy that he had turned an honest profit by helping the town.

This man was an entrepreneur.

EXPLORING • PROBLEMS OR OPPORTUNITIES?

1. How did the townspeople respond to the weather forecaster's pronouncements?
2. Where did the entrepreneur learn about the impending problem?
3. How did the entrepreneur tend to look at problems?
4. How did he respond to these problems?

AGENTS OF CHANGE

Claris Rudkowski, a Labrador Metis, decided that the tranquillity of her home town and the Metis' traditional way of life of were being threatened by the effects of low-level flying. She organized the Mokami Project Group to bring together representatives of government, business, labour, and Natives to encourage better relationships. One woman's concern brought harmony out of turmoil.

Looking for Opportunities

Entrepreneurial people tend to look at reality in a different way. The townspeople in this profile looked at the impending drought and saw a problem. The drought seemed to threaten their well-being and frighten them into concentrating only on the problem: What would they do with no rain? What would they do about crops that would not grow? The entrepreneur, on the other hand, looked at the problem and saw only the opportunities — opportunities to create ventures that would meet the people's needs and bring about positive change. Entrepreneurs are never moved to action by the problems they see. They are, however, always on the lookout for the opportunities they see in problems.

Problems = Opportunities = Successful Ventures

YOUR TURN

1. Ask your school librarian to help you find other readings about inventions or innovations. Prepare a list of at least three that were market-pulled and three that were product- or service-driven. Write a short description of the entrepreneurial process used in each venture.
2. In small groups, identify the need or want that each invention or innovation satisfied.
3. Prepare a display of your descriptions separated into two categories: Market-Pulled Innovations and Product- or Service-Driven Innovations.

The Change Process

Entrepreneurs see opportunities arising from change.

Entrepreneurs watch the process of change and take note of the **trends** or movements that they see in the change process. They study these trends, identify potential changes in needs and wants, and seek out opportunities for new ventures.

Alvin Toffler, in his book *The Third Wave*, talks about three major waves of change. He labels the First Wave the **Agricultural Age**, in which most people were either farmers or farm workers. The Second Wave he labels the **Industrial Age**, in which most people were labourers. The Third Wave he calls the **Information Age**. At the beginning of each new wave, new concepts are introduced. These new concepts help bring about changes in the way people live. They open the doors to opportunity and entrepreneurship.

Toffler suggests that the following concepts were used to bring about change in the Industrial Age:

- **standardization** - one way to do it
- **specialization** - concentrate on only one part of the process
- **synchronization** - do it with routine procedures
- **centralization** - control it from one spot
- **concentration** - work on one area at a time

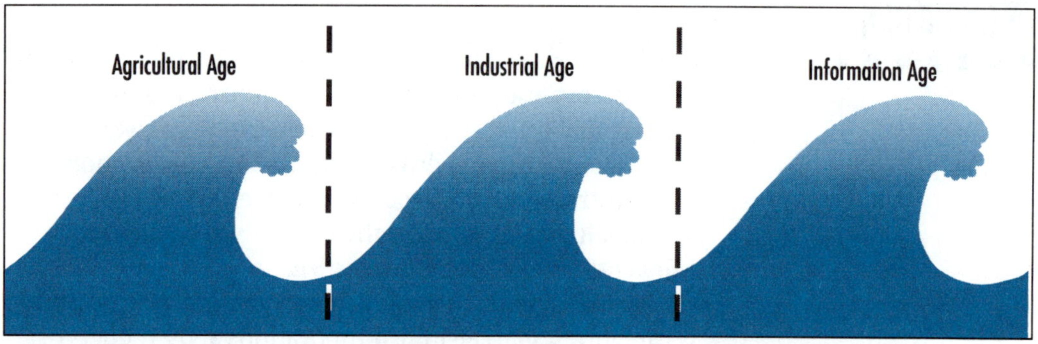

Figure 4.3 Alvin Toffler's Three Waves of Change

These key concepts were picked up and followed by business, government, entrepreneurs, and society as a whole. At the end of the Agricultural Age and at the beginning of the Industrial Age, many entrepreneurs identified a variety of new and different opportunities for individual and collective enterprise. The assembly line was a spin-off from the concepts of standardization, specialization, and synchronization. Strong federal governments which allowed regional specialities were spin-offs from the concepts of centralization, concentration, and specialization.

Today, we are entering the Third Wave. The concepts of the Industrial Age are no longer acceptable.

A technological upheaval has brought about a drastic change in our everyday lives.

People no longer want the results of standardization, specialization, synchronization, centralization, and concentration. They want to be unique. They are looking for individual and societal challenges as well as satisfactions. Toffler suggests that the Second Wave, the Industrial Wave, is now in real crisis. He maintains that the entrepreneurs of the Third Wave will turn this crisis into opportunities and step out into creative and innovative ventures.

AGENTS OF CHANGE

Everyday living can be difficult for physically challenged people. Janet Hawkins, Janet de Saint-Sardos, and Sheila Banks formed AccessAbles, a company that designs and produces handy gadgets to ease this difficulty. As the world is made more accessible, people can meet and overcome greater challenges.

The giant corporations that developed during the Industrial Age are **downsizing** (reducing their number of employees) and even merging to stay alive. These "giants" are no longer creating the new jobs that they once did. Small business (100 employees or less) has begun to take its place in the job creation field. Over the past five years, small business has generated close to 90 per cent of new jobs. There are now more than 800 000 small businesses operating in Canada, and these businesses are creating more new jobs than ever before.

Small business ventures are founded by people who look for little opportunities, gaps in the marketplace that are not being filled by anyone else. They can effect change quickly without working their way through layers of corporate management. They know what their customers want, because they are small enough to stay in close contact with the people who use their services or buy their products.

YOUR TURN

4. In groups of four or five, brainstorm key concepts or words that might describe the Third Wave.
5. Through class discussion, narrow the list down to about five concepts. In small groups, brainstorm opportunities that might develop because of these concepts.

Trends and Fads

Entrepreneurs know what's going on.

Entrepreneurs are curious. They watch. They listen. They read. They think. They dream. They look for changes in the marketplace or in society's needs and wants. These changes trigger opportunities, and entrepreneurs are excited by opportunities. Changes in society can be long term or of very short duration. Long-term changes are referred to as trends. Short-term changes are **fads**. Innovations like those described in the Sony Venture Profile can result in lasting changes. The trends that can be charted, from the first wireless recorder to the high-technology products we purchase for our homes today, reflect changes that are long lasting.

Changes that lead to temporary or short-term adjustments in the way we live are called fads. Fads make quick entrances and quick exits. Consider the impact of such fads as mood rings, hula hoops, rock 'n flowers, or paper clothing. The entrepreneur who created rock 'n flowers, flowers which rock in time to music or to any sound, found a fad and "rocked" the eighties. He produced a product and took advantage of a fad. When the fad wound down, he took his venture out of the marketplace and went on to other things.

Figure 4.4 Rock'n Time

If there is no need or no want for a better mousetrap, you can design and manufacture the greatest new and improved mousetrap the world will ever see and nothing more will happen. A better mousetrap will not automatically bring thousands of customers to your door. Only if there is a market opportunity and a need or a specific want for such an invention will an invention ring up a million dollars in sales. The entrepreneur must learn to differentiate between fads and trends.

AGENTS OF CHANGE

An entire life was often how long it took to produce only one book. Johann Gutenberg, a German printer, is thought to be the person responsible for introducing a movable-type printing process. With the Gutenberg press, books could now be produced in a fraction of the time and were available to countless people who had never even seen one before.

Trends indicate that a lasting change is taking place.

John Naisbitt, for his 1982 best-seller, *Megatrends*, monitored 6000 local newspapers over a period of a dozen years. From this monitoring, he compiled a data base from which he was able to plot 10 major trends or changes. He called these trends **megashifts,** or transformations. Although the book was published in 1982, the trends or megashifts he predicted are a very real part of our lives today. One of the trends he predicted was that North America was moving from an industrial society to an information society. Alvin Toffler made this same prediction in his book, *The Third Wave*. Naisbitt also predicted that countries would move from powerful federal governments to more local control by provinces, cities, neighbourhoods, and private associations.

YOUR TURN

6. In small groups, discuss Toffler's or Naisbitt's predictions. Find contemporary examples to prove or disprove each prediction. Share your group's examples with the rest of the class. (You may want to read Toffler's and Naisbitt's books for other predictions.)
7. Pick one trend predicted by Naisbitt and, using the techniques of brainstorming, generate a list of entrepreneurial opportunities.
8. In small groups, select one of the words on your brainstorming list and generate ideas by making a word cluster.

Forecasting Trends

A **forecast** is a vision or perspective on the future. Although it is difficult to predict with any degree of accuracy exactly what the future will hold, carefully analyzing past events will help you paint a picture of what the future is likely to be. Such a picture or forecast will certainly resemble the future more closely than a picture created using simple guesswork.

Accurate forecasting depends on your ability to organize data into effective information — information upon which you can confidently base your predictions. Being able to chart or plot data, analyze it, and forecast trends will help you identify opportunities for entrepreneurship in the Information Age. The entrepreneurs who, a few years ago, plotted and then forecast the trend towards physical fitness and good health had an edge. They saw the potential opportunities in this field and introduced fitness clubs, sports facilities, health foods, exercise equipment, sports and exercise clothing, and even specialized fitness newsletters and magazine publications all related to this new trend. These entrepreneurs have now duplicated their services throughout the community, province, or country, and in some cases, even around the world.

Trends indicate that a change is taking place and opportunities are available.

AGENTS OF CHANGE

Marvin Moore is the President of Canadian Organic Producers Marketing Cooperative Ltd., in Saskatchewan. He heads a steadily growing co-operative of farmers who believe that organic farming is an innovative and creative solution to the agricultural crisis in Saskatchewan. This new wave of farmers may be the agent of change for agriculture in many parts of the world.

Forecasting can be a complicated and sophisticated process or it can be relatively straightforward. Business sections of daily newspapers and specialized financial or business and investment weeklies use trained statisticians to report a variety of forecasts related to Gross National Product, unemployment, inflation, and technological, social, and other changes likely to affect the Canadian community. They sometimes use computer programs to predict and simulate future events. General economic trends are typically forecast in this way. Magazines and newspapers employ staff writers to study forecasts and trends and make predictions that will interest their reading audience. Large industries use opinion polls and attitude surveys to predict consumer tastes, employee preferences, and political choices. Accounting, legal, and management consultants regularly produce newsletters or journals to indicate major trends and help their clientele take advantage of the opportunities identified by these trends.

The Marketing and Economics Group of Clarkson Gordon/Woods Gordon in its 22nd edition of *Tomorrow's Customers* identifies the following trends for the Canadian community.

The "New" Family

Many businesses catering to the singles market in the 1970s and early 1980s must now adopt a more family-oriented approach. Witness Club Med's moves to transform its young singles image to a more family-oriented image to attract baby-boomer families.

Changing Age Profile

While the predominant theme of the population in North America is that of aging, there are, within certain age groups, some interesting developments, especially among teenagers, those 30-50, and among seniors.

Teenagers: Consumers in Training

Teenagers have decreased as a proportion of the total population, but their economic power has increased. Children buy and influence the purchases of an increasingly wide range of products.

The 30 to 50s

This group allocates more available income to housing (31 per cent of expenditures) than does any other age group, but will still be affluent enough to be major purchasers of discretionary products and services.

Over 65s

Seniors will represent 13.5 per cent of the Canadian population in the year 2000, compared to 10.7 per cent in 1986. Of these, 1.7 million will be over 75.

AGENTS OF CHANGE

Food always came in packages that were larger than needed for people who lived alone. Myra Sable and Carol Rosenfeld began manufacturing gourmet food products packaged in 115 g jars designed for single servings. Today, Myra oversees an empire of gourmet condiments that are stocked in more than 3000 stores across the continent, proving just how needed the idea was.

Clarkson Gordon/Woods Gordon also make the following predictions about lifestyle trends:

Table 4.1 Lifestyle Trends

Tradition	The '50s and '60s are back in style. So are marriage and family life.
Back to the Home	Consumers are spending more on their homes and doing more entertaining there.
Adventure	Excitement and fantasy are in vogue — adventure vacations and exciting sports.
Individuality and Style	Consumers want to make a personal statement through what they wear, how they live and work, and what they eat and drink.
Indulgence	Consumers want top-quality products and will pay for them.
Convenience	Easy to buy and easy to use are the criteria for the '90s.
Fitness	The desire for good health is creating a new way of life for many.

The Time-Series Forecast

A number of forecasting methods exist to provide the entrepreneur with accurate information about possible opportunities. The easiest method for a beginning entrepreneur to use is the **time-series forecast**. This involves plotting a trend of the past and present on a chart. You can then analyze this trend, make comparisons to other trends, and project it into the future.

A **growth trend** will be indicated by a line on your chart that is increasing or upward sloping over time.

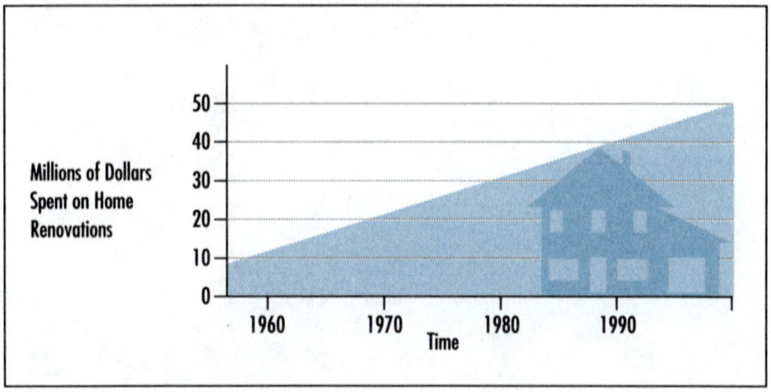

Figure 4.5 Growth Trend

A **declining trend** will be indicated by a line that is decreasing or downward sloping over time.

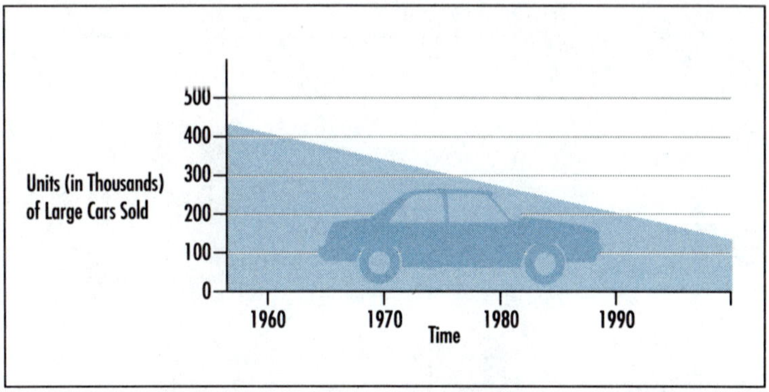

Figure 4.6 Declining Trend

A **stable situation** will be indicated by a line that is neither increasing (upward sloping) or decreasing (downward sloping) over time.

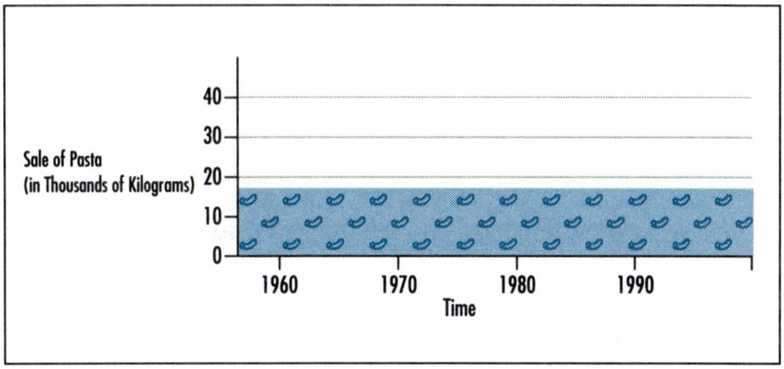

Figure 4.7 Stable Situation

Lines plotted for any of these three situations (growth, declining, or stable) may be **linear** (a straight line), **irregular** (indicating an irregular up and down movement), or **cyclical** (indicating a regular pattern of increases or decreases).

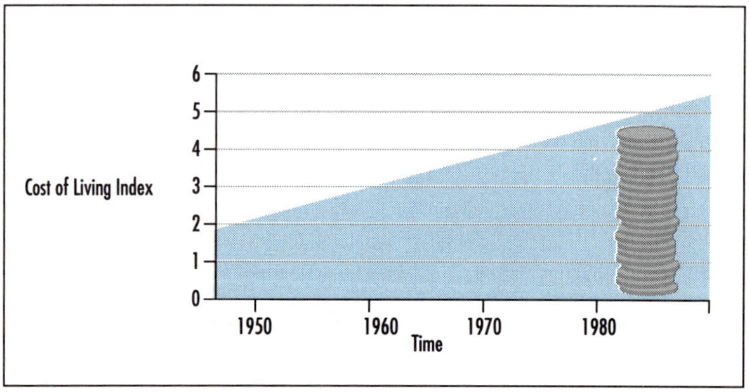

Figure 4.8 Linear Line

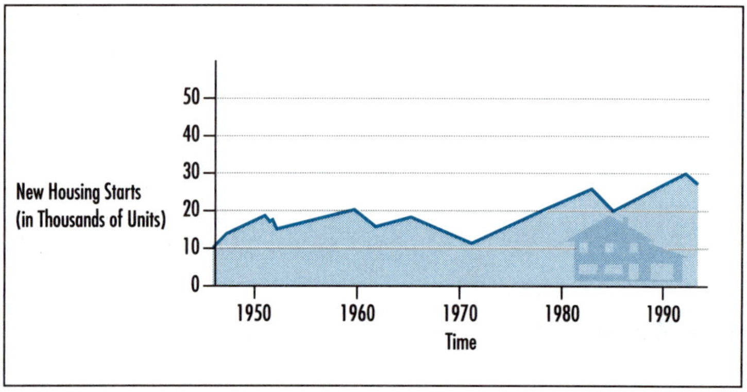

Figure 4.9 Irregular Line

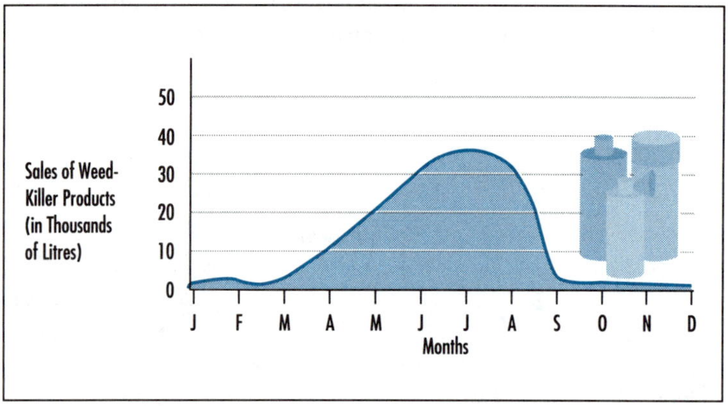

Figure 4.10 Cyclical Line

Using Research

Trends can be identified by plotting and analyzing data or they can be identified by using common research techniques. The word "research" suggests a patient, objective, and accurate search for information.

> Research is usually defined as the systematic and objective process of gathering, recording, and analyzing data for decision making.

> To guess is cheap. To guess wrongly is expensive.
> *An Old Chinese Proverb*

The process of doing the research should be organized and designed so that it will provide the kind of information that is needed to help you identify opportunities or evaluate your ideas more effectively.

Research should be goal oriented; that is, it should be designed to provide exactly the kind of information required. The person organizing the research will therefore need to know what kind of information you are looking for.

There are two kinds of research: primary research and secondary research.

Primary Research

Primary research is the technique used when you observe, experiment, interview people, or use questionnaires to find out what is happening. It also involves identifying the interests or needs of a select group of people. If you were trying to identify opportunities for transportation in a particular city, for example, you might observe traffic patterns, count the number people who ride a bus to work each day, note what stops they get off at and at what times they travel. If you wanted to develop a specific product or service in response to an identified need, you would experiment with a variety of possible models until you found an acceptable one. Interviewing or using a questionnaire to determine specific kinds of

AGENTS OF CHANGE

Hoping to use the results of her research to prevent the destruction of valuable vegetable crops, Dr. Verna J. Higgins is busy documenting information about disease resistance in the tomato plant. Plant breeders and molecular biologists will be able to put this information to good use. Her work may change the way tomatoes are grown in the future.

information requires that you carefully word your questions so that you will get exactly the kind of information you need. It is always helpful to try out your questions on a sample audience first, to make sure the information you obtain will be useful to you in solving your problem.

Secondary Research

Secondary research is the technique of reading second-hand data that has already been collected. By accessing information already prepared by someone else, someone looking, for example, at the camping industry for entrepreneurial opportunities could learn how many tourists spent how many camping nights in Canada by province and by month, for any specific year. There would also be information available on how much money campers spent for accommodation, or whether they travelled by car or by van. Trends can be identified, predictions made, and opportunities recognized by reading articles in trade journals, magazines, newspapers, or by watching movies, television shows, or by studying advertisements. Your school or community librarian will be able to help you use special indices to locate reading material that will be helpful to you when using secondary research to evaluate an idea or identify an opportunity.

The Seven Steps of Research

A company preparing to manufacture a new toy would first need to check that there is an opportunity for this toy in the marketplace. What age group might want this toy? What kind of marketing would do the best job of selling it to the public? Is the toy something that would sell in other countries? How long would the toy last under normal play conditions?

Using the seven steps to effective research outlined in Figure 4.11, this same toy manufacturer would be able to provide answers to the following questions and then analyze and summarize the data to come to a decision about the idea. For example:

Step 1: Why do I need to research this? Is there a market for this toy? If so, what is it?

Step 2: What research technique should I use? Will I bring in children to observe them playing with this toy? Will I send a sample toy out to a sample of children and have their parents observe them playing with it? Will I look at the sales of other similar toys and estimate the market, based on my findings?

Step 3: Who will I involve in this research? What age, sex, education, background of child or adult am I looking for?

Step 4: How will I collect the data? How will I organize it as it comes in?

Step 5: How will I analyze the data?

Step 6: Prepare a summary of my findings.

Step 7: Determine whether or not to manufacture the toy, make changes to it and then manufacture it, or abandon the idea altogether.

Figure 4.11 Seven Steps to Effective Research

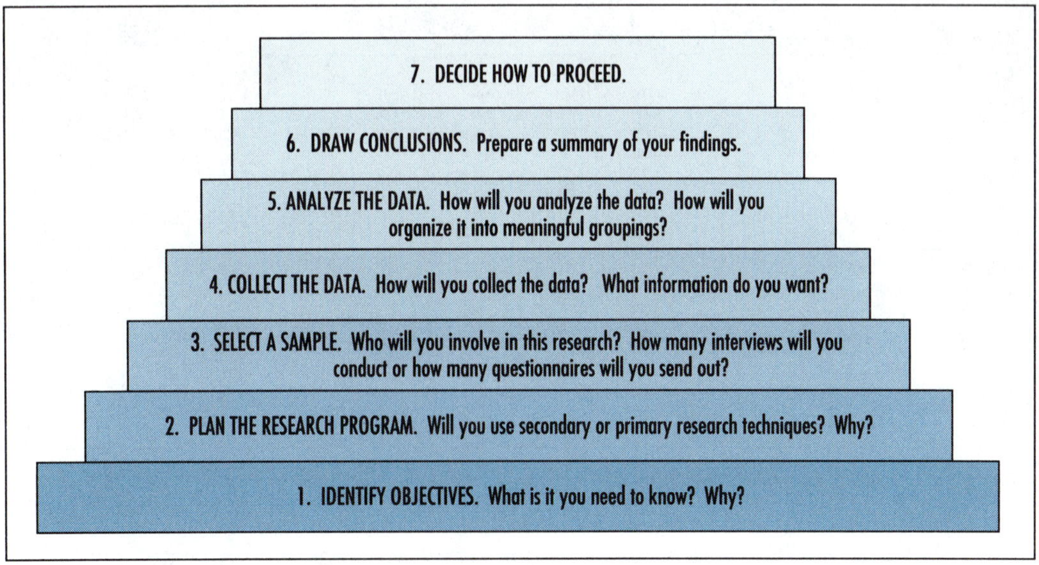

YOUR TURN

9. Visit your local library and, using the techniques of secondary research, look at a copy of a Yellow Pages Telephone Directory that is at least ten years old. Compare

the listings in that edition with a current Yellow Pages. Prepare a list of three kinds of business ventures that are no longer operating and three that are in business today that were not ten years ago. In small groups, prepare a statement about the trends you have found.

10. Plot these trends on a graph using a time-series forecast. Indicate whether they are growth, declining, or stable, and linear, irregular, or cyclical.
11. Using the data in Table 4.2, identify and plot the trends in violent crime, marriage, divorce, and unemployment rates from 1981 to 1988.

SOCIAL INDICATORS

	1981	1982	1983	1984	1985	1986	1987	1988
FAMILY								
Birth rate (per 1,000)	15.3	15.1	15.0	15.0	14.8	14.7	14.4	*
Marriage rate (per 1,000)	7.8	7.6	7.4	7.4	7.3	6.9	7.1	*
Divorce rate (per 1,000)	2.8	2.9	2.8	2.6	2.4	3.1	3.4	*
Families experiencing unemployment (000s)	693	984	1,066	1,039	990	915	872	789
LABOUR FORCE								
Total employment (000s)	11,001	10,618	10,675	10,932	11,221	11,531	11,861	12,244
- goods sector (000s)	3,711	3,376	3,317	3,404	3,425	3,477	3,553	3,693
- services sector (000s)	7,290	7,242	7,359	7,528	7,796	8,054	8,308	8,550
Total unemployment (000s)	898	1,308	1,434	1,384	1,311	1,215	1,150	1,031
Unemployment rate (%)	7.5	11.0	11.8	11.2	10.5	9.5	8.8	7.8
Part-time employment (%)	13.5	14.4	15.4	15.3	15.5	15.5	15.2	15.4
Women's participation rate (%)	51.7	51.7	52.6	53.6	54.6	55.3	56.4	57.4
Unionization rate - % of paid workers	32.9	33.3	35.7	35.1	34.4	34.1	*	*
JUSTICE								
Crime rates (per 100,000)								
- violent	666	685	692	714	749	808	856	898
- property	5,873	5,955	5,717	5,607	5,560	5,714	5,731	5,630
- homicide	2.7	2.7	2.7	2.7	2.8	2.2	2.5	2.2

- Not available * Not yet available ^{p} Preliminary estimates ^{m} Figures as of March.
[1] For year ending May 31st.
[2] Includes Protection of Persons and Property; Health; Social Services; Education; Recreation and Culture.

Table 4.2 Statistics Canada Data. Social Indicators

12. In small groups, using the trends you have just plotted, prepare forecast statements or predictions that:
    a) state the assumption(s) you are making
    b) indicate what you think the change(s) will be
    c) state the probability of the change occurring
    d) indicate the time period to which your forecast applies

13. As a class, review and analyze the trends forecast and come to a consensus on common forecast statements for the class.
14. As a class, brainstorm entrepreneurial opportunities that might flow from the trends forecast in your common forecast statements.
15. Using some of the techniques of primary research to determine what is happening in your local marketplace, in small groups identify one of the following kinds of stores: specialty shop, department store, variety store, catalogue store, discount store. Visit a store of this nature in your local community to observe what is happening.
    a) What is a typical customer for the store you have identified?
    b) What is happening in this store? What is on sale? What is new? What is not there? What is the store promoting? What is dusty?
    c) If you are visiting a department store or one that is large enough to have several departments in it, note which department has the shortest and which has the longest lines of customers at the cash register.
    d) Draw conclusions about the trends and opportunities you see there.
16. Refer to back issues of newspapers or *The Market Research Handbook*, produced by Statistics Canada. These should be available at your local library. Use the techniques of secondary research to develop a data base for your city or province on one of the following topics:
    a) the total dollars spent on automobiles and related products
    b) the percentage of households earning more than the national average income
    c) Total city/country population

    Draw conclusions about trends and new opportunities.
17. Fisher Price still produces the toy barn and animals that it produced 15 years ago. But Fisher Price has added an entire range of new toys, such as a grocery checkout with scanner and food items, and a McDonald's hamburger drive-in. Using the seven steps of research, determine what Fisher Price might have done at each step before putting one of these new toys on the market.

Venture PROFILE

Pathfinder helps students learn.

NEW WAVE VENTURE MARKETING The Pathfinder Learning System

In the last three decades, North American society has experienced a population decline. Over the next two decades, this trend will result in a demographic deadline: by the year 2020, most of the baby-boom generation will have retired. The bulk of Canada's population will be living off the economy rather than sustaining it. Supporting the baby-boomers in their retirement will require a level of productivity greater than anything we have seen.

Tomorrow's super-producers will have to be our youth of today. They will have to embody the advanced skills, education, technological sophistication, and productive efficiency necessary.

YES (Youth Employment Skills) Canada closely examined the following trends:

- Nearly one-third of Canadian Grade 9 students will drop out of school before they graduate.
- 17 per cent of high school graduates find reading difficult.
- 85 per cent of all occupations require some reading at a Grade 9 level or higher.
- Low literacy not only lessens performance on the job, but also eliminates possibilities of advancement.
- Illiteracy and low literacy cost business $4.2 billion each year in industrial accidents, lost productivity, and training costs.

In Canada today, there are more than 374 000 disadvantaged young Canadians between the ages of 16 and 24 who are out of school and out of work. Many of these young people lack the basic skills necessary to find permanent employment or to advance their careers through job-training.

YES Canada saw an opportunity to satisfy the needs of a group of disadvantaged people and provided an answer. The Pathfinder Learning System ™ was developed in Canada by improving on an American experience. It has the capacity to deliver and administer a complete, individualized educational program that is especially suitable for the disadvantaged youth or adult learner who may require remedial upgrading in areas such as reading and writing, science, mathematics, the social sciences, or employment and life skills.

YES Canada is now looking at a number of opportunities to advance the marketing of Pathfinder. Possible avenues include the development of an ESL (English as a second language) component in the system, creating an "Americanized" version to sell in the United States, and fostering partnerships with industry to address adult illiteracy among workers.

EXPLORING • PATHFINDER LEARNING SYSTEM

1. What trend did YES Canada observe?
2. What source do you think YES Canada used to obtain the data on which the trend was charted?
3. What opportunities did it identify?
4. Did it originate the idea used to meet this opportunity?
5. What other opportunities is YES Canada looking at now?
6. Is it using a market-pulled or a product- or service-driven process of entrepreneurship?

New Wave Entrepreneurs

New wave entrepreneurs, like YES Canada, will look for opportunities by carefully plotting trends or changes as we continue to move from the Industrial Age into the Information Age.

New wave entrepreneurs will observe, read, and talk to people to determine where new opportunities might lie.

They will drop into bookstores, notice what books are on display, ask salesclerks what items are best sellers, and draw conclusions about potential opportunities. They will read newspaper and magazine advertisements to find business and social opportunities. They will keep a clipping file of interests, opportunities, and ideas. They will subscribe to and read trade journals related to their special field of interest or skill in order to keep up with the trends and take advantage of new opportunities. They will develop a list of contacts in banking, law, accounting, manufacturing, community service, politics, and education. People in these fields hear about new ideas, have a "feel" for new opportunities, and can help entrepreneurs put their finger on gaps in the marketplace.

New wave entrepreneurs will keep their eyes and ears open for opportunities. They will look for opportunities associated with special events. The opening of a new sports stadium will shout out for ideas. A visit of a special person like the Queen, or the Pope, will open a door for an entrepreneur. A spell of bad weather, a hurricane or tornado, will present opportunities for community service organizations and entrepreneurs to rush into action.

Venture PROFILE

New Wave Entrepreneurs

One of the most common success principles is finding and filling a special niche in the market. Dufferin Cue Ltd. is one such example. Owners Al and Elizabeth Selinger knew that snooker was the premier TV sport in Britain and that snooker booms were underway in Japan, Hong Kong, and China. They gambled that it was only a matter of time before Canadians caught billiard fever. Their efforts to clean up the game's image in this country by opening a chain of brightly decorated, family-oriented retail snooker outlets promised to turn their $12-million cue manufacturing firm into a $35-million business by 1990. How is that for dropping the eight-ball in the right pocket?

Another company that has filled a niche is Diagnostic Chemicals Ltd. of Charlottetown. But owner Regis Duffy has done more than that; he has also capitalized on a demographic trend. With an aging North American population that will require increasing amounts of medical attention, Diagnostic Chemicals is assured a continued market for its low-cost medical test kits. These kits are in demand from doctors and hospitals for on-site diagnosis of everything from sexually transmitted diseases to pregnancy.

"The Canadian kitchen was bland ten years ago," says Sam Geraci, owner of Derlea Brand Foods Inc. and probably Canada's first genuine garlic king. "But people have immigrated to Canada from all over the world, bringing recipes that require lots of garlic and other spices. Now garlic is next in line to salt and pepper." That's a pretty succinct summary of what led to Geraci's success selling processed garlic and other odiferous variations on the same theme, including frozen garlic bread and garlic juice. But here's some food for thought: entrepreneurs should be aware that passing fads may be their downfall. Geraci's decision to package food products for other companies could provide him with a safety cushion if the bottom falls out of his $2-million-a-year business.

EXPLORING • NEW WAVE ENTREPRENEURS

1. What do all of these new wave entrepreneurs have in common?
2. What trends were these entrepreneurs watching?
3. Where would they each have received the information they needed to identify the opportunities?
4. What needs or wants did each venture meet?
5. What trends can you think of that will provide opportunities for innovation in the near future?

Figure 4.12 People who have collected the most ideas when they die have had the richest lives.

Problem Solving Is a Three-Step Process

The problem-solving process, as mentioned in Chapter 3, involves the three stages of identifying a problem or opportunity, generating ideas to meet that opportunity, and, finally, evaluating options and coming to an appropriate solution. In some cases, the idea comes first; in others, the opportunity comes first.

In Chapter 3, we used the problem-solving process to identify problems and ideas. In this chapter, we talked about identifying opportunities. When you already have the idea, you must then evaluate it against opportunities which exist. In Chapter 5, you will put on your Judge and Warrior hats and evaluate both opportunities and ideas to arrive at a viable solution to a problem.

P·O·I·N·T·S T·O R·E·M·E·M·B·E·R

- Ideas need opportunities for success; either can come first.
- We are now in the Third Wave, the Information Age, in which technology has a major impact on our lives.
- Entrepreneurs follow trends to observe changes and identify opportunities.
- Trend analysis may be plotted on graphs to indicate growth, decline, or stable situations and linear, irregular, or cyclical problems.
- Primary and secondary research are used to evaluate ideas and identify opportunities.
- New wave entrepreneurs use a variety of techniques to search for opportunities.

W·H·A·T H·A·V·E Y·O·U L·E·A·R·N·E·D·?

1. Define "market-pulled entrepreneurship".
2. Define "product- or service-driven entrepreneurship".
3. Distinguish between trends and fads.
4. What is a forecast?
5. List the seven research steps.
6. Briefly describe the three different waves described by Alvin Toffler.
7. Name five concepts that were used to bring about change in the Industrial Age.
8. Define "research".
9. Distinguish between primary research techniques and secondary research techniques and give one example of each.
10. Provide a brief description of how new wave entrepreneurs look for opportunities.

V·E·N·T·U·R·I·N·G O·U·T

1. In his book, *Megatrends*, Naisbitt says that "Trends, like horses, are easier to ride in the direction they are going." In small groups, use the techniques of primary research to compile a list of opportunities that might be associated with one of the predictions stated below. You may choose to design a questionnaire to send to a select group of people, or you may prepare a list of interview questions and interview fellow students or individuals in your community.
   a) New technology will continue to change our lives at home and at work. Some years ago, people talked about machines that would fly. Today, we hear people talking about machines that will think. Soon machines that can think will be as commonplace as machines that fly.
   b) Changing age clusters will be a significant factor in defining business and social opportunities in the future. Baby-boomers are getting older. Some are already looking forward to retirement.
   c) People are living longer. As they grow older, their psychological and physical needs change.
   d) People today are generally more diet and health conscious.

2. In small groups, identify a different prediction from the list in Question 1. Use secondary research techniques to determine opportunities that might exist for innovation and entrepreneurship. You may want to search newspaper or magazine articles or use statistics available from Statistics Canada.
3. Canadian society has developed some new values. These values include a deep concern for community, meaningful relationships, meaningful work, and a clean environment. What effect will the development of groups such as consumer activists, environmentalists, and people concerned with the quality of work life have on any one of the following industries:
   a) retailing
   b) health and fitness
   c) food and drink
   d) furniture and housing?
4. The number of women and members of minority groups joining the work force has increased steadily for more than 20 years. The sexes and minorities are reaching a new balance at work, at home, at the fitness club, in the board room, and even in parliament. What opportunities will be available if this trend continues?
5. People are becoming conservationists. Waste is no longer tolerated. In Canada, we are growing more concerned and more thoughtful about our forests, our fish, and our farms. Consumers have adopted a new respect for restraint, a new attitude toward waste, and a new thrift in the way they use their resources. As a class, use the techniques of brainstorming to compile a list of ideas that will meet these opportunities.
6. In groups of two, identify a trend and prepare a statement such as: "People are becoming more aware of the need to protect the environment." Post your statements on the class bulletin board. In groups of four or five, select one statement and list opportunities that would meet a need or a want resulting from that trend.

"One opportunity will be special." Chapter 5 will show you how to look at trends, target customers, and life cycles in order to determine the best opportunity for your idea.

CHAPTER 5

Evaluating Opportunities and Ideas

LEARNING OUTCOMES

At the end of this chapter, you should be able to:

- determine the importance of selecting the best opportunity
- distinguish the roles of the Judge and the Warrior in evaluating opportunities
- understand the concepts of trends, target customer, lifestyles, and product or service life cycle
- develop a definition of innovation
- identify examples of intrapreneurship and describe conditions that promote it
- identify criteria used for evaluating ideas

ENTREPRENEURIAL LANGUAGE

patent
target customer
target market
lifestyle
customer profile
market niche
life cycle
classic product
introduction stage
growth stage
maturity stage
decline stage
window of opportunity
global market
Canada/U.S. Free Trade Agreement
European Common Market
tariff
Pacific Rim
opportunity cost

Venture PROFILE

Students create own jobs with paper for job-seekers

By Pat Brennan, *Toronto Star*

The three publishers of the student newspaper *Afterschool Opportunities*, (L to R) Paul Pijuan, Nenad Milekovic, and Allen Lising, check out their latest edition—while visiting the newsroom of a competitor, The *Toronto Star.*

When Allen Lising went hunting for an after-school job, it was like being turned loose in a candy store.

"Practically every third shop had a help-wanted sign in the window," said Lising about the large Brampton Mall where he began his search.

Nenad Milekovic and Paul Pijuan already had part-time jobs, but they joined Lising on his job hunt because that's what good friends do.

After landing a lucrative job for Lising,the three teenagers kept on noticing help-wanted signs.

And a light went on.

Why not introduce these job opportunities to job seekers?

Within a couple of months, the three had launched a newspaper called *Afterschool Opportunities*.

While maintaining a full academic schedule, the teens used their spare time and lunch periods to get their first edition out.

Volume 1, Issue 1 of *Afterschool Opportunities* was published in December, 1988, with 6000 issues distributed to 14 high schools in the Brampton-Bramalea area.

Its 12 pages carried 15 paid ads and about the same number of free ones, listing part-time jobs.

By the time the fifth edition hit the streets on June 1, *Afterschool Opportunities* had grown to a circulation of 12 000 at 40 schools in Peel Region and 1000 home deliveries.

The newspaper's pages had doubled in size and its 32 pages were crammed with 52 paid ads.

"Our fourth issue made a profit and we did even better with the fifth issue," said Milekovic, nicknamed Nad, and largest of the three 19-year-olds.

Although the three are heading off to university this fall, they're serious about their newspaper and plan to continue publishing.

They've created a publishing company called Triax Youth Services and hired high school students to sell advertising.

They negotiated a $7500 youth venture bank loan, bought newspaper display racks, and a fax machine.

"The fax machine helped us put out the June issue in two weeks," said Lising. "It took two months to get the first issue out."

The racks are used to display the newspaper in school cafeterias, libraries, and guidance offices.

It is also available in some Garfield and W.H. Smith stores and in government employment centres in Peel Region.

The teens persuaded The *Brampton Guardian* to insert 1000 copies of the June issue in home deliveries on a Sunday. The last two issues were printed by Metroland Printing and Publishing, a division of Torstar Ltd. that publishes community newspapers.

"Apparently our newspaper didn't take up much of their press time," said Pijuan.

The publishers had to visit each school and obtain the principal's permission to distribute their newspaper on campus. "Nobody turned us down, but that might be because we got the permission of their area superintendents first," said Milekovic.

They also roamed their community and tried to sell an ad each time they saw a help-wanted sign in a store window.

Milekovic, Pijuan, and Lising did all this while holding down their original part-time jobs.

The OPP (Ontario Provincial Police) took a full-page, $345 career ad in the latest edition and so did ten other clients, from business schools to supermarkets to fast-food outlets.

The newspaper has expanded its contents, adding ads for full-time jobs, careers, and goods and services.

"It's very direct advertising to reach the high school market," said Pijuan. "There are more than 44 000 students in the schools our newspaper goes into."

The young publishers have had guidance counsellors write articles on how to perform in job interviews. They also publish articles by young people starting out in interesting careers.

The September issue will be a tabloid size newspaper, and its three publishers insist they can run an efficient newspaper and meet deadlines while attending universities in Toronto and London.

EXPLORING • AFTERSCHOOL OPPORTUNITIES

1. In six small groups, discuss the merits of this venture from the point of view of the six thinking hats.
2. In what way did Milekovic, Pijuan, and Lising take on the roles of von Oech's Explorer and Artist?
3. As an Explorer, what other ideas can you suggest for this newspaper business?

4. What ideas can you suggest as an Artist?
5. How did this threesome identify the opportunity?
6. What need or want does the newspaper satisfy?
7. In this case, what came first, the idea or the opportunity?
8. How would your Judge react to the new ideas that the Explorer has developed and the Artist has added form and value to?
9. As the Warrior, how would you implement these new ideas?

Identifying Opportunities

AGENTS OF CHANGE

Billy Diamond believed the Cree nation could prosper in Canada's economy. He mobilized the Cree peoples, spread throughout the country, to negotiate with the government for the return of their lands. Through Grand Chief Diamond's efforts, the Cree nation has gone on to found its own airline, Air Creebec. Determination brought change to the Cree nation.

Identifying opportunities is an important part of the process of evaluating your ideas. Turning ideas into viable opportunities is both the reward and the challenge of entrepreneurship. It is important for the entrepreneur to assess each idea generated to determine if, in fact, there is an opportunity to satisfy a need or a want with this idea.

In the process of venture creation, the entrepreneur relies on both the Judge and the Warrior. The Judge enables entrepreneurs to identify opportunities which others do not see. The Warrior then brings the venture together.

The Role of the Judge

The Judge is associated with the solution-finding stage of the problem-solving process. Unlike the creative Artist, the Judge is a critical thinker. He or she must carefully analyze every alternative to determine which one is best.

The Judge establishes the criteria that will be used to test every idea the Artist produces. He or she decides whether the idea should be modified, discarded, or used as is. The Judge asks questions such as:

- What is the idea trying to do?
- What are the positive and negative aspects of this idea?
- What are the chances that the idea will fail?
- If the idea does fail, what will the costs be?
- Is this the right time for this idea?

The Judge has to evaluate each idea from a negative and a positive viewpoint. The black and yellow hats help by giving the Judge the tools to conduct this evaluation. The black hat provides logic tempered with scepticism and the yellow hat provides positive reaction.

> "Good judges remember their overall purpose is to help get good ideas produced, not to revel in the beauty of their criticism."
> *Roger von Oech*

> Our Judge is developed within us from an early age. We learn from family, teachers, and friends to judge what is right and wrong, better or worse, helpful and hurtful.

A Judge with creativity will look beyond the suggestion for something to build upon. He or she will treat temporary setbacks as stepping stones towards an ultimate solution or a better idea.

The Judge's role is also to examine each opportunity and assess the risk it represents. Few entrepreneurs set out to fail; however, trying something new always has an element of risk attached. Entrepreneurs can learn a great deal from failure. Learning from early mistakes can lead to greater success when undertaking a major entrepreneurial venture.

> "No one ever achieved greatness by playing it safe."
> *Harry Gray, Entrepreneur*

Developing our Judge is necessary if we are to successfully use the creative problem-solving process introduced in Chapter 3. Not every concern is a real problem. Not every idea represents an opportunity. Not every solution is a good solution. The role of the Judge helps to sort out and evaluate all the material the Explorer has discovered and all the ideas the Artist has created.

YOUR TURN

1. Reread the Bombardier Venture Profile in Chapter 3. Make a list of the criteria Bombardier's Judge used to evaluate each idea his Artist had.
2. If you were designing your own snowmobile today to compete with Bombardier's, what criteria would you consider before producing your model? (Think of what your customers would want most in a snowmobile.)
3. The creative problem-solving process is a useful tool. It can be used by individuals or by groups of people. In small groups, complete the following:
   Use your Explorer to discover things you would like to change in your classroom or school. Focus on one of the things you have listed and use your Artist to generate as many ideas as possible. Use brainstorming techniques to generate the ideas. When the ideas stop flowing, use your Judge to establish criteria you can use to evaluate all the suggestions. Consider now what you should do to make your idea work. Report back to the class on the results of your problem-solving process.

Venture PROFILE

Chip's better wiper idea

by David Elsner, *Chicago Tribune*

Chip Haney's classmates did not elect him "most likely to succeed" when he graduated from high school last year.

Today he probably would stand a better chance.

Chip Haney, who will not turn 19 until October, has invented a better windshield wiper. He is close to signing a contract with a Michigan firm to manufacture and distribute it. General Motors Corporation has shown some interest in buying it.

He has his own company, Haney Manufacturing Industries Inc. His business cards read "Alonzo J. Haney III, Chief Executive Officer". In the corner of the card is a logo of the world.

College is on hold. He sits behind a large desk in a North Michigan office building surrounded by etchings and other works of art. There he puts in 10 hours a day researching and otherwise figuring out how to become a millionaire by age 20. He is very bright, very thoughtful, and very, very serious.

"I have always been interested in money," says Alonzo J. Haney III.

His quest for fortune began on a rainy October afternoon in 1986 when he went to pick up his mother from her machinist's job. "The wiper blades weren't working the way I envisioned they should," he said.

Millionaire by 20? Alonzo J. Haney, 18, holds two of his inventions that he hopes will make him a millionaire. GM says it will test his patented windshield wiper.

His mother was late, so Haney took out a pad and pencil and in 15 minutes sketched his first drawing for a wiper blade with a curved centrepiece capable of scooping rain, ice, and snow and tossing it up to 1.2 m away. That night he made his first prototype, cutting up a garden hose for raw material, something his father didn't discover until the following spring, when he tried to water the lawn of their North Chicago home.

Soon after, Haney rifled through the Yellow Pages to find an attorney to write a patent application. But when the attorney said it would cost $10 000, Haney decided to do it himself. With the help of a friend, Mike Mathis, he read up on patent law at the Chicago Public Library, did the necessary research to make sure that he wasn't infringing on an existing idea, and wrote a detailed, 19-page document.

The U.S. Patent Office was impressed. It called Haney's invention "A Device To Clean the Windshield More Efficiently" and awarded it patent No. 1194432.

"He was always talking about the wiper," said Joseph N. Stephenitch, Haney's teacher in four business courses at Warren Township High School in north suburban Gurnee.

"Chip was very persistent. It got so the other kids joked about it."

"But the Monday after he graduated, Chip was sitting in the office of a GM executive in Detroit talking about his idea."

That meeting came about because Haney picked up the telephone and, by mistake or persistence — probably a bit of both — got through to a senior vice-president.

In Detroit, a buyer with the Buick-Oldsmobile-Cadillac group helped him put his business plan on paper and guided him to two potential manufacturing sources.

Alofs Manufacturing Co., a small maker of auto assembly parts in Grand Rapids, Michigan, was willing to take Haney on as a partner.

"We have a verbal agreement," says Alofs' owner Eugene DeFouw, "and our attorney is writing a contract draft right now."

DeFouw cautions there is still a long way to go before the wiper blade becomes a reality. "GM still has some reservations," he said. "They feel it should be smaller in profile and have asked us to resubmit samples. But they have agreed to test it."

Haney thinks GM will buy 14 million wiper sets for about $9 million for its 1990 models, and that "aftermarket" auto supply stores will purchase at least another $10 million worth.

DeFouw says he would be "delighted" to sell 1 million units to GM by 1992, "but I'm not counting on it."

Still, he says, it has been an unusual experience to work with Haney. "I did have a certain apprehension dealing with someone so young. But Chip is very intelligent and extremely creative. I like to think of this as the beginning of a relationship."

Haney is thinking about the future, too.

"At my age, you have to be serious a lot, with little joking, to show others that you are serious and mean business," his school newspaper quoted him in a recent article. He added that he found that companies "were really happy to see someone so young go for something in which they believed."

So Haney is continuing to invent. He has designed a device that can dispense shampoo and lotions through a shower head. He made it from a laundry softener bottle cap, part of a plastic siphon pump and a garden hose attachment. He calls it Moisexcel and thinks there is a market in hotels and health clubs. Patents are pending.

AGENTS OF CHANGE

Can you imagine driving a car without windshield wipers? Until 1903, that's exactly what you would have had to do. Mary Anderson of Alabama decided to do something about it and invented one of the first windshield wipers for cars. Mary hit upon an idea that's still helping us today.

"To put your ideas into action is the most difficult thing in the world."
Goethe, a German Philosopher

EXPLORING • CHIP'S BETTER WIPER IDEA

1. In what way did Haney use his Explorer and Artist to develop his product?
2. What role has the Judge played in this venture?
3. What goals has Haney set for himself?
4. What evidence is there of a plan to achieve these goals?
5. Put on your black hat, then your yellow hat, and evaluate this new windshield wiper.
6. What role is Haney taking on as he continues to invent? Why?
7. Put on your red hat and explain how you feel about the health and beauty device Haney has invented.

The Role of the Warrior

The skills of the Explorer, Artist, and Judge must be complemented and implemented by the skills of the Warrior. It is the true entrepreneur who is able to play the role of the Warrior in the creative process. The Warrior carries an idea from the world of "what if" to the world of action. The Warrior transforms an idea or inventive solution into the reality of a useful good or service and delivers it to those who need it.

Warriors are not afraid to try new ideas. They know how to minimize risk through planning, researching, and seeking help when necessary. Warriors are also confident in their ability to bring about change and are able to withstand criticism.

Warriors are like orchestra conductors. Each section of the orchestra—the woodwinds, strings, brass, and percussion—knows how to implement its part, but without the conductor to bring the different parts together and put them in sequence, the orchestra will not succeed. The Warrior mobilizes all the necessary resources to organize the venture and get it going.

The blue hat has the same job description as the Warrior. The blue hat makes things happen by controlling the other hats.

The Warrior uses blue hat thinking to transform a dream into a reality.

Figure 5.1 The Warrior and the blue hat thinker carry an idea into action.

Four Roles Working Together

Knowing when to use each of the four thinking roles will help the entrepreneur be successful. Each of the roles—the Explorer, the Artist, the Judge, and the Warrior—has a specific place in the entrepreneurial process. Chip Haney used his Explorer to identify the need for a new kind of windshield wiper. His Artist designed the wiper and made the prototype. Haney's Judge evaluated and modified the prototype, and his Warrior is carrying the wiper to the marketplace. If Haney had used his Warrior before his Artist, he probably would not have had a successful venture.

YOUR TURN

4. Consider the possibility that there is a great deal of garbage littered around your school property. In small groups, examine this problem as each of von Oech's four thinkers would: the Explorer, the Artist, the Judge, and the Warrior. Remember to put on the different coloured hats for the different thinking phases. Present your ideas to the class. From the group presentations, select one or two ideas that could be presented to the student council for implementation throughout the school.

Venture
PROFILE

JOSEPH ARMAND BOMBARDIER
The Entrepreneur

Once Bombardier had solved the problem of traction and power with the invention of the sprocket wheel and rubber tread, he set up his garage to produce six more snow machines. Each vehicle was sold and on the road as soon as the last bolt was in place. He was so happy with his progress that he decided to close down his regular garage business and to manufacture snow vehicles year round. His father urged him to be careful. He reminded him that he had established a very successful garage repair business and that he had a family to support.

Bombardier went ahead anyway and recruited a small but skilled team of employees who worked six days a week. He decided he would be the travelling salesman for his idea and drove around Quebec in his new machine doing all kinds of stunts to gain publicity. He applied to the Canada Patent Office for a **patent** which would protect his sprocket wheel and track system. The patent, which was granted on June 29, 1937, made it illegal for anyone to copy his invention for 17 years.

And so began a venture which today is known as Bombardier Inc. By the end of 1988, it was the seventy-eighth largest company in Canada. Its total sales were nearly $1.5 billion and it employed more than 10 000 people. Today it produces a wide variety of vehicles. Municipal transit cars and military vehicles now account for most of its sales, but it still produces various types of snow machines and all-terrain vehicles which are used around the world for work and leisure.

EXPLORING • BOMBARDIER: THE ENTREPRENEUR

1. In what ways did Bombardier use the skills of the Warrior to make his dream come true?
2. Identify examples in the Venture Profile where Bombardier used blue hat thinking.
3. In your opinion, is Bombardier an inventor or an entrepreneur? Give reasons for your answer.

Looking Before You Leap

AGENTS OF CHANGE

Mostly self-taught, Paul Cunningham of New Brunswick built his first water wheel when he was 10 years old. He now builds and sells residential-sized hydro electric systems to people living far from hydro lines. His next step is to set up shop in Third World countries where electricity is desperately needed. An age-old idea may come back to solve some modern energy problems.

Figure 5.2 Consider all factors before you leap into action.

The Bombardier Venture Profile demonstrates the importance of understanding the complete picture and seeing how your venture fits in with changing trends before you act. Confirm your hunches and redefine your venture to ensure it is consistent with the needs of the marketplace. Also protect yourself and your new invention by applying for a patent.

You increase your chances of success still further if you can gain work experience beforehand in the type of venture you wish to start.

Did you know that, in 1890, a patent was granted to a Calgary woman who had invented a mechanical skirt lifter? It was designed to lift the hem of her skirt ever so discreetly when crossing muddy or dusty streets.

Venture PROFILE

Life in the doghouse

Anita Lusterio was a bank manager whose hobby was breeding, raising, and training prize-winning dogs. When her grandfather died, he left her an inheritance of $250 000. Anita used the money to purchase a boarding kennel and retired from the bank, forever.

The kennel needed a great deal of work. It had the capacity to board 100 dogs, but there were only 40 dogs there. Anita did everything she could to make the place better for the dogs. She bought the best quality food, she brushed the dogs regularly, she painted the inside of the kennel. She gave the dogs the best care money could buy.

When the dog owners did not continue to bring their dogs to Anita's kennel, she could not understand. She treated the dogs like her children. Within the first year of operation, Anita was so behind in her payments, she decided to sell the boarding kennel and go back to work as a bank manager.

EXPLORING • LIFE IN THE DOGHOUSE

1. Who were Anita's real customers?
2. Who did she cater to?
3. What were some of the things her real customers might have wanted a boarding kennel to offer?
4. Did Anita "get the big picture" before she bought the kennel?
5. What roles did the Explorer, Artist, Judge, and Warrior play in this situation?
6. Which thinking hats did Anita wear? When?
7. What mistake(s) did Anita make?
8. What do you think she could learn from her mistakes?

Know Your Customers

The consumers who you are hoping will buy your product or service are your **target customers** or your **target market**. As an entrepreneur, it is important to probe the **lifestyle** of your potential target customers before you plunge into a new venture. Look for clues to their lifestyle preferences.

- How many cars do they have?
- What makes and models of cars?
- How old are the cars and what condition are they in?
- What sports or recreational activities do your target customers participate in?
- Do they have pets, hobbies?
- Do they live in houses, apartments, town houses, detached homes, condominiums?
- How many bedrooms and bathrooms do they have?
- How large are their homes?

Study your target customer from all angles and develop a **customer profile** of the person you are going to sell your product or service to.

Consumers today are generally looking for products and services that can enhance their lifestyles. Examination of recent trends shows that consumers today are most interested in quality, service, and convenience. What can you offer consumers?

Clarkson Gordon/Woods Gordon is predicting that consumers are becoming part of the "two-of-everything" household. A generation ago, it was unusual for households to have more than one car or more than one television. Today, with the number of two-income households increasing, two cars and two televisions are no longer unusual. How will this "two-of-everything" household affect the lifestyle of your target customer?

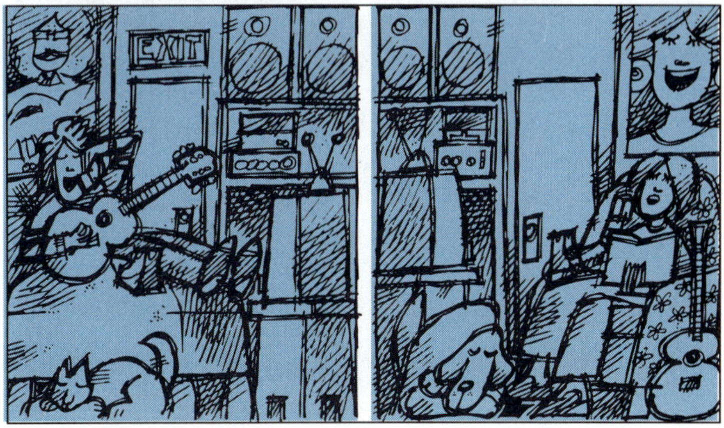

Figure 5.3 Today's consumers may be from a two-of-everything household.

Your target customer is likely to be educated, well travelled, and demanding.

Many consumers know exactly what they want, some think they know what they want, and others have no idea what they want or need. If an entrepreneur is going to be successful in creating a **market niche** for his or her product or service, the entrepreneur needs to identify the needs and wants of the customers.

Knowing your customer or target market means knowing the business you are really in. Are you selling a product or a convenience? Are you producing a necessity or a luxury? The entrepreneur must have a solid knowledge base of his or her product or service. An entrepreneur with inaccurate or limited knowledge will not be an effective champion of the product or service.

Anita Lusterio thought her business was to care for dogs. She put all her energy into making the dogs more comfortable. However, the dogs were not her customers. The owners of the dogs were her real customers and she did nothing to directly satisfy them. Without satisfaction, customers do not return.

YOUR TURN

5. What opportunities are likely to arise as a result of the "two-of-everything" household?
6. If your target market is better educated, well travelled, and more demanding than ever before, how should you, the entrepreneur, prepare to respond?
7. What could Anita have done to ensure repeat business from her customers?
8. In small groups, identify the businesses that the following industries are really in. What needs and wants should be satisfied for each industry?
   a) banking
   b) medicine
   c) railway
   d) social services

Venture PROFILE

Lacteeze—an alternative to milk

Kingsmill Foods Company had been in the business of producing hot chocolate mix for industrial clients for over 45 years when Dorion Kingsmill became a second-generation owner of the company. Dorion developed a product called Lacteeze. Lacteeze is milk that is free of lactose, a substance many people are allergic to. Dorion markets this product directly to the consumer. She has carved out an excellent market niche by responding to the needs of customers who could not tolerate drinking regular milk. Her concern is that she is unable to reach a large part of her potential market because many potential customers have not recognized their need for a lactose-free milk.

EXPLORING • LACTEEZE

1. What are the needs and wants of the customers of Kingsmill Foods Company?
2. How can Dorion Kingsmill get her customers to recognize their needs?
3. Are there any similarities between Anita Lusterio and Dorion Kingsmill? What are they?

AGENTS OF CHANGE

Goat's milk is in demand by people who are allergic to cow's milk. Maxine Joyce started Forever April with one goat called "April". Her herd quickly grew to 150 goats. She finally sold the name, production, and distribution rights to The Elm Avenue Dairy, which plans to provide other products made of goat's milk. Now more people who could not drink cow's milk could get an inexpensive, tasty, and healthy alternative.

Life Cycles and Timing

It is crucial that an entrepreneur knows the **life cycles** of the industry or service field he or she plans to enter. Innovations are more successful and bring greater rewards when they are injected into an industry or service field while it is still young and growing. Blue jeans are a classic example of a product introduced at the very early stages of the leisure clothing industry. They have had the staying power of a **classic product** and have become a symbol of conformity.

The four essential stages in the life cycle of a product or a service are: **introduction**, **growth**, **maturity**, and **decline**.

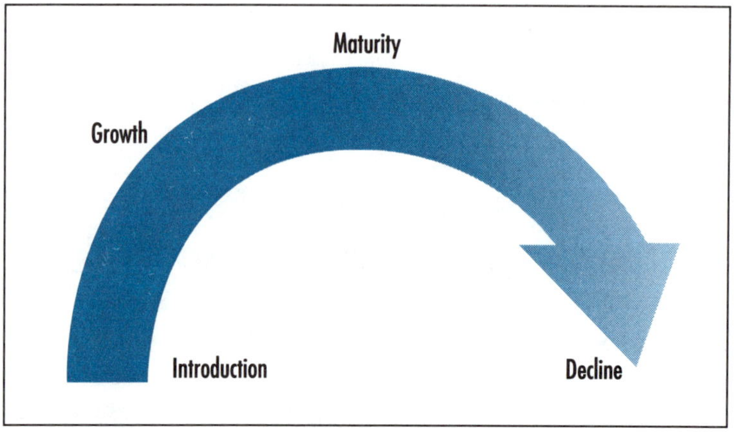

Figure 5.4 The Life Cycle of a Product or Service

The designer-jean craze started as a new industry in the early 1980s. A few years later, some designer jeans had moved from the introduction stage, through growth, into the maturity stage and now can be purchased at discount stores for less than a third of their original price. Figure 5.5 indicates at which stage some of the products we know today might be placed on the life cycle curve.

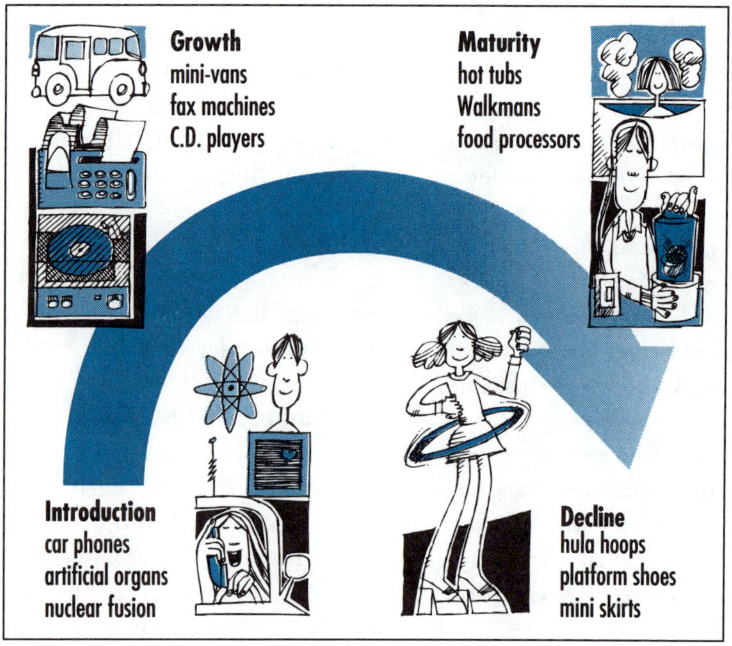

Figure 5.5 Stages in the Life Cycle of a Variety of Products

The time at which a product or service is introduced into the market is also important to its success. Disposable diapers were introduced to the market in the 1950s and sales were poor. Society frowned upon mothers who would consider using these "paper" diapers on their children. As more women began to work outside the home, using cloth diapers became a burden. When disposable diapers were reintroduced in the 1960s, they were an overwhelming success. Today, the disposable diaper is under fire and the cloth diaper is making a serious comeback because of the disposable diaper's long-term effects on the environment.

YOUR TURN

9. Develop a complete picture of the target customer for each of the following products or services:
   a) glow-in-the-dark necklaces
   b) first-class air travel
   c) frozen gourmet dinners
   d) skills upgrading courses
   e) maid service
10. How would you adjust the product or service in each case to accommodate your target customer?
11. Place the following industries or products on a life cycle chart similar to that in Figure 5.5.
    a) laser technology
    b) slinkies
    c) computer software
    d) silly putty
    e) stereo sound system
    f) leather jackets

Windows of Opportunity

Before you enter into a venture, it is important to consider the big picture and then determine where your venture will fit. This process is sometimes referred to as looking at the **window of opportunity**. Some windows are large while others are small. Timing your venture so that it will fit into the window, however large or small, is crucial to success.

AGENTS OF CHANGE

African-Canadians had no voice of their own in Nova Scotia until 1946, when Carrie Best began publishing a church bulletin. That bulletin grew from a bi-monthly newspaper to *The Negro Citizen*, a newspaper that gained national circulation between 1949 and 1956. A small venture became headline news and helped change the way African-Canadians viewed themselves!

The Wall Walker fad found the window very small. Its creator assessed the opportunity, decided the timing was right, entered the market, and left as the window was closing. Imagine what might have happened had the timing been off for this fad. Wall Walkers might have entered the marketplace after the window had closed and the venture would never have received the acclaim for having hit the marketplace at exactly the right time. Consumers were ready to accept such a whimsical product and make it into a fad.

Windows of opportunity can be predicted by using the research skills or trend analysis skills outlined in Chapter 4. Whatever method is used, windows of opportunity are very important in the success or failure of a venture.

The Process of Innovation

In Chapter 1, you saw how the E.D. Smith Company encouraged its employees to generate money-saving ideas by rewarding them with a cash bonus based on the annual savings generated by the ideas. This case illustrates the importance of intrapreneurship, or entrepreneurship within the company. The time is now ripe for corporations to encourage innovation among their employees. Canada needs to be competitive at the local, national, and international levels.

> Recognizing the window of opportunity in large corporations is sometimes difficult because of the layers of employees through which an idea has to pass before it becomes a reality.

To compete against small entrepreneurial businesses in a **global market**, it is essential for larger companies to encourage innovation among their employees by urging them to come up with new and better ideas.

Companies which encourage innovation are continually trying to improve their existing products or services and to discover new products and services which are better than the competition. They recognize the fact that it is important to be innovative to survive.

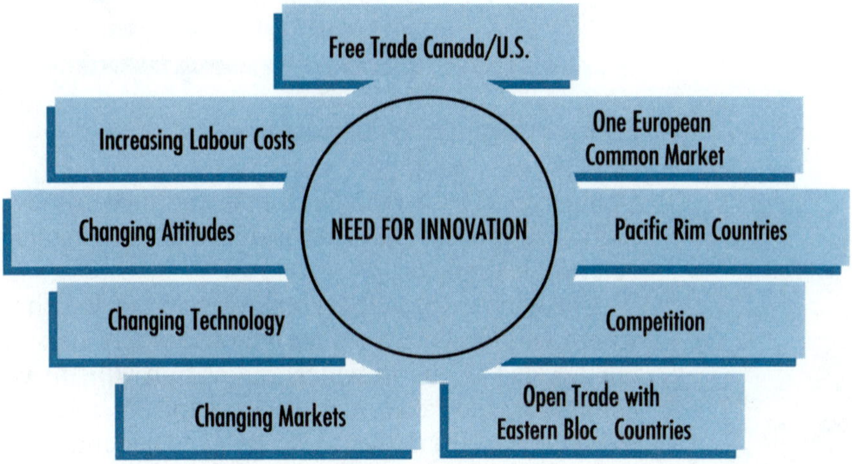

Figure 5.6 Innovation helps ensure the survival of the venture.

Entrepreneurs bring a spirit of innovation to an economy and to society. As companies face the challenge of an increasingly competitive world, entrepreneurs and the spirit of innovation that they bring become more essential. The 1990s will see the **Canada/U.S. Free Trade Agreement** fully implemented. This will allow more products to pass freely between these two countries, thus increasing competition while opening up new markets.

By 1992, there will be one **European Common Market**. All citizens of the Common Market will be free to relocate to a different country depending on where their expertise is required. Products and services will be allowed to cross borders without **tariffs** (duties or taxes), thus creating new opportunities and markets for entrepreneurs.

The **Pacific Rim** countries—especially Japan, Singapore, Thailand, Korea, and the Philippines—will continue to compete with North American businesses due to their lower costs, abundant labour force, and increased use of technology. For example, most countries outside North America are now using a new, innovative keyboard designed to increase the speed of keyboarding. International companies can transfer information by satellite to these countries and have documents produced rapidly at considerable savings.

To compete in these rapidly changing markets, North American companies need to be more innovative.

Encouraging Innovation

Companies which recognize that employee innovation is their greatest asset have learned to train their employees to be creative thinkers.

An environment where employees do not feel threatened, where employees are supported, and where new ideas are encouraged is one in which innovation will thrive. Some companies, such as Hewlett Packard and 3M, reward creative thinkers for their ideas. By helping, encouraging, and rewarding their innovative employees, companies gain entrepreneurs inside the organization.

Many companies also ask their customers for suggestions on how to improve aspects of the company. Although this is not intrapreneurship, it can make the company more competitive and innovative.

As you have been learning throughout this text, there is no shortage of ideas. Ideas are the seeds of innovation. Companies should create a supportive environment, encourage employees to talk to each other, set time aside for groups of employees to get together to brainstorm, and reward the innovations that are developed. The major methods for encouraging innovation and intrapreneurship are:

- generating new ideas
- managing the innovation process
- managing the intrapreneurs
- providing leadership

AGENTS OF CHANGE

Ted Dixon, a physics professor at the University of Waterloo, developed a crude prototype of a scanning laser microscope. When he discovered that the business sector was reluctant to develop a prototype product at the forefront of technology, he started Waterloo Scientific Inc. His company now sells to customers such as Intel, Motorola, and IBM. Here, necessity truly was the mother of this company.

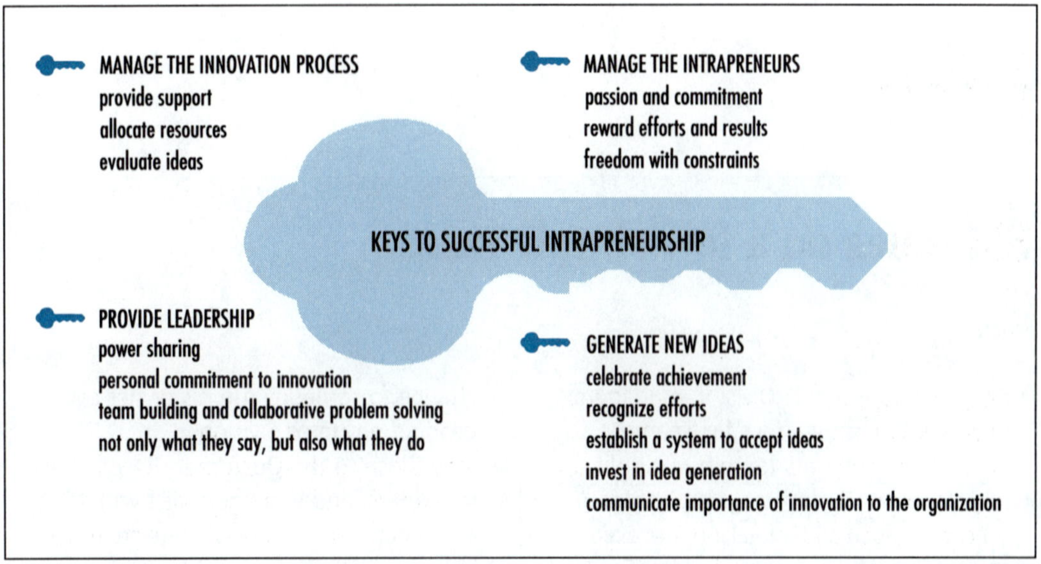

Figure 5.7 Keys to Successful Intrapreneurship (Courtesy of the Coopers and Lybrand Consulting Group)

YOUR TURN

12. In pairs, contact one of the larger corporations in your community and arrange to interview one of the managers about innovation and intrapreneurship within the organization. The following questions could be used in your interview:
    a) How has the rate of change affected your organization?
    b) In what ways has your organization been innovative?
    c) What aspects of your business have you been paying close attention to?
    d) In what ways do you communicate the importance of innovation to the organization?
    e) How does your company celebrate or reward employee achievement?
    f) What do you do to encourage team building and collaborative problem solving?
    g) How will innovation and intrapreneurship help your company compete in a global market?

Venture PROFILE

3M relies on a few simple rules

Business Week

- Keep Divisions Small: Division managers must know each staffer's first name. When a division gets too big, it is split up.
- Tolerate Failure: By encouraging plenty of experimentation and risk-taking, there are more chances for a new-product hit. The goal: Divisions must derive 25 per cent of sales from products introduced in the past five years. The target may be boosted to 30 per cent.
- Motivate the Champions: When a 3Mer comes up with a product idea, he or she recruits an action team to develop it. Salaries and promotions are tied to the product's progress. The champion has a chance to someday run his or her own product group or division.
- Stay Close to the Customer: Researchers, marketers, and managers visit with customers and routinely invite them to help brainstorm product ideas.
- Share the Wealth: Technology, wherever it's developed, belongs to everyone.
- Don't Kill a Project: If an idea can't find a home in one of 3M's divisions, a staffer can devote 15 per cent of his or her time to prove it is workable. For those who need seed money, as many as 90 Genesis grants of $50 000 are awarded each year.

EXPLORING • 3M'S RULES

1. How do 3M's rules relate to the Keys to Successful Intrapreneurship (Figure 5.7)?
2. In what way do you think keeping the divisions small helps to encourage innovation?
3. Are there any similarities between 3M's approach to innovation and E.D. Smith's (in Chapter 1)? If so, what are they?
4. How would staying close to the customer help contribute to new ideas?
5. How would staying close to the customer help to identify the window of opportunity?

6. Innovators like to see their ideas succeed. How does 3M ensure that this happens?
7. If the E.D. Smith Company that you read about in Chapter 1 had some simple rules, what do you think they would be?

Evaluating Your Ideas

Put on your blue hat, become a Warrior, and evaluate your idea before you enter a particular venture.

Each idea will have its own evaluation criteria. The suggestions offered below are very general and should be used only to help you prepare a checklist to evaluate your ideas before entering into a venture.

Cost

- Will the idea cost more than you can afford or more than the client or customer will pay?
- Will costs be high initially and then be reduced over a period of time?
- What marketing costs will have to be covered?
- What personnel or labour costs will have to be covered?

Opportunity Cost

- How much of your time will it take?
- What personal commitments or pleasures will you have to give up as part of the **opportunity cost**?
- How stressful will your venture be?

Time

- Should your venture be started now or should it wait?
- When it is started, will it be ready for the marketplace in time to fit into the window of opportunity that you have charted?
- Will your venture be a long-lasting one or will it be a fad?
- When should you get out of the venture?

Feasibility

- Is the idea going to work?
- Do you have sufficient resources and facilities to start it now?
- Will it be manageable once it has started? Do you have the right procedures in place for effective management?

Acceptability

- Will your venture serve a specially targeted market?
- Have you carefully described your customer?
- Does your product or service exactly meet your customer's needs or wants?
- Is your product or service consistent with accepted values and attitudes?

Usefulness

- Will your product or service meet a real need?
- Will it prove more advantageous than other similar products or services already available?

P·O·I·N·T·S T·O R·E·M·E·M·B·E·R

- Identifying opportunities is part of the evaluation process for ideas.
- The Judge in the entrepreneur establishes the criteria by which the ideas are evaluated.
- The Judge uses black and yellow hat thinking to analyze and evaluate what the Artist has developed.
- The Warrior in the entrepreneur transforms the idea from the "what if" stage to the "what is" stage.
- It is important to watch the marketplace to learn about your target customer, your product or service, and life cycles and timings.
- Try to "fit" your venture into a window of opportunity.
- Intrapreneurship and innovation within corporations are essential for their survival.

WHAT HAVE YOU LEARNED?

1. What is the role of the Judge in evaluating opportunities?
2. How is the role of the Judge related to black and yellow hat thinking?
3. What role does the Warrior take on?
4. Compare the role of the Warrior to blue hat thinking.
5. Why is it important to "get the big picture" before venturing out?
6. What impact will the "two-of-everything" family have on entrepreneurial opportunities?
7. List the four stages in the life cycle of a product. Give an example of a product or service at each stage in the life cycle.
8. Briefly explain the difference between life cycles and timings.
9. Why is it essential for corporations to be intrapreneurial?
10. Suggest four ways corporations can encourage innovation.
11. List the six criteria used for evaluating ideas.

VENTURING OUT

1. The computer, the television, penicillin, and the zipper are all relatively modern innovations. What impact has each of these innovations had on society?
2. In groups of three or four, develop a statement that begins: "Innovations we would like to see in our school would be...." Include at least six innovations in your statement.
3. Differentiate between an innovator and an inventor. Which one is an entrepreneur? Find two examples of each in the Venture Profiles contained in Section 1 of the text.
4. In groups of four or five, brainstorm opportunities in your local community.
5. Prepare a list of key factors that should be considered when evaluating an entrepreneurial opportunity. Then use this list to evaluate the opportunities brainstormed in Question 4.
6. In what ways are banks becoming innovative?

"Behind every successful venture is a good plan." This chapter will show you how to use the problem-solving process, the four creative roles, and the six thinking hats to complete each major part of a venture plan.

CHAPTER 6

Moving into Action: The Venture Plan

LEARNING OUTCOMES

By the end of this chapter, you should be able to :

- use the problem-solving process, the four roles, and the six thinking hats to begin planning a venture
- understand why both organization and a written venture plan are crucial to the success of a venture
- use the components of the Research Assistance Grid
- list and describe the five major sections of a venture plan
- relate each major section of a venture plan to the entrepreneurial process through spokes in the venture wheel
- recognize the need for flexibility in the venture plan
- write a preliminary venture plan.

ENTREPRENEURIAL LANGUAGE

venture plan
game plan
launch
Research Assistance Grid
needs assessment
market analysis
short listing
description
resource analysis
operating strategy
financial strategy

Venture PROFILE

Rule 1 for entrepreneurs

By Paul Lebel, *The Globe and Mail*

Like a road map, a venture plan provides specific direction.

Despite the romantic notion that intuition alone will lead an entrepreneur along the road to success, the reality is that a good map is necessary. John Gilbert, president of Metalon Technology, credits the New Ventures program with forcing him to take a hard look at his dream.

Ontario's New Ventures program guarantees personal loans of up to $15 000 from financial institutions. Entrepreneurs must invest an equal amount and agree to hire at least one full-time employee during the term of the guarantee. They must also prepare a comprehensive business plan.

"I'd written a cursory business plan before I applied for the loan," Mr. Gilbert said. "I think it was one page. By the end of the loan process, I had a 20-page document."

Metalon uses an electro-chemical process to restore precision machine parts. Mr. Gilbert's detailed business plan has paid off in the form of a 45 per cent annual growth rate since the company was started in 1986.

Peter Friedman, director of the small business branch at the Ontario Ministry of Industry, Trade and Technology, supports the importance of planning. "We did extensive research on startups four years ago. The results were clear. If you do a formal business plan before you start, the chances of your business succeeding rise significantly."

Despite this fact, most entrepreneurs set off without a formal plan and often have business records of the shoe-box variety. The result is a failure rate that is much higher than it should be.

EXPLORING • RULE 1 FOR ENTREPRENEURS

1. Why did John Gilbert end up writing a detailed plan of his venture?
2. How did the writing of a detailed plan help John Gilbert's business?

3. Make a list of the major undertakings you have been involved in during the last year. Your list might, for example, include a trip, a major purchase, or a major assignment at work or school. How much planning did you do beforehand? Did you create a written plan?

The Research Assistance Grid: A Basic Planning Tool

Entrepreneurs use the creative problem-solving model, the six thinking hats, and the four roles described in Chapters 3 and 5 to organize resources and create a venture that will satisfy needs. Although entrepreneurs are action oriented, the most successful ones think and plan before acting. Planning is a very important part of the action process. The **venture plan** acts as a bridge between the thinking and the doing.

A venture plan is a strategy statement describing how the entrepreneur plans to accomplish the specific task of starting a venture.

It outlines the goals and objectives for a particular venture and provides a thorough description of the roles of the "players" involved. You might call it the **game plan** the entrepreneur uses as he or she works towards a successful **launch** of the venture.

While every venture plan is unique, every plan attempts to do much the same thing. Whatever its size and however simple or complex it may be, your plan should outline specific goals and objectives and should describe planning strategies. It should identify and assess potential risks. If your venture is a for-profit undertaking, preparing a venture plan will help you, the prospective entrepreneur, predict future profits. It will also reveal whether or not you can expect to earn enough to carry the venture through the first few months after startup. If the venture is not-for-profit or a community service, a venture plan will help you consider the costs and benefits of such a service. Doing the research necessary to write a venture plan helps entrepreneurs identify what ideas represent the best opportunities.

AGENTS OF CHANGE

The Women's World Banking Association is a 20 000 member co-operative that lends close to $100 000 annually, usually to women who want to start a business in developing countries. Eight years ago it loaned $2500 to a woman in Cali, Colombia, who started a bicycle repair shop. She now has two shops, 13 employees, and a factory. A small boost helped create jobs and opportunities.

A good planning model enables the entrepreneur to identify the questions to ask before beginning a venture. Table 6.1 presents a **Research Assistance Grid**. Each of the six sections of the grid contains a one-word question. Beneath this one-word question are more specific questions which anyone starting a venture should answer before he or she begins. A venture plan should contain the answers to these questions and more.

Table 6.1 Research Assistance Grid

WHAT?	**WHY?**
WHAT good or service will I produce?	WHY should I spend my time and energy on this venture?
WHAT will I do to control the costs of production?	WHY will others buy my good or service?
WHAT will I do to maintain quality standards?	WHY will my venture be unique and offer something special?
WHAT is the venture's potential for growth?	WHY is it necessary to start this venture from scratch?
WHERE?	**WHEN?**
WHERE will I find a suitable site?	WHEN is the demand greatest for my good or service?
WHERE will I find the equipment that is needed?	WHEN will I be able to start my venture?
WHERE will I find the right people to work with?	WHEN should I order the inventory I will need?
WHERE will I find supplies at competitive prices?	WHEN should I raise or lower my selling price?
WHO?	**HOW?**
WHO will my customers be?	HOW will I provide my good or service at the lowest cost?
WHO are going to be my major competitors?	HOW strong is the competition now and how strong will it be in the future?
WHO will I get to do the things I cannot do?	HOW will the competition react to a new competitor?
WHO do I need to help me during the startup?	HOW large is the market and what share can I get?

YOUR TURN

1. Why are most of us, like many entrepreneurs, reluctant to make written plans?
2. Make an hour-by-hour plan of how you would like to spend the rest of this day. What are the advantages of this kind of planning?
3. Assume that you wish to start a small venture to make and deliver home-made pizza. Think of all the *what, why, where, when, who*, and *how* questions your venture plan would have to answer. Make up your own Research Assistance Grid listing specific questions that must be answered during your planning process.

Venture PROFILE

Ms. Chang's Class: Part 1

Ms. Chang and her Entrepreneurship Studies class had been making good progress with their course, but there were some difficulties. The class met every morning at 8:30 a.m. and neither Ms. Chang nor her students were at their best at that time of day. The earlier enthusiasm of September was dwindling almost as rapidly as the hours of daylight. It was now a cold, grey, rainy day in November, and no one liked getting up in the dark every morning to get to school on time.

By the time Ms. Chang had completed attendance, the late arrivals had finished trickling in. They sat silently in their rows, struggling with their own internal "timeclocks" which told them it was not yet time to be awake and alert. The subject of the lesson today was the role of the Warrior in the creative problem-solving process.

After Ms. Chang completed her explanation of who the Warrior was and what the Warrior did, she asked if there were any questions. There was dead silence. Not a hand moved. "Do we have a problem?" she asked.

From the back of the class came the immediate response, "This Warrior is tired of fighting sleep. I want to go back to bed!"

"I'm hungry," added someone else. "I need to study for my Physics test," contributed a third student.

Ms. Chang then broke in. "It's quite clear that we do have a problem, perhaps many different problems. We have already studied the creative problem-solving process, the four roles, and six thinking hats entrepreneurial individuals use to create ventures which satisfy needs. I want you to use what you have learned to see if you can solve your own problems. So where should we begin?"

Several hands went up and the students suggested that they should begin by trying to find out exactly what the problem was. They decided it would be best if each student took five minutes to think about and write down exactly how he or she was feeling and what was making learning difficult that morning. Ms. Chang gave them time and then asked them to share with the class what they had written. She agreed to act as the class secretary and to write down everything they said on the board.

In no time, they had a long list which included, among others: "I'm tired!" "I had an argument with my best friend just before class." "I missed breakfast and left my lunch at home." "I can't concentrate this early in the morning." "I had to work the late shift last night and am exhausted this morning." "These seats are uncomfortable!" "I was up too late last night finishing an English assignment." "It's just one of those days!" ...and so the list went on.

Ms. Chang looked at the board which was full of notes and asked the students what was next. One student noted that some of the feelings and difficulties on the list were personal and unique, while others seemed to be shared by many members of the class. She suggested that they form groups which would try to identify the common difficulties.

The groups were formed and, after some discussion, Ted, the spokesperson for one group, summarized the feelings of the class in the following way: "Many of the things people mentioned as a problem or difficulty were personal. We, as a group, can't do much about them. There are others which seem fairly common. Our group decided that what we seem to need at 8:30 in the morning is something to wake us up and get us going. This classroom is also a pretty dull, uncomfortable place to be, particularly on a dark, wet, November morning." The other groups agreed.

"Since many of you seem to have some common needs and some common problems," said Ms. Chang, "perhaps you, as a group, can do something. Let's begin by changing the problems and needs you identified into challenges or opportunity statements by asking:

In what ways might we:

a) change this class to make it a more comfortable, inviting place to be; and
b) increase our level of alertness and ability to concentrate?"

> "The basic difference between an ordinary man and a Warrior is that a Warrior takes everything as a challenge while an ordinary man takes everything either as a blessing or a curse."
> *Carlos Castenada*

EXPLORING • MS. CHANG'S CLASS: PART 1

1. At what stage of the creative problem-solving process have the students in this profile been working? (Reread Chapter 3, pages 61 to 63 to review the problem-solving process.)
2. What creative role(s) are they playing? (Review Chapter 3, pages 66 to 67.)
3. What thinking hat(s) are they wearing? (Review Chapter 3, pages 67 to 71.)

Structure of a Venture Plan

Venture plans are written for new ventures whether they are small or large. They are written for established ventures that are trying to do something new. They are written for business ventures or community service ventures. Simple ventures have simple plans. Larger or more complex ventures have more complex and detailed plans. A venture plan is comprised of five major sections:

Sections of a Venture Plan

- Section 1: the description (which is written last, but appears first)
- Section 2: the market analysis
- Section 3: the resource analysis
- Section 4: the operating strategy
- Section 5: the financial strategy

You will notice from following Ms. Chang's class through its problem-solving process that a venture plan can be used by students to resolve a class problem.

Market Analysis

The students in Ms. Chang's class are using the creative problem-solving process, creative roles, and thinking hats to work through the Self and Opportunity Spokes of the Venture Creation Wheel.

Figure 6.1 The Self and Opportunities Spokes of the Venture Creation Wheel are used during market analysis.

First they analyzed their individual needs. Then they tested to see whether others had the same needs. In other words, they were testing to see whether an opportunity existed to do something to satisfy the needs of the class. **Needs assessment**, or, as it is more often called in commercial business ventures, **market analysis**, is an important part in the process of creating any venture.

The market analysis section of a venture plan describes precisely who and how many will benefit from the venture and provides a profile of the venture's target market.

YOUR TURN

4. Refer back to what took place in Ms. Chang's class and make a list of all the needs of the students in the class.
5. Write the market analysis section of a venture plan for Ms. Chang's class by answering the following questions:

- What specific needs will be satisfied by the venture?
- Whose needs will be satisfied?
- How many will benefit from the good or service offered by the venture?

6. Describe this venture's target market.
7. Why does the venture not try to satisfy all the students' needs?

Venture PROFILE

Ms. Chang's Class: Part 2

Ms. Chang asked the students to work in groups to consider ways of dealing with class needs. "I want you to come up with as many suggestions as you can," she said. "It's quantity, not quality, we want at this point. When all the groups are finished, I will have you put all your suggestions on the board."

The level of activity and noise in the room rapidly rose. Within ten minutes, the board was filled with suggestions ranging from a lighthearted "Let's start each day with a movie about business", to the more serious "Let's get some comfortable seats in here", to the truly grand schemes such as "Let's paint the walls and put a carpet on the floor". There were over twenty-five suggestions to consider.

Ms. Chang surveyed the board and noted that having too many ideas could be just as serious a block to bringing about change as not seeing any alternatives. The students decided to reduce the options to a more manageable and practical few which they could more fully investigate. To do this, they decided to establish criteria for a useful suggestion. The students agreed to eliminate any suggestions which had only been made in fun, any which would not bring benefits to a large number of students in the class, and any which would take too long or cost too much money to achieve.

One after another suggestion was erased from the board. In some cases, two or more suggestions were joined together. Eventually, the list was reduced to the following three major suggestions for more serious investigation:

a) Change the physical environment by painting the walls and replacing the one-piece chair-desks with a more flexible variety of seating arrangements.
b) Provide food and something to drink in the classroom.
c) Provide some music of the students' choice which they could listen to before class or during work periods.

EXPLORING • MS. CHANG'S CLASS: PART 2

1. What part of the problem-solving process have the students been working through in this part of the Profile?
2. What creative role(s) are they playing?
3. What thinking hat(s) are they wearing?

The Description

Ms. Chang's students in this section are working through the Ideas Spoke of the Venture Creation Wheel.

Figure 6.2 The Ideas Spoke of the Venture Creation Wheel is used when writing the description.

They began by generating a long list of creative possibilities. Then they made a short list of those ideas which offered the greatest chance for change and decided to work on them. This process of **short listing** ideas to determine which are the most feasible is essential when starting to create the venture plan.

The first major section of a venture plan is the **description**.

> The description serves as an introduction which contains general information without specific details.

It should be accurate and should tell readers enough so that they can decide whether they are sufficiently interested in the ideas behind the venture to read further.

The description answers questions such as:

- What is the venture?
- What are its objectives?
- What good or service will it provide?
- How unique is this good or service?
- Where will the venture be located?
- When and for how long will it operate?
- Who are most involved in starting and managing the venture?

Although the description appears first, it cannot be written until all the other sections of the venture plan have been completed.

YOUR TURN

8. You cannot yet write a description of Ms. Chang's students' plan. They have not yet decided what they intend to do. However, they have decided on three ideas that merit further investigation. What are they?

Venture PROFILE

Ms. Chang's Class: Part 3

Now that they had some specific ideas, the students realized that they must try to identify what was needed in order to accomplish each of their suggestions. That meant identifying what resources were needed, what obstacles had to be overcome, and what help was required and could be obtained from others. The class began by dividing itself into three groups, one group to investigate each suggestion. The groups met separately and all three made a list of what they needed to begin their investigations. Ms. Chang gave them a class period to work things out. The next day, each group reported the results of its work.

Group 1, whose task was to change the physical environment, reported that it had investigated:

a) locating a supply of different desks and chairs
b) getting Mr. Dezamba, who also used the room to teach Math in period four, to agree to the changes

c) obtaining the principal's permission to paint the walls
d) finding the best source of supplies

Group 1 also reported that its investigation revealed there was little hope of bringing about significant change in a reasonable amount of time and at a reasonable cost. Mr. Dezamba was not very supportive because his Math students did most of their work individually at their desks, so the existing seating arrangement was the best for them. Moreover, there was no other classroom available for his class. Some members of the group also found from speaking with the principal and head custodian that there were no other types of tables and chairs available in their school, nor could they be borrowed from other schools in the system. They would have to be purchased at considerable expense, which had not been provided for in the budget. Redecorating the room by painting the walls would be difficult because the Board of Education's agreement with its maintenance workers specified that all painting in the schools was to be done by these workers and they had work scheduled for months ahead. The study group recommended that the class abandon its attempts to bring about these changes.

Group 2 reported that it was possible to organize food and something to drink in the class on a daily basis. The group had asked Ms. Chang if she would permit it. She had no objections provided the students organized and ran it themselves, that they kept the room clean, and that it did not interfere with other things she had planned. The group had conducted a survey and found the class wanted coffee, hot chocolate, or tea to drink. They had also identified a member of the class who was willing to donate the use of a percolator which could be used to boil water. The group recommended that the students bring their own mugs. Ms. Chang agreed to donate part of a filing cabinet for storage. All the supplies would be purchased as needed. Each student would have the responsibility of providing cookies or donuts for the class one day a month at his or her own expense. The class accepted all these recommendations except the last one, which was rejected as being too expensive.

Group 3, which was investigating the addition of music to the class, found a mixed response among the students to the idea. This group had also conducted a survey and found that some class members found any music disturbing and preferred to work in quiet surroundings. Others worked best with music in the background. The group had found a tape deck which the Business Department was willing to loan to the class on a daily basis. The students could bring their own tapes. The group therefore recommended that the tape deck be borrowed and that music be played, with the permission of the teacher, before and during class when the students were working individually or in groups on an assignment. It also recommended that the use of music in the class be reviewed every two weeks. The class accepted this suggestion.

EXPLORING • MS. CHANG'S CLASS: PART 3

1. What stage of the problem-solving model were students working through in Part 3 of this Profile?
2. What role(s) were the students playing in Part 3?
3. What thinking hat(s) did they wear?

Resource Analysis

In Part 3 of the Venture Profile the students have moved on to consider the Resources Spoke of the Venture Wheel.

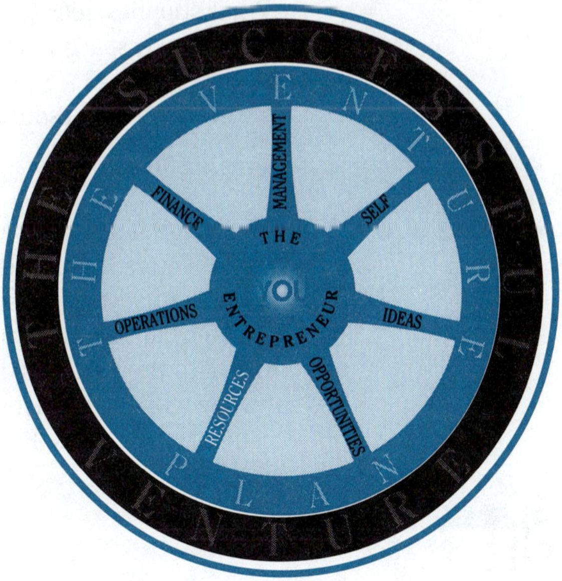

Figure 6.3 The Resources Spoke of the Venture Creation Wheel is used during resource analysis.

They are planning to take action! They are moving out of the classroom and into the school to talk with people in search of resources. In the process, they find that some of their ideas are too difficult to achieve. The resources simply do not exist or are, like new furniture, too costly. Other ideas, such as painting the classroom, are difficult because of existing rules and regulations. Rules can be changed or modified, but the effort of doing so must be weighed against the benefits received. The students have, however, identified some resources which are useful and available. They have been investigating those questions which are answered in the third major section of a venture plan. This section of the venture plan is called **resource analysis.**

> The resource analysis section of the venture plan is primarily concerned with identifying what resources the venture will need in order to provide its good or service.

It considers questions such as:

- What tools or equipment is needed?
- What human resources are required?
- What supplies does the venture need?
- How much space is required and what is the best space for the venture?
- What will these resources cost?

YOUR TURN

9. Ms. Chang's students have identified the resources they believe will be required to provide beverages and music for the class.
   a) Make a list of the resources they identified under the two headings: Beverages and Music
   b) Add to the students' list any other resources you think they will need which have not been specifically mentioned in the Profile.

Venture PROFILE

Ms. Chang's Class: Part 4

"It seems to me," said Ms. Chang, "that you are making excellent progress with your planning, but you have overlooked one or two vital questions. In your study groups, I would like you to decide who will do what and when will they do it!"

The group planning the music found this a relatively easy task. Each day someone would have to get the tape deck from the Business Studies office and return it. That same person could also be responsible for bringing the tapes. The members of the class who keenly wanted music agreed to organize a daily duty roster among themselves. The same group would also prepare and administer a survey to see whether the music would continue or not.

Those planning the provision of something to drink soon realized their task was more difficult. Who would get the water each day and see that it was boiled? Who would purchase the needed supplies? How would the supplies be paid for and how would everything be cleaned up? This group also decided to draw up a daily schedule. Each day, one student would see that everything was ready and, at the end of class, that everything was cleaned up. The task was rotated among all those students who wanted something to drink so that each student only had to do it twice a month. Students would contribute money as needed to a central fund, and all supplies would be purchased from the fund. One student volunteered to collect the money and purchase the supplies.

EXPLORING • MS. CHANG'S CLASS PART 4

1. What stage of the problem-solving process are the students working through in Part 4?
2. What role(s) are they playing?
3. What thinking hat(s) are they wearing?

Operating Strategy

The students are now deciding how to acquire and organize the resources they need for their venture. This accomplishes the tasks that make up the Operations Spoke of the Venture Creation Wheel.

The venture plan must also contain a section called **operating strategy.**

The operating strategy explains how the resources will be organized and used on a day-to-day basis.

The operating strategy should answer the following questions:

- How is the production process to be organized?
- Who will do what?
- What records must be kept?
- How can the venture keep costs to a minimum?
- What rules and regulations apply to how the venture uses resources?

Figure 6.4 The Operations Spoke of the Venture Creation Wheel is used when preparing the operating strategy.

AGENTS OF CHANGE

The victims of war and disease had few hopes in 17th century Canada. But in 1642, Jeanne Mance and Paul de Maisonneuve, settlers from France, came to Ville-Marie, Quebec, and built a hospital. Their new hospital served Native and European casualties alike. Two people changed the health conditions of a nation!

Financial Strategy

Finally, every venture plan must include a section known as the **financial strategy**.

The financial strategy uses numbers to forecast the financial needs and rewards of a venture.

Unlike most financial statements, which are accounts of past performance, the financial strategy is based on projected results. In general, the financial strategy will answer the following questions:

- How much money will it take to start the venture?
- How much money will it take to keep it going after the startup?
- What are the expected costs and revenues of the venture?

- When will the capital be required?
- What sources of capital are available to the venture?

Figure 6.5 The Finance Spoke of the Venture Creation Wheel is used when preparing the financial strategy.

The financial strategy of Ms. Chang's students who were planning the music was simple and straightforward. They were able to acquire all the resources their venture needed — a tape deck, tapes, and labour — by donation. No payments were necessary. This is how many resources for small venture startups are acquired. They are donated by those who are interested in, or who will benefit from, the venture.

On the other hand, the plans that Ms. Chang's students made to provide the assorted drinks were neither complete nor precise. The class believed the best way to acquire supplies was to have everyone contribute money rather than have individuals donate supplies. A financial strategy requires precision. It must provide specific numbers. How much money is needed? How much should everyone pay? Without specific numbers, there can be no financial strategy. Without a financial strategy, there is no venture plan.

When the students in Ms. Chang's class complete their financial analysis, they will have completed the major components of venture planning. They can now write up the description section. In the beginning, the students were investigating three possible ways to respond to the needs they identified. You may return to your answer to Question 8 on page 163 to review what they were. Two of these ideas resulted in specific, thoroughly planned ventures. The students can now write a description of each venture.

YOUR TURN

Use the Research Assistance Grid (page 156) and the Venture Plan Summary, Table 6.2 (pages 172-73) to answer the following questions:

10. Write a description for the two ventures Ms. Chang's students plan to undertake.
11. Assume that your own class wanted to organize itself to sell small, individual pizzas and soft drinks to students in your school to raise money for a class trip. You have been given the task of writing up both an operating strategy and a financial strategy.
    a) As a class, make a list of everything you will need to know and, using a Research Assistance Grid, prepare a list of questions you must ask in order to prepare both an operating strategy and a financial strategy.
    b) Once you have the questions, research the answers and write up your class operating strategy and financial strategy for this school venture.
12. Assume that a group of students from your school came to you seeking advice. They wanted to put on their own drama production and, hearing that you had learned how to organize a venture, have come to you for help. Write out for them, using the headings of the venture plan, a list of specific questions which they should answer that would help them organize the resources to produce their drama. Beneath each question, jot down any suggestions you think might help them answer the question.

AGENTS OF CHANGE

The cotton gin, a remarkable invention that was instrumental in allowing us to manufacture cotton material and clothing, is commonly attributed to Eli Whitney. It was really the brainchild of his landlady, Catherine Greene. Whitney simply helped make the prototype.

AGENTS OF CHANGE

Employment opportunities have often been hard to create in Prince Edward Island. Carol Livingstone founded the not-for-profit West Point Development Corporation. It has helped people tackle the challenges of business startups, improved the local craft industry, and encouraged tourism in the area. By looking at one problem, Carol created solutions to many more.

The Importance of the Venture Plan

Planning and organization are important to the success of any venture.

Lack of proper planning is one of the leading causes of failure.

Without planning, some ventures get started that should never have seen the light of day. Perhaps they were not based on a good idea. Perhaps the good or service produced was no better than what was already available. Perhaps the huge market the entrepreneur was sure about existed only in his or her imagination. Perhaps people were just not willing to buy the good or service at the price that had to be charged in order to make the venture worthwhile. Perhaps the entrepreneur was unable to produce the good or service efficiently.

Other ventures may start smoothly, experience some growth, but eventually fail. Perhaps they ran out of capital. Perhaps new competitors stole the market. Perhaps the entrepreneur was not interested in, or good at, managing and allocating resources. Perhaps the market simply vanished. Needs and interests can change quickly.

There are many advantages to writing a venture plan. First, writing the plan provides a summary and a record of what has been decided for future reference. A written plan can save time, resolve disputes, and provide clear direction. Secondly, putting a plan in writing will help ensure that all the details have been thought through. A written plan is more thorough than an unwritten plan. Finally, a written plan can be used to impress others and gain their support. This is particularly important if other people have some resources your venture needs.

Table 6.2 The Venture Plan Summary

Section of Plan	**Questions Addressed**	**Spoke in the Venture Creation Wheel**
1. Description	This section serves as an introduction. It contains general information without specific details. It should be accurate and concise, yet interesting and informative. Questions addressed are: • What is the venture? • What are its objectives? • What good or service will it provide? • How unique is this good or service? • Where will the venture be located? • When and for how long will it function? • Who are most involved in starting and managing the venture?	Ideas
2. Market Analysis	This section analyzes the need for the good or service provided by the venture. It also provides data on how well that need is currently being met. Finally, it forecasts what share of the market this venture hopes to acquire. Questions addressed are: • What needs will be satisfied? • Whose needs will be satisfied? • How many will benefit from the good or service offered by the venture?	Opportunities
3. Resource Analysis	This section identifies what resources the venture will need to provide its good or service. Questions addressed are: • What tools or equipment is needed? • What human resources are required?	Resources

	• What supplies does the venture need? • How much space is required and what is the best space for it? • What will these resources cost? • What, according to the rules and regulations, must the venture acquire? • What can be done to protect the venture or the idea on which it is based?	
4. Operating Strategy	This section of the plan deals with how resources will be organized and used on a day-to-day basis. Questions addressed are: • How is the production process to be organized? • Who will do what? • How will the venture sell its good or service? • What records will have to be kept? • How can the venture keep costs to a minimum? • What rules and regulations apply as to how the venture uses resources?	Operations
5. Financial Strategy	This section of the plan uses numbers to forecast the financial needs and rewards of a venture. Questions addressed are: • How much money will it take to start the venture? • How much money will it take to keep it going during the startup? • What are the expected costs and revenues of the venture? • When will the capital be required? • What sources of capital are available to the venture?	Finances

Figure 6.6 Computers with spreadsheet and word processing software make the job of producing a venture plan much easier.

AGENTS OF CHANGE

Thirteen Cape Breton teenagers have won a spot in the national record book of Junior Achievement. They manufactured and sold genuine pieces of Cape Breton coal incorporated into oak pen sets. After selecting a board of directors and conducting a market survey, they went into production. They used an old product in a very different way.

Preparing a venture plan will take you through the process of assessing potential risks and identifying any problems that might arise. Preparing a venture plan will force you to look at what future profits might be and whether or not you have enough capital to carry you through the first few months after startup. It will help you prepare for some of the seasonal, market, and labour influences.

A venture plan can and should be used to help the entrepreneur develop a better understanding of the many factors that can, and probably will, influence a new venture. A carefully thought-out venture plan will accommodate the special needs and expectations of financial institutions, creditors, shareholders, customers or clients, employees, and local community groups.

A well-prepared venture plan will prove (or disprove) that the proposed idea is realistic and that the process for putting the idea into action is (or is not) workable.

It will establish that a real opportunity exists and show how that opportunity can be met and what is needed to do so. You can also reduce the risk of failure and prevent many potential problems by carefully examining different aspects of a proposed venture and selecting an approach that seems to work out best on paper.

Many entrepreneurs fail to plan; few plan to fail.

Venture plans are not only appropriate for startup ventures. Many businesspeople have found that venture plans prepared for startup have proven to be even more helpful as their ventures grow and develop. They provide a framework against which businesspeople can monitor their ventures' progress. Existing businesses prepare or review a venture plan to examine internal opportunities, such as reorganization, expansion, addition of new lines of business, or even selling out completely.

Venture plans should be dynamic, living documents which are constantly revised and updated. Any plan must remain flexible enough to adjust to changing circumstances. Under extreme circumstances, it may have to be abandoned altogether. The plan is a means to an end. It is not an end in itself. It exists to benefit the venture. Many a venture has been lost because a plan did not exist or did not anticipate and accommodate change and the entrepreneur was not prepared to abandon it.

Your Turn

13. List five possible reasons for the failure of a venture.
14. When might an existing business require a venture plan?
15. For what reasons is flexibility important in creating the venture plan?

Venture PROFILE

Ross Fedele's Port-a-Tray is batting 1000

by Robert Hough, *Financial Post Moneywise Magazine*

Young Inventor/Entrepreneur Ross Fedele enjoys a Coke at the SkyDome using his Port-a-Tray.

Ross Fedele of Toronto is the inventor and purveyor of the Port-a-Tray, a 27-cm-long plastic drink holder. Unique in the world of beverage caddies, the Port-a-Tray snaps onto the seat arms in the world's biggest retractable-roof dome, thus ending the peril of spilling your Coke every time George Bell hits a homer.

An avid baseball fan, Fedele designed Port-a-Tray because he was tired of having no place to rest his drink at Blue Jays games. Last year, with the opening of SkyDome looming, Fedele quit his Seneca College business course and paid $350 to have a prototype tray made. He then badgered SkyDome. "I just wouldn't let up," Fedele recalls, grinning at his own persistence. "I called, I wrote letters, I finally just went down there. You know, there are patents out there that are conceptually similar. But they've gone nowhere, and I think it's because they all gave up too soon."

Fedele eventually found himself in the office of David Garrick, SkyDome's vice-president of marketing. "It was unique," Garrick says of Port-a-Tray. "It was perfect for SkyDome. In fact, I ended up taking him under my wing. It's nice to see a young guy wanting to go out and be an entrepreneur." Garrick agreed to market the product in the Dome.

Nine months and $50 000 in startup costs later (his financing was a combination of personal savings, a loan from his parents, and a federal Youth Venture loan), Fedele is now selling Port-a-Trays to SkyDome for $2.75 each. SkyDome sells them for $6 (which, Fedele says, is *not* a huge markup compared with other souvenirs). After manufacturing costs, taxes, and SkyDome's 10 per cent, Fedele makes about a buck per unit.

He describes sales as "somewhat better than expected." By the ninth Jays home game, SkyDome had sold several thousand. The most profitable avenue of the business, however, is selling "blank" Port-a-Trays to corporations, which slap on their own logo and then give them to clients and employees. "It's an easy way to get your logo into the SkyDome," Fedele says. "Otherwise, you have to be IBM to afford any of the stadium advertising." Since starting his company, Global Innovations, six months ago, Fedele has sold about 10 000 trays through this one route.

The future looks promising for the young CEO (Chief Executive Officer).

His company is almost turning a profit, he's arranging a distribution deal in the U.S. (Port-a-Trays fit most standard stadium seats), and he is in the early stages of designing other stadium products. But along with his youthful success, Fedele has also gleaned some idea of the travails facing the Blacks and Reichmanns of the world.

"It's funny, but I find I'm starting to have a few sleepless nights. If you work for someone else, when you leave the office you also leave your problems behind. With this, as soon as I wake up, my mind starts racing. With a new product, you can't predict how it's going to do. You just throw your dice and take your chances."

Venture PROFILE

Kelowna's Sunshine Theatre true community effort

By Arnold Edinborough, *Financial Post*

Kelowna, B.C. — There's lots of sunshine in the Okanagan Valley, which ripens all those Delicious apples, peaches, and cherries. So it's quite natural for the professional theatre that runs a summer season there to name itself the Sunshine Theatre Company.

The company was founded in 1977 by Joan Fanton, a professional actress who lives in Kelowna but who had worked several seasons for the Kawartha Festival in Lindsay, Ontario. Right from the start, she had the support of Kelowna City Council, and was able to rent the community theatre, with its more than 800 seats.

Over the years, the Sunshine Theatre has developed to the point where, over the past winter, the city council built an addition to the theatre, giving the company a splendid rehearsal space that matches the spacious front-of-house and the foyers.

As the theatre's fact sheet points out, the Sunshine Theatre reaches more than 34 000 people who attend its shows, support events to raise money, and make donations as members. Its 17 member board of trustees is drawn from the area. The board and a group of 237 volunteers who usher, sell tickets, help with rehearsals and special events, donate more than 5000 hours of help a year.

Though tourists and visitors are a major part of the audience — Kelowna and the Okanagan are tourist centres — there are 2600 local subscribers in summer, 500 in the winter season, and 231 for its theatre for young audiences.

On the financial side, the theatre has 100 individual donors; 52 local businesses and service clubs offering sponsorships and help in kind; and 17 national companies.

At the opening of its thirteenth season on July 6, the house was sold out. When one thinks back to the straw-hat theatre common in this country 30 years ago, the Sunshine Theatre Company is a shining example of how far we have come.

What comes through, however, to a visitor from the East, is the intense feeling of community the Sunshine Theatre inspires. It has a media sponsor for each production — three radio stations and the television station. There are four national sponsors — du Maurier Council for the Arts, Petro-Canada, Shell, and Labatt — along with local companies such as Ehmann Printing, Calona Wines, the Coast Royal Anne Hotel, Mission Hill Winery, and Hyperion Trust.

The theatre now has a budget of $433 000 (up from $55 000 12 years ago). Revenues are 52 per cent box office and earned revenue; 18 per cent from private fund raising and sponsorship; and 30 per cent grants from all three levels of government.

Though Kelowna has not moved entirely into the age of Aquarius, both the community and the audience are happy that at least in one respect they have "Let the sun shine in."

EXPLORING • PORT-A-TRAY AND SUNSHINE THEATRE

1. How are these two Venture Profiles different? How are they similar?
2. Identify the market to which each venture has aimed its product or service.
3. What resources were needed for each venture?
4. How were these resources used?
5. Using the concept of a Research Assistance Grid, prepare a list of questions that should have been asked before the two ventures you just read about were undertaken.
6. Assume the role of the entrepreneur in each case and answer the questions you prepared in Question 5 as best you can.
7. Using the information contained in your response to Question 6, prepare a draft venture plan for each venture.
8. Recognizing that plans must be flexible:

a) Make a list of five specific changes which could affect each venture.

b) How would you change the venture plan you wrote in Question 7 to reflect these changes?

P·O·I·N·T·S T·O R·E·M·E·M·B·E·R

- A Research Assistance Grid is an important device for identifying the variety of questions to be answered before starting a venture.
- A venture plan is a written account of all the thinking and research which has gone into a proposal to create a venture to bring about change.
- Like a blueprint, a venture plan describes what is being created and determines what will be needed to create it.
- A venture plan consists of five sections:
  1. a description, which describes the idea in general terms;
  2. a market analysis, which defines the size and characteristics of the market to be served;
  3. a resource analysis, which identifies all the resources the venture will need to make it a success;
  4. an operating strategy, which explains how the resources will be organized and used together; and
  5. a financial strategy, which forecasts costs and revenues to determine how much capital will be required to start and keep the venture going and when it will be needed.
- A venture plan must be continually re-evaluated throughout the life of the business as changes continually occur.

W·H·A·T H·A·V·E Y·O·U L·E·A·R·N·E·D?

1. What are the six basic questions which form the Research Assistance Grid?
2. Match each of the Spokes in the Venture Creation Wheel with the section of the venture plan which deals with it.

Spoke in the Venture Creation Wheel	*Section of the Venture Plan*
Operations	Market Analysis
Opportunities	Financial Strategy
Resources	Description
Ideas	Resource Analysis
Finances	Operating Strategy

3. In what part of a venture plan would each of the following questions be answered:

a) How will the resources be organized?
b) Who are my main competitors?
c) How much do I need to borrow?
d) What good or service will the venture produce?
e) How many employees will I need to hire?
f) When can I expect to start making a profit?
g) What are people willing to pay for my good or service?
h) What are the objectives of the venture?
i) Who are my customers?
j) What supplies will I need to purchase?
k) What records need to be kept?
l) Where should I locate my venture?

4. List five advantages of writing a thorough plan for a venture.

V·E·N·T·U·R·I·N·G O·U·T

Individually or in a small group:

1. Using the idea generating techniques you learned in Chapter 3, decide on a venture you might like to start to solve a problem or satisfy a need in your school or

community. It may be a profit or not-for-profit venture.

2. Prepare a Research Assistance Grid of all the questions you think must be answered during the planning process.
3. Investigate each question and outline in point form what you would describe in each section.

"Marketing makes the difference." Targeting the right market and working out the right marketing strategy is vital to the success of your venture. This chapter will outline the steps you need to take in order to develop the right marketing strategy for your venture.

CHAPTER 7

Analyzing Your Market

LEARNING OUTCOMES

By the end of this chapter, you should be able to:

- understand the classifications of marketing research
- use the three major forms of marketing research
- list the four components in the marketing mix
- describe how and why target markets, market segments, and life cycles need to be identified
- collect, record, and analyze data related to marketing issues
- understand why sales forecasts need to be prepared
- prepare a market analysis section for your venture plan

ENTREPRENEURIAL LANGUAGE

marketing research
questionnaires
surveys
observation
experimentation
exploratory research
specific research
causal research
internal research
census
sample
research instrument
attitude scales
marketing strategy
homogeneous segments
final user
marketing mix
market segmentation
culture
market segments
demographic
socioeconomic
geographic
psychographic
behaviour patterns
consumption patterns
sales forecast
market potential
sales potential
sales prediction

Venture PROFILE

Dialing for dollars

By Paul McLaughlin, *Canadian Business*

What does my business need next?

The owner of a small service firm wants more customers, so he needs to advertise. One newfangled option is to let computers pitch his services by phone. But do machines have the right touch?

Jack Fisher's intuition told him it was time to expand, and his intuition had never failed him in the 12 years he'd been running his own business. New Interiors Ltd., his Toronto-based painting and home decorating company, was a great success, with revenues for 1988 topping $1 million. But most of his sales came from nearby neighbourhoods. With the renovation market in Toronto booming, he wanted to tap into other areas of the city, and he knew from experience that the way to do this was through advertising.

Fisher, 48, attributed his company's success to two factors: his dedication to providing quality workmanship at competitive prices; and to an aggressive marketing campaign. "What good is it to be the best painter around if nobody knows who you are?" he repeatedly asked his son Bryan, 24, who had recently joined the family business as the general manager. "You gotta spend the dough so they know where to go."

True to his philosophy, Fisher sent out flyers four times a year to the suburban neighbourhoods near his office and regularly purchased ads in community newspapers. In addition, he worked actively in several community organizations to maintain a high local profile. "Call me a traditionalist," he would tell Bryan, "but I believe that if I shake a man's hand, there's a greater chance that hand will dial my number when there's work to be done."

When Fisher informed his son — whom he was grooming to take over the business — about his plans for expansion, Bryan responded with enthusiasm. But when he outlined his marketing strategy, Bryan was less receptive. "I'm going to blitz most of the city with flyers and take out ads in the major newspapers," Fisher said. "I'm also thinking about radio commercials."

"Newspaper ads are too expensive for the one shot that they give you," Bryan replied, "and flyers have an extremely low response rate. You're not going to get nearly as high a response in areas where you're not known, compared to what you're getting right now. However, I have another suggestion. There's a new sales method called automatic call dialing." Bryan explained that the system he was proposing consisted of a computer that calls numbers out of the telephone book and presents them with a recorded message describing New Interiors' services. At the end of the message, listeners are asked to leave their names if they want more information. "I have a friend in an advertising company who told me about this," Bryan said. "He was very persuasive about the way it could reach a lot of people at a relatively low cost."

Fisher did not like the idea. "Look, I had one of those machines call me a while ago. Something to do with life insurance. And you know what I did as soon as I realized it was a computer?"

"You hung up."

"I hung up. You know your father, which is good. What is not good is that you think you can get new customers by using some impersonal machine. People hate these things. They'll get mad at us and we'll get a bad reputation."

Bryan countered by saying that flyers weren't any more personal than a recorded message. "Lots of people hate junk mail," he said. "You should be open to new ways of doing things. You can't shake hands with two-and-a-half million people. But this is a way that you can send them a message, and your voice if you want, directly into their home."

Fisher wasn't convinced, but he also didn't want to arbitrarily crush his son's initiative. Their conversation ended with Fisher asking Bryan to research the automatic call dialing services available. He doubted that he would change his mind but he wanted to give his son another chance to make his case.

EXPLORING • DIALING FOR DOLLARS

1. On what basis was Fisher planning to expand his business?
2. What kind of advertising was he accustomed to using?
3. From where did most of his business come?
4. Should Fisher have a more open attitude toward automatic call dialing?
5. What are the benefits of call dialing compared to sending out flyers?
6. What would you do if you were Fisher?
7. What would you do if you were Bryan?
8. Where would you start to research automatic call dialing advertising?

Marketing Research

Marketing research is a systematic and objective way of collecting, recording, and analyzing data that relates to a particular marketing issue or problem. In Chapter 6, you learned that marketing research or market analysis uses the Opportunities Spoke of the Venture Creation Wheel.

Figure 7.1 Marketing research uses the Opportunities Spoke of the Venture Creation Wheel.

It is undertaken to determine:

- What needs will be satisfied?
- Whose needs will be satisfied?
- How many will benefit from the goods and services offered by the venture?

Entrepreneurs who create a product or service first and then try to find the consumers (or customers) to purchase may be taking a big risk. They may have to wait some time before finding their target market, as was the case with Akio Morita in a Chapter 4 Venture Profile, or, worse still, they might be unable to find a customer match for their idea. It often makes greater sense to determine first what customers want or need, how many customers might want or need it,

AGENTS OF CHANGE

No one had connected genetic and environmental factors to rheumatic fever or Down Syndrome before Dr. Irene A. Uchida's Ph.D. work. Her research led others to study the part that the environment plays on various heart conditions and on the genetic factors in Down Syndrome families. One researcher's work initiated change in medical research!

who these customers are, and then create a product or service that meets their needs.

Marketing research is used more and more frequently by entrepreneurs to give them the data they need to make marketing decisions. Deciding what to produce, what services to offer, how to advertise, and even what to do about their competition is often the result of what marketing research has been able to tell them.

In the introductory Venture Profile, the Fishers really have to decide more than just how to advertise their expanding business. They must also consider whether to expand at all, who their new customers might be, and how their competition might react to the expansion of their company.

Thomas Edison, although he may not have known what the term "marketing research" meant, made deliberate efforts to identify people's needs and wants. He developed the electric light bulb to meet identified needs. Houses would no longer be lit by a gas flame. A Canadian researcher and doctor team, Best and Banting, identified the need for something to help people suffering with diabetes. They developed insulin to meet that particular need. For years, some people maintained that post offices across the country were not meeting the need for fast and efficient parcel delivery. So new business ventures were established to provide fast and efficient courier delivery service to compete with Canada Post and to meet the needs of a growing number of people.

Advantages of Marketing Research

Marketing research can be used to provide data about customers, products, services, prices, advertising, and consumer behaviour. It can also be used to project future sales.

> Correct use of marketing research can give you a tremendous advantage over your competition.

Effective marketing cannot exist without it. Entrepreneurs may use marketing research to identify a certain number of potential consumers for a particular product. They can use information they obtain from marketing research to refine and adapt their products and services so that they appeal to more customers. They can direct all their resourses towards that segment of the public whom they have identified as their potential customers. Entrepreneurs will use marketing research to determine what their competition is doing and then offer a more competitive product or service that is more appealing to potential buyers.

Classifications of Marketing Research

Marketing research is usually conducted by asking questions and noting answers. **Questionnaires** or **surveys** can be used to conduct marketing research by mail, telephone, or in person. Some entrepreneurs use **observation** to conduct their marketing research. They may, for example, actually count the number of people entering a certain kind of restaurant in order to estimate the number of potential customers for a new restaurant in a particular location. **Experimentation** is another method of conducting marketing research. Entrepreneurs will manufacture a small number of units and provide them, for the purpose of experimentation, to a small group of people. The results of this experiment can then be used to refine and improve the product, or, if the results are positive, large-scale production may commence.

Figure 7.2 Observation is a popular method of marketing research.

Three main classifications of marketing research are exploratory research, specific research, and causal research.

AGENTS OF CHANGE

Eighty per cent of the mistakes athletes make are vision related. Karen Muncey worked with Phil Jones of the Edmonton Eskimos football club to develop a vision training system called DYNAVISION 2000. This equipment trains athletes to take in information faster, concentrate better, and reduce stress levels.

Exploratory Research

Exploratory research is used to define a problem more clearly or to obtain ideas for solutions. It is usually conducted through in-depth interviews with a relatively small number of people. Questions asked in this kind of research are often very open-ended. They invite more than just a simple yes or no response. They encourage the kind of answers that will generate ideas or identify opportunities for the entrepreneur. The Fishers might decide to use exploratory research to give them an idea about what other kinds of decorating services they might offer should they decide to expand. They might even consider using exploratory research to identify other forms of advertising to announce their expanded service. Should they decide to use exploratory research, they might ask: "What decorating services will you need in the next six months?" "What house renovations do you dream about?" "How would you like to be informed about new decorating services?"

Specific Research

Specific research is used to determine specific information related to an already clearly defined problem. It is typically used with a larger group of consumers. Fisher, for example, could use specific research kinds of questions to confirm the kind of decorating that his customers might be interested in. He might ask: "Will you need your interior walls (a) plastered, (b) painted, (c) papered, or (d) fabric covered?"

Causal Research

Causal research is used to explain the relationship between a particular cause and its effect. It is used in situations where a particular incident has caused a particular result. Causal research might be undertaken where a price increase, for example, has resulted in either a higher or, more typically, a lower sales figure. If the Fishers were reluctant to select a particular form of advertising because they felt their customers might be offended by it, they could use causal research questions to determine why the effect might be negative. They might ask: "Would you use our services if you received a flyer describing them?" "Why?" "Would you use our services if you received a computer telephone call telling you about them?" "Why?"

YOUR TURN

1. In small groups, select one of the following issues or choose an issue of particular importance in your community. Design exploratory, specific, and causal questions that might be asked to provide the kind of data needed to resolve the issue you select. Share these questions with the rest of your class.
   - Should a new mall be constructed across from your school?
   - Should your class sell chocolate bars in the neighbourhood to raise money for a special charity?
   - Should you sell raffle tickets to raise money for a class field trip?
   - Should you hold a "garage sale" to raise money for new computers for your school?
2. Try these questions out on some of your schoolmates to see if your exploratory questions are open-ended, if your specific questions are specific enough, and if your causal questions elicit answers to why something has happened.

Forms of Marketing Research

In Chapter 4, you read about secondary and primary forms of research. **Internal research**, introduced in this chapter, involves using your own records for information about sales, products, customers, or complaints. It can be used by entrepreneurs who have operated the same venture for a number of years. It is easy and inexpensive to conduct. All the information needed is right at hand, in company files.

Bryan could use internal research to access data already available in the files of New Interiors Ltd. He could find out how effective distribution of flyers was in the past by looking

AGENTS OF CHANGE

A new film using both computer graphics and live action premiered at the 1990 World's Fair in Osaka, Japan. The Canadian IMAX SYSTEMS CORPORATION, which invented and developed large film format motion picture systems, used full-colour stereoscopic images in a wide-field, wraparound screen theatre.

at company records to determine the names of customers listed just after the last distribution of flyers.

If he chooses to use secondary research, he might consult periodicals or trade magazines to determine which areas of renovation or decorating are on the increase in specific communities.

On the other hand, if Bryan decides to use primary research, he will have a considerable amount of extra work to do. A questionnaire will have to be designed or sample interview questions prepared. He will have to conduct the interviews, see that questionnaires are mailed out, or surveys conducted. He will then have to analyze and summarize the data collected.

Whether you use primary, secondary, or internal research, whether you decide to distribute a questionnaire, conduct a survey, or launch a series of personal interviews, you will still need to design the right kind of research method to collect the data you need.

Selecting a Sample

A survey conducted with the total population of a country is referred to as a **census**. Marketing research, however, is usually conducted with a much smaller group of the population, people who have been carefully selected to represent the whole population. This smaller group is referred to as a **sample**. The composition of the sample is dependent upon the objectives of the research project and the size of the sample needed to represent a target population.

Knowledge is power.

YOUR TURN

3. Prepare a questionnaire that Bryan might use to find out who his customers are. Set the questionnaire up in a professional manner. If desktop publishing software is available, make use of this to help make your questionnaire look attractive.
4. In small groups, design an internal market research project for New Interiors Ltd. Use a data base program, if available, in your design. Consider the information the Fishers might already have on file and outline a course

of action that would tell them where most of their customers are located, what form of advertising they might best respond to, and how many new customers might respond to a particular advertising campaign.

5. In small groups, use secondary research techniques to identify five different ways in which a product or service might be advertised. Prepare a description of each form of advertising. Share your descriptions with other members of your class.
6. In small groups, outline how Bryan might use primary research to determine whether or not the kind of customers New Interiors Ltd. attracts would respond to flyers or automatic call advertising.

Steps in Marketing Research

As you read in Chapter 4, marketing research usually follows a systematic procedure in order to remain effective and objective. This sequence of steps is reinforced for you in Figure 7.3

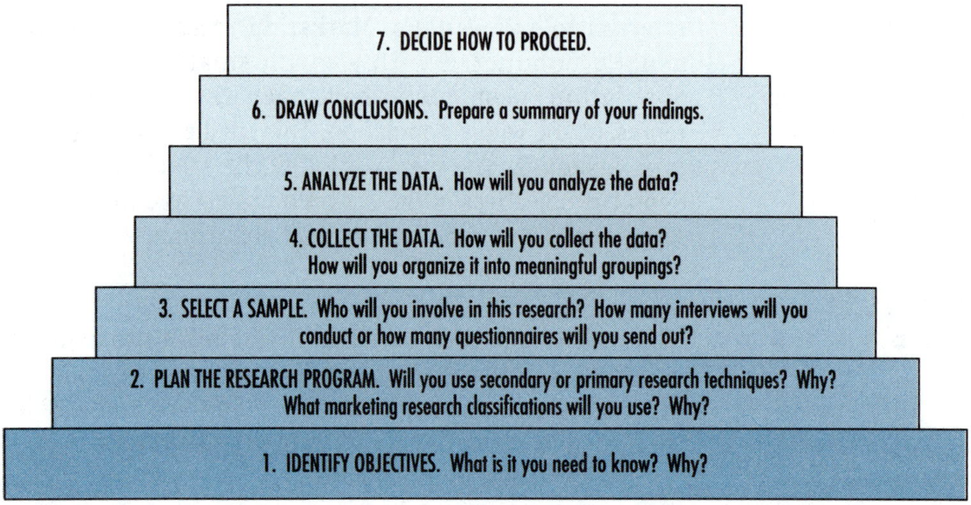

Figure 7.3 Steps in Marketing Research

YOUR TURN

7. Bryan was asked to research a specific issue for his father. If you were Bryan, what would your response be at each of the seven steps? In small groups, discuss how you would work through the steps in marketing research outlined in Figure 7.3.
8. Bring the results of your group discussion to the whole class and decide on one course of action that Bryan might take.
9. If Bryan chose to use secondary research to help his dad decide whether or not to use automatic call advertising, prepare a list of sources that he might use.

Venture PROFILE

What the experts say about automatic call dialing

Bryan actually used secondary research and went to three organizations for information. This is what the experts said.

Tony Rothschild, President of Phonetix Corporation
Coincidentally, our company recently completed a test of an automatic call dialing system using a Toronto paint company as the prospective client. Among other information, we wanted to determine the kinds of responses the system generated. Almost 50 per cent of the people that we called listened to the complete message. When you consider that people could slam the phone down on a machine without feeling that they're upsetting someone — unlike a direct personal call — that was a very healthy response. About 40 per cent just hung up, while the rest consisted of fax machine numbers, no answers, operator intercepts, and so forth.

The format that we used consisted of a message followed by a tone like an answering machine so that people could leave their names if they wanted more information. About 40 per cent did leave a short message. Some were abusive and quite a few asked not to be called again. Under Canadian Radio-Television and Telecommunications Commission guidelines, you must comply with their request by taking them off the data base. The percentage of positive responses was about 4 per cent — that's quite encouraging compared to the responses usually elicited by flyers, which usually range from 0.05 per cent to 2 per cent. Now, those aren't all going to end up as customers, but it's a good number of leads.

For various reasons, our company usually doesn't offer this kind of service, although we will sell a company a complete turnkey system so that they can do it themselves, which costs about $25 000 for a four-line system. I would advise Fisher to consider using automatic call dialing because I think it is well suited for businesses such as painting and home decorating. However, I think he should go to a company that will do it for him on a fee-for-service basis. In other words, he should test it out before risking the considerable expense of buying a system.

This type of advertising is becoming more accepted, just as the answering machine is now quite commonplace. It's effective for situations such as the police issuing emergency information to an area (the calls can be targeted with any parameters you want); school boards informing parents of closing due to bad weather; and airlines notifying passengers of cancellations.

The Canadian Red Cross Society doesn't use the system to advise people of blood donor clinics because it prefers to rely on volunteers and finds automatic call dialing dehumanizing. However, they may use it in the future if they don't have enough volunteers to make the calls. Although there will be people who will get upset at being called, and who will feel that their privacy is being invaded, I don't think that should deter Fisher. There are people who get angry at flyers coming in the mail, too.

Marvin Fine, President of D.F.D. Telebroadcasting Inc.

We provide an automatic call dialing service to clients such as fitness clubs, home renovators, stop smoking clinics, life insurance companies, headhunters, and so forth. We make about three million calls a week. I think it's a method of advertising and promotion that's suited to certain types of businesses; from my experience, I believe it would work for Fisher's company, especially because he wants to reach a large number of people across a city.

We charge a minimum of $2520 a month plus Bell charges of about $600 a month. That gets you 12 lines a day (a line is like an operator) with any additional lines costing $7 a day. For a two-month period, which is our minimum rental, the cost for 12 lines will be about $6500. In two months, 12 lines will place about 800 000 calls. A script will be written and prepared for about $60. In addition to the basic system that asks people to leave a message after they've listened to the ad, we can produce interactive ads that ask the listeners to indicate certain responses by pushing numbers on their touch-tone phones.

We would offer Fisher a four-day free trial after which we would guarantee him in writing a certain number of leads a day, which is an obvious difference from using a flyer. We've found the response rate to be in the 4 to 8 per cent range. The key for Fisher is that he must follow up on the leads quickly. He must have people in place to do that before the leads get cold, or else he's just wasting his money.

We do get some resistance and a few "scoldings" from people who don't like being called by a machine, but it's not that many. Out of the three million calls we make each week, there are only about 2500 complaints. A lot of people really seem to enjoy it. I had an evangelical organization that ran a 13-minute message for a year and a half. People expressed happiness at getting the call.

This kind of advertising is effective because of the importance of the telephone in our society. If the phone rings, people answer it, no matter what else they're doing. A flyer, on the other hand, often gets thrown into the garbage without even being looked at. The bottom line is that the phone gets results that no other form of communication can offer.

David Scheib, Member Services Representative, Scarborough Chamber of Commerce

I became interested in telemarketing 18 years ago, long before it became as popular as it is today. Over the years, I've sold just about everything over the phone, such as real estate, contracts for construction jobs, investments, even chimney sweeping. I'm a great believer in selling anything over the phone if you know what you're doing. I definitely think personal telemarketing is more effective than a flyer, but when it gets down to an automatic call dialing machine, I have some reservations.

I would tell Fisher that in theory automatic call dialing is a good system for his type of business. However, it requires a sophisticated, well-produced message in order for it to be effective. Most of the messages that I've heard are not well designed. If it wasn't for my professional interest in hearing them, I'd hang up on almost all of them right away. One exception was a travel agency that knew what it was doing. I was pushing numbers on my dial phone to answer certain questions and it pulled me in the whole way with its five-minute call. Fisher should spend the money to have a professional produce the message he wants to send out, someone who understands the psychology involved in getting people to listen to a machine.

This is vital because a poor message can really turn people off. I know many people who've told me they find the calls a great annoyance. It also doesn't help that there are a lot of scam-type people involved in marketing products over the phone, so it's crucial that the right impression is created immediately off the top. There are only a few seconds to capture people's interest before they hang up.

Because of the volume of calls a system like this can make, Fisher could get good value for his money from it. But he has to follow up those calls within three days or risk losing the leads.

EXPLORING • WHAT THE EXPERTS SAY

1. According to the experts, how many responses could you expect from flyers, automatic call dialing, and personal telephone calls?
2. What did you learn about how automatic call advertising works?
3. How do you feel about automatic call advertising? About flyer advertising?
4. If you were Bryan, what would you advise your father to do, based on what the experts said?

AGENTS OF CHANGE

During the student uprising in Beijing, in 1989, students in China and around the world used fax machines to compile and disseminate information about what was happening in Beijing. This information was sent out of and back into urban and outlying areas of China. A modern invention was used to inform the world and get around official censorship.

Designing the Primary Research

Primary research is conducted mainly through mail questionnaires, telephone surveys, or personal interviews. In each case, a carefully designed **research instrument** must be created to collect the data in a consistent format. The questions asked on this instrument must be designed to reflect either the exploratory, specific, or causal classification of the research.

The form of research you have chosen to use will determine the appearance of your instrument. An internal form of research might require only a chart or graph with places for a clerk to enter or check off data obtained from company files. If your instrument is to be mailed, you will need to design an attractive, easy-to-read questionnaire to collect your data.

If you decide to mail out questionnaires, your administrative costs will be relatively low. They would include the cost of printing the questionnaire, the cost of addressing and mailing the envelopes, and the cost of including self-addressed, stamped envelopes for the responses.

Table 7.1 Questionnaires and Their Characteristics

If your questionnaire is to be:	It should be designed to:
mailed to customers or particular groups of individuals	• motivate readers to respond • be easy to read and understand, but not so simple that it loses its significance • be short enough to hold the attention of the reader • leave the right amount of space for answers • contain all the questions needed to provide complete and accurate data • include questions worded according to the objective of the marketing research study (exploratory, specific, or causal)
used with telephone surveys	• keep respondents interested • be easy to understand, but not so simple that it loses its significance • be short enough to hold the attention of the respondent • contain all the questions needed to provide complete and accurate data • include questions worded according to the objective of the marketing research study (exploratory, specific, or causal)
used with personal interviews	• be as long as necessary to elicit the data required • include questions that require detailed responses • include alternate wording in case the person being interviewed has trouble understanding the wording of the original questions

If you decide to use telephone surveys, you will require extra telephone and supervisory personnel.

Personal interviews are the most expensive to conduct. You would need to hire and train interviewers and supervisors and pay their travelling expenses.

Designing a Questionnaire

Questionnaires should be kept as short as possible. Respondents are more likely to complete a shorter questionnaire than one that is several pages in length. One-page questionnaires are best. If necessary, you could use both sides of one page. Remember to include only questions that are easy to answer.

> The harder the questions, the less likely your respondents are to complete the questionnaire.

WILD RICE CONSUMER STUDY

Good afternoon/evening. I'm ______________ of Co-op Research and I'd like to ask you some questions about rices. It will just take about 5 to 10 minutes of your time.

1. How often have you eaten any kind of rice at home in the past 6 months?
   Would that be: *(Read statements)*

More than once a week?	1	Once a month?	4
Once a week?	2	Less than once a month?	5
Twice a month or more?	3	Never?	6 *(thank and end)*

2. What kinds of rice have you eaten? *(Write in answers and probe:)* Any others?__________________________

3. IF RESPONDENT HAS EATEN WILD RICE (Q.2), ASK: How often have you eaten wild rice in the past 6 months?

4. Have you, or has someone else in your household bought wild rice in the past 6 months?

Yes	1	
No	2	SKIP
Don't know	3	TO Q.7

5. Was it a planned purchase or did you buy it on impulse?

Planned	1
Impulse	2
Don't know	3

6. Was it for your own consumption or was it for a gift?

Own consumption	1
Gift	2
Other (SPECIFY) ________________	

7. Have you ever ordered wild rice in a restaurant?

Yes	1
No	2
Don't know	3

8. IF WILD RICE NOT MENTIONED IN Q.2, OR Q.7 ASK:
   Have you ever eaten wild rice?

Yes	1
No	2
Don't know	3

9. On what occasions might you serve wild rice? *(Write down in order and probe:)* Any others? ______________

Figure 7.4 Extract from a Co-op Research Questionnaire

AGENTS OF CHANGE

Many small towns in Canada find themselves with the dilemma of how to strengthen their local economies. Chemainus, British Columbia, commissioned Canadian artists to paint larger-than-life murals on the outside walls of its downtown buildings. Tourists now flock to Chemainus to see its unique downtown splash of colour. Chemainus found a beautiful way to help itself and its art community.

A questionnaire that is mailed out to individuals or used to collect data from a telephone survey should be designed to include the following four sections:

Section 1

Questions that will gather basic data, including the name of the person responding, his or her address, and any other information that you might need for your records.

Section 2

An introductory statement that explains the purpose for the questionnaire or survey and establishes a positive relationship with the respondent. This section could be in the form of a covering letter that is mailed with the questionnaire. If the questionnaire is used with a telephone survey, the individuals making the call should be encouraged to put this introduction into their own words so that the interview will seem less formal.

Section 3

Simple questions of an impersonal nature that can be used to gather general impressions about the product or service offered. These questions should be designed to provide information about such things as quality, price, where the consumer would go to purchase the product or service, and how he or she would respond to different kinds of advertising. If the research is exploratory in nature, the questions should be open-ended. If the research is specific in nature, alternative answers should be provided. **Attitude scales** (see Table 7.2) or multiple choice questions are commonly used in these cases.

Table 7.2 Attitude Scales for Boomers Pizza

Rate Boomers Pizza on the following qualities:							
Taste	Poor	1	2	3	4	5	Excellent
Temperature	Poor	1	2	3	4	5	Excellent
Amount of Cheese	Poor	1	2	3	4	5	Excellent
Price	Poor	1	2	3	4	5	Excellent
Delivery Service	Poor	1	2	3	4	5	Excellent

If the intent of your research is to improve your product, you might want to include questions that will identify why consumers might purchase one product over another. If you want to know how much they are prepared to pay for your product or service, you should group price ranges together and ask in which price range they would be prepared to purchase your product or service. When you have received completed responses, you can tabulate the results and determine the most acceptable price range.

Sequence your questions to motivate your respondents to keep working through the questionnaire. Go from easy to more difficult questions and then back to easier ones again. Watch for questions that might influence answers in later questions. For example, a question such as: "Boomers Pizza has recently added more cheese to its regular pizza. Have you enjoyed the extra cheese taste?" may influence a following question such as: "What do you think of the new Boomers Pizza?"

Section 4

Include questions here that are more personal in nature, such as age, education, and income. Never ask for specific answers here. Indicate a range of ages, education, and income and ask your respondents to indicate which range they fit into. Always close with a simple but friendly appreciation and thank you. You might want to call on them again.

Your Turn

10. In small groups, design a questionnaire that could be mailed to the students in your school to determine the kind of bicycle sales and repair services needed in your school community, the price range for new and used bikes that would be acceptable, and the best location for such a venture.
11. Try out your questionnaire on other members of your class. Refine your questions. As a class, select the best features of each questionnaire and prepare a class questionnaire. Then try it out on other students in the school. If desktop publishing is available, use it to set up the questionnaire in a professional manner.

12. Design a questionnaire that could be used in a telephone survey of members of your local community to identify the products and/or services that should be available in drug stores, pet care shops, or children's clothing stores.
13. With other members of your class, roleplay telephone calls to test your survey questions for Question 12.

Venture PROFILE

Marketing research leads to profits

A 1965 Ford Mustang

In the early 1960s, Ford, along with other major American motor car companies, started developing smaller, compact cars to compete with smaller foreign cars that seemed to be making significant inroads in the American automobile market. But after a year or two, sales of Ford's Falcon, along with sales of other American compact cars, showed a significant decline. Instead of deciding to simply forget their small car initiative, Ford decided to conduct marketing research to find out more about why Falcon sales were decreasing.

They discovered an interesting and important fact. While sales of the Falcon were declining, sales of sporty options, such as bucket seats and a special interior, were increasing. This was due primarily to the greater number of young adults who were purchasing cars in the early 1960s.

Ford's careful research in the market led them, in 1965, to put out a new product — the Ford Mustang. This sporty vehicle topped all previous records for sales and developed a new market for competitors to envy and try to emulate.

AGENTS OF CHANGE

In 1913, automobiles were still outrageously expensive. Henry Ford applied the concept of mass production to the automobile industry, making cars on assembly lines, and the prices dropped to a level that the average consumer could afford. A radical concept created an exciting change: an ordinary person could own a car.

EXPLORING • FORD: FROM FALCON TO MUSTANG

1. Put on your different thinking hats to examine what Ford did. Which of von Oech's characters played a role in Ford's decision making?
2. On what kind of information did Ford probably base its decision to market a Ford Mustang?
3. Where might Ford have found this information?
4. What kind of information would Ford have had on hand to enable it to use an internal form of research?
5. What was the real advantage to Ford from this marketing research?

Identifying a Marketing Strategy

A **marketing strategy** or plan is important to any kind of venture. Fisher, in our opening Venture Profile, struggled with advertising decisions because he did not have a marketing strategy. Business ventures and not-for-profit ventures need well-designed marketing strategies in order to succeed.

Developing a marketing strategy is the first step in the preparation of a marketing plan. A marketing plan or market analysis section is the crucial first step in the building of a venture plan.

Whenever "something of value" is offered for "something of value" received, a specially designed marketing strategy has probably been used to achieve success. Business organizations offer products or services and accept financial rewards in return. Fund raisers offer special services and accept donations in return. Politicians offer promises and accept votes. Special government health campaigns, like PARTICIPACTION, offer a healthier way of life and accept a healthier population in return. Marketing strategy probably played an important role in all of these ventures. It is a major force in both business and non-business ventures.

Requirements of a Marketing Strategy

A marketing strategy has three major funtions. It should:

- identify your target customers and describe the product or service they are prepared to buy. It should classify or group these customers into relatively **homogeneous segments** according to common, identifiable characteristics. It should indicate where these potential customers are located and whether they would purchase your product or service because of its price, quality, or the service that you plan to provide. It should note potential customers who have expressed an interest in a particular product or service and describe why they have indicated this interest.
- indicate the possible size of a potential market and outline potential trends. It should identify any competition that exists within this potential market and note the strengths of the proposed product and how it differs from the competition. It should outline how the company plans to take the idea for a product or service from the production stage to the consumer or **final user** stage.
- identify the sales expectations for a particular product or service and what kind of promotion or advertising activity is necessary to achieve those sales. Almost all subsequent sections of the business plan depend on the sales estimate developed in the marketing plan. Plans for manufacturing, advertising, selling, distributing or delivering, and financing all depend on the sales estimate.

Marketing Mix

The success of any marketing strategy depends on whether or not the entrepreneur has planned the right combination or mix of the following marketing elements. These elements are referred to as the **marketing mix**:

• Product (or Service)	Is the product or service something customers will want to purchase? Will it be of benefit to them? Will it meet their needs?
• Place	Where will the product or service be made available?

• Price	How much are customers willing and able to pay?
• Promotion	How will customers be made aware that the product or service is available?

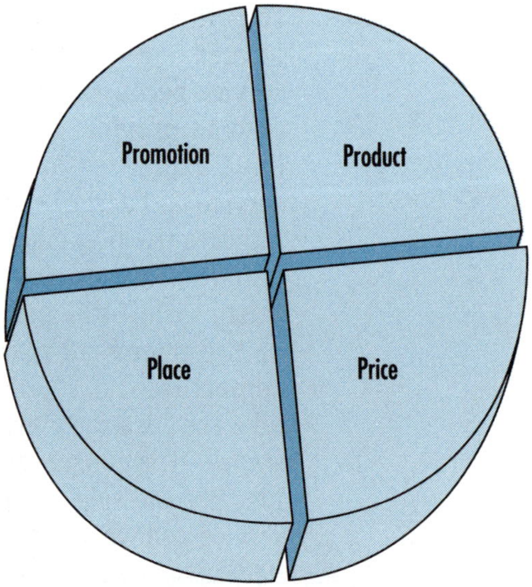

Figure 7.5 The Four Marketing Elements in the Marketing Mix

In this chapter, we will discuss the first element in the marketing mix — the product or service you plan to develop, who your customers will be, what competition to expect, and how to forecast sales. The other elements of the marketing mix will be discussed in Chapter 9.

Confirming a Target Market

Whether your idea for a venture involves a product or a service, you should start by confirming a target market — those individuals or organizations who are likely to want to use what you produce.

In Chapter 4, you examined trends and identified opportunities that might arise as trends change. You discovered that one person's problems can become another person's opportunities. Coffee companies, for example, might see the decline in coffee drinking as a problem, whereas soft-drink manufacturers would see it as an opportunity. Pepsi and Coke are now introducing advertising to encourage people to use their products instead of coffee for breakfast. No well-established company willl develop a new product for the marketplace without first using all the available marketing research techniques at its disposal to confirm that there is a market for the product. Confirming a market involves identifying those people who have a particular need or want for a product or service.

When you write your venture plan, you will need to explain why you chose a particular target market for your product or service. The Sony story, in Chapter 4, illustrated how Akio Morita and his team were able to plan for and achieve success only after they realized that they needed to find individuals who had a special need or a want for the product they were developing. Fisher, in the introductory Venture Profile for this chapter, does not seem to know who his target market is. He is thinking about using automatic call dialing to identify potential customers.

Figure 7.6 Targeting your product or service towards a particular consumer need is the key to a successful venture.

Market Segmentation

Categorizing individuals who share common characteristics into defined target markets, a process known as **market segmentation**, will result in the development of a more focused product or service, one that is more likely to meet the common needs and wants of a specific group of individuals.

Most products or services appeal to only a small section of a country's total population. The Canadian market, for example, consists of more than 25 million people. These people live in different parts of the country, work at different occupations and career levels, and have a variety of different lifestyles, needs, wants, and consumer behaviours. They range in age from less than one year to more than 100 years of age. Their per capita income ranges from zero to over a million dollars per year. Very few products or services can be designed to appeal to all members of this entire market.

AGENTS OF CHANGE

Irene Murdoch, like many similar farmers' wives, worked only "in the home". When her marriage broke down in 1968, she claimed a share of the family ranch. The denial of this claim by the courts mobilized women and women's groups to press for change. The Murdoch case went to the Supreme Court of Canada. It changed the laws of the land regarding spousal rights.

Target markets are made up of individuals who:

- belong to a homogeneous group
- share the same wants or needs for a particular product or service
- have the purchasing power to be able to afford the product or service
- are willing and able to use their money for that purpose

A 16-year-old would not fit into the target market of a politician's campaign because the legal voting age is 18. Men or women with post-secondary education might be in the target market for luxurious ski holidays in Europe, but only if they were willing to spend their money in that way. Men or women between the ages of 20 to 40 might be in the target market for new expensive sports cars, but only if they were in an income bracket that allowed them to spend a great deal of money on automobiles.

Consumer behaviour is also affected by the **culture** to which the consumer belongs. Culture is a combination of beliefs, understandings, morals, values, customs, and habits. It varies from place to place around the world and, since Canada is comprised of a number of ethnic groups from a variety of different countries, within one country.

Finally, consumer behaviour is affected by the values or goals that consumers hold important, either by their status or rank, or by the norms or rules of conduct they observe.

Each consumer is a member of a number of common groupings or **market segments**. Consumers in a particular market segment can be expected to follow similar patterns of behaviour and make similar purchases because they:

- belong to the same culture
- have similar tastes and preferences
- share the same values or goals
- have the same expectations of individuals holding particular status or rank
- respect their group's norms or rules of conduct

To confirm a target market, you must first identify a market segment, or group of consumers, with common characteristics. The best segmentation will be the one that identifies the most meaningful target market. After you have identified a target market, you should prepare a description of a typical consumer in this market. This description is often referred to as a customer profile.

AGENTS OF CHANGE

Ezekiel Hart was the first Jewish member of government to sit in Lower Canada's Legislative Assembly. His term of office was short. The first time the assembly met after he was elected, a law was passed forbidding a Jew to sit or vote in the legislature. Benjamin, Hart's own grandson, many years later introduced a law giving equal rights to Jews.

Common Market Segments

Market segments can be defined by any number of common characteristics:

Demographic	People of the same sex, age, marital status, family size, or in the same stage of the family life cycle
Socioeconomic	People of similar occupation, education, income, social class, or culture
Geographic	People who live in regions of the country that could be defined by specific climate, or political or population boundaries
Psychographic	People with similar lifestyles or personality attributes
Behaviour patterns	People who can be identified by when, where, and how often they shop, as well as by their media habits

Consumption patterns People who can be identified by their knowledge about, and loyalty to, particular products or brands

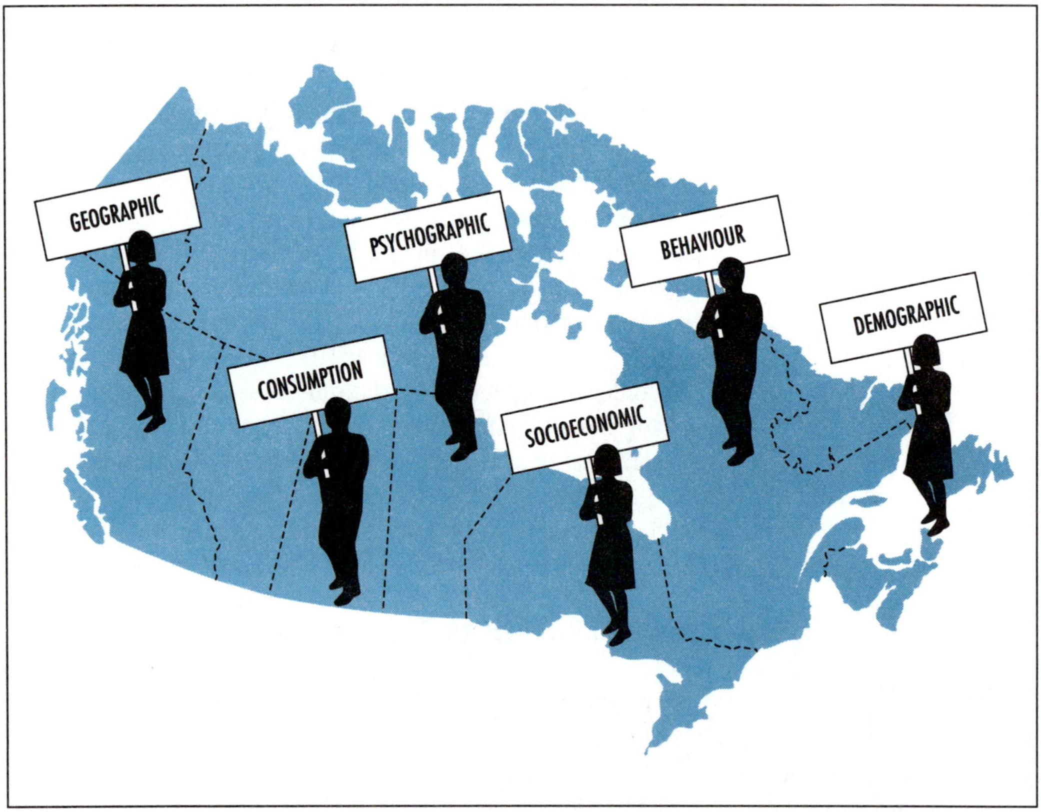

Figure 7.7 Canada is made up of a variety of market segments.

It is important to note that even though members of a target market may share particular characteristics, these characteristics may not be measurable and meaningful in relation to the product or service offered. For example, people who share the same birth date would be difficult to identify and measure in the marketplace. A target market should be one that can be reached easily. Moreover, for most products and services provided, a particular birth date would probably not be a very meaningful characteristic.

Identifying a small target market is not going to be worth the effort required.

A target market needs to be large enough to warrant the time and effort required to provide a specific product or service.

YOUR TURN

14. a) In small groups, select one of the following products. Identify the characteristics of the market segment that would purchase the product and describe your target market.
    - tacos
    - videos
    - leather jacket
    - apartment-sized washers and dryers
    - mountain-climbing equipment
    - fishing and hunting tours
    - easy-to-open medicine bottles

    Share your findings with the rest of the class.

    b) In the same small groups, prepare a description or profile of a typical consumer in your target market.
15. In the same small groups, research the competition for the product you selected.
16. Examine the statistics for Yourtown in Table 7.3 (page 210). Describe the kind of people who live in this community and state what their needs might be. Name the goods and services that are likely being provided to meet their needs and suggest some that are not. In small groups, prepare a list of businesses that you feel might succeed in this community and explain why.
17. In groups of two or three, visit your library, Board of Trade, Parliament Buildings, local Chamber of Commerce, municipal office, or real estate office to collect demographic data that describes the population of your community. Collect as much information as you can about the kinds of businesses already established in your community. As a class, tabulate the data collected. Use a data base program if one is available.
18. As a class, prepare a visual display that describes your community.

Table 7.3 Demographic Statistics for Yourtown

Age and Gender		
	Males	Females
Total population	7 163	8 547
Under 5 years of age	901	1 290
Age 5 - 13	927	1 078
Age 14 - 17	887	916
Age 18 - 24	920	1 010
Age 25 - 34	912	1 028
Age 35 - 54	1 014	1 163
Age 55 - 64	849	1 018
Age 65 - 74	561	699
Age 75 and over	192	345

Income		
Total number of households	5 603 —100%	
Less than $25 000	1 121	(20%)
$25 001-30 000	1 793	(32%)
$30 001-40 000	1 177	(21%)
$40 001-50 000	616	(11%)
$50 001-60 000	784	(14%)
Over $60 000	112	(2%)

Education		
Total population 25 years of age and older	10 891 — 100%	
Elementary: 8 years	1 307	(12%)
Secondary: 4 years	7 950	(73%)
College/University	1 634	(15%)

Occupation		
Total employed (18-65 years of age)	7 914 — 100%	
Professional	791	(10%)
Owners/Managers	950	(12%)
Sales/Service	1 108	(14%)
Clerical/Office	871	(11%)
Mechanics/Construction	712	(9%)
Factory Workers	2 612	(33%)
Miscellaneous	554	(7%)
Unskilled	316	(4%)

19. In small groups, write a consultant's report in which you:
    a) select and describe a venture for your community
    b) prepare a description of a typical customer (a customer profile) and a target market. Use word processing and graphics programs, if available, to enhance the appearance and readability of your report.
20. In small groups, identify and evaluate the target markets for the following products or services:
    a) the *Financial Post*
    b) United Way
    c) the Edmonton Oilers
    d) a science magazine
    e) anti-smoking courses
    f) health and fitness clubs
    g) rate-payer associations
21. Use secondary research to identify:
    - who invented the sandwich
    - where the telephone was first used
    - why penguins are black on one side and white on the other
    - what is meant by "geostationary orbit"
22. Discuss what effect the baby-boom will have on marketers in the year 2000.
23. Prepare an article for a daily newspaper describing how opening up the Eastern European countries will affect marketing in the year 2001.

Life Cycles and Competition

In Chapter 5, you charted the life cycles or stages of development of a number of different products or services. You recognized that they all went through the same stages, or cycles, but that the rates of change and the length and height of the cycles varied greatly from one product to another.

> Life cycle analysis can be used to determine when to enter a market and what elements of the marketing mix to use to compete effectively.

In the introductory stages of a product's life cycle, emphasis is usually placed on the product. Later, the focus changes to promotion and price.

Introduction

As you learned in Chapter 5, when a product or service is first introduced into the marketplace, it is in its introduction stage. If the company is successful at this stage, it will show a profit and its sales will increase. There is little or no competition during this stage.

Growth

As it begins to establish a presence in the marketplace, a product is in a growth stage. Some competitors have moved in at this point and entrepreneurs need to watch competition very carefully. They can modify the product, reduce prices, and launch special advertising campaigns to take a larger market share.

"The next best thing to knowing something is knowing where to find it."
Samuel Johnson

Maturity

When a product has reached its peak of popularity, has established itself in the marketplace, and is as popular with consumers as it will ever be, it is in a maturity stage. Competition is at its peak at this stage. Promotion and advertising campaigns need to be in full swing at this point.

Decline

When sales begin to drop off, a product is considered to be in its decline stage. Many competitors have already left the scene by this time. It is at this point that the company must decide whether to abandon the product entirely, or to modify it to meet new needs in the marketplace.

Figure 7.8 "I want to know everything about the competition for Friday's game. No detail is too small."

Just as a baseball or football coach needs to know as much as possible about an opposing team, so too do business organizations need to know as much as they can about their competition and about the life cycle of their product or service. You will want to identify any competitive advantage that your venture might have.

YOUR TURN

24. Research the life cycle of the following products and identify the kind of competitive activity in each stage. Where possible, indicate at what point the company moved its emphasis from product to promotion and price:
    - microcomputers
    - fitness centres
    - sail boards and wind surfers
    - frozen yogurt

Forecasting Sales

A **sales forecast** is an estimate of how much of a product or service will be sold during a specific period of time. Most sales forecasts are prepared for one-, three-, or five-year periods. With products or services that sell in a wildly fluctuating market, the period of time used to forecast sales might be considerably shorter. A fad item, for example, might have a three-month sales forecast, whereas a piece of furniture might require a five-year forecast.

> A carefully designed sales forecast is the basis for any sound planning in any kind of venture.

It is impossible to purchase the right amount of raw materials, hire the right number of people, plan the right amount of production time without first preparing a well thought-out sales forecast. An accurate sales forecast can play an important role in setting the price of a product or service. It can also be used to set goals for a company and then evaluate the company's performance against these goals at the end of a particular period of time.

Figure 7.9 Sales forecasts must be made with a great deal more analysis and thought than is shown here.

Forecasting sales requires that you take what you believe is happening in the market today, project it into the future, and predict what might happen with respect to the product or service you offer in the future. People who prepare sales forecasts ask such questions as:

- What are the market conditions now?
- What changes can we anticipate in the next period of time?
- What is our target market?
- Given what we believe to be happening in the marketplace today and what we believe will happen in the future; given that this is the size of our target market for this particular period of time; given that this is what we expect to happen in the future, what will the size of the market be for the next period of time? and the next?
- How large a share of the market will we have in the next three years? five years?
- How many units of our product or service will we sell to this market over the next one-, three-, or five-year period?

Sales forecasts are usually created in terms of:

Market potential — the upper limit of expected sales of a particular product for the entire industry (all of the companies that produce the product)

Sales potential — an estimate of how much of a product or service an individual company would be able to sell over a given period of time

Sales prediction — a prediction of the expected actual sales volume for the next given period of time. This amount is usually lower than the sales potential to accommodate for unpredicted market restraints, or incentives offered by other companies in the industry.

Forecasts or future predictions are usually delivered with some conditions attached. Sales forecasts are no different. Sales forecasters will preface their forecasts with statements about what is happening in the industry that might (or might not) have an effect on actual sales for an individual company. The forecast may even be presented in terms of a range, from the most pessimistic to the most optimistic prediction.

Steps in Forecasting Your Sales

The first step in forecasting your sales is to estimate the market potential for your product or service. You will need to consult with local businesspeople, your Chamber of Commerce office, or your public library. If your product or service is connected with a particular trade association, the office nearest you should be able to help you determine the market potential. To increase your degree of accuracy, a total market potential for each of the next three to five years should be estimated.

In Chapter 4, you looked at the projection of trends to identify opportunities. Sales trends are also used to determine a total market's potential. If, for example, sales have increased in a particular industry by 10 per cent annually for the past five years and marketplace conditions have not changed to any great extent, you can reasonably predict that sales will continue to increase by at least 5 per cent per year for the next few years. Your next step, then, in preparing a sales forecast for your product or service would be to look for any definite trends in the industry and adjust your total market potential figures to reflect them.

Your final step is to determine your share of this total potential market. If there are three businesses in your area producing and marketing the same product or service, add your business to that number and divide the total marketing potential for the area by four (to include your business in the total market share). However, it would be naive of you to expect that your company would automatically reach that percentage of market share. Based on what you know about the qualities of your product or service, you should be able to predict how successful you might be at launch, after three months, after six months, and by the end of the first year.

> Adjust your sales forecast to reflect what you know about your sales potential and you have a sales figure on which to base your production, personnel, and pricing strategies.

Venture PROFILE

What actually happened (in the Fisher story)

Bryan Fisher arranged for his father to visit a company offering automatic call dialing. Fisher was impressed by the demonstration but was still reluctant to go ahead with it. He had talked to many of his friends who almost exclusively expressed their dislike of receiving calls from a computer. Fisher decided to go ahead with his original marketing plan of using flyers and some radio ads, but said that if the results weren't satisfactory after a few months, he would reconsider the automatic call dialing system.

EXPLORING • FISHER'S DECISION

1. How did your recommendation for Fisher compare with what he finally chose to do?

POINTS TO REMEMBER

- Marketing research is used to collect, record, and analyze data that will be used to make decisions on marketing related issues.
- Marketing research follows a systematic procedure that includes:
  - — identifying and stating the objective
  - — planning the program
  - — selecting a sample
  - — collecting the data
  - — analyzing the data
  - — drawing conclusions
- An effective marketing mix provides the right combination of product, place, price, and promotion.
- Target markets are defined in order to identify customer needs and wants and to focus the resources available.
- Markets are segmented by the following characteristics: demographics, socioeconomics, geographic, psychographics, behaviour or consumer patterns.
- Products go through four stages of development: introduction, growth, maturity, and decline.
- Sales forecasts are prepared in order to plan production, purchases of raw materials, distribution of finished goods, and promotion activities.

WHAT HAVE YOU LEARNED?

1. What is "marketing research"?
2. Marketing research has three main classifications. Name each classification and describe how it is used.
3. There are three main forms of marketing research. What are they?
4. Outline the seven steps of marketing research.
5. What important qualities should be considered when planning the appearance of a research instrument?

6. Which of the following marketing research routes is most expensive: mailing a questionnaire, conducting a telephone survey, or conducting personal interviews? Why?
7. Describe the four major sections of a questionnaire designed to be mailed out for response.
8. Outline the four elements of the marketing mix.
9. Define a "target market".
10. Why is a sales forecast an important ingredient in the marketing plan?

V·E·N·T·U·R·I·N·G O·U·T

In Chapter 6, you examined the five major components of a simplified venture plan. In this chapter, you investigated the challenges involved in conducting a thorough marketing analysis. This Venturing Out section has been designed to help you gather the facts and figures that you will need to convince the reader of your plan that your venture's product or service has a substantial market in a growing industry and that it is worth pursuing.

In preparation for the development of the market analysis section of your venture plan, write out:

a) the objective of your venture
b) the product or service you plan to provide
c) your target market. Describe your target customers' common and identifiable characteristics. Identify where your potential customers might be found and note whether they would likely purchase your product or service because of its quality, price, or the service that you are prepared to provide.
d) a profile of your target customer
e) a description of any potential customers you have identified and why they have indicated they would purchase your product or service
f) a description of your competition and an evaluation of your product or service in relation to theirs

g) a description of any special trends or conditions in the marketplace that might have an effect on the success of your venture
h) a sales estimate for the next three years

"Successful entrepreneurs will identify the resources they will need." This chapter will outline the many different kinds of resources that you might need and indicate where you can go to find them.

CHAPTER 8

Rolling up Your Sleeves: Team Building and Structuring Your Venture

LEARNING OUTCOMES

By the end of this chapter, you should be able to:

- differentiate among the three major types of resources
- develop a list of the human resources to consult when launching a venture
- understand the importance of building the right team to get your venture off the ground
- distinguish among the four major forms of business ownership
- understand the process of protecting and promoting your company and product through registration, patent, trademarking, and choosing a logo
- develop a list of criteria to use when choosing a site for your venture
- identify the variety of municipal, provincial, and federal regulations that apply in venture creation
- prepare the resources analysis section of your venture plan

ENTREPRENEURIAL LANGUAGE

resources
capital goods
depreciates
expense goods
human resources
mobilize
partnership agreement
lease
bylaws
lending agencies
loan application
cashflow
network
crown corporation
sole proprietorship
corporation
in trust
partnership
general partnership
joint venture
limited partnership
limited partner
general partner
silent partner
corporate charter
co-operative
trademark
logo
vendor's permit
letter of patent
copyright

Venture PROFILE

Simply Marbleous: the power of partners

By Larry Krotz, *Canadian Business*

Despite his inexperience, Bruce Johnson's good idea brought good times to Winnipeg.

Winnipeg is renowned for many things, but a sizzling nightlife isn't one of them. In fact, it used to be the kind of city where those under 25 in search of a good time crowded into pubs where the rock music split eardrums, and people a little older frequented lounges so soothing they risked snoozing over their drinks. But that was before Bruce Johnson. "I'd seen nightclubs in other North American cities when I travelled as a semipro hockey player, and I thought to myself, 'I could do that.'"

It didn't seem to matter that the 27-year-old had no club experience or that he was still in community college studying communications. And it didn't seem to matter that he had no cash or assets. What mattered was that he was determined to realize his goal.

Five years later, Johnson stands proudly in the middle of the Rorie Street Marble Club. Behind him, throngs of professionals, office workers, and school teachers pack the big main bar; in the back corner is a smaller bar and a group of tables where customers chat while purchasing trays of hot hors d'oeuvres. On the other side of the room is a 33 m^2 dance floor. Beside it is a podium for the club's live music. A vivacious insurance company analyst cradling a wine spritzer declares: "This is a place you can visit with your friends to really have fun."

Catering to the desires of those seeking an informal, lively place to meet has made the Marble Club the hottest spot in town. Up to 3000 customers a week flood through the club's doors, a testament to the fund-raising, promotional, marketing, and operating talents of Johnson and his three partners. But getting this far took some time. "I thought it would take me six months to open," says Johnson. "It took me two years."

While he miscalculated on the club's opening date, Johnson, the club's founder and general manager, more accurately pinpointed what would make it thrive. After talking to dozens of people, he realized that most saw nightclubs as dangerous, smoke-filled places. "I knew we had a perception problem we'd have to try and overcome," he says. Future patrons also told him to "offer food, make sure the band doesn't play too loud, and make sure there's lots of room to stand up and move around in."

Armed with his knowledge of what the market wanted, Johnson, who was still in his last month at Red River Community College, called real estate broker Terry Moss. At first Moss misunderstood; he thought Johnson's search for a suitable site was just a student project. When he realized that Johnson was serious, Moss identified three areas where Johnson felt a club would work. Although he knew what he was looking for — a central downtown building with large windows and good parking facilities that would attract both the lunchtime and after-work trade — Johnson didn't understand "what a tough business he was getting into," says Moss. He laughs about having to drive Johnson around because he didn't have a car of his own. But what impressed Moss was Johnson's determination. "It kind of reminded me of myself when I was starting out," he says.

If Johnson got co-operation with finding a site, coming up with half a million dollars was tougher. That's the amount he had calculated he would need to design and renovate the kind of room he wanted, to equip a bar and kitchen, and to do the necessary promotion. Johnson, who had no money of his own and lived with his parents, put the plans for his club into his briefcase and travelled by public transit looking for financing. Now he laughs about it, though a bit ruefully. "I had no clothes, no car; I walked everywhere because I was too cheap to take taxis. Can you imagine this guy coming in and asking you for half a million dollars?"

Without collateral, the four bankers he approached for funding wouldn't touch him; some, in fact, were quite rude. Even his own branch of the bank refused to float a $1000 loan while he worked on the deal.

Undeterred, Johnson started to look around for private investors who had done this sort of financing before. Three times he thought he had the money; three times the deal fell through. Twice it was because investors got cold feet over Johnson's lack of experience. Once Johnson himself backed out when a middleman demanded too much management control. After a year of dead ends, he was at a low ebb. His father had been advancing him survival money but was urging him to get a real job. Johnson was on the verge of heeding his advice.

But by this time he had found partners: Harry Holbrook and Ron Gregory, whom he had met while working at Brandy's, a local restaurant and bar. Holbrook was a disc jockey and entertainment manager at Bogart's, one of the cities first stand-up bars. He'd considered going into business for himself a number of times and when Johnson came along, the pair clicked. "Bruce had a reputation as a straight guy," says Holbrook. "And we both wanted to set up a club that would be around for a while." Gregory was operating manager of Brandy's. But, like Holbrook and Johnson, he didn't have any money either. After putting together a business plan, the three approached Murray Palay, a lawyer at the Winnipeg firm of Buchwald Asper Henteleff.

"They had everything," says Palay, whose specialty is putting together financial packages. "A good concept; a restaurant systems man [Gregory]; a man with a great talent for marketing and promoting [Johnson]; and an entertainment man [he refers to Harry Holbrook as Mr. Party]. What they were missing was the financial and administrative wherewithal. They had all the research and information in their package, but it wasn't in quite the right shape to take to investors." Palay helped to smooth out their business plan, refining the concept, description of personnel and management, discussion of location, projections of startup time and sales possibilities. When he realized they couldn't afford to pay him for his services, he agreed to become a fourth partner.

The quartet registered themselves as Bannatyne Ventures Inc. and decided, on Palay's advice, to break their financing needs into more manageable sums. The partners needed 10 investors willing to put up $25 000: $7500 cash plus a $17 500 letter of credit. To avoid registering with the Manitoba Securities Commission, Palay suggested that they make the offering a private one.

Equipped with a professionally prepared prospectus, the quartet started selling shares to people they knew — a doctor, a couple of dentists, a petroleum engineer, and so on. Physician Ron Watson heard about the offering from his daughter. "She convinced me," he says, "that Winnipeg needed such a place."

On the strength of the gathering investment, the partners paid a $7000 rental deposit on space near the intersection of Portage and Main streets in Winnipeg's warehouse district, which was just then beginning to be popularized and renovated. Then they went to the Manitoba Liquor Control Commission for a liquor licence.

Before it would consider issuing a permit, the commission wanted the partners to have enough financing in place to guarantee that the club would open. This meant that they needed six of their ten potential investors; they had five. On the night before their application expired, the partners prevailed on Johnson's father to become the sixth backer.

From there the venture seemed to take off. They found three more private investors. The Bank of Nova Scotia, impressed by their outside financing and with its investment guaranteed by the federal government, gave them a $100 000 small business investment loan and a $50 000 operating line of credit. The Winnipeg Core Area Initiative, a government body in charge of rejuvenating Winnipeg's central core, came up with a $25 000 small business grant.

Almost before Johnson knew it, the club was ready to open. That was when he realized he had budgeted pitifully little — only $10 000 — for pre-opening publicity. With such limited funds, he couldn't afford to hire an advertising agency; relying on his communication training, he developed a strategy himself. Johnson created a series of radio teasers and newspaper ads that said nothing more than "Simply Marbleous" or "Marbleous Good Times Coming". The ads worked. The Marble Club opened to long lineups. The queues continued every night, alleviating any worries Johnson might have had with cashflow.

Still not quite believing that they'd done it, the partners remained frugal for the first few months. Even though the club was booming, Johnson and Holbrook, the club's entertainment manager, refused to pay themselves any more than their bartenders made. For the first three weeks, Johnson continued to sneak out the back door every night to ride the bus home to his parents' house in south Winnipeg. The result was that the club paid off its bank loan in seven months rather than the anticipated fourteen, releasing the letters of credit held as collateral. Since then the investors, who are in roughly a 50-50 profit-sharing relationship with the partners, have seen more than their original investment in profits.

Group sales play an important part in keeping the operation profitable. Holbrook calls on local businesses to promote the club as a site for company parties, prepares special menus for groups, even provides door prizes.

With experience and assets behind them, the founders of the Marble Club feel ready to act as consultants to other businesses, or as managers for other club owners. Although Ron Gregory has now left the partnership to start his own club, Johnson, Holbrook, and Palay have maintained their relationship. As Marble Management Inc., they are ready to take on whatever life rolls their way.

EXPLORING • SIMPLY MARBLEOUS

1. What did Johnson need to do to bring his venture to a startup?
2. What was the hardest thing to acquire?
3. List all the people Johnson contacted for help.
4. How many of these people actually helped? How did they help?
5. Why were some people unwilling to help?
6. Is there anything Johnson could have done to ensure co-operation from everyone he contacted? Why or why not?
7. How did Johnson determine his target market?
8. Why are the partners of the Marble Club willing to help other new businesses start up?
9. In what ways did the government help this new venture?
10. What made Palay think that Johnson, Gregory, and Holbrook "had everything" when they came to him?

The Resources Spoke of the Venture Creation Wheel

When listing the **resources** that Johnson and his partners needed to get their Marble Club up and running, you probably included everything from a building with furniture and equipment, to food and drink supplies, money to cover startup costs, people to provide advice and moral and financial support, and employees to provide the service. The Resources Spoke on the Venture Creation Wheel includes all resources needed to start up and operate a venture.

Most ventures require a great many resources to start up.

Figure 8.1 Numerous resources are needed to start up a venture.

> One of the most challenging aspects of launching a venture is acquiring the needed resources.

Some resources, such as furniture, equipment, and supplies, must be purchased. The entrepreneur has to find the financial resources needed to fund these purchases. Some resources, such as advice, moral support, and financing, must be sought out. Where this is the case, entrepreneurs need to know where to find the right people with the right skills. Some resources, such as trained consultants, lawyers, accountants, and employees, must be employed or hired on a contract basis. All ventures, whether business or community service, require their own special kinds of resources. And the entrepreneur usually spends a great deal of time looking for and acquiring the right ones.

AGENTS OF CHANGE

By the mid-1800s, cable wires still could not withstand the attack of the ocean's salt; therefore, they were unreliable. Frederick Gisborne, of Nova Scotia, invented a method of insulating these wires from the salt, opening the door to trans-continental communication by telegraph. Another step towards modern telecommunications was taken.

Resources Required for a Successful Venture

Resources are generally categorized into three major groups:

Capital Goods

Capital goods are usually expensive. They last a long time and their cost **depreciates** (lessens in value) over a number of years. They include such items as land, buildings, furniture, and equipment installations.

Expense Goods

Expense goods, or intermediate goods, are goods that are usually consumed during the process of doing business. They include such items as parts and supplies, such routine services as hydro and telephone, and raw materials.

Human Resources

Human resources usually come in the form of advisors, consultants, professional counsellors, financial backers, partners, startup teams, and/or employees.

The decision to purchase needed capital and expense goods and human resources services must be made wisely after examining the venture's needs and the finances available. Successful entrepreneurs not only have to acquire the right kind of resources, they also have to **mobilize**, or use them, in the most effective way.

The team of human resources that you put in place should be designed to offer the knowledge and expertise that you do not have. For this reason, you will have to carefully assess your own strengths and weaknesses. You will have to identify what has to happen in order for your venture to be successfully launched and then identify what you feel you are lacking. Once you have identified your own strengths and weaknesses, you are in a good position to identify exactly what you are looking for in the way of advice or advisors. Hiring employees to work in the venture once it has been started will be discussed in Chapter 9.

The successful launch of the Marble Club required the mobilization of a large number of people. Without the assistance of the real estate agent, the bankers, the government, the management consultant, and the lawyers, Johnson might not have been able to turn his idea into a reality.

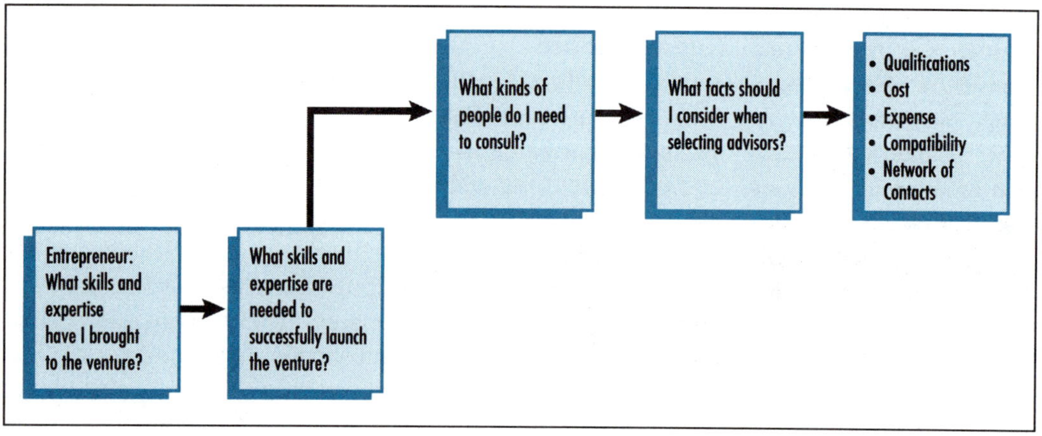

Figure 8.2 Venture Team Formation

YOUR TURN

1. Under the headings, Capital Goods, Expense Goods, and Human Resources, classify the list of the resources that Johnson needed to start up. Identify those that were the most expensive to acquire in each category.
2. a) Reread the following Venture Profiles from previous chapters:
   Chapter 1 - Rick Hansen, Man in Motion
   Chapter 2 - Superstar Bryan Adams: Rock 'n Roll Inc.
   Chapter 3 - Ron Foxcroft: The Fox 40
   b) For each Venture Profile, list the Capital Goods, Expense Goods, and Human Resources required to launch the venture.
3. Consider the venture that you are planning. Make a list of your own skills and the skills you would have to look for in other people.

The External Venture Team

The external venture team is made up of advisors, consultants, and support groups who will offer advice and services to help entrepreneurs organize and start their ventures. Entrepreneurs should recognize the potential benefits of seeking expert advice and deliberately search it out whenever there is a gap in their own knowledge or experience. The following provides an introduction to some professional advisors.

The Lawyer

> "A new idea is delicate. It can be killed by a sneer, or a yawn; it can be stabbed to death by a frown on the right man's brow."
> *Charles Brower*

A lawyer can offer advice on:

- choosing the best legal form of ownership for your venture
- registering a name
- knowing and applying the federal, provincial, and/or municipal laws and bylaws that relate to your venture

Johnson needed a lawyer to properly close the **partnership agreement** between Holbrook, Palay, Gregory, and himself. A lawyer would probably have been used to help the Marble Club venture negotiate the **lease** on the premises and understand any **bylaws** that applied.

Figure 8.3 Lawyers provide helpful information and advice.

> He who acts as his own lawyer has a fool for a client.

Lawyers are trained to give legal advice, but it is the responsibility of the entrepreneur to make all the final decisions. To get the best advice possible, it is important to ensure that the lawyer selected has a clear understanding of the needs of the entrepreneur and the venture as well as experience dealing with small business.

The Banker

The banker can be an important person to an entrepreneur starting out. Bankers lend money and provide advice. Competition in the Canadian banking industry is keen; it is therefore a good idea to shop around for any financing and advice you need. Banks, and other **lending agencies**, require that the entrepreneur carry some of the risk by putting up a portion of the capital required.

Figure 8.4 Bankers offer advice as well as capital.

Selecting a banker with experience in the area of a particular venture can make it easier for the entrepreneur to obtain financing.

Bankers have a limit on the amount of capital that they can approve. It is therefore a good idea to make sure that the banker selected has an approval limit higher than the amount required by the venture.

If the banker's approval limit is not sufficiently high, the **loan application** will have to go to head office. When this happens, the loan decision will be made based on facts and figures and not on the characteristics and skills of the entrepreneur, the merits of the team, the idea, or the opportunity.

The Accountant

Figure 8.5 Accountants ensure that decisions are made on a sound financial footing.

An accountant should be hired early in the planning stages of a venture. He or she will help to ensure that decisions are made on a sound financial footing. The accountant can help at the stage when the entrepreneur must prepare **cashflow** and other financial statements in order to justify a request for financing. He or she may even aid the entrepreneur in writing the financial section of the venture plan. The accountant can also help with the procedures the venture might use to monitor growth.

The Real Estate Agent

Figure 8.6 Real estate agents will help select the right location for the venture.

The real estate agent will help in selecting a location for the venture. It is essential that the real estate agent knows exactly what the venture requires in terms of size, traffic patterns, price, and access to the street and parking. The more information the real estate agent has, the better assistance he or she can offer. Moss offered Johnson an excellent service in finding a location for the Marble Club because Johnson knew exactly what he was looking for in a location and he was able to articulate that to Moss.

Management Consultants

Figure 8.7 Management consultants offer a wide range of consulting services.

Management consultants are in business to help entrepreneurs through the startup and management of a venture. They offer a wide variety of services, from conducting marketing surveys and determining whether or not there is a real opportunity for a particular product or service in a specific location to the preparation of financial statements and the acquisition of startup capital. Management consultants use their **network** of specialists — lawyers, accountants, real estate agents, bankers, and insurance agents — to ensure that the venture is correctly placed on the road to success.

Networking, or the drawing together or connecting of key advisors, is at the core of the management consultant's business.

YOUR TURN

4. As a class, prepare a list of questions that you would need to ask each of the following in order to understand the role that each plays in advising new entrepreneurs on how to create and start up a venture: a banker, a lawyer, an accountant, and a real estate agent. Select one of these professions and ask the questions you have prepared to a representative of that profession in your local community.
5. Invite a representative from each of the following professions to speak to your class about his or her role in helping new entrepreneurs: credit union manager, representative from the Chamber of Commerce, an insurance agent, and a management consultant.

Venture PROFILE

Can Students Consult?

By Cathy Hilborn, *Small Business Magazine*

Canada's student consulting services say they can spot market opportunities and dangers for aspiring entrepreneurs.

Christopher Ross rewrote his business plan 27 times before he got started, and paid $60 000 in fees to professional management consultants. When the business plan still misfired, he turned for help to low-cost student consultants; in the end, it was the students, says Ross, who really helped him launch the company.

More than a dozen university business faculties across Canada have laid out a welcome mat. For fees well below those of their professional counterparts — sometimes for nothing — student consultants provide similar services, from developing a business plan to studying the market feasibility of a proposed product.

Since 1984, the University of Calgary's Faculty of Management has operated the Centre for New Venture Development. Each year, some 100 companies seek its assistance. The cost is about as low as you can get; clients only pay for expenses associated with their projects.

For Ross, President of Pulse Composites Corp. of Blairmore, Alberta, the Centre was his company's lifeline. "Without the New Venture Program, this company would never have started," he says.

Pulse manufactures fibre-reinforced composite materials. Ross personally invested more than $100 000 cash into his project, but he needed $2 million - $3 million in capital.

"Administration and staff went over our application, looking for two criteria. We had to have a commitment to our idea, to see it through. And they had to establish that our product had market potential."

Once Ross got the green light, five MBA students worked with him over the course of their 13-week semester. Because the students use the entrepreneur's ideas rather than a hypothetical case, it's important for the client to have a lot of input.

The students' projects included a cross-Canada telephone survey to determine the market potential for window frames made from Pulse's composite material.

The students completed a feasibility study to determine whether Blairmore, which lies in the Crow's Nest Pass, was a good place to locate Pulse's manufacturing plant. They also examined the product and found that it met Canadian standards for a variety of uses.

Through the Centre, Pulse received legal and financial advice regarding such things as patent rights and how to sell shares. He also attended workshops on how to develop a business plan.

EXPLORING • CAN STUDENTS CONSULT?

1. In what way did the Centre for New Venture Development help Ross with his startup?
2. Where else could Ross have received this same assistance?
3. Student consultants charge much less than professional management consultants. Do you think the savings compensate for the students' more limited experience?
4. Contact your local university or community college and find out if it offers similar services as the University of Calgary to entrepreneurs.
5. If Ross had come to you for advice, what would you have told him?

Government Resources

In support of new venture creation, the federal and provincial governments have established services to work with entrepreneurs. The Federal Business Development Bank is a **crown corporation**, owned by the federal government but operating independently. It provides financial support and consultative services to new ventures. These services are offered on a one-on-one basis, through seminars or booklets.

The Federal Department of Regional Industrial Expansion offers a number of free services to help new ventures. These include a data base of trade fairs at which entrepreneurs can display their products or services, market surveys that give statistics on sales, imports, and exports, and a service that matches foreign opportunities with Canadian ventures. In addition to the services rendered, the Department of Regional Industrial Expansion annually recognizes companies that excel in productivity, entrepreneurship, innovation, invention, technology, and marketing with the Canada Awards of Excellence.

There are 27 federal departments or agencies that offer a service to new ventures. Each provincial government also has agencies that assist entrepreneurs through the startup phase.

YOUR TURN

6. Contact your provincial government and find out which departments and agencies serve small business.
7. In small groups, select one department or agency and describe the kind of support it offers.
8. Contact an entrepreneur in your community and ask him or her what type of advice he or she sought, and from whom, when starting up the venture. Is the support the entrepreneur seeks different now?

Choosing a Form of Organization

Within each of the two classifications, for profit and not-for-profit, ventures can be small, medium, or large. They can be privately owned and operated or publicly (government) owned or operated. Each successful venture will, however, use a specific form of organization to maximize its effectiveness and to operate efficiently.

Some people may select a form of business ownership without adequately evaluating all of the alternatives. They may choose a **sole proprietorship**, for example, because it appears to be the easiest way in which to begin a business. A sole proprietorship is generally a good form of organization for a business venture where the startup costs are expected to be low. Others may decide, unnecessarily, to form a **corporation** because they feel that the word "Limited" or "Inc." at the end of their business name will add prestige or importance to the venture. In general, even if a business venture starts as a sole proprietorship, it should incorporate when something of major significance, such as signing an important contract, is undertaken. Incorporating offers protection in the form of limiting liability.

Before you decide on a form of business ownership for your venture, you should review the various forms of organization that your venture might take and select the one that will best meet your needs.

Sole Proprietorship

A sole proprietorship is an unincorporated business venture that has only one owner.

> Most people starting a small business venture will select a sole proprietorship because it is the simplest form of business ownership.

Figure 8.8 A sole proprietorship is the simplest form of business ownership.

You may conduct any type of business as a sole proprietorship. Usually, all that is legally necessary to operate as a sole proprietorship is that the business has been registered and that proper licences have been obtained. The owner is held responsible for everything that happens within it, including any debts, contracts, or other legal obligations. On the other hand, since income or losses are considered part of the owner's personal income, any losses incurred during the first few years of operation can be deducted from the owner's previous year's income. The tax refunds which might result can then be used to help finance the business. The sole proprietor assumes unlimited liability for the business. If the business is in any financial trouble, the owner's personal assets may be seized to cover any debts or obligations of the business. However, a lawyer may be able to arrange to have your personal assets held **in trust** to protect you from personal liability.

Table 8.1 Advantages and Disadvantages of a Sole Proprietorship

Advantages	***Disadvantages***
• quick, easy, and inexpensive to establish • only requires registration and appropriate licences • owner makes all decisions • owner includes all business profits or losses with personal income	• limited in terms of employee compensation plans offered • all business income is taxed • profits may be taxed at a higher rate than they would be for an incorporated organization • harder to raise capital than for a partnership or a corporation

Partnership

A **partnership** is a formal commitment to work together to achieve the goals and objectives of a particular business venture.

For best results, partners should have similar goals, work ethics, management philosophies, and values.

Each partner must contribute something towards the partnership. This contribution may be in the form of startup money, material, talent, skill, experience, knowledge, or business contacts.

People who depend on "handshakes" and "good friend" agreements in their partnerships often end up regretting the arrangement. The most important procedure in setting up a partnership is the writing of a partnership agreement, which is a legally binding contract.

Figure 8.9 A balance of skills makes for a sound partnership.

The Partnership Agreement

A partnership agreement usually covers:

- the goals and aims of the partnership
- the initial contribution made by each partner and their continuing roles and responsibilities in the everyday activities of the partnership
- the amount of money each partner may draw out of the business
- authorizations for financial commitments
- the procedure for:
  - — distribution of profits and losses
  - — admitting new partners
  - — releasing (or buying out) one of the partners
  - — dealing with the death or extended illness of one of the partners
  - — selling or liquidating the partnership
  - — the appointment of authorized persons for signing cheques and other documents
  - — dealing with disagreements between or among the partners

Types of Partnership

A **general partnership** (or unincorporated partnership) is registered in the same way (and for about the same cost) as a sole proprietorship. At income tax time, the profits or losses of the partnership are divided according to each partner's percentage of interest or ownership in the venture. Each partner then applies that amount of profit or loss to his or her personal income for tax purposes. However, all debts and obligations of the partnership, regardless of whose responsibilities they were, are still the responsibility of each partner. If, in the event of a bankruptcy, one partner does not have enough personal assets to cover his or her share of the losses, creditors can file claim to the personal assets of any of the other partners in the **joint venture.**

Table 8.2 Advantages and Disadvantages of a Partnership

Advantages	*Disadvantages*
• quick, easy, and inexpensive to establish • each partner may deduct business losses (in proportion to the amount invested in the business) from whatever is earned within the business or from other sources • favourable tax treatment, especially for startup losses • combines the talents and resources of two or more people	• general partners assume unlimited liability for all debts or obligations incurred by the partnership • both business and personal income are taxed • profits may be taxed at a higher rate than they would be for an incorporated organization • unless otherwise stated in a partnership agreement, the partnership is automatically dissolved when one of the partners dies • if the partners cannot agree on the day-to-day operation of the partnership, decisions become difficult to make

A **limited partnership** consists of one or more **limited partners** with liability limited to their investment in the venture. It may also, depending on the terms of the partnership agreement, contain one or more **general partners** who have unlimited liability with respect to the debts and obligations of the partnership. **Silent partners**, who invest money in the partnership but do not take an active part in the management of it, may also be involved in a limited partnership. Any involvement, such as giving advice

AGENTS OF CHANGE

In the early 1920s, farmers in Saskatchewan were frustrated with the grain handling and marketing systems they had to deal with. To give them stability in the marketplace, they created The Saskatchewan Wheat Pool. Their co-operative has now grown from a band of hopeful farmers into one of the largest grain-handling organizations in Canada.

or helping out in any way in addition to financial investment, may make a silent limited partner into a general partner, liable for debts and obligations incurred by the partnership. For more specific information on partnerships, refer to the Limited Partnership Act of each province or consult your lawyer.

Corporation or Limited Company

A corporation or limited company is a legal person created by law and established by **corporate charter** that stands separate and apart from the persons who own it. It is given the term "limited" because, just as with limited partners, the liability of the shareholders or owners is limited to the amount of money that they originally invested in the corporation (or what they paid for the shares that they purchased).

A corporation owns all the assets and is responsible for all the liabilities of the business.

The personal assets of shareholders cannot be claimed to cover any debts or obligations that the corporation incurs. Likewise, shareholders cannot deduct, from their personal income, any losses that the business might experience. As an owner of a corporation or limited company, you may adjust the amount of personal income you take out of the business and reflect this in the amount of taxes that you pay.

The inventors of the board game *Trivial Pursuit*, for example, sold shares to friends and venture capitalists. They not only raised all the capital they needed, but they also avoided risking everything to get it. By forming a corporation, you spread the risk of failure among a group of people rather than assuming it all yourself. In return, you give these people a small share in the future profits of your venture. Bankers and other lenders may be more willing to make loans based on the level of equity investment in the corporation. In fact, you should have more flexibility overall regarding the different kinds of shares and debt instruments you can offer.

Table 8.3 Advantages and Disadvantages of a Corporation

Advantages	***Disadvantages***
• corporations have an unlimited life, and day-to-day business continues despite the illness or death of their owners • ownership is easily transferred and does not affect the licences held by the company • profits can be removed from the corporation in the form of dividends, which can be a tax benefit to the owner • tax advantages in the form of tax credits and choice of year end • the corporation can be eligible for such benefits as group insurance or registered pension plans • capital is raised by selling shares • personal liability of the owner is limited	• more costly to set up because of government fees, name searches, legal fees • requires more formal annual activities (i.e., an annual meeting with formal minutes and an annual report) • losses cannot be used by the owner to offset personal income • business losses incurred during the startup period can only be deducted against future profits of the corporation • owner's personal assets may be seized by the lending agency if he or she has put up personal collateral for a business loan

AGENTS OF CHANGE

A consumer co-operative is a business owned and operated by the people who use it. The first known consumer co-operative was started in Rochdale, England, in 1844. Since then, consumer co-operatives have sprung up throughout the western world, ranging in size from small buying clubs to large supermarket chains. The co-operative movement attempts to put control of the venture into the hands of the users so their specific needs are met.

Co-operative

A **co-operative** is a member-owned enterprise. Co-operatives are responsible neither to outside owners, nor to government, but rather to their own members. Each member of a co-operative has a voting right, independent of his or her investment in the co-operative. There are a variety of different kinds of co-operatives operating in Canada. The most common are:

- consumer or supply co-operatives, organized to purchase goods required by their members
- service co-operatives, organized to provide services, such as housing, for members
- financial co-operatives, organized to provide financial services to members
- worker co-operatives, organized to produce commodities such as wheat or dairy products

Figure 8.10 Co-operatives are common in our society.

Table 8.4 Advantages and Disadvantages of a Co-operative

Advantages	*Disadvantages*
• less expensive to operate • members take an active interest in the co-operative and feel a sense of ownership • provides goods and services at a reduced cost to membership	• depending upon the legal form of ownership that is chosen (partnership or corporation), the same disadvantages would exist

Franchise

A franchise is a system that allows the owners of a successful business to duplicate it in another location without having to raise additional money or capital themselves. A franchise operation is not a new or innovative entrepreneurial venture. Each individually owned franchise operates as though it were part of a large chain. Each uses the same trademark, equipment design, and operating procedures. Each franchise produces the same standardized product or service. It doesn't matter how many Burger King restaurants you eat in, the Whopper will taste the same in every one of them.

A franchise purchase is a continuing agreement between the franchisor, the company that originated the venture (or seller), and the franchisee, the individual(s) purchasing the right to operate a copy of the venture (or buyer). The franchisor's knowledge, image, success, manufacturing, marketing, and management techniques are part of the agreement. Generally speaking, franchisees are not free to run the business as they see fit. They must follow the franchisor's policies, standards, and operating procedures.

Advantages and Disadvantages of Each Form of Business Organization

Your choice of ownership form will have a significant effect on the future of your venture. It is important that you take the time to study the tables provided in this chapter, including Table 8.5 which follows. Match your needs with the advantages and disadvantages of each structure and select the one that offers the most positive environment for a successful venture. You will then be in a better position to either seek the advice of professional consultants or decide on your own which form would be best for your particular venture.

Table 8.5 Characteristics of the Four Forms of Business Ownership

Sole Proprietorship	Partnership	Corporation	Co-operative
Name Usually the owner's name. If any other name is used, the term "Registered" or "Reg'd" is added.	*Name* Identified by the name of the firm (Dorset Plumbing and Heating) or by a name made up of the names of some or all of the partners (Clark and Wojack Waste Disposal). The abbreviation "Reg'd" is only compulsory when the firm's name includes the name of a person who is not a partner (e.g., Amin and Eyton Consultants, Reg'd).	*Name* Only a business that is incorporated may use the terms "Limited", "Ltd.", Inc.", or "Corp." after its business name.	*Name* Only a co-operative that is incorporated may use the terms "Limited", "Ltd.", Inc.", or "Corp." after its business name. Otherwise the same rules as apply for a partnership.
Jurisdiction Any province or territory in which the business operates.	*Jurisdiction* Any province or territory in which the partnership operates.	*Jurisdiction* May be incorporated under either federal or provincial jurisdiction.	*Jurisdiction* May be incorporated under either federal or provincial jurisdiction
Set-up Completion of a simple registration form with the local provincial government. Keep the description of your venture general enough to enable you to expand into other related business areas.	*Set-up* Created by a verbal or written agreement between the parties concerned and then registered with the province or territory. Proper operating licences or permits must also be obtained from each province, territory, and municipality.	*Set-up* Must obtain a corporate charter or file articles of incorporation describing the company name, how and to whom shares will be issued, names of the officers of the company, and what their responsibilities will be.	*Set-up* Can be set up as partnerships or corporations with the same conditions applying to each.

Sole Proprietorship	Partnership	Corporation	Co-operative
Legal costs Minimal.	*Legal costs* Minimal if registration of the partnership and operating licences are required. If a partnership agreement needs to be drawn up, varying legal fees will need to be added.	*Legal costs* Costs of incorporating will include legal and government filing fees.	*Legal costs* Same costs apply as for a partnership or a corporation.
Term Business may be closed whenever the owner wants, or automatically when the owner dies. Even after the business has been closed, the owner is responsible for all debts or obligations to employees, creditors, and customers.	*Term* If the partnership has been created for a fixed term, it will automatically dissolve at the end of that term. If the partnership agreement spells out another alternative, it will end by: • an agreement of parties involved • the bankruptcy, death, retirement, admission, or withdrawal of a partner • unlawful partnership practice	*Term* Corporation legally continues to exist even if the owner(s) or shareholder(s) change, die, or retire. A majority vote of all shareholders is required to dissolve a corporation as well as special resolutions and tax clearances.	*Term* The same conditions apply for a co-operative as for a corporation or a partnership
Financing Sole proprietors will usually use their own assets or borrowing power as startup capital.	*Financing* All partners involved will use their own capital or borrowing power for startup financing.	*Financing* Easier to find investors because they hold "limited" liability.	*Financing* Co-operatives may choose to record their members' investment as shares or loans or any combination of these.

Sole Proprietorship	Partnership	Corporation	Co-operative
Taxes Business profits and losses are reported on the owner's personal income tax return and payments are made according to federal and provincial income tax schedules.	*Taxes* Business profits and losses are reported on the personal income tax returns of each of the partners in accordance with the sharing ratio described in the partnership agreement.	*Taxes* In smaller corporations, owners pay tax at a corporate level for any profits of the corporation over and above operating expenses. Shareholders are taxed individually on dividends paid by the corporation.	*Taxes* The same laws apply as for a partnership or a corporation, depending on the form of co-operative established.
Liability Owner's personal assets may be claimed to cover unpaid debts incurred by the business venture.	*Liability* Claims may be made on each partner's personal assets to pay for any outstanding debts or obligations of the partnership.	*Liability* Personal assets of any owners (or shareholders) cannot be seized to cover liabilities of the corporation.	*Liability* If incorporated, the same rules apply as for a corporation. If a partnership, the same rules apply as for a partnership
Administration Is easily understood and administered. Fewer government forms and reports are required than with any other form of organization.	*Administration* Requires a general agreement on contribution of money, talent, skill or expertise, and administration from each partner.	*Administration* May have one or more directors responsible for administration, though shareholders may act as directors. Information about meetings, shareholders, directors, capital, and income tax must be maintained and updated regularly.	*Administration* Policies are set and the co-operative administered by the membership itself.

YOUR TURN

9. Review the following Venture Profiles and identify the form of ownership for each:
   Chapter 5 - Students create own jobs with paper for job-seekers (page 128)
   Chip's better wiper idea (page 133)
   Joseph Armand Bombardier, the Entrepreneur (page 136)
   Chapter 7 - Dialing for dollars (page 184)
10. As a class, prepare a list of the restaurants in your community and identify the form of ownership for each. Select one or two restaurants from each category and ask the owner why he or she chose that particular form of ownership.

Choosing a Name, Trademark, and Logo

Once you have selected a form of organization, you will need to decide on a name for your new venture. Try to stay away from names that will not add anything to your business. Names like A and B Contractors, or AAA Carpet Cleaners, will not help sell your product or service.

> Some business advisors suggest that you should use the "3M rule" for selecting a name for your venture. The name you select should be "Memorable", "Mellow", and have "Mass" appeal.

If the quality of the product or service you offer is reflected in the name of your venture, you will have free advertising for the duration of your venture.

If you are planning to keep your business venture small, either as a sole proprietorship or as a small partnership, you can, after you have selected a name, fill out a simple form at your local Ministry of Consumer and Commercial Relations or provincial equivalent. The provincial ministry office will look through its records to make sure that no other business is using the name you have selected.

If, on the other hand, you think that your venture will someday be quite large, with perhaps a national or international market, you should have a national corporation name search conducted to make sure that the name you have selected is not already in use. The cost of such a search is minimal but, unless you have incorporated your venture, your name can only be reserved for you for six months. If you are not ready to incorporate, you can repeat the search every six months to protect your name until you are ready to incorporate. Special name search houses are listed in the Yellow Pages of major centres.

Your lawyer will help you when it comes time to protect your company name. Many companies will protect their name by establishing a reputation associated with a name. Other companies will register a **trademark** to protect the name of their company. A trademark is a symbol, phrase, word, picture, drawing, shape, method of wrapping or packaging, or a combination of these, that is used to differentiate your goods or services from somebody else's.

Once you have a company name and a trademark, your next step will be to produce a **logo.**

Unless you are a talented and professional graphic artist, do not try to design your own company logo.

Your company logo will appear with your company name and address on your business cards, letterheads, invoices, advertising, trucks, and anything else you wish to have identified. You might be satisfied with something you can design now as you start up your venture, but try to think ahead and ask yourself whether you will be satisfied with that logo when your company grows in size and in importance in the business world. Examine some of the company logos you see around you and employ a professional artist or ask a graphic arts student from your nearest community college to design one you can be proud of.

Choosing a Site

The selection of the best site for your venture will depend to a great extent on what kind of business you are setting up and on how large you expect it to be soon after startup.

A community service, for example, should be located close to the people it is designed to serve and will require that you have enough space to conduct the service adequately.

A small service business, one that responds to telephone calls from customers, can be set up in an extra room in your home. You will probably only need a desk, filing cabinet, telephone, and maybe a telephone-answering machine. If your service requires that you keep an inventory of special material or equipment, you will also need storage space.

A retail business will require a great deal more attention to location. You will have to ask yourself such questions as:

- What kind of customer am I looking for?
- Where will these customers be during a normal working day?
- What kind of retail space might be available close to where these customers are?
- Will potential customers drive to my location? Will I need parking facilities?
- What kind of business would I want to locate close to?
- What kind of business would I want to stay away from?
- What kind of interior and exterior space should I be looking for?
- What kind of window space will I need?
- What rent can I afford?

When you have answered all these questions, and any others that you can think of, you can start looking for a potential site. Real estate agents, signs in the windows of existing stores, classified advertisements in your local newspaper, and even information from friends and business associates will give you a good start.

Narrow your selections down to four or five that seem the most promising and draw up a chart like the one illustrated in Table 8.6. Include your financial resources and any special factors that reflect the needs of your business. List all the selections you want to consider further and check off the criteria for each potential site. Examine each set of criteria and reduce your selections to one or two final choices.

AGENTS OF CHANGE

Children who have been missing for long periods of time might often not be found because they have aged, and no one recognizes them. Two University of Chicago researchers developed a computer program that can age the picture of a person. Police are now using this program to age pictures of missing children so they can be recognized even several years after going missing. A new use for computers has changed the way police search for missing children.

Table 8.6 Location Evaluation

Potential Site	Location (Corner/Strip Plaza Mall/Town Centre)	Surface Area (in square metres)	Parking	Rent
A B C D				

Knowing the Laws and Regulations

It is important to be familiar with all the municipal, provincial, and federal laws and regulations that will affect your venture. You should determine whether a business permit or tax licence is required, whether a special building code or labour law applies to your industry, and what zoning bylaws pertain. If you plan to open a retail business, you should obtain a **vendor's permit** (or retail sales tax licence) from your Provincial Ministry of Revenue. If you plan to be in manufacturing, you will need to contact the local office of the Customs and Excise Tax Division of Revenue Canada about federal sales tax requirements. You should also contact Revenue Canada for information about salary, benefits, and deductions for prospective employees. Since regulations vary from province to province, and in some cases from municipality to municipality, it is best to investigate them yourself with the help of a lawyer, banker, accountant, or your local Chamber of Commerce.

Protection for Products and Ventures

It is also important to consider legal protection for your venture and products.

Trademark registration requires the services of a registered patent attorney.

A trademark is good for fifteen to twenty-five years, depending on the country in which it is registered, and is renewable every term for a small renewal fee.

New products can also be protected. If you have a great idea for a product, you might want to consider having it patented. A **letter of patent** is a legal document issued by the federal government through the Department of Consumer and Corporate Affairs. It gives the patent holder the right to exclude others from using, claiming, or selling the invention within the country of patent for a specific number of years. You should contact a registered patent attorney or agent for advice.

Copyright is the simplest form of protection. All that is required to register a copyright, as the author or creator of a piece of work, is to send in an application along with a cheque. In fact, the procedure is so simple that you can do it yourself, though it is still wise to have a patent attorney review it first, especially if the work may be of considerable market value. The legal fee should be minimal, if anything. The registration process is usually completed within two months and a certificate will be issued on approval of your application.

Unlike trademarks, copyrights fall under two international conventions, which means that you might need only to register it in your country to be automatically protected in most countries around the world.

In Canada, a copyright typically lasts for the life of the author or creator plus fifty years.

Protecting ideas is a different matter. Very little protection is available. If you have an idea and are concerned that it might be stolen, make an appointment with a patent attorney and explore the specific legal options that may be available in your particular circumstances.

The names and locations of some of the agencies and government offices you can contact to identify the laws and regulations that apply to your business are included in the Appendix.

YOUR TURN

11. Evaluate company names such as Marble Club and Timeposters using the "3M rule."

12. Contact your municipal government office to determine what bylaws are in place for special kinds of business establishments. Include such businesses in your list as food stores, restaurants, manufacturing businesses, and daycare services.
13. What type of site should you look for if you are planning a venture in the following categories: a ladies' fashion boutique, a fast-food restaurant, a hardware or drygoods store, a fabric centre, and an automobile repair shop?

Venture PROFILE

Tasia Richards' Waterproof Signs

Financial Post Moneywise

Tasia Richards successfully patented her waterproof lawn signs, a simple idea that's worth millions.

Not every invention involves complex technology. Take the waterproof lawn signs that first appeared nationwide in a recent election. The candidate's name and party logo are printed on both sides of a rectangular plastic bag. A piece of stiff cardboard and a wooden stick are slipped inside, the unit is stapled together, and — voilà! — a cheap sign that far outlasts the old cardboard ones, especially in rainy weather. The inspiration of entrepreneur Tasia Richards, of White Rock B.C., this simple concept is now covered by both Canadian and U.S. patents.

Richards came to Canada from Greece and settled in B.C. Employed as a sales representative, marketing plastic sleeves to protect floral arrangements during shipping, she began sprucing up this plain packaging item with colours and graphics, and soon went into business for herself. She also had experience as a volunteer in political campaigns. In late 1983, she conceived the lawn sign and, at the urging of her husband, tried and found she was able to patent it. In the 1984 federal election, she cranked out 60 000 of them for B.C.'s Tory candidates. Working madly for one month, she cleared a tidy $20 000 profit. Provincial and municipal elections in Ontario followed, and she sold her signs to other parties as well. Between elections, flower sleeves remain her bread and butter.

Holding a patent, Richards quickly learned, is no guarantee of protection. During one campaign, she won an injunction against a candidate who had identical signs made by a competitor, but this has not stopped the infringement. For the 1988 federal campaign, she sold well over 300 000 signs, but at least six other companies in three provinces also made them. Not only is it expensive to sue each of them, Richards learned, but the political party as well as the manufacturer is liable. And law firms which often have close ties to the parties are very reluctant to take such cases: "They ask, 'Who is this woman who wants to sue the Liberal party?' It just isn't *done*." One law firm refused outright. Yet, she realizes, if she doesn't defend her patent rights, "next time around, everybody's going to be doing it."

The dilemma is magnified when she looks at the U.S. and considers a more durable version for real estate signs, potentially a huge year-round enterprise. How, she wonders, can she expand to service this market and defend her patent as well? Dealing with lawyers has already proven expensive and time-consuming. So, she plans to license her concept to large U.S. companies with the resources to market it properly *and* fight the inevitable lawsuits.

Recently Richards took on a partner and doubled the size of her small manufacturing operation. Her simple idea, if handled properly, could make her millions. "But that doesn't mean that I'll get the big money and just retire." Already onto new hush-hush schemes, she hopes to leave the routine work to others and focus on her strength — creative marketing. "Everything you do in life," she says, "you have to sell."

EXPLORING • WATERPROOF SIGNS

1. What form of business organization do you think Tasia Richards is using for her waterproof lawn sign business?
2. Why did she feel it was necessary to patent her idea?
3. Why do you think she would need to hold both U.S. and Canada patents on this product?
4. What does she mean when she says she plans to "license her concept to large U.S. companies" and how will this be beneficial for her?
5. What reasons does she have to keep her new schemes "hush-hush"?

POINTS TO REMEMBER

- Entrepreneurs need to mobilize their resources effectively in order to launch a successful venture.
- A startup team should represent a balance of abilities.
- Lawyers, bankers, accountants, real estate agents, and management consultants are effective advisors for a starting entrepreneur.
- There are four major forms of business organizations:
  — sole proprietorship
  — partnership
  — corporation
  — co-operative
- Selecting a name, trademark, and logo for your venture requires careful thought.
- The best site for your venture will depend on the type of business you establish.
- It is important to know the laws and regulations that apply to your venture before you start.

WHAT HAVE YOU LEARNED?

1. What is meant by the terms: "capital goods", "expense goods", and "human resources"?
2. What strengths should a startup team have?
3. What can the following people do for a starting entrepreneur: lawyer, banker, real estate agent, accountant, management consultant?
4. Describe the services that the Federal Department of Regional Industrial Expansion might offer an entrepreneur.
5. Describe the advantages and disadvantages of a :
   a) sole proprietorship
   b) partnership
   c) corporation
   d) co-operative
6. To what does the "3M rule" apply?
7. How would you apply for a patent to protect your product?
8. What is a copyright?
9. Where would you go for a vendor's permit?
10. Where would you go for information about federal sales tax?

V·E·N·T·U·R·I·N·G O·U·T

1. In preparation for the development of your venture plan, identify the most suitable form of organization and prepare reasons for your selection.
2. Identify the laws and regulations that apply to your venture and describe how you will follow them.
3. Prepare the resource analysis section of your plan considering such questions as:
   a) What equipment do I need?
   b) What human resources will I require?
   c) What supplies does this venture need?
   d) Where do I want to locate and why?

"Profit, Price, Production, People and Productivity, and Promotion are the six P's of entrepreneurship." The OPERATIONS spoke of the Venture Creation Wheel in this chapter will focus on each one of these and show you how to use each in your venture.

CHAPTER 9

The Six P's of the Entrepreneurship Process

LEARNING OUTCOMES

By the end of this chapter, you should be able to:

- list and describe the 6 P's of entrepreneurship
- understand the relationship between profit and entrepreneurship
- distinguish between various pricing strategies used by entrepreneurs
- determine the importance of accurate costing, appropriate materials, equipment, and productivity to the production process
- understand that employees are crucial to venture creation
- distinguish between the four major promotional activities
- prepare a preliminary operating strategy section for your venture plan

ENTREPRENEURIAL LANGUAGE

6 P's of entrepreneurship	cost-plus pricing	labour intensive	publicity
economic resource	markup	capital intensive	sales promotion
total profit	follow the competition pricing	fringe benefits	AIDA formula
total revenue	penetration pricing	Canada Pension Plan	rate cards
total cost	skimming	Unemployment Insurance	word-of-mouth
fixed costs	psychological pricing	Workers' Compensation	point-of-purchase display
variable costs	loss-leader pricing	profit sharing	cents-off merchandise
price takers	productivity	advertising	
pricing strategy	raw materials	personal selling	

Venture PROFILE

Rug seller finds his wares by blanketing rural India

Shashi Sharma shows off a Moslem prayer rug, one of the $8 million worth of oriental coverings that Indo-Persian Rug Company will sell in Canada this year.

Toronto Star

When the road ends you get out of the car and walk, or try to hitch a ride on a bullock cart.

That's how Shashi Sharma approaches the rug business.

And it's often the way he has to approach hundreds of rural villages in north-central India to meet master rug weavers in their homes.

Sharma's approach — bypassing the luxury hotels to head into the field — has helped him become one of North America's largest independent retailers of oriental rugs.

His life savings amounted to $16 000 when he started the Indo-Persian Rug Company five years ago on Sheppard Avenue East in Scarborough, Ontario, but that is not why he avoided the five-star hotels in Delhi.

He was eliminating the layers of middlemen bumping up the prices on hand-knotted rugs as they moved a couple of hundred kilometres from the weavers in the countryside to the North American purchase agents waiting back in the comfortable hotels.

"The purchasing agents from the department stores have big buying budgets and they don't like roaming the countryside where there's no air-conditioning, no room service, sometimes no roads, and you can't drink the water," said Sharma.

"So they have the dealers come to them and pay much higher prices."

Sharma, 50, who grew up in a small village in the rug-weaving belt of India, expects to sell $8 million in rugs this year. But on his trips back to India every two months, he and his sons still avoid the nice hotels of Delhi.

"When we go to the home of the master weavers to meet their families and eat meals with them, we not only get a much better price, but we also get control of the quality of the wool and the workmanship," said Sharma.

Plus, Sharma has been buying wool for the weavers, which helps out the weaver but also gives him control of materials and colours.

Sharma never learned to weave. He earned a master's degree in economics from the University of Allahabad and went to work for one of India's largest import-export firms.

He was the company's head man in Kuwait for 10 years but said he didn't want to raise his family there.

Sharma, his wife, Manju, and their three young sons emigrated to Canada in 1973 and he went to work as a salesman in the downtown Hudson Bay store, selling, among other things, oriental rugs.

Half of the family's savings were used to open a 418 square metre store in Scarborough and to send Sharma on his first buying trip to India.

He was able to buy $90 000 worth of rugs in the villages totally on credit and his family's good name.

"I was able to buy rugs on credit because of my family, but if I didn't pay for them in 30 days I would disgrace my family and I wouldn't be able to go back into the villages to buy again," he said.

About 65 per cent of the rugs in his store come from Uttar Pradesh province of India, but Sharma and his sons also buy from weavers in Iran, Pakistan, Afghanistan, and Kashmir.

There are more than 2000 villages throughout the rug-weaving belt of India, and Sharma has hired hundreds of master weavers in these villages to create rugs only for his store.

"It takes a year for a family to weave a large rug, and if they are busy working for me they won't be producing for somebody else," he said.

EXPLORING • THE INDO-PERSIAN RUG COMPANY

1. Is Sharma motivated by profit? How can you tell?
2. How does Sharma select his products?
3. What is unique about his method of purchasing?
4. Did Sharma have a clear vision of what he wanted to accomplish when he set out? How can you tell?
5. Sharma's method of organizing his business resulted in success. Explain how each of the following contributed to his success:
   a) bypassing the luxury hotels
   b) going directly to the homes of his suppliers
   c) buying and supplying wool for his weavers
   d) using his family's good name
6. What action did Sharma take to gain a competitive edge over other importers? How did he plan to keep it?
7. Who does Sharma have working for him and advising him?

The Operations Spoke of the Venture Creation Wheel

The operations spoke of the Venture Creation Wheel encompasses the **6 P's of entrepreneurship**: profit, price, production, people and productivity, and promotion. In Chapter 7, you learned about the four P's of the marketing mix. In this chapter, you will see how the marketing mix is intertwined with the 6 P's of entrepreneurship. Together, the 6 P's form a strategy to implement your venture plan. They help entrepreneurs articulate their visions and develop a process to help them make their visions a reality.

A specific plan to implement the 6 P's shows investors that the entrepreneur understands how to start the venture and how to ensure that the product or service reaches the target market.

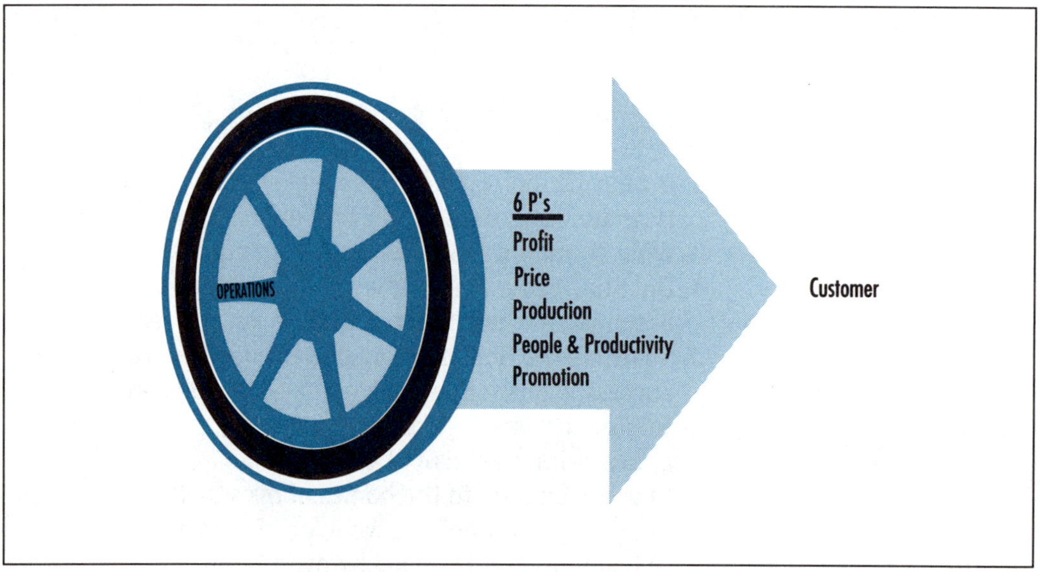

Figure 9.1 The Operations Spoke of the Venture Creation Wheel incorporates the 6 P's of entrepreneurship.

Entrepreneurs need to know the answers to many questions before determining the course of action to take. The Research Assistance Grid, introduced in Chapter 6, can help formulate a course of action for each of the six P's of entrepreneurship. Table 9.1 asks the questions that entrepreneurs must answer before determining the price of their product or service.

Table 9.1 Research Assistance Grid for Price

What? WHAT is the cost of the raw materials? WHAT are the costs of labour, production, and distribution? WHAT is the competition charging for similar products or services? WHAT is the best price to charge for growth and profit?	*Why?* WHY should I offer my product or service at this price? WHY will others buy my good or service? WHY will my venture be unique and have something special for the price? WHY is it necessary to price my product or service at this amount?
Where? WHERE will I find raw materials at competitive prices? WHERE will I find the equipment that is needed? WHERE will I find the right people to work with? WHERE will I find supplies at competitive prices?	*When?* WHEN is the demand greatest for my good or service? WHEN should I order the inventory I need? WHEN should I raise or lower my selling price?
Who? WHO will be willing to pay this price for my product or service? WHO will be able to pay this price? WHO will I get to do the things I cannot do at a fair price?	*How?* HOW will I provide my good or service at the least cost? HOW strong is the competition now and in the future? HOW will the competition react to a new competitor?

YOUR TURN

1. In small groups, complete a Research Assistance Grid for two of the other 6 P's of entrepreneurship: profit, production, people and productivity, or promotion.

Profit

Profit is the first "P" of entrepreneurship and the major goal of the entrepreneur. It is the incentive for mobilizing resources, taking risks, and starting ventures. Without profit as a goal, few entrepreneurs, except perhaps those involved in not-for-profit social or community service ventures, would produce goods and services to satisfy consumer wants and needs. Even not-for-profit organizations, though, must be concerned with covering their expenses; otherwise they would be unable to stay in business.

To earn profits, entrepreneurs must produce goods and services efficiently, without wasting **economic resources**, that is, land, labour, and capital. Efficient use of resources lowers production costs. Consumers then benefit by paying lower prices. Society benefits by having a greater number of economic resources available to produce other goods and services.

"Nothing contributes so much to the prosperity and happiness of a country as high profits."
David Ricardo

For many entrepreneurs, profit is like a scorecard for measuring success. If the venture is meeting the needs and wants of the target market, the scorecard will reflect a high score. If the score is low, there may have been a change in the perception of the market. It may be time to review the way the goods and services are produced, pricing policy, or promotion materials needed. Profits indicate a demand for the products or services and encourage entrepreneurs to continue.

Name	Date	Win	Lose
		✔	
		✔	
			✔
		✔	
		✔	
		✔	
			✔
			✔
		✔	
		✔	

Figure 9.2 To make a healthy profit, an entrepreneur should try and ensure as many wins as possible.

The amount of profit is dependent on the price of the good or service, the quantity that is sold, and the costs of producing it.

$$\text{Profits} = \text{Price} \times \text{Quantity} - \text{Costs}$$

If, for example, it costs a toy manufacturer $45.50 to produce and sell 10 rubber duckies at $6.00 each, the manufacturer's profit would be: $6.00 x 10 – $45.50 = $14.50.

The quantity sold is influenced by the demand for the product or service and the number of customers who are willing and able to pay the price for it. Decisions made by both the entrepreneur and competitors, as well as the level of risk assumed, will influence the level of profits.

YOUR TURN

2. Analyze the following table. Which entrepreneur made the greatest profit?

Entrepreneur	*Price*	*Quantity*	*Costs*	*Profit*
Mohan	$3	2000	$ 500	
Samantha	$2	4000	$1000	
Jeanne	$2	3000	$ 750	

3. Ms. Raphael and Mr. Tsao are both in the landscaping business. They design, plant, and market gardens. Their philosophies on how to run a business differ, and this is reflected in the following figures.

Item	*Ms. Raphael*	*Mr. Tsao*
Labour Costs	$160 000	$ 80 000
Costs of Materials	$ 90 000	$ 50 000
Utilities	$ 10 000	$ 10 000
Advertising	$ 40 000	$ 20 000
Rent	$ 60 000	$ 40 000
Income (PxQ)	$400 000	$240 000

a) Which entrepreneur will make the greater profit?

b) Comment on the difference between how they operate their businesses.

Price

The price a venture receives for its goods and services pays for production and distribution costs.

Sometimes selling a large quantity will be the most profitable, but not always.

Total profit equals **total revenue** minus **total cost**. Total revenue is determined by multiplying the price of each unit by the quantity sold of that unit. Total cost is determined by adding together **fixed costs** and **variable costs**. What would happen to the quantity sold if the price went up? The answer to this question depends on consumer behaviour. If consumers perceive the increase in price as an indication of improved quality or popularity, the demand will probably remain steady or increase, thus yielding a higher profit. If, however, the price increase makes the unit price higher than consumers are willing and able to pay, the quantity sold will drop and so will the profit.

The best price to charge is the one that allows you to earn the maximum profit, not to sell the most.

Table 9.2 Price and Quantity Sold and Their Effect on Profit

Price per Unit	*Quantity Sold*	*Total Costs*	*Total Revenues*	*Total Profits*
$50	100	$2000	$5000	$3000
$40	120	$3000	$4800	$1800
$30	150	$5000	$4500	$ (500)

Entrepreneurs can use market research to help them determine how much will sell at each price level. Table 9.2 demonstrates that as price increases, the number of consumers willing and able to buy a particular product decreases. It also reveals that even with increased price and decreased demand, total revenues have increased, total costs have decreased, and total profit is higher.

If the price is increased, the demand for the product or service may drop a little. This may not hurt the venture at all, as shown in Table 9.2. However, the demand may also disappear completely.

Knowing what the customer is willing and able to pay is an essential ingredient in determining price.

What does the customer perceive the value of the good or service to be? Are there any substitute products? What price is the competition asking?

Cabbage Patch Dolls are a good example of a product where the perceived value was higher than the actual value of the doll. The demand was so great that the doll was constantly in short supply. This pushed the price up further. There were no substitutes for the product.

It is interesting to note that small ventures generally tend to be **price takers**. In other words, they follow the existing price in the market. When competition exists, both prices and profits for any ventures involved are lowered. Sometimes, the entrepreneur can regain some control over price by differentiating his or her product or service from the competition and offering something really unique.

Venture PROFILE

An Admission at the British Museum?

The Victoria and Albert Museum

In the mid-1970s, the British Parliament passed an act requiring its top museums to charge admission for the first time in history. This created a storm of protest. The proponents of the admission price supplied the following arguments: (1) the government could no longer afford all of the annual cost of $44 million to maintain the museums; (2) visitors from abroad were getting something free by not being charged; (3) visitors would better appreciate the institutions if they were charged; (4) museum directors would have the incentive to put on better shows and be more responsive; (5) the money could be used to finance extensions and better collections; and (6) museums on the continent and in North America charged admission fees.

Those who opposed the admission price countered with the following arguments: (1) the charge would discourage attendance by slum children, students, and the elderly; (2) the cost of collecting the money — more attendants, gates at the entrance, more paperwork — would reduce much of the benefit; and (3) museums should not be forced into the entertainment business to please the public but should concentrate on presenting serious exhibits. Despite these counter-arguments, the act was passed and the British museums began to consider the best form of charging admission. They examined three major pricing approaches:

1. Museums could charge daily admission except for one day of the week. A free day would allow the poor or young to visit the museum. The admission charge could be varied for different visitors, being lower (or waived) for children and students, people over 65, disabled people, and veterans.
2. Museums could encourage donations from visitors rather than charge a fixed price. At the Metropolitan Museum in New York, people are encouraged to contribute $4.00, or anything they can. The voluntary nature of the donation allows the poor and young to enter without cost if they choose.
3. The museums could charge a small admission fee and also sponsor a membership plan which provides members with special benefits, such as a monthly magazine, an annual report, invitation to exhibit openings, a discount at the gift shop, and a waiver of admission charges. The museum would establish different levels of membership and membership privilege, with dues going from $15 (regular membership) to $100 (special membership) to $500 life membership.

The various museums considered these and other alternatives, and soon realized that the key issue was what objectives they were seeking to accomplish through the price mechanism.

EXPLORING • MUSEUM ADMISSION CHARGE

1. Why did the British government pass the act requiring its top museums to charge admission?
2. What effect do you think an admission charge will have on visitors?
3. What are the benefits and drawbacks of each of the pricing approaches being considered?
4. What factors should each museum consider when deciding on a price?
5. Would these factors be different for a privately owned movie theatre?

Pricing Strategies

Costs, the target market, competition, and demand are all important factors in determining which **pricing strategy** to use. The pricing strategy selected has to give your product a competitive edge while yielding enough profit to maintain its share of the market after the venture is launched.

Entrepreneurs can choose from the following pricing strategies:

Cost-plus Pricing

In **cost-plus pricing**, costs are determined for each unit produced. A **markup** is added on to yield a profit. In the example given in Table 9.3, the most profitable point of production is 266 units. The cost per unit is \$2.03 [(\$120 + \$420) ÷ 266]. (The selling price per unit is \$3.00.) The markup on cost price is 97 cents or 48 per cent.

Table 9.3 Maximizing Profit

Number of Personnel	Units Produced and Sold	Fixed Costs	Variable Costs	Total Revenue (P*x Q)	Total Profit or Loss
0	0	\$120	\$ 0	\$ 0	(\$120)
1	4	\$120	\$ 60	\$ 12	(\$168)
2	28	\$120	\$120	\$ 84	(\$156)
3	72	\$120	\$180	\$216	(\$ 84)
4	128	\$120	\$240	\$384	\$ 24
5	190	\$120	\$300	\$570	\$150
6	240	\$120	\$360	\$720	\$240
7	266	\$120	\$420	\$798	\$258
8	280	\$120	\$480	\$840	\$240
9	288	\$120	\$540	\$864	\$204
10	290	\$120	\$600	\$870	\$150

* Price = \$3.00 per unit

$$\text{Markup} = \text{Selling Price} - \text{Cost Price}$$

$$\text{Markup Percentage} = \frac{\text{Selling Price} - \text{Cost Price}}{\text{Cost}} \times 100$$

AGENTS OF CHANGE

Robert Bateman, a well-known wildlife painter, retains the instincts of a naturalist and a teacher, and uses his popularity as a wildlife painter to support worthy causes and broaden public awareness of the human threat to the environment. Bateman builds his fame as an artist into a platform for teaching environmental responsibility.

Follow the Competition Pricing

In **follow the competition pricing,** an entrepreneur can price his or her product or service at the same level or slightly lower than the venture's major competition. This can be effective for increasing market share; however, new ventures often have costs that are higher than existing businesses. The price the competition is charging may not cover the costs incurred in a new venture. It is wise to continually check to ensure costs are adequately covered by the price.

Penetration Pricing

In **penetration pricing**, new ventures can price their products or services significantly lower than the competition in the hope of taking away a large part of the competition's market share. The premise is that if you sell large amounts at low prices, you will gain customers and profits. Table 9.3 illustrates that producing more can sometimes lower profits, indicating that a penetration pricing policy should be used only after careful thought and with continuous monitoring. Your competition may respond by lowering its price, in which case everyone may end up with reduced profits.

Skimming

Using the strategy of **skimming**, new products or services can enter the marketplace at a high price because there is no competition. As competition increases, the prices have to be decreased to maintain market share. The prices of fax machines have, for example, been lowered as competition increased.

Psychological Pricing

Some entrepreneurs price their products or services at odd number amounts. This is referred to as **psychological pricing**. It leads the customer to believe the item is less expensive than it actually is. Gasoline is usually priced at an odd amount, for example, 54.9 cents per litre. Most people would think of the price as being 54 cents per litre, not 55 cents. Consumers think they are getting a bargain.

Figure 9.3 Psychological pricing leads the customer to believe the item being purchased is less expensive than it is.

Loss-Leader Pricing

In **loss-leader pricing**, selected products or services are sold at cost or less than cost to attract customers. It is hoped that, once there, customers will buy other products or services to compensate the venture for loss of profits. Many carpet-cleaning businesses, for example, advertise carpet cleaning of three rooms for a low price. Once the cleaners arrive at the customer's home, they offer scotchguarding, deodorizer, and other cleaning services at full price.

Figure 9.4 Loss leaders attract customers.

The pricing strategy selected will depend on the product or service, consumer behaviour, and the objectives of the entrepreneur. It must be carefully thought out before you embark on your venture. It should reflect to potential investors that you have thoroughly considered such factors as quality and costs of your product or service, your target market, the demand, and the competition.

YOUR TURN

4. Selenia's Skateboard Factory produces and sells skateboards at a price of $22 each. Selenia's fixed and variable costs are indicated in Table 9.4

Table 9.4 Selenia's Skateboard Factory

Number of Skateboards Produced and Sold in 1 Day	*Fixed Costs*	*Variable Costs*	*Total Revenues (P* x Q)*	*Total Profit or Loss*
0	$200	$ 0		
10	$200	$ 170		
20	$200	$ 320		
30	$200	$ 440		
40	$200	$ 580		
50	$200	$ 800		
60	$200	$1100		

* Price per skateboard = $22.00

a) Calculate the Total Revenues and Total Profit or Loss columns of the table. Enter the amounts in your notebook.

b) What is the most profitable number of skateboards to produce? Why?

Production

Production is the mobilization of resources to yield a product or service that consumers want or need. The entrepreneur has to organize his or her resources: employees, materials, and equipment. An entrepreneur's resources are often limited, so they must be used efficiently.

Resources are used best when they are organized in a way which reduces the cost per unit produced to a minimum.

AGENTS OF CHANGE

Pierre Burton is one of Canada's best-known journalists. He works in every media, appearing regularly on television, radio, and on the printed page. His books focus on Canada and remind us of our special Canadian heritage. Burton helped Canadians gain pride in their own history.

Entrepreneurs have to streamline their operations to produce the best quality and sufficient quantity with the resources available to them.

Every business has fixed costs, such as mortgage payments or rent, the cost of equipment, tools or vehicles. Fixed costs are the same amount every month, regardless of how much the venture produces or sells. Businesses also incur variable costs: labour, raw materials, inventory, electricity and gas. Variable costs differ every month, depending on the demand for, and output of, the product or service. The greater the demand, the higher the variable costs. More raw materials and labour will be required to meet increasing demands.

When writing the operations strategy section of a venture plan, the entrepreneur should describe in some detail the production facility required and the personnel needed to operate the facility. Most ventures are designed with a specific number of personnel in mind. This is the optimum number to generate maximum use of the facility. If the facility is operating at full capacity in response to demand for the good or service and more personnel are hired, **productivity** may be lowered.

Productivity is typically measured in terms of output per worker employed. For example, if five workers can produce 100 000 bushels of wheat, their productivity would be 100 000 ÷ 5, or 20 000 bushels. If demand for wheat increased and the wheat farmer could sell more wheat if he or she produced it, one more worker is hired. The additional worker produces 8000 bushels of wheat. What has happened to productivity? It is now 108 000 ÷ 6 workers or 18 000 bushels per worker, not 20 000.

Decreasing productivity increases the cost of production which will decrease profits.

Figure 9.5 Productivity is measured in terms of output per worker employed.

Motivating employees to increase their productivity is one of the "P's" of entrepreneurship. We will examine this under People and Productivity.

With limited space and equipment, adding personnel will increase variable costs without sufficiently increasing the number of units being produced to cover the increase in variable costs. It will no longer be more profitable to produce more units.

In the example given in Table 9.3 (page 267), producing and selling 266 units yields the highest profit. If fewer than 266 units are produced and sold, the fixed and variable costs take up a large part of revenue. If the entrepreneur decides to hire more personnel and sell more units, the profit begins to decrease. Adding more personnel increases variable costs more than it increases profits. This causes total profits to decline, even though more units are being produced and sold.

The Ingredients of Effective Production

Employees should have up-to-date technological equipment. To compete effectively in the global market, the decision on what equipment to purchase or lease must be made carefully.

Because the cost of most tools and equipment is high, once the purchase is made, it is difficult to change. It is a fixed cost. The right equipment can improve the quality of the product or service, minimize maintenance and time off for repairs, and be linked to other equipment to extend its use.

The quality of the tools and equipment purchased by a business is of equal importance as the quality of the goods and services the business produces.

AGENTS OF CHANGE

Ray Bateman, Jr. is a 15-year-old computer hacker. He uses his computer to do his homework, but after school he works with Dr. Glenn Tisman on cancer research. Together, they discovered a drug that provides effective chemotherapy on certain kinds of tumours.

Raw materials should be purchased on the basis of cost, availability, and quality. A steady supply of materials is required to maximize the use of equipment and to ensure that the employees remain productive. If materials are stored for a long period of time with employees idle, profits will be reduced. If there is an insufficient amount of materials, production will slow down resulting in customers turning somewhere else to purchase the product. This will also lower profits. The quality of the materials should be compatible with the cost. The quality of the materials will be reflected in the finished product or service.

Work should be scheduled to co-ordinate the supply of materials and the availability of equipment and employees. This will lower production costs and increase efficiency. Consumers will benefit by paying lower prices.

Ultimately, when planning production, the foremost question is: How can it be done best? How can resources be organized and used to produce a good or service of the desired quality at the lowest possible cost? How can resources be mixed together in the most efficient way?

If a greater amount of labour than equipment (capital) is used in production, the method of production is said to be **labour intensive**. If labour can be replaced by machinery in a cost-efficient way resulting in more units produced, this is a **capital intensive** method of production. Because entrepreneurs are often searching for a market niche, which may be quite small, their ventures are often small scale and more labour intensive. However, if research shows that the entrepreneur can capture a large market, investment in capital equipment is warranted.

Table 9.5 Labour and Capital Needed for Output

	Labour-Intensive Method				*Capital-Intensive Method*			
Total Output	*Units of Capital Used*	*Number of Workers Employed*	*Total Costs*	*Efficiency (Cost per unit produced)*	*Units of Capital Used*	*Number of Workers Employed*	*Total Costs*	*Efficiency (Cost per unit produced)*
1000	1	10	?	?	10	5	?	?
5000	2	100	?	?	10	30	?	?
10 000	3	250	?	?	10	50	?	?

YOUR TURN

5. Table 9.5 shows how many units of labour and capital must be used to produce a certain amount of output. The data gives you two choices. You may produce using either a labour-intensive or a capital-intensive method of production. Calculate the total costs of production and the efficiency (cost per unit produced) for each. Assume that the cost of each unit of capital used is $10 000 and the cost of each worker is $1000. Enter the results in your notebook in a table like the one shown here. When you have completed the table, answer the following questions.
   a) Would the labour-intensive or the capital-intensive method of production be more efficient if you wanted to produce:
      i) 1000 units?
      ii) 5000 units?
      iii) 10 000 units?
   b) If a labour-intensive method of production is used, what happens to efficiency as additional workers are employed? Why does this happen?
   c) If a capital-intensive method of production is used, what happens to efficiency as more is produced? Why does this happen?
   d) When does it seem to you that a capital-intensive method of production is more efficient?

e) Assume that there is a demand for 10 000 units of an item and that ten small businesses each produce 1000 units in a labour-intensive way, as shown in the table. If a new company built a factory that produced 10 000 units using a capital-intensive method of production, what would likely happen to:
   i) the market price of the product?
   ii) the profits of the ten labour-intensive businesses and the one capital-intensive business?

6. Visit a local entrepreneur and ask to see the production facility of his or her business. Sketch the layout of the facility, marking where the equipment is, where the employees are, where the raw materials are received and stored, and where the finished goods are stored. Comment on the efficiency of this plan. Try to suggest possible ways to improve the organization of resources.
7. Complete a Research Assistance Grid to help an entrepreneur determine his or her production needs.

People and Productivity

Did you know that Walt Disney was fired from a job working on a newspaper because he had no good ideas?

In Chapter 7, you learned that entrepreneurs need to assess their own skills and expertise in order to determine what outside help they should consult before launching a venture. While the experience and knowledge of an external advisory team is invaluable to any entrepreneur, it is the employees the entrepreneur hires who conduct the day-to-day business and are crucial to the venture's day-to-day success.

Employees are hired by the entrepreneur on a full- or part-time basis. Employees who have skills that complement those of the entrepreneur should be chosen. Employees should also be selected for their commitment to the venture. It is important for an entrepreneur to involve his or her employees in the problem solving and decision making of the venture if they demonstrate this commitment and enthusiasm for the venture.

Good employees should be considered the most valuable asset if the new venture is going to succeed.

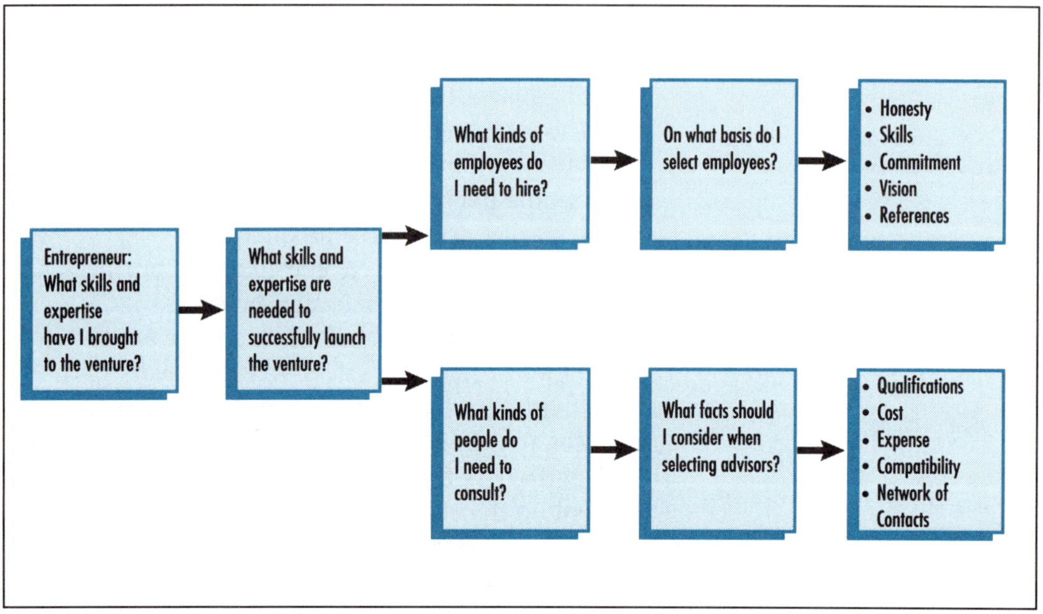

Figure 9.6 Employees are a crucial part of the venture team.

Co-operation and collaboration on the job are important. If the team is to be effective, employees must trust each other, communicate openly, and enjoy their working environment.

"The working team is like four horses pulling a carriage, they must not only pull, but all in the same direction."
Raymond Kao

Figure 9.7 Working together as a team builds trust and co-operation.

In Chapter 4, you learned about creativity and the importance of developing creative thinking skills. Tapping the creativity in employees can be a major benefit to your venture. Creative people generally see problems as opportunities. Giving creative employees the time, space, and support to explore, develop, question, and think will yield better products or services, satisfied customers, and happy, challenged, committed employees. Employees who can express their ideas confidently in the workplace are an invaluable asset.

It is important to have a good "fit" between the entrepreneur and his or her employees.

Employees' Fringe Benefits

Employees also add costs to the venture. Salaries and wages are negotiated between the entrepreneur and the employee. The availability of employees, the specifications of the job, and the **fringe benefits** will all contribute to the amount paid in wage or salary. Federal and provincial governments are responsible for legislating a minimum wage for all employees in Canada.

It is important for employees to recognize that it pays to work harder and that this translates into opportunities for growth and advancement. Salary increases should be tied to improved performance, not just to seniority and inflation. If each employee receives a raise every year and productivity does not improve, costs will increase, efficiency will decline, and the venture will not survive.

"Second wave industries see factories and machines as assets and their employees as expenses. Third wave industries see their employees as assets and factories and machines as expenses."
Alvin Toffler commenting on changing perception in The Third Wave.

In addition to salary and wages, most employees receive fringe benefits. The federal and provincial governments legislate employee and employer contributions to the **Canada Pension Plan**, **Unemployment Insurance,** and **Workers' Compensation.** Tables and instructions on how to calculate and remit these contributions are available from your local Revenue Canada office. In addition to these financial contributions, employees must receive time off for statutory holidays, vacation time, and maternity leave.

HOSPITAL

Should you incur hospital expenses for room and board and other necessary services and supplies above those paid by your provincial government hospital plan, your health insurance plan will pay the reasonable and customary charges incurred, provided the confinement is medically necessary and is not for chronic or custodial care.

- For regular hospital room and board, the insurance company pays up to the usual daily charge of the hospital concerned for semi-private care.
- The plan will also pay for charges for confinement in an Intensive Care Unit.
- If you or one of your dependents are confined in a convalescent hospital, the insurance company will pay up to the usual daily charge of the hospital concerned for semi-private convalescent care, provided the confinement
  - (1) is recommended by your physician, and
  - (2) follows a 3-day confinement in a hospital as a registered bed-patient and is for the same condition.
- If you or one of your dependents require treatment as an out-patient, the insurance company will pay the actual charges incurred for services and supplies received for such treatment.
- Hospital confinement for pregnancy is covered

Please Note: No benefits will be payable for a hospital confinement which began before your insurance became effective.

Out-of-Province Expenses

If an expense would have been covered if incurred inside the person's province of residence, such expense will also be covered if incurred outside the province of residence but only:

(1) for an emergency or unexpected sudden illness if the insured person is temporarily out-of-province for business, vacation or furthering education, or

(2) if the required medical treatment is not readily available in the province of residence and the person is forced to seek such treatment elsewhere.

If the medical treatment is readily available elsewhere in Canada, but you seek treatment outside Canada, benefits will be limited to the reasonable and customary charges of the nearest Canadian medical centre equipped to provide the necessary treatment. It is suggested you submit a Treatment Plan; in this way you will know the amount of your coverage before you incur the expense.

Continuation of Hospital Benefits

If you are totally disabled when your Hospital Insurance terminates, and you have expenses for that illness which would have been paid had your coverage continued, your benefit payments will continue until the earliest of the following:

- the date your disability ceases,
- the date which is 90 days after the group policy terminates,
- the date on which you have received benefits for a period equal in length to the period for which you were insured,
- the end of the calendar year next following the calendar year in which your insurance terminates.

Table 9.6 Excerpt from a Handbook on Employee Benefits

In addition to the legislated benefits, many businesses may offer such fringe benefits as dental plans, additional paid vacation, pension plans, life insurance, disability insurance, **profit sharing**, bonuses, educational plans, and stock ownership. The demand for skilled employees in the marketplace and the size of the venture will determine how many and which benefits the entrepreneur should offer his or her employees. If there is a high demand for the employee, the entrepreneur might want to offer a larger compensation package to attract and keep that employee.

Basic compensation packages must be equal to or close to those of the competition.

Fringe benefits may also be used to help increase employee productivity. As performance improves, employees can receive additional benefits. This is an incentive for employees. For a new venture, profit sharing is probably the best fringe benefit to offer. The entrepreneur pays a percentage of the profit to employees if the financial goals of the venture are met or exceeded. Employees will want to work together co-operatively to achieve this common goal.

Benefits such as dental plans, life insurance, and disability insurance are very costly. If a venture has only a few employees, the costs of including these benefits in a compensation package is often too high.

Although compensation may be a major contributor to the level of employee motivation and productivity, a sense of belonging, involvement in decision making and problem solving, and positive communication between the entrepreneur and employees also contribute to improved productivity.

Improved productivity ultimately yields an improved standard of living. Resources are used more efficiently, costs to consumers are kept down, and profits are increased. Selecting, training, motivating, and encouraging employees to improve productivity are important tasks for the entrepreneur.

YOUR TURN

8. Telephone your local Canada Employment Centre and discover the current minimum wage.
9. Contact three entrepreneurs in your community. Ask each of them the following questions:
   How many employees do you have? What fringe benefits do you offer employees? How do you involve your employees in the problem-solving process? How do you motivate your employees to improve productivity? What is your cost of providing fringe benefits per employee?
10. Using the Research Assistance Grid, prepare ten questions an entrepreneur could use when interviewing a prospective employee.

Promotion

Promotion is the vehicle through which entrepreneurs tell the world about their products or services. Promotion is a key element in the success of any new venture. The target market has to know that a product or service is available before consumers can make the decision to buy.

With the results of their market research, entrepreneurs can use promotion to bring their product or service to the attention of their target market. Promotional activities include **advertising**, **personal selling**, **publicity,** and **sales promotion.**

All the components of promotion involve communication. Communication is the key to effective promotion. Entrepreneurs communicate with their target markets to inform them of the product or service, to persuade the target market to try the product or service, and to remind their customers that their venture is around and thriving.

"If the circus is coming to town and you paint a sign saying, "Circus coming to town", that's Advertising. If you put the sign on the back of an elephant and walk him or her into town, that's Promotion. If the elephant walks through the mayor's flowerbed, that's Publicity."
Margaret Norman

Venture PROFILE

Aspen Cleaners sell good clean fun

By Nathan Rudyk, *Small Business Magazine*

Marketing experts say value sells services and personal contact creates value. And if you don't believe the experts, get your pants pressed at Aspen Cleaners.

In the mornings, she greets her drive-through customers with *The Globe and Mail*; in the afternoons, she serves popcorn, and at Christmas, she dresses up as an elf to give away candy canes. Who is she?

Sarah Ferris, 27, is the owner/manager of Aspen Cleaners Ltd., a dry-cleaning business in Toronto's chic Yorkville shopping district. She is confident that her company will report sales of $750 000 in its first year. The drive-through and sundries are free. As is membership in the Team Aspen Customer Club, the smiles and hellos from Ferris and her friendly staff, and a sign that reads "Caution, Lions. Stay in Car". The dry-cleaning is expensive, 10-15 per cent more than average Toronto prices, but customers don't seem to notice. They're too busy being pampered and having fun.

According to marketing consultants, the reason many service companies don't survive is that they really don't understand what they're selling — an intangible called value. "Dry-cleaners clean and press your clothes, but what they really do is make you look and feel better," says Jean Booth, President of Booth Associates in Toronto. Booth says the key to selling value is people: "It's the personal transaction that will make or break the sale."

Carol Vipperman, co author of *Marketing Your Service*, published by Self-Counsel Press, goes further: "It doesn't matter what benefits you promise or what your company's reputation is, if you don't build an emotional bond with the client, there's no incentive for that client to come back."

Ferris understood this when she started Aspen Cleaners. "I didn't like traditional dry-cleaners. Usually you have to go to some out-of-the-way shopping mall, find a parking spot, drag your clothes across the parking lot, and drop them off at an ugly store. It's inconvenient, impersonal, and boring."

Ferris wanted a service that would be convenient, deliver high quality and, above all, be friendly. Along with a silent partner who had dry-cleaning experience and the wherewithal to finance Aspen's $1 million in startup costs, she rethought the dry-cleaning business.

The drive-through, where customers drive in off the street and wait for a sprinting Aspen attendant to exchange the laundry for the morning news, is the major convenience feature. The transaction takes about a minute, and customers with pre-authorized credit can make the drop in about 30 seconds. Hours are geared to convenience as well. After a brief flirtation with 24-hour service, Aspen now stays open 6:30 a.m. to 11 p.m. Monday to Thursday, and from 6:30 a.m. to 8 p.m. on Friday and Saturday.

Quality is orchestrated by a production manager with 20 years of experience who oversees $200 000 worth of dry-cleaning equipment in a 446 m^2 plant.

The friendliness is infectious, and Ferris insists her 18 full-time and eight part-time staff regularly greet customers. "The personal contact keeps our customers very loyal," says Ferris.

The personal contact also keeps the employees loyal. Ferris starts them at typical wages for service businesses. But she keeps them motivated with monthly market-research assignments on nearly 500 local competitors and "event-planning" meetings. At these meetings, the staff decide on seasonal promotions they think would entertain customers. At Hallowe'en, for example, everyone dons costumes and the customers get to vote on the best one. Each promotion is different, in keeping with Ferris's fight against boredom.

This fight is important to a service's marketing success. "You have to use more than one type of promotion," says Vipperman, "because different stimuli prompt different clients to use any service. You just have to find out which combination of techniques works best."

But, says Booth, remember that your best promotion value comes from your existing customer base: "Traditionally, 90 per cent of marketing dollars are devoted to securing new business when 70 per cent of revenues come from past customers." For this reason, Booth recommends steering the dollars back to their source by spending them on after-sale service, bonuses for frequent customers, or cash discounts. She also recommends polling clients, either verbally or through a small questionnaire, on a regular basis to see if you can improve the value of your service. "For this you need to maintain a good customer list."

Ferris practises many of the consultant's suggestions. Virtually all of her promotion is done at her Yorkville location. She regularly gives out Aspen Bucks, her version of Canadian Tire Money, and frequent customers can join Team Aspen. Membership privileges include an official Team Aspen laundry bag emblazoned with the customer's name and a personal file that lists preferences — no crease on jeans, for example.

As for customer suggestions, Ferris says they're creating traffic jams at the drive-through. "Our customers love to stop their cars and chat with us about what they'd like to see for the Grey Cup promotion or how much salt on the popcorn. It's wonderful, but it forced us to put up the lions sign. I'm changing it to sharks!"

EXPLORING • ASPEN CLEANERS

1. What did Ferris do to promote her dry-cleaning service?
2. If her service was a product, do you think she would have done things differently?
3. In what ways is Aspen Cleaners different from other dry-cleaners?
4. What do the experts say about promotion?
5. Did Ferris understand the true value of promotion? How could you tell?
6. What evidence is there that Ferris made her decisions based on the research grid: Who, What, Where, When, Why, and How?

Advertising

"Advertising isn't a science. It's persuasion. And persuasion is an art."
Bill Bernbach

Advertising is a message paid for by the venture and directed toward the target market. Advertising helps customers move through the **AIDA formula** — Attention, Interest, Desire, Action. Advertising should attract the attention of the cus-

AGENTS OF CHANGE

In 1953, when Queen Elizabeth II was crowned, people all over England watched the ceremony on a new invention called "television". Today, TV programs, telephone calls, news releases, and weather photographs are sent world wide via satellite. World-wide communication systems have moved us closer to the "global village".

tomer, create an interest in the product or service, stimulate a desire to have the product or service, and thrust the customer into acting — buying the product or service.

Advertising can be conveyed through a variety of media: newspapers, magazines, radio, TV, direct mail, transit, directories, or outdoor billboards. The medium selected will depend on the following factors:

- its reach
- the number of people who will see the advertising
- the frequency and scheduling of the advertising
- the trading area to be covered
- the budget
- the impact the entrepreneur is seeking
- the suitability of the medium to the product or service

If the product is skateboards, for example, the most suitable media would be television, magazines, and transit advertising. This is because the target market for skateboards is young people aged 10-19. This age group watches television, reads magazines, and travels on public transit. The television show or magazine selected must be one that appeals to this age group — *DeGrassi High* for a television show and *Teen* for a suitable magazine.

The cost of the medium will be a budget consideration. Prime-time television advertising is very expensive because of the large viewing audience. An advertisement aired on a morning television show costs much less.

If a newspaper is chosen as the most suitable medium, the section, page, and size of the advertisement will all need to be considered in the cost.

The cost of media is determined by the audience, the frequency, and the size of the advertisement.

Rate cards are printed by each of the media listing the cost of advertising.

Personal Selling

Selling is what keeps the venture alive and well. A good salesperson makes the customer feel as if he or she is the most important person around. A salesperson interprets the features of a product or service by describing the benefits and advantages to the customer. Thorough product knowledge is necessary for a salesperson to answer questions customers might have. This sound knowledge of product features and benefits will add to the reputation of the venture and **word-of-mouth** will draw more customers to the business.

In a sense, every employee is a salesperson. Attitude toward the venture and the product or service are easily picked up and conveyed to potential customers. Positive attitudes attract customers while negative ones will drive them away.

Publicity

Publicity is an unpaid message delivered by the media to the target market. The media decide whether a product or service is newsworthy. The reporter gives a factual account of the product or service without trying to persuade customers to buy.

Jocelyne Casavant got some free publicity for her business when the following article appeared in the *Toronto Star*.

Venture PROFILE

She nails down problems

By Dale Anne Freed, *Toronto Star*

The nail-care business is a growth industry, and entrepreneur Jocelyne Casavant is the proof.

Three years ago, the energetic former Mary Kay director began to market her own line of nail products and opened two esthetics centres and schools — first in her native Quebec, on Montreal's St. Denis Street and, more

Hitting the nail on the the head: Jocelyne Casavant's patterned nail wrappings are currently available in Europe.

recently, on Toronto's Avenue Road. In her first full year of operation, she did $500 000 worth of sales and made $60 000 in profit.

Casavant's speciality is the treatment of problem nails. Broken, split, or pitted nails — sometimes due to exposure from toxic products — can be helped or at least disguised.

Her most recent innovation — one that could make her a name in Europe — is a patterned or plain coloured silk wrap called French batik. With a patent pending, the new wrap has been snapped up and marketed in Europe and distributed to 1200 outlets of the large French cosmetics company, Yves Rocher.

"There's nothing new about nail wraps, ancient Egyptians used them," says Casavant matter-of-factly, as she picks up a piece of white silk and shows how it is draped and fitted over a nail and coated with resin.

What's new about Casavant's nail wraps is that the silk fabric she uses is patterned and coloured. "In the U.S. when they wrap nails and add a pattern, they have to paint it on each time, that requires artistry and time, whereas the pattern on mine is already printed on the fabric, it's a no fail method," she explains.

EXPLORING • SHE NAILS DOWN PROBLEMS

1. Why do you think the reporter found Casavant's business newsworthy?
2. What was Casavant's speciality?
3. What was unique about it?
4. Why do you feel it is so successful?

Sales Promotion

Sales promotion is any activity directed at increasing sales and supporting adverising. **Point-of-purchase displays** are set up near cash registers to encourage customers to buy on impulse. Businesses sponsor contests to entice customers to come to their location and fill in an entry form. The information on the entry form can be used for future mailings. Free samples are distributed to encourage customers to try the new product.

Trade shows are a promotional vehicle in which entrepreneurs can display their products or services. Some trade shows are for a particular industry only. For example, Manstyle is a trade show in which manufacturers of men's clothing display their products to retailers of men's clothing.

Coupons offer **cents-off merchandise**. Coupons encourage consumers to try new products or switch brands.

Figure 9.8 Sales promotion takes various forms.

YOUR TURN

11. Reread "Calendars that have no dates allow you to wipe out the past" in Chapter 1 and "Students create their own jobs with paper for job-seekers" in Chapter 5. What

do you think would be the best methods of promotion for each of these ventures? Give reasons for your answer. Compare your suggestions with the person sitting on your left.

12. Obtain a rate card from a local newspaper or radio station. Select three advertisements from this medium and determine the cost of each.
13. Visit a local retail store and observe a salesperson in conversation with a customer. Listen for whether the AIDA formula is followed in the sales talk, and evaluate the salesperson on his or her effectiveness.

P·O·I·N·T·S T·O R·E·M·E·M·B·E·R

- The Operations Spoke of the Venture Creation Wheel encompasses profit, price, production, people and productivity, and promotion, known also as the 6 P's of entrepreneurship.
- Efficient use of resources increases profits for the entrepreneur and benefits society by yielding more resources in general.
- Pricing a product or service is dependent upon fixed and variable costs, demand, and profit objectives.
- The co-ordination of employees, equipment, and materials is essential for effective production.
- Employees should be selected on the basis of their skills and qualities, creativity, commitment, and sense of co-operative effort.
- The federal and provincial governments legislate certain benefits to which the employee and the entrepreneur are required to contribute. Many businesses enhance this compensation package with additional fringe benefits.
- The promotional mix — advertising, personnal selling, publicity, and sales promotion — must be carefully selected to reach the target market.

W·H·A·T H·A·V·E Y·O·U L·E·A·R·N·E·D·?

1. Why is planning the 6 P's important to entrepreneurs?
2. In what way does society benefit from the efficient use of resources?
3. How does each of the following influence profits:
   a) price?
   b) demand?
   c) productivity?
   d) efficiency?
4. Differentiate between fixed and variable costs.
5. What dangers lie in pricing your product or service:
   a) at the same level as the competition?
   b) above the competition?
   c) below the competition?
6. In what ways does up-to-date equipment affect a new venture?
7. What criteria should be used in selecting an employee for a new venture?
8. How can creative employees benefit the venture?
9. On what basis should the media be selected to advertise a product or service?
10. List four types of sales promotion activities designed to increase sales.

V·E·N·T·U·R·I·N·G O·U·T

Using your own idea for a venture, answer each of the following questions:

1. What price are you planning to sell your product or service at? Determine the costs of materials, resources (such as employees and equipment), and the level of profit you want. Conduct a market survey to determine the price your customers are likely to want to pay for your product or service.
2. How will you organize your production facility? Draw a diagram illustrating the layout.
3. How many employees do you need? What skills should each of them have? What will be the function of each job? How will you motivate employees to be creative and productive?

4. What promotional strategy will best suit your product or service? How much will it cost? Which media will you select for advertising?
5. Using the above information, write up the preliminary version of the operating strategy for your venture plan.

"Profit is the bottom line." All ventures, whether they are for profit or not for profit, need financial resources. This chapter looks at the kind of financial information an entrepreneur needs and shows you how to use it.

CHAPTER 10

By the Numbers: Financing the Dream

LEARNING OUTCOMES

By the end of this chapter, you should be able to:

- identify the eight steps in financial planning
- list the various types of financial objectives an entrepreneur might pursue
- calculate total revenues, total costs, break-even points, profit margin, return on investment
- distinguish between and calculate fixed and variable costs, startup and operating expenses
- interpret, complete, and explain the use and importance of:
  - a personal budget
  - a cashflow forecast
  - a personal balance sheet
- prepare a partial financial strategy for your venture plan

ENTREPRENEURIAL LANGUAGE

break-even point
market share
profit margin
return on investment
startup costs
operating expenses
personal budget
personal drawings
equity
capital gain
dividend
cashflow forecast
accounts receivables
accounts payable
cash rich
cash poor
cash in
cash out
net cash
monthly surplus
monthly deficit
personal balance sheet
assets
liabilities
net worth

Venture PROFILE

The Plastic Engine Technology Company

The Empty Petco Plant

Petco, the Plastic Engine Technology Company, was a dream come true. Inventor Leon Lilley had developed a prototype of a plastic engine that ran so cool you could put your hand on it. Because most of the engine was made from injection moulded plastic rather than metal, it was lighter, more fuel efficient, and cheaper to build than traditional engines. It would revolutionize the huge market for small engines. Dr. Lilley and co-founder of Petco, Gerry McKendry, believed they could produce and sell 400 000 engines by 1989.

For several years, Petco used an old bakery as its factory. It produced conventional small engines while gathering orders for its plastic engine. The company had no problem getting orders but did have trouble producing enough to fill the orders they had. In December of 1988, Petco opened its new multimillion dollar headquarters in Kingston Township. More than 880 guests showed up to celebrate with the high tech company that was going to create 500 jobs and build two million small engines by 1991. With 1449 m^2 of floor space, the plant rivalled the largest plants in the Kingston area.

Four months later in April, 1989, the company folded, throwing 130 people out of work and sending millions of dollars down the drain. The cause — a cashflow problem. The company had raised $6 million but that and more had been used up. By March, it needed $11 million more to pay off its creditors and keep going. When creditors finally cut the company off, it owed $7 million but had assets worth less than $1 million.

What had happened? The idea of a plastic engine had caught the imagination of investors and, in the beginning, there was no shortage of money. The company had been able to acquire a large number of orders, but had been unable to produce enough engines to fill those orders. While it aimed at producing 1500 engines a week, it was never able to produce more than 200. The company's growth had been generated by interest in the plastic technology and sales and not by its ability to produce. It now needed $11 million more to get into full production and the money was not there. The dream came to an abrupt and messy end.

EXPLORING • PETCO

1. "Build a better mousetrap and the world will beat a path to your door." How does this saying apply to the Petco case?
2. What do you think was the cause of Petco's problems?

The Principles of Financial Strategy

Generating a financial strategy involves the Finance Spoke of the Venture Creation Wheel.

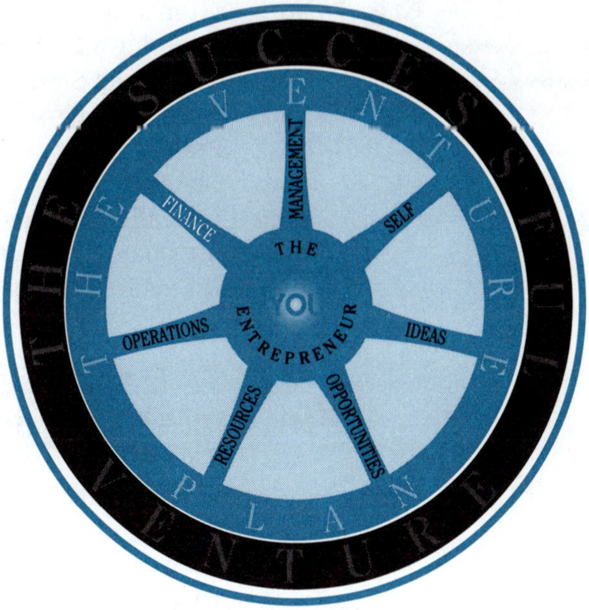

Figure 10.1 A financial strategy utilizes the Finance Spoke of the Venture Creation Wheel.

It requires the qualities of the Explorer, the Judge, and the Warrior. The Explorer, wearing his or her white hat, must search the market to accurately estimate how many customers there are and what price they are able and willing to pay. He or she must also price all the resources and supplies the venture will require in order to produce its good or service.

The Judge must be able to wear the black hat of negative criticism as well as the yellow hat of positive optimism to assess the worst, best, and most likely outcome. More than a few aspiring entrepreneurs have been fired up by an idea only to go down in flames because their Judge deserted them when they most needed a healthy dose of realism. Financial planning requires work. It involves careful attention to detail and long hours of research. The more effort one puts into it, the more precise and useful it becomes. It requires the persistence of the Warrior to see it through, and, once completed, the financial plan forms an important part of the foundation on which a successful venture can be built.

AGENTS OF CHANGE

In France, in 1863, vat after vat of wine was turning into vinegar. The Emperor asked Louis Pasteur to investigate. This request led Pasteur to discover pasteurization, a process which kills the micro-organisms in milk that threaten people's lives. A mystery spawned a scientific breakthrough.

The process of financial planning consists of several steps:

No. 1 - Establishing Financial Objectives
No. 2 - Preparing a Personal Budget
No. 3 - Estimating Revenue and Expenses
No. 4 - Preparing a Cashflow Forecast
No. 5 - Calculating Startup Costs and Operating Expenses
No. 6 - Preparing a Personal Balance Sheet
No. 7 - Preparing Projected Balance Sheets and Income Statements

Steps 1 - 6 will be covered in this chapter. Step 7 will be addressed in Chapter 11, where the process of acquiring capital for the venture will be examined in detail.

Step 1: Establishing Financial Objectives

Every venture, no matter whether it is a not-for-profit collective or a profit-making private corporation, needs money. It will, therefore, require financial objectives. A small business specializing in desktop publishing might have a financial objective to purchase $20 000 worth of sophisticated computer equipment. A neighbourhood food co-operative might have a financial objective of reducing food bills by 20 per cent through bulk buying. A community hockey league run by volunteers might aim to raise just enough money to have each team play one game and have one practice per week. All three will require money to pay for their costs, in this case computer equipment, food, or ice time. All ventures must strive to break even at the very least. Total revenues of all money flowing into the venture must equal or exceed the total costs of providing the good or service. As we learned in Chapter 9, total revenue is determined by multiplying the selling price by the number of units sold. Total cost is determined by adding together all fixed and variable costs. The point at which total revenues equal total costs is known as the **break-even point**.

> If a venture cannot at least cover its costs, it will go bankrupt, cease operations, and fail to satisfy the need it was created to serve. If a venture takes in revenue above its break-even point, it begins to make a profit.

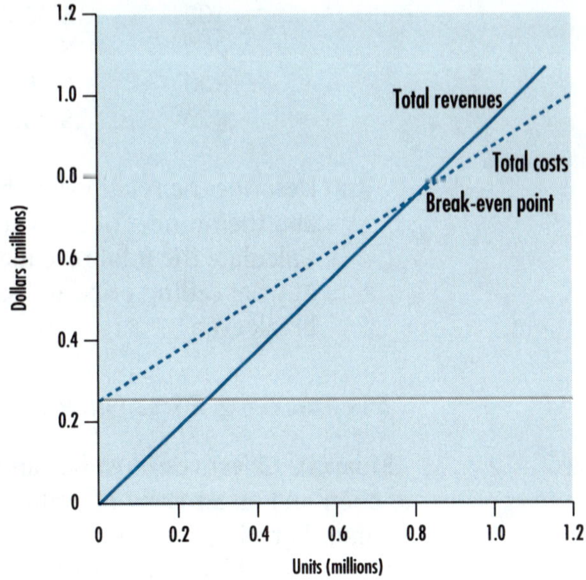

Figure 10.2 A Break-Even Chart

YOUR TURN

Calculate the break-even point in each of the following cases. (If a spreadsheet software package is available, you may use this to complete your calculations for these and subsequent Your Turn assignments in this chapter.)

1. If the XYZ Company's total cost of production was $1000 and the selling price of its product was $5, how many units would it have to sell to reach the break-even point?

2. What would the XYZ Company's break-even point be if:

	total costs were	*and*	*selling price was*
a)	$ 1000		$10.00?
b)	$ 1000		$ 2.00?
c)	$ 1000		$ 0.50?
d)	$ 3000		$ 5.00?

3. The ABC Company calculated that for a total cost of $5000 it could produce 200 units. What would it have to sell each unit for in order to break even?
4. Assume you had the following information:

Units Sold	*Total Costs*	*Selling Price*
100	$ 800	$ 15
200	$ 1400	$ 10
300	$ 1800	$ 6
400	$ 2000	$ 3

a) Describe the relationship between the selling price and the number of units sold.
b) Calculate the total revenue at each level of sales.
c) At what selling price and sales level will this venture break even?

Measuring Financial Success

Financial objectives must be carefully prepared as a guide for action and as a means of evaluating how well the venture is doing. Forming specific financial objectives helps the entrepreneur establish criteria that the entrepreneur's Judge can use to determine whether an idea really does represent an opportunity. In the event that a number of opportunities exist, the Judge can use the financial objectives to test which represents the best opportunity.

Those who start a venture in the hopes of making a profit will, of course, not be satisfied by breaking even.

Financial objectives may be expressed in terms of capturing a defined **market share**, attaining a particular **profit margin**, earning a certain **return on investment**, or reaching a specific level of profit.

Market Share

Market share refers to the percentage of total sales which the venture has. If a venture has, for example, a market share of 18 per cent, this means that its sales represent 18 per cent of the total sales of all companies producing the same good or service.

Profit Margin

Profit margin refers to the percentage of the final selling price which is greater than the cost of producing the good or service. If, for example, a good costs $15 to produce and sells for $20, then the profit margin is 25 per cent. The equation to calculate profit margin is:

$$\text{Profit Margin} = \frac{\text{Selling Price} - \text{Cost Price}}{\text{Selling Price}} \times 100$$

Return on Investment

Return on investment refers to how much income or profit is being earned on the capital which has been invested in a venture. If $10 000 was invested in a venture which was worth $15 000 at the end of the first year, then the return on investment was $5000 or 50 per cent. The equation to calculate return on investment is:

$$\text{Return on Investment} = \frac{\text{Net Income}}{\text{Amount Invested}} \times 100$$

Most people who invest in a new venture which they hope will be profit making expect a return on their investment which is substantially greater than what could be earned by putting the money in the bank or into government bonds. The higher return compensates them for the greater risks they take.

YOUR TURN

5. If the value of total sales by all producers was $850 000 and your objective was to capture 25 per cent of the market, at what sales level would you reach your objective?
6. How much would your sales have to be if your objective was to capture 20 per cent of the market?
7. a) If the selling price of your product is $10 and your profit margin is 25 per cent, how much has it cost you to produce the product?

b) If something cost you $20 to produce and you wanted to realize a 50 per cent profit margin, at what price should you sell your product?

8. a) Calculate your return on investment if you invested $20 000 in starting a venture which had total revenues of $125 000 and total costs of $120 000.
   b) If you invested $10 000 in a venture and you wanted to earn a return of 25 per cent, how much must you receive from your investment each year?

Covering the Costs of Production

When entrepreneurs plan their financial strategy, regardless of the objective, they must be careful that they have enough financial resources available to cover both the **startup costs** and the **operating expenses**. The startup costs are all those expenses which are required to open for business. Startup costs include all fixed costs of production plus the variable costs incurred in providing the good or service during the startup phase.

Operating expenses are those expenses required to keep a venture going once it has successfully completed the start-up phase.

Operating Expenses = Total Costs – Startup Costs

Although operating expenses may take the form of fixed costs, many of the expenses are variable. It is important that all operating expenses, or as many as possible, be paid for from the sale of the good or service the venture is producing. Petco went into bankruptcy because it did not have enough money to continue paying its operating expenses. Its financial plan should have forecast this problem and determined a way to cover these costs in advance. As it was, Petco was not producing quickly enough to maintain a sufficient flow of revenue to pay its suppliers. When they did not receive payment for past shipments, Petco's suppliers finally refused to ship more supplies on credit; the company then went bankrupt because it could not produce at all.

YOUR TURN

In Chapter 6, Ms. Chang's class was planning to provide itself with something to drink. Its financial objective was simply to raise enough money to cover expenses or, in other words, to break even. The class made a list of things it needed, along with the prices of each item and how often each item would have to be purchased. The list looked like this:

Item	*Cost*	*Frequency of Purchase*
hot chocolate	$5/can	1 can each week
sugar cubes	$1/box	1 box every 2 weeks
creamer	$4/bottle	1 bottle every 3 weeks
coffee urn	$40	once
tea	$2.50/box	1 box every 2 weeks
cups	$1.25/package	3 packages a week
coffee	$5/jar	1 jar every 2 weeks
storage cabinet	$60	once

9. Classify each of the above costs as fixed or variable.
10. Copy and complete the following table of operating costs for Ms. Chang's class for its first month.

Item	*Time in Weeks*			
	Week 1	Week 2	Week 3	Week 4

11. What are the total startup costs of the venture?
12. Assuming each month has four weeks, calculate what the operating expenses would be for:
    a) month 1 b) month 2
13. High startup costs often discourage people from starting a new venture. Make a list of ways Ms. Chang's students could reduce the startup costs.
14. Calculate what the new startup costs would be if the suggestions made in Question 13 were followed.
15. Assume:
    a) there are 25 students in the class
    b) they decide to share all the costs evenly
    c) they raise their capital at the beginning of each month through a donation

    If the venture is to break even, how much should each student pay:

    i) at the beginning of month 1 ii) at the beginning of month 2?

Venture PROFILE

Going Whole Hog

By Danièle Walker, *Your Money*

Coombes' racing pigs are a popular attraction at Maritime county fairs: "They have a lot of personality."

Forget hog futures on the stock market: Jenny Coombes is making money on the real thing. Pigs. "Jenny's Racing Pigs," says Coombes, "is putting me through school."

Coombes, 20, studies animal science at the Nova Scotia Agricultural College in Truro, N.S. At least that's what she does during the winter months. In the summer, Coombes travels the county fair circuit in the Maritimes showcasing her nine porcine racers and her own portable racing track, Porkchop Downs.

Jenny's Racing Pigs made its debut last summer and met with instant success — people love watching pigs race. Fair organizers have been vying all year for a place on this summer's tour.

Coombes buys her pigs in July when they're six weeks old and puts them into training for about a month. By the time they're ready to race, they're about two months old, four months short of when they'll no longer be physically able to run. In October, the fair season ends: Coombes returns to her studies and the plump racers go to market.

Last summer, the Windsor, N.S. native made only about $2000, but she covered all of her one-time expenses, including a four-horse trailer (converted to house the pigs), fencing for the miniature race track, and hundreds of bags of Oreo cookies. Oreo cookies? "For the winning racer," explains Coombes. "Pigs have a sweet tooth...they just love them." This summer she expects to clear at least $15 000.

Life on the road is old hat for Coombes. She's a seasoned horse trainer and show jumping competitor, and she has been attending horse shows throughout Eastern Canada since she was seven. The difference now lies in the people she meets en route. While she once chatted with tense fellow competitors, she's now more likely to chat with old farmers, children, and pig lovers of all ages. "Actually, the children and farmers ask about the pigs, everyone else asks how I got started."

Coombes' previous summer jobs involved training or caring for horses. At age three, she rode her first pony; at 13, she landed her first summer job as a stablehand; and by the time she was 17, she was an experienced stable manager, albeit parttime. There was never any doubt that she would work to pay her way through university. The question remained "how" until her father suggested pigs.

"My father is the secretary/manager of several fairs including the Atlantic Winter Fair in Halifax. He saw a pig race at the New York State Fair, but he couldn't bring the show to Halifax because of quarantine laws. He said, 'Jenny, if you can train a horse, you ought to be able to handle pigs,' as a joke. He thought I'd be angry...I thought it was a great idea."

Coombes sold both of her horses to pay for last summer's pigs and some of the startup costs. After initial success at the Atlantic Winter Fair, the Hants County Exhibition, and the Nova Scotia Provincial Exhibition, she was able to book this year's tour. Her grandfather travels with her to drive the camper and help her care for the pigs.

Other family members help out, too. Her sister designed "I love racing pigs" buttons, signs, T-shirts, and hats, which Coombes sells, and her father donates accounting help. "And I've arranged business co-sponsorship this summer for small fairs that can't afford me on their own."

In the short term, her racing pigs are helping to pay her college tuition. In the long term, Coombes plans to use this experience to work with animals, maybe running a veterinary practice or business of her own. This summer, however, Coombes is concentrating on pigs. "They look so silly in their racing togs, tutus and bow ties, but they have a lot of personality. It'll really be sad to see them go."

EXPLORING • GOING WHOLE HOG

1. Describe Jenny Coombes' business.
2. What were her profits last year? What does she expect to clear next year?
3. How do family members help out in the business?
4. What are Coombes' short-term and long-term goals with respect to the business?
5. Why is there such a difference in profits between the first and second year?
6. Make a list of the costs of the venture and classify them as:
   a) fixed or variable b) startup or operating costs
7. How did Jenny get the idea of raising pigs?
8. How was she able to expand her market?
9. How did she get the money to cover her initial costs?
10. How is she able to keep her costs down?

Step 2: Preparing a Personal Budget

If the entrepreneur is going to rely on a venture for his or her income and livelihood, then breaking even is not good enough. The entrepreneur must focus attention on his or her own financial affairs to determine how much income the venture must generate to meet personal living expenses. This personal financial analysis represents a return to the hub of the Venture Creation Wheel. No income generating venture should be contemplated without first analyzing the entrepreneur's specific financial needs. The analysis can be done by exercising the Explorer and using some white hat thinking to complete a **personal budget**.

Table 10.1 A Personal Budget

Regular Monthly Payments		*Food Expenses*	
Rent or House Payments	______	Food at Home	______
Car Payments	______	Food away from Home	______
Appliances/TV Payments	______	TOTAL	______
Home Improvements	______	*Personal Expenses*	
Personal Loan Payments	______	Clothing, Cleaning	______
Life Insurance Premiums	______	Laundry, Shoe Repair	______
Other Insurance Premiums	______	Drugs	______
Miscellaneous Payments	______	Auto: Gas, Repairs	______
TOTAL	______	Doctor & Dentist	______
Household Operating Expenses		Education	______
Telephone	______	Dues	______
Gas & Electricity	______	Gifts	______
Water	______	Travel	______
Other Repairs	______	Books, Magazines	______
TOTAL	______	TOTAL	______
		GRAND TOTAL	______
		(Add all previous totals together)	

Entrepreneurs who start their own successful business may earn money in a variety ways. First, they may choose to have the venture pay them a wage or a salary. Such payments are referred to as **personal drawings**. While they represent a form of income for the entrepreneur, they are a cost from the venture's point of view and are included as such in the venture's cashflow statements. Secondly, entrepreneurs may choose to take very little from their venture in the form of a wage or a salary but instead elect to reinvest any profits in the venture to make it grow. This choice is common among entrepreneurs who are just starting a venture. Reinvesting profits increases the value of the entrepreneur's **equity**, or personal financial investment, in the venture. The value of the asset, the venture itself, increases, but the increased value can only be recovered or realized in the form of a **capital gain** when the venture is sold. A capital gain refers to the profit acquired as a result of selling the venture. Thirdly, owners of the venture may decide to take their share of the profits in the form of a **dividend**, or amount of money paid out to shareholders. How money is derived from the venture is up to the owners of the venture to decide. They will often choose the method which yields the most income after taxes.

At present, income received as a wage or salary is taxed most heavily. Dividends and capital gains are taxed at a lower rate or, in some cases, not taxed at all.

YOUR TURN

16. Make out a personal budget detailing the expenses you presently face in a typical month.
17. Now assume that you have graduated from high school, left home, and are attending a university or community college. What would your personal budget for a typical month look like now?
18. Ask your parents or some other adult who is close to you to fill out their personal budget for a month.
19. From a financial point of view what are a) the advantages and b) the disadvantages of being young and wanting to start your own venture?

Venture PROFILE

JASSO PERSAD
Making Plans

Jasso Persad is an 18-year-old student who is just completing her final year of high school. She has decided that she wants to go on to university and has not only selected a university, but has also carefully analyzed how much it would cost to attend. She is astonished to find that it is almost $10 000 a year when all the costs of tuition, room and board, textbooks, and personal living expenses are added up. She is a good student but not a top student and is unlikely to earn a scholarship. Both her parents work but earn only enough to meet the basic needs of a large family. Jasso is the eldest of four children and she has had jobs since the age of 10 when she started delivering papers. She is also a good saver and, over the years, has managed to accumulate $5000 which she invested in a term deposit which earns her 10 per cent annually.

She now has a job at a pizza restaurant where she earns $6 per hour working 20 hours per week. The restaurant has offered her employment for the summer working 40 hours a week during July and August. Between April and the time she has to go to university in mid-September, she estimates she could get 600 hours of work. Unfortunately, not all the money she earns can be saved for university. Some of it must be spent covering current expenses which she estimates at approximately $1000 for the period from April to mid-September.

EXPLORING • JASSO PERSAD: MAKING PLANS

1. What is Jasso's specific financial objective?
2. Will she achieve her objective if she continues to work at the pizza restaurant for the summer?

Step 3: Estimating Revenue and Expenses

All ventures, whether for profit or not for profit, should engage in financial planning. A careful consideration of the size and timing of expenses makes up part of a planning tool known as a **cashflow forecast.**

The cashflow forecast is the single most important financial planning tool for a new venture.

The purpose of the cashflow forecast is to estimate the size and timing of a venture's expenses and its revenue. It forecasts when money will actually flow into the venture, from, for example, cash sales and **accounts receivable**. It also forecasts when money will flow out of the venture, for example, in salaries and expenses and **accounts payable**. It identifies for the entrepreneur when the venture will be **cash rich** and when it will be **cash poor**. A venture becomes cash rich when revenues are greater than expenses. When expenses exceed revenues, the venture becomes cash poor. The entrepreneur must make sure that there is always enough money on hand in its cashflow reservoir to cover cash poor periods. If this fails to happen, the venture will be unable to pay its bills and will be forced to cease operations. The Petco case, at the beginning of this chapter, is an excellent example of what happens when entrepreneurs do not manage their cashflow well.

AGENTS OF CHANGE

Canadian scientists became known as world leaders in the design, construction, and operation of communication satellites. As a result of their efforts, we have grown quite accustomed to watching live TV coverage of international events. Canadian science is bringing the world closer together.

Estimating Revenue

A venture's total revenue may be estimated by determining the demand for its good or service. The entrepreneur must try to determine the potential sales of a product at different price levels. This, of course, is the objective of the market analysis done as part of the Opportunities Spoke of the Venture Creation Wheel. The entrepreneur uses the information collected by market analysis methods to estimate how much total revenue the venture might generate. These same projections may now be used as a basis for calculating how much money can be expected to flow into a venture over a specific period of time. While this analysis is basically straightforward, it does require some careful calculation. When forecasting actual cashflows, it is not enough to estimate sales alone. With cash sales, the money flows into the venture immediately. Other sales, where credit buying is involved, may not be completely paid off for months, or even years. The cashflow forecast records revenue when it is received, not when it is earned. Credit sales are recorded in future months as payments are received.

Many a cashflow crisis occurs during a period when a venture's sales are booming but, since most sales are on a credit basis, full payment is not received immediately.

Venture PROFILE

JASSO PERSAD
Entrepreneur

When Jasso's Explorer discovered the facts, it joined with her Artist and came up with a new idea. She decided that her restaurant job was not lucrative enough to meet her financial needs. She decided to investigate the possibility of starting her own business during the summer, painting house exteriors. Her Explorer then conducted some informal market research to determine the demand for her service and how much she could charge. She phoned established painters and one other student painting operation and felt a rate of $14 an hour would be reasonable. She then conducted a brief door-to-door survey to determine the size of the market and prepared the following forecast of revenues for her venture. She assumed that all jobs would be paid in full upon completion.

CASH IN	*April*	*May*	*June*	*July*	*August*	*Sept.*	*Total*
Estimated Sales	$1200	$3640	$4900	$4900	$2900	$800	$18 340

EXPLORING • JASSO PERSAD: ENTREPRENEUR

1. Jasso's revenue estimate follows a pattern. Describe the pattern and the reasons for it.
2. What would happen to her revenues in each of the following cases:
   a) if she had to cut her hourly rate to $12?
   b) if she had underestimated demand by 20 per cent?
   c) if the summer was unusually wet, which reduced her business by 25 per cent?
3. What other factors could influence her projected revenues?

Estimating Expenses

Estimating expenses involves determining all the resources the venture will need and costing them. This is the task undertaken when working through the Resource Spoke of the Venture Creation Wheel. The entrepreneur's Explorer and Warrior must doggedly seek out sources of supply and negotiate the best price and terms for the resources the venture needs. A venture's suppliers can be its best friends or its worst enemies. Suppliers may provide information about customers. They may offer production advice and special financial terms, such as discounts and credit. On the other hand, they may fail to deliver on time or provide shoddy materials. The venture may have to pay its suppliers before it has received payment for its output. Making sure there is always enough cash to cover expenses can be a tricky balancing act.

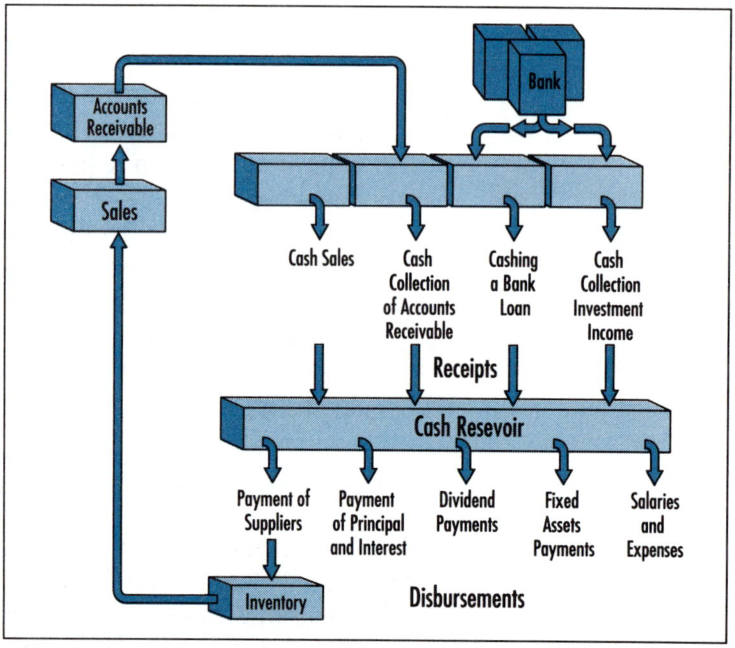

Figure 10.3 A Cashflow Reservoir

YOUR TURN

Assume a new venture has the following revenues and expenses in its first four months of operation:

	Month 1	Month 2	Month 3	Month 4
Total Value of Sales	$10 000	$12 000	$20 000	$25 000
Total Monthly Expenses	$12 000	$ 9 000	$15 000	$20 000

20. a) Calculate the venture's profit or loss for each of its first four months.
    b) Calculate its total profit or loss after four months of operation.
21. Now assume that it receives only half of its sales in cash and the remainder is paid in 30 days. Further assume that it must pay all its expenses in cash as they are incurred. (This is not unusual for a new venture.)
    a) Calculate how cash poor or cash rich the venture will be at the end of each month. Remember, to do this you must calculate actual money received and paid out for each month.

b) How much capital would the entrepreneur need to have on hand to cover operating expenses for the first four months?

22. Expenses do not always have to be paid as they are incurred. Assume the entrepreneur has been able to negotiate terms with his or her suppliers whereby if half of the expense is paid in cash, the other half may be paid off in 30 days. Now calculate whether the venture is cash rich or cash poor at the end of each month.

Step 4: Preparing the Cashflow Forecast

A simplified cashflow forecast has three components. They are referred to as: **cash in**, **cash out**, and **net cash.**

Table 10.2 A Simplified Cashflow Forecast

	Time Period (Months, Years) 1 2 3 4 5 6
Part 1: Cash In This section keeps track of the flow of money which is actually received by the venture from sources such as sales, loans, and contributions. Income is recorded only when it is received. (If a firm sells something in month 1 and does not receive payment until month 3, the sale is registered in month 3.)	
Part 2: Cash Out This section keeps track of all expenses as they are paid. If supplies are purchased in month 1 but not paid until month 2, this expense would be listed under month 2.	
Part 3: Net Cash This section records the balance of cashflow for the individual period. The value of the Cash Out is deducted from the value of the Cash In to determine whether a surplus or deficit exists for that period. The balance is recorded as either a **monthly surplus** (when revenues exceed expenses) or a **monthly deficit** (when expenses exceed revenues). The last line in the forecast records the cash surplus or deficit since the beginning of the accounting period under the heading of Cumulative.	

YOUR TURN

23. If before doing this activity you would like to see what a partially completed cashflow forecast looks like, turn to Table 10.6 on pages 315-316.
    Create a cashflow forecast for Ms. Chang's class for the first eight weeks of operation of the beverage project assuming:
    a) the cost of supplies and the frequency of purchase remain the same as given in the example on page 299
    b) the students must purchase the coffee urn and storage cabinet and decide to pay them off 50 per cent in week one and the rest in week five
    c) the class decides to collect money in advance every four weeks (in weeks one and five) sufficient to cover expenses for the following four-week period

Step 5: Calculating Startup Costs and Operating Expenses

When you last encountered Jasso Persad in the previous Venture Profile, she was forecasting revenue for her house painting business. At the same time, Jasso's Explorer is busy working through the Resources Spoke of the Venture Creation Wheel to identify and cost all the items she will need to offer a first-class service. Her list of expenses includes the following:

Table 10.3 Jasso Persad's List of Expenses

Purchase of Equipment:	- used pick-up truck .... $ 1 500
	- ladders 350
	- miscellaneous (brushes, scrapers, etc.) 200
	- Total $2 050
Rental of Equipment:	- sprayer, extension ladder
Labour Expenses:	- allowance of $10/hour
	- hiring 1 employee for April and September, 2 employees during busy months ($4.50/hour for wages plus employer's contribution for Canada Pension Plan and Unemployment Insurance Commission benefits)
Materials:	- paint, turpentine, primer etc. used in providing services
Business Licences:	- for registering the company name

Advertising:	- community newspaper advertisement, flyers, and lawn signs
Insurance:	- for the truck and business liability
Office Expenses:	- business phone and answering machine
Other:	- allowance for gas and truck repairs

Jasso then estimates when her expenses will occur and prepares the following cashflow forecast. She assumes she will purchase everything on a cash basis.

Table 10.4 Jasso's First Cashflow Forecast

CASH IN	*April*	*May*	*June*	*July*	*Aug.*	*Sept.*	*Total*
Estimated Sales of Goods or Services	$ 1200	$3640	$4900	$4900	$2900	$800	$18 340
CASH OUT							
Purchase of Equipment	$ 2050						$ 2050
Rental Expenses	$ 75	$ 75	$ 75	$ 75	$ 50	$ 25	$ 375
Labour Expenses (including employer's contributions to UI and CPP)	$ 200	$1600	$2400	$2400	$ 600	$150	$ 7350
Personal Drawings	$ 50	$ 200	$ 250	$ 250	$ 150	$100	$ 1000
Materials	$ 100	$ 200	$ 300	$ 300	$ 200	$100	$ 1200
Business Licences and Fees	$ 10						$ 10
Advertising	$ 150	$ 100	$ 100	$ 50			$ 400
Insurance	$ 725						$ 725
Office Expenses	$ 200	$ 50	$ 50	$ 50	$ 50		$ 400
Other (Gas and Truck Repairs)	$ 125	$ 100	$ 250	$ 200	$ 75	$ 50	$ 800
Total							

NET CASH: (Cash In - Cash Out)	*April*	*May*	*June*	*July*	*Aug.*	*Sept.*	*Total*
Monthly Surplus							
Monthly Deficit							
Cumulative (to date)							

YOUR TURN

24. Calculate Jasso's total expenses for each month of operation and the total estimated expenses for the entire venture.
25. Some of Jasso's costs were fixed and some were variable. Classify each of her costs as fixed or variable.
26. How much were Jasso's projected startup costs?
27. Suggest two ways Jasso could have reduced her startup costs.
28. How much were Jasso's operating expenses for the venture?
29. Compare Jasso's projected revenues and expenses and calculate the Net Cash section of the Cashflow Forecast. A monthly surplus will exist if revenues are greater than expenses. If expenses exceed revenues, she will record the difference as a monthly deficit.
30. What problem does Jasso's Cashflow Forecast reveal?
31. How much money will Jasso need to cover her venture's startup and operating expenses?

Step 6: Preparing a Personal Balance Sheet

Jasso's financial analysis reveals that her venture, like many others, cannot generate enough sales to cover its startup costs. Where will she get the capital she needs to get started? This is a major startup problem faced by entrepreneurs.

The best source of capital is most often the entrepreneur himself or herself.

Using your own savings is better than using someone else's money. It costs less since there is no interest to pay and no profits have to be shared with others. The entrepreneur can also retain more control over the venture and maintain greater freedom of action. However, entrepreneurs often lack sufficient personal assets to finance the startup phase of a new venture. An important part of financial planning therefore is determining how much personal capital can be used and how much will have to be obtained from other sources.

Researching and writing a **personal balance sheet** will provide this information. A personal balance sheet consists of three sections. The first section lists all the entrepreneur's **assets**. The assets are everything the entrepreneur owns which have a cash value. The second section lists all the entrepreneur's liabilities. A **liability** is a debt; a sum of money the entrepreneur owes. The third section calculates the entrepreneur's **net worth.** Net worth is determined by subtracting the value of liabilities from the value of the assets.

An entrepreneur's net worth will help determine how much capital may be raised for a venture from personal sources. The amount of an individual's net worth tends to overvalue the amount of capital which can be raised because not all assets may be sold quickly for the amount they are worth. Lending institutions, such as banks, credit unions, and government agencies, may be unwilling to accept some assets as collateral for a loan. Nevertheless, preparing a personal balance sheet will indicate personal financial resources available to finance a venture and what the entrepreneur must give up in order to make the dream a reality.

Table 10.5 A Personal Balance Sheet

ASSETS		
Cash	$	.00
Bank Accounts	$	.00
Stocks, Bonds, and Other Securities	$	.00
Money Owed	$	.00
Life Insurance Cash Value	$	.00
Income Tax Refunds	$	.00

Vehicles	$	.00
Real Estate	$	.00
Pension Plan/Retirement Accounts	$	.00
Personal Assets (furnishings, jewellery furs, cameras, etc.)	$	.00
Other	$	.00
Total Assets	$	.00
LIABILITIES		
Bank Loans	$	.00
Mortgages	$	.00
Credit Card Debts	$	.00
Income Tax Owing	$	.00
Life Insurance Loans	$	.00
Other	$	.00
Total Liabilities	$	.00
NET WORTH (Total Assets – Total Liabilities)	$	.00

YOUR TURN

32. You have the following information about Jasso's personal finances:
    a) She has $165 in her bank account.
    b) She has a $5000 term deposit.
    c) She owns a motorbike worth $1200, but still has to make payments totalling $500 to the bank.
    d) She lent her younger brother $200.
    e) She owns a stereo system worth $400.
    f) She has an income tax refund of $150 coming.
    g) She still owes her father $600, which was the additional cost of insurance so she could drive his car.

    Construct her personal balance sheet.
33. Which of her assets could she easily sell for cash or would the bank accept as collateral for a loan?
34. Does Jasso have sufficient assets to finance her venture herself?
35. Assume that Jasso does go to university. How would her personal balance sheet look by the end of her first year?
36. Assume that Jasso is now 40 years old with two children of her own. Suggest how her personal balance sheet might change.

37. What are the advantages and disadvantages of:
    a) being young
    b) being older
    when it comes to raising personal capital?
38. Jasso's Explorer finds that there is in existence a special government program designed to encourage young people to start ventures. It would loan her up to $3000, interest free, if the venture created summer jobs for students and if the loan was fully paid off by September 30 of the year in which it is borrowed. Any balance which remained unpaid after that date would incur the going rate of interest. Should Jasso apply for the government loan or should she use her savings? Why?
39. Assume that Jasso decides to apply for the Student Venture Loan, though not to the maximum available amount. Like other entrepreneurs seeking financing, she is required to submit her financial forecast, which she prepared in the form of the Cashflow Forecast in Table 10.6. Calculate the missing figures in Jasso's revised Cashflow Forecast.

Table 10.6 Jasso's Revised Cashflow Forecast

CASH IN

	April	*May*	*June*	*July*	*Aug.*	*Sept.*	*Total*
Estimated Sales of Goods or Services	$1200	$3640	$4900	$4900	$2900	$800	$18 340
Student Venture Capital Loan	$2500						$2500
Other (Specify)							
Total	?	$3640	$4900	$4900	$2900	$800	?

CASH OUT

Purchase of Equipment	$2050						$2050
Rental Expenses	$ 75	$ 75	$ 75	$ 75	$ 50	$ 25	$375

	April	*May*	*June*	*July*	*Aug.*	*Sept.*	*Total*
Labour Expenses (including employer's contributions to UI and CPP)	$200	$1600	$2400	$2400	$600	$150	$7350
Personal Drawings	$ 50	$ 200	$ 250	$ 250	$150	$100	$1000
Materials	$100	$ 200	$ 300	$ 300	$200	$100	$1200
Business Licences and Fees	$ 10						$10
Advertising	$150	$ 100	$ 100	$ 50			$400
Insurance	$725						$725
Office Expenses	$200	$ 50	$ 50	$ 50	$ 50		$400
Other (Gas and Truck Repairs)	$125	$ 100	$ 250	$ 200	$ 75	$ 50	$800
Loan Repayment (To be completed by September 30 of this year)			$ 500	$ 500	$ 700	$800	?
Total	?	?	?	?	?	?	?

NET CASH: (Cash In - Cash Out)

Monthly Surplus	?	?	?	?	?	?	?
Monthly Deficit	?	?	?	?	?	?	?
Cumulative (to date)	?	?	?	?	?	?	?

YOUR TURN

40. In one month she projects a cash deficit.
    a) What were her fixed and variable costs of production that month?
    b) Why would she not just stop and shut down completely that month?

c) At what point is it best for a business to shut down completely?

41. According to her Cashflow Forecast, how much does Jasso intend to take from the business in the form of income and how much will she realize in the form of profit?
42. Will her venture raise enough money to cover her costs at university?
43. What else could Jasso do to raise income from her venture even after she has shut it down? (Hint: What would the venture's balance sheet look like on October 1?)

The Importance of Planning a Financial Strategy

The Finance Spoke of the Venture Creation Wheel is vital to the creation of a successful venture for two reasons. First, completing the required financial research helps entrepreneurs to synthesize or combine and pull together everything they did as they worked through all the other spokes. Secondly, it helps entrepreneurs to make their research more precise by requiring them to define and assess all aspects of their venture in specific numerical terms.

To do a thorough job of planning a financial strategy, entrepreneurs are forced to examine their needs and their objectives. Then they must state those objectives in precise, measurable terms, such as break-even points, profit margins, market share, and return on investment. Developing the financial strategy subjects the wild, creative fantasies of the Artist to the cold, calculating, reality-based analysis of the Judge. How many people will purchase the good or service and what price will they be willing to pay? What specific resources are required and how much will they cost? How much capital will the venture require and how much profit can be made? Are the returns worth the risks?

Finally, when all the financial analysis is done, the entrepreneur is left with a forecast of what his or her venture can be, described in the specific detail of numeric projection. Bankers and other investors who have the financial resources the entrepreneur seeks can relate to this forecast. A good financial strategy is the best promotion any idea ever receives. It is also a blueprint the entrepreneur can use to guide the venture through the startup stage.

POINTS TO REMEMBER

- No venture plan is complete without a thoroughly researched financial strategy.
- The financial strategy should establish the specific financial objectives of the venture.
- If the venture is intended to generate income for the entrepreneur, a personal budget should be prepared to determine how much income is needed.
- Accurate estimates of future total revenues the venture can earn and total costs of production should be calculated and a cashflow forecast prepared.
- The forecast should be used to calculate how much capital is needed to cover startup costs and short-term operating expenses.
- The entrepreneur should prepare a personal balance sheet to determine how much of the needed financial capital can be supplied by the founder(s) of the venture.
- The need for outside financing should also be determined.

WHAT HAVE YOU LEARNED?

1. List three different financial objectives a venture might use to guide its decisions.
2. Explain which roles must be played and which thinking hats must be worn to complete a thorough financial strategy.
3. Define the following terms or phrases:
   a) break-even point
   b) profit margin
   c) return on investment
   d) share of market
   e) startup costs
   f) operating expenses
   g) net worth
4. Explain three ways in which income may be received from a venture.
5. Identify and explain the function of each of the three sections of a cashflow forecast.
6. Explain two important facts which can be learned from an accurately completed cashflow forecast.
7. If a person's total personal assets were $50 000 and his or her total liabilities were $30 000, how much would this person's net worth be?

8. If a person's assets were $30 000 and his or her liabilities were $50 000, would this person be poor, bankrupt, or able to get a loan?
9. Listed below are some of the things which should be done as part of developing a financial strategy for a venture. Which items do not belong in the list?
   a) establishing specific financial objectives
   b) coming up with a money-making idea
   c) determining the cost of legal fees to start the venture
   d) preparing a cashflow forecast
   e) finding out the legal regulations which apply to the venture
   f) asking parents for a loan to startup
   g) estimating personal financial needs
   h) establishing what prices and terms suppliers will charge
   i) marrying a wealthy person
10. Briefly explain why a financial strategy is vital to the creation of a successful venture.

V·E·N·T·U·R·I·N·G O·U·T

Prepare a partial financial strategy section for your venture plan referring to the information below. (This section of the venture plan is to be completed in Chapter 11 when you examine financial statements in further detail.)

a) State the specific financial objective(s) your venture will pursue.
b) Specifically calculate projected revenues by month for the first 12 months under three headings: least favourable, most likely, and most favourable scenario.
c) Prepare a personal budget for yourself and any others who may be involved as partners to determine how much income the venture must generate.
d) Calculate all costs of production by month for the first 12 months using once again the three headings: least favourable, most likely, and most favourable scenario.
e) Draw expenses and revenues together by completing a cashflow forecast.
f) Draw up a personal balance sheet for yourself and each partner to determine whether you have enough capital to cover the startup and operating costs or how much you will need to find.

The FINANCE spoke in this chapter will identify a number of different sources of startup capital for your venture. It will help you prepare such necessary financial statements as an income forecast and balance sheet, before you talk to a potential investor.

CHAPTER 11

Knocking on the Right Door: Financing the Venture

LEARNING OUTCOMES

By the end of this chapter, you should be able to:

- identify a variety of sources for startup capital
- distinguish between debt and equity financing
- understand the purpose of income forecast and projected balance sheet financial statements
- prepare an income forecast and projected balance sheet
- compare the advantages and disadvantages of buying an existing business to starting a venture from scratch

ENTREPRENEURIAL LANGUAGE

equity financing
venture capital
private placement
"love money"
credit rating
share purchase
stock option plans
debt financing
tax deductible
debt to equity ratio
fixed asset
character
capital
collateral
capacity
circumstances
coverage
6 C's of credit
line of credit
term loan
mortgage
grant
guarantee
"matchmaking service"
income forecast
projected balance sheet
creditor
income statement

Venture
PROFILE

Indian Business of the Year — Meadow Lake Tribal Council buys sawmills

By Marie Mendenhall, *Saskatchewan Business*

Ray Ahenakew (r) and Laurie Banagan, NorSask production superintendent, checking the sawmill's operation.

It's a long way from facing off over traditional native hunting and fishing grounds to facing each other as equals around a boardroom table.

That's the road treaty Indians, Metis, and sawmill employees in the Meadow Lake area of northwestern Saskatchewan have travelled over the past two years. The vehicle for this change has been the privatization of the Meadow Lake and Green Lake sawmills, which made mill employees and the Meadow Lake Tribal Council into business partners.

The two groups each purchased 50 per cent of the $6 million mill operation in June, 1988, forming a new company called NorSask Forest Products Inc., with support from the provincial and federal governments. They purchased the mill in an original package including $3 million in mill modernization and development of an $11 million chopstick factory and an $80 million hardwood pulp mill over the next two years.

As a western diversification project, the sale to employees and a local organization was unprecedented, especially when government could not interest a larger operation in purchasing the two mills. As a business venture, it has proven to be a winner: an operation known to lose about $1 million a year boasted a $90 000 profit in its first quarter since the takeover, and expectations of close to $1 million in profits for this year.

Mill managers and employees came up with the idea over the past two years. After the Papco pulp mill in Prince Albert was sold to Weyerhaeuser, they found themselves running operations alone and started changes designed to make the mill financially viable, including changes in equipment and operations that saw even unionized employees taking drastic cuts in benefits.

But even with changes, employees alone couldn't get financial backing for the take-over.

That's when the Meadow Lake Tribal Council stepped in. While day-to-day operations are left up to management and employees, the tribal council's investment has gained its share of potential profits and a say in the policy and decision making. The tribal council has two representatives on the seven-member board of directors, while the employee company has two, the government nominates one, and two more are members at large.

Raymond Cariou, a Meadow Lake lawyer who served on the mill's advisory board and is now chairman of NorSask's board, says the tribal council is an asset in many ways. It has been involved in business transactions and joint ventures over the past few years, and Cariou says experience has made its members "tough negotiators" and "capable business men."

The tribal council has taken an active role negotiating for and dealing with the concerns of the northern people. During the past few years, northern Indian and Metis people were frustrated to the point of roadblocks and confrontations over logging operations seen to threaten traditional woodland-dependent lifestyles including hunting, fishing, and trapping, without their consent or consultations.

Cariou says one of the important parts of the mill package is the Forest Management Leasing Agreement, which puts NorSask in charge of harvesting and reforestation in northern woodlands. It also gives the new company responsibility to carry out on-going consultation with those communities which may be affected by new logging operations, including those of independent mill operators in the area. Under the agreement, 15 per cent of the northern portion called the Vermette Block must also be set aside for northern communities, and they must have the first right to harvest and reforest the area.

The tribal council's experience in forest management joint ventures, as well as training programs like the National Indian Forestry Institute which is based on the Flying Dust reserve near Meadow Lake, make it a valuable ally in this policy area, Cariou adds.

While Cariou says administrating the agreement fairly will be a challenge for the board, working together hasn't been difficult so far. There is no evidence of racial tensions, hidden agendas, or block voting on the part of any board member. All vote as individuals, with a common goal of making mill operations as economically viable as possible. They are interested in knowing where the company is going and expect management to keep them informed of this, he adds.

At the same time, the tribal council gained its business expertise acting as a government for its 10 member bands, Cariou says, and shows a strong concern for social programs and the lifestyle of northern people.

"The tribal council started on the road to self-government by looking after its own affairs," he comments, "and I think we should be proud of that in this community."

Ray Ahenakew, executive director for the tribal council, says it has learned to conduct business with a view to long-term objectives, taking into account treaty rights, the need to handle its own programs and services, and the opportunity to build a solid economic base in the region.

"There's no stop to the spin-offs that might not produce an actual hard dollar in some cases, but might produce a livelihood for maybe five or ten people," Ahenakew says. "I think we call that a business, a positive business where you're going to leave something more than just the money value."

The tribal council represents a large region, with diverse bands spread over an area stretching north to La Loche, south to Loon Lake, east to Canoe Lake, and west to Pierceland. Business ventures like the mill package have the added attraction of keeping potential profits within the local community, he adds.

"The bottom line is probably a commitment to a better way of life," Ahenakew says. "Maybe that's where our percentage of profit is really realized."

EXPLORING • MEADOW LAKE SAWMILL

1. Who are the entrepreneurs in this venture?
2. How did the entrepreneurs obtain financing for this venture?
3. How has this venture proven to be a winner?
4. In what way do the investors participate in the business venture?
5. What experience did each of the investors bring to the venture?
6. What are the benefits of this financial arrangement?

The Process of Raising Capital

Money — a capital idea from the start.

Starting a venture requires capital. Often this capital is more than the entrepreneur has available through personal sources. The employees of Meadow Lake sawmill wanted to finance the venture by reducing expenses and making their sawmill operation more efficient. They hoped this would help them to attract investors. In the end, the financing came from an unexpected source. There are numerous sources that an entrepreneur may tap to raise money for a venture.

The first source of financing is usually the hardest to obtain because many investors are reluctant to take on unknown risk.

Entrepreneurs may have to knock on many doors before securing financing. This can be very frustrating. In order to increase the likelihood of a positive response to the request for financing, entrepreneurs should try to generate excitement about their venture and show evidence of strong commitment and a belief in success.

One who asks not, receives not.

The process of creating a venture plan, discussed initially in Chapter 6, takes entrepreneurs out into the community to talk to people, to do research, to seek advice, and to interact with other entrepreneurs. This helps entrepreneurs develop a network of contacts who may be able to assist in seeking a source of financing. Someone in the entrepreneur's network may know an investor willing to back a startup venture.

It is important to note that investors will rarely lend money without having a sound knowledge of the venture. The venture plan must provide thorough and carefully considered answers to the following questions:

- How will the venture earn revenue?
- What is the potential profit?
- How long will it take to attain this profit level?
- How much of an investment is required?
- Is the investment secured?
- Can the investment be converted to cash at any time?
- Who will be involved in the day-to-day management and decision making of the venture?
- Will the investor have an opportunity to be involved in the management of the venture?

A detailed, professional, and well-presented venture plan will attract investors, build their trust, and encourage them and their investments to grow with the venture.

YOUR TURN

1. Review the initial research you prepared for your venture plan in Chapter 6 and study your partially completed financial analysis section created in Chapter 10. Are all the questions listed above answered in your plan? If not, take the time to expand your preliminary plan to include any missing answers.

Equity Financing

Equity financing is a form of financing in which the investor receives ownership in the venture in exchange for a financial contribution. The investment may come from the entrepreneur's personal savings or from friends, relatives, or business partners. It may be acquired by forming a partnership, establishing a limited business and selling shares, or through **venture capital**, **private placement**, or business employees.

Table 11.1 Advantages and Disadvantages of Equity Financing

Advantages	*Disadvantages*
• A large capital investment by the owner(s) increases the venture's borrowing power. • Suppliers will offer more generous credit terms to ventures that are equity financed. • Ownership of the venture is shared by more people, thus the risk is spread out. • Investors have a genuine interest in the success of the venture.	• The entrepreneur may end up being an employee of the other investors, depending on their relative contribution of capital. • The entrepreneur may lose some of his or her independence. • Investors share in the profits according to their investment. • Additional expenses may be incurred; for example, legal fees or bookkeeping expenses.

Weighing the advantages of equity financing against the disadvantages can help entrepreneurs determine if this is the best form of financing for a venture.

Personal Savings

Entrepreneurs who have sufficient personal savings and who do not wish to share the decision making, profits, or ownership of the business may choose to use only their own savings to start the venture.

> The entrepreneur may be more motivated to succeed when the risk is not shared by anyone else.

AGENTS OF CHANGE

Emily Carr's love for the Indians, her fondness for animals, her innate artistry, and singleness of purpose made her an outstanding woman not only in British Columbia, but also in all of Canada. For years she was known as the interpreter of Indian life.

Using personal savings can be a great financial and personal sacrifice for the entrepreneur. However, it conveys a high level of confidence in the venture and that may make it easier to obtain a personal loan.

Friends and Family

Friends and family may wish to invest money because they believe in the entrepreneur and are willing to risk some of their savings to help start the venture. This type of investment is commonly referred to as **"love money"**. The inventors of the board game *Trivial Pursuit*, for example, obtained their startup capital from friends and relatives. They had tried unsuccessfully for several months to raise capital. Some people they approached thought the board game was not a marketable idea, others thought the lack of the inventors' business experience was a real deterent to success. But these young entrepreneurs persevered. They approached friends and relatives and asked for only a small investment — $1000 in exchange for five shares of equity in the business. They were finally able to raise $75 000 to test market the game. The rest of the story, as they say, is history. The friends and family members who invested have had returns of over 50 times their investment.

Figure 11.1 "Mom, Dad, I am certain you will be able to retire on your investment."

Although not every venture is as successful as *Trivial Pursuit*, if the investors know the entrepreneur, have confidence in his or her ability and can envision the success of the venture, they may be persuaded to part with some of their savings. The potential disadvantage to investment from friends or family is that the personal relationship could be hurt if the money is lost or not repaid.

Partnership

As you read in Chapter 8, a partnership is formed when two or more entrepreneurs get together to start a venture. With each of the partners making a financial investment in the venture, there may be no need to raise additional capital. However, if further capital is required, there will be a higher **credit rating** which will increase borrowing power. The partnership agreement illustrated in Table 11.2 provides information on the kinds of financial issues which must be decided when two or more individuals join forces in venture startup and management. Here we again meet Jasso Persad, the young entrepreneur from Chapter 10 who wished to finance her university costs through profits earned from her painting and renovation business. She has decided to take on a partner, David Epstein.

Table 11.2 A Partnership Agreement

Article 1: Name of Partnership
Jasso Persad and David Epstein hereby form a partnership named Jasso and David Painting (hereinafter referred to as the "Partnership") under the provisions of the Partnership Act of the Province of Thisplace. All regulations applying are the same as those provided in the act, unless otherwise provided for in this agreement.

Article 2: Purposes
The purpose of the Partnership is to operate a company that provides painting and renovation services and to:

- enter into, perform, and carry out such contracts necessary, in connection with, or incidental to the operation of the Partnership.
- acquire any real or personal property, in fee or under lease, or any rights necessary or appropriate for the continued operation of the Partnership.

- borrow money, issue evidences of indebtedness, or to secure the same by mortgage, deed or trust, pledge or other lien, to further the purposes of the Partnership.
- sell or otherwise dispose of all or any portion of the assets or properties or the Partnership.

Article 3: Name and Place of Residence of Partners
This Agreement is between: Jasso Persad, 48 King Haven Road, in the City of Yourtown, Province of Thisplace, and David Epstein, 116 Glendale Street, in the City of Yourtown, Province of Thisplace.

Article 4: Location and Principal Place of Business
The principal address of the Partnership shall be located at 2220 Queen Street North, in the City of Yourtown, Province of Thisplace or at such other location as Jasso and David Painting decides to maintain its principal office.

Article 5: Term of Partnership
The term of the Partnership shall commence on October 1, 199_ and continue until the Partnership is dissolved as provided for by one of the articles of this agreement.

Article 6: Contributions of the Partners
Each Partner shall contribute the following amount of money on or before the date specified below. Additional contributions shall be determined in accordance with Article 7.

Name of Partner	Amount	Date
Jasso Persad	$10 000	October 1, 199_
David Epstein	$20 000	October 2, 199_

Article 7: Capital Accounts
An individual capital account shall be maintained for each Partner to which shall be credited or debited his or her contributions to capital or withdrawals or returns of capital and his or her share of profits, losses, and other distributions of the Partnership. The capital account of a Partner shall not be subject to withdrawal by the Partner without the consent of the other Partner and shall not bear interest.

Article 8: Advance Drawing
Each Partner may draw out of the business, in anticipation of expected profits, an amount agreed upon in writing between the Partners. Any such advance shall be deducted from the Partner's share of the distribution of profits in the accounting period that the advance took place or in an accounting period that the Partners agree upon.

Article 9: Distribution of Capital
The respective amounts of the Partners' capital interest in the Partnership may be returned to them, in whole or in part, at any time that the Partners may decide. Such returns shall be made either pro rata to each Partner in proportion to his or her interest in the Partnership. Notwithstanding the foregoing, it must be determined that all liabilities of the Partnership have been paid or the Partnership has property sufficient to pay them before the capital interest of any Partner shall be returned to him or to her. No Partner shall have priority over the other Partner either as to the return of investment or as to the distribution of net profits.

Article 10: Charges to Capital
Any and all distributions of profits or capital to a partner shall be charged to his or her respective capital account on the date when they are made.

Article 11: Year End
The fiscal year of the Partnership shall end on September 30 of each year.

Article 12: Distribution of Profits and Losses
In this initial year and in each succeeding year the net profits or losses of the Partnership shall be determined using the accounting methods chosen by the Partners. Such methods shall also provide the net profit or loss of the Partnership for income tax purposes unless any of the aforementioned accounting methods is prohibited from such use by law.

Profits of the Partnership shall be determined at the end of each fiscal year and allocated to each Partner on the basis of his or her respective percentage of contribution as set out in Article 6. All losses occurring in the course of the business shall be borne in the same manner, unless the losses were caused by the willful neglect or default, and not by mistake, of any of the Partners, in which case the loss so incurred shall be made good by the Partner through whose neglect or default the losses occurred.

Incorporating the Business

If the venture requires a great deal of capital, incorporating and selling shares may be the wisest route to take. The advantages and disadvantages of incorporating and going public have been carefully examined in Chapter 8.

Venture PROFILE

Public ownership means public scrutiny

By Mary Ann Prychoda, *Small Business*

Going public has some alluring advantages, but deciding when and where to list is crucial.

Is your company ready for its first public share offering? Start the decision-making process with some critical self-examination. Realize first that going public means sharing your company with hundreds of new partners. Can you live with answering to others? Will you be able to take guidance from your board of directors? Or will the reporting required of public firms become overly burdensome? And can you live with the idea of arch competitors knowing key financial information that you once shared only with your accountant?

These can be difficult questions for some owner/managers. For others, the advantages of equity financing far outweigh the potential loss of privacy and freedom. For one thing, unlike debt financing, equity financing injects new money into the company that you never pay back: You aren't borrowing the funds, you are selling part-ownership in your company. And once a company goes public, future equity financing can be raised more quickly and cheaply than the initial offering. The influx of cash, and the growth it allows, can also make supplier credit and debt financing easier to obtain.

Other advantages include the ability to offer share purchase and other stock plans as employee benefits and incentives. Having shares with liquidity and an established market value can facilitate financing an acquisition or merger through a share exchange, and you can offer shares as collateral to your creditors. Remember, too, that public companies enjoy a heightened public profile through articles and analysis in the business press and through daily listing in newspaper stock-market tables.

If you decide that going public is an option you want to explore, you must next decide if the business itself is ready. "In general, the time to go public is when you are sufficiently mature that you can maintain earnings growth and report quarterly" without the kind of earnings dips that might scare off investors, advises Linda Willis, a partner in the Entrepreneurial Services Group of Clarkson Gordon/Woods Gordon in Toronto.

To make your initial offering, you must convince first an underwriter (the investment dealer who undertakes to sell your first share issue to the public) and then public investors that your company has significant potential for earnings growth. And you must be able to show how you will use the funds raised in the offering to fuel that growth. An established business will have to demonstrate strong management and a good track record, including rising profits in recent years. If you have no track record because you're going public with a startup company, underwriters and investors will have to base their assessments on just two factors: the expertise of management and the market potential of the product or service to be produced.

EXPLORING • GOING PUBLIC

1. In what ways does going public affect the venture?
2. How can an entrepreneur determine if his or her venture would be best suited to going public?
3. What does an underwriter do to assist the entrepreneur?
4. What do investors look for in a share offering? Does it differ if the shares are being offered for the first or third time?
5. Refer back to the Venture Profiles in Chapter 5: Students create own jobs with paper for job-seekers (page 128) and Chip's better wiper idea (page 133). Would either of these ventures benefit by going public? In what ways?

Venture Capitalists

Venture capital comes from private individuals or companies who are interested in investing in new ventures in hope of a high return on their investments. The venture capitalist, often introduced to the entrepreneur through a network of contacts, sets goals for the level of return he or she is looking for and will make investment decisions based on the projected ability of the venture to reach these goals. For example, if a venture capitalist has $100 000 to invest, he or she may be looking for a return of 25-30 per cent.

Venture capitalists like to see a precise breakdown of how much money is required and will weigh this against how much they are prepared to invest.

AGENTS OF CHANGE

Ellen Fairclough was forced to leave school at the age of 16 when her father's farm failed. She held a number of jobs until 1946, when she developed an interest in local politics. In 1957 she became the first female Cabinet Minister in Canadian history.

Figure 11.2 This venture capitalist has decided that this business opportunity is too good to miss.

Some venture capitalists like to be involved with the venture either in a day-to-day management role or on the board of directors of the business. The entrepreneur forfeits some independence because he or she has to regularly report to the venture capitalist and the business cannot be sold without the venture capitalist's permission.

Private Placement

Private placement is similar to venture capital; however, usually a small group of investors get together to invest. This group of investors is gathered together by one of the partners of the venture or by a member of the external venture team.

> It is faster and cheaper to raise money through private placement than it is through going public.

Each of the group of investors may, however, want a say in the day-to-day operation of the business and this may detract from the entrepreneur's sense of independence and vision for the venture.

Employees

Employees of the Meadow Lake and Green Lake sawmills saw that their jobs would be eliminated if the mills did not start to produce at a profitable level. They implemented changes to make the mills financially viable in the hope of obtaining some financial backing for the takeover. As part owners, the employees became even more motivated to keep expenses down and efficiency up.

Employees who have been with a company for a specified period of time or who are in senior positions may be invited to invest in a venture on a limited basis. Inviting employees to become owners in a venture can have very beneficial results. **Share purchase** and **stock option plans** often serve to motivate employees to work more productively, to resolve problems more efficiently, and to be more committed to the venture.

AGENTS OF CHANGE

Sarah Day and Michelle Morneau knew they wanted to be self-employed, but they rejected all the traditional student businesses such as lawn care, house painting, and selling T-shirts. When a friend suggested they sell chimney caps, they decided they had the right idea. Today, they are inundated with orders. Recognizing the right idea at the right time changed their lives.

YOUR TURN

2. Review the Venture Profiles listed below. In your notebooks, complete the chart by writing down the form of equity financing each venture used.

Entrepreneurs	Forms of Equity Financing
Ross Fedele, Port-a-Tray (Chapter 6, page 176)	
Joan Fanton, Sunshine Theatre (Chapter 6, page 177)	
Bruce Johnson, Simply Marbleous (Chapter 8, page 222)	
Shashi Sharma, The Indo-Persian Rug Company (Chapter 9, page 258)	
Sarah Ferris, Aspen Cleaners (Chapter 9, page 280)	
Gerry McKendry, Petco, The Plastic Engine Technology Company (Chapter 10, page 292)	

3. In groups of three, interview five local entrepreneurs. Discover whether their startup funds came from personal savings, family or friends, a partner, selling shares, a venture capitalist, employees, or any other source not discussed here.

Debt Financing

Debt financing refers to the borrowing of money to start a venture.

> Debt differs from equity in that the entrepreneur does not give up any ownership; however, the loan must be paid back and there is an interest charge for the use of the money.

The entrepreneur borrows money and pays it back after the venture is more firmly established

It is a relatively easy process to obtain a business loan. Most lenders will approve a loan within a few weeks. Compare this to finding a partner to share your vision and you can see why many entrepreneurs use debt financing to at least partially finance their startup costs.

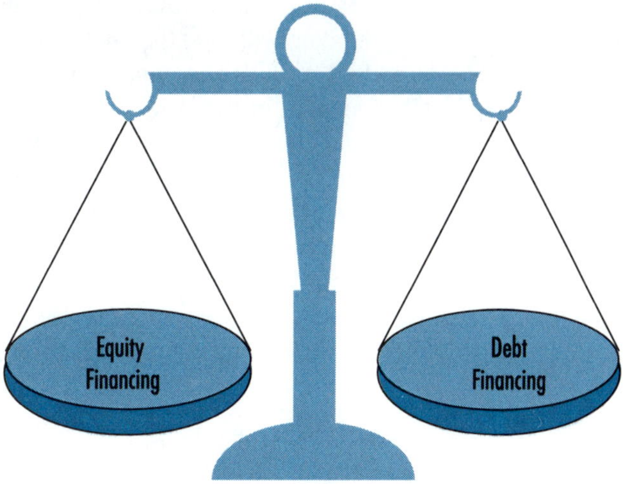

Figure 11.3 Balancing debt with equity requires knowledge and planning.

It is important to note that all the costs incurred in borrowing money for the venture are **tax deductible**. This means that interest on the loan and any costs associated with setting up the loan reduce the amount of income tax the venture has to pay. This actually reduces the interest rate of the loan in terms of real dollars. The entrepreneur must ensure, however, that he or she does not borrow more than can be repaid from the income generated by the venture.

It's much easier to look for a good loans officer if you understand how loans officers look at you.

It is the entrepreneur's responsibility to find a lender who is compatible with the venture. The lending institution with the lowest interest rate is not always the best one. Some lenders place limits on what the entrepreneur can and cannot do. The lender must understand the requirements of the venture and must be able to assess the financial risk with a fair degree of knowledge.

New ventures pose a great risk to a lender because the venture has no track record and the lender has no knowledge of whether the entrepreneur can be relied upon to repay the loan. Lenders usually feel more comfortable lending to entrepreneurs who have previous business experience and some expertise in the current venture. They also like to feel confident that the entrepreneur understands the elements of financial management. It is important too that the entrepreneur has invested his or her own money or some form of equity in the venture as security. Depending on the lending institution, the individual involved, and the particular venture, lenders will look for a **debt to equity ratio** of anywhere from 1:1 to 4:1, with the debt portion equalling four times the equity portion, in the latter case. Debt financing through government agencies and ministries tends to have a 1:1 lending ratio for such programs as New Venture Loans or Youth Venture Loans. This is because the government is taking a big risk and is responsible for repaying the loan to the financial institution should the entrepreneur be unable to do so. The case of a 4:1 ratio might exist where the entrepreneur has considerable financial and management expertise, a proven record of past earnings, and a **fixed asset**, such as real estate, as security.

AGENTS OF CHANGE

Casimir Gzowski, the son of a Polish count, landed in New York as a poor Polish exile. He moved to Upper Canada in 1841 and organized the building of roads, bridges, and lighthouses. His greatest engineering feat was the designing and building of the International Bridge across the treacherous Niagara River.

"There are bankers who will loan you an umbrella when the sun is shining and then want it back when the rains come."
Mark Twain

The Six C's of Credit

When applying for a loan, the entrepreneur must be prepared for a full investigation. Lenders are interested in knowing about the entrepreneur's **character**, **capital**, **collateral**, **capacity**, **circumstances**, and **coverage**. These are known as the **6 C's of credit** and are used as the basis for evaluating the loan application.

Character is honesty and reliability. The lender is able to trust the entrepreneur with character to protect the assets of the venture and pay the loan back as scheduled.

Capital is the amount of money the entrepreneur has invested in the venture from his or her own savings.

Collateral is the personal assets the entrepreneur uses to ensure that a loan will be paid back should anything happen to the venture. If the entrepreneur is not prepared to put personal assets on the line, the lender may not make a loan.

Capacity is the ability of the entrepreneur to manage the venture effectively and efficiently. If there is a complete business plan that indicates the goals of the venture and the path to reach the goals, the lender will be more confident in making the loan.

The circumstances that the lender considers when making a loan decision include: the competition, the current state of the economy, the rate of inflation, and the nature of the product or service. If the lender views the product or service as a luxury and the economy is tight, the loan may not be granted. The circumstances are largely out of the control of the entrepreneur; however, the entrepreneur should address the current circumstances in the venture plan and demonstrate an understanding of how to manage the venture in light of these circumstances.

Coverage refers to insurance protection for the venture and the entrepreneur. In the event of fire, liability, or death, the lender wants to be paid back.

Banks

Chartered banks, such as the Toronto Dominion Bank, the Bank of Montreal, and the Royal Bank of Canada, are financial institutions organized under federal legislation. Banks can offer the entrepreneur a **line of credit**, a **term loan**, or a **mortgage**. A line of credit allows the entrepreneur to draw extra money whenever it is needed for a short period of time. Pay back is flexible as long as the interest is paid every month. A term loan is usually made to purchase equipment and there is a defined pay-back period with specified payments. For example, if the entrepreneur borrows money to purchase a delivery truck, the loan would have to be paid back before the value of the truck has depreciated to nothing. A mortgage is a loan made for the purchase of real estate. The term on a mortgage is much longer than on most other types of loans. The real estate purchased is used as collateral for the loan. The maximum rate of interest that the bank can charge on any type of loan is regulated by the Bank of Canada.

Figure 11.4 Chartered banks offer a variety of debt financing options.

YOUR TURN

4. Interview a local bank manager. Make an appointment before you go and be sure to send a thank-you note after the interview. Ask the bank manager the following questions:
   a) What types of loans does your bank offer to entrepreneurs?
   b) What is the rate of interest charged on each of these types of loans?
   c) What other costs are associated with obtaining a loan for a new venture?
   d) What factors do you consider when deciding whether or not to lend money to an entrepreneur?

Credit Unions

Credit unions are financial institutions organized under provincial legislation. To obtain a loan from a credit union, the entrepreneur must be a member.

Credit unions are organized as co-operatives with an equity participation by all the members.

Members have a common interest, that is, they work in the same industry or live in the same neighbourhood. For example, the Scarborough Education Credit Union serves those individuals who live in Scarborough or work in the education field in the Scarborough vicinity.

Credit unions operate very much like banks. They offer operating lines of credit, term loans, and mortgages. The manager of the credit union will evaluate each loan application on the basis of the 6 C's of credit; however, sometimes credit unions will take a risk on a member that other financial institutions might not. Because the credit union is operated for its members, if there is a surplus of money at the end of the year, the borrowers may receive a rebate on their loan interest.

Figure 11.5 Credit unions are formed by individuals with a common bond.

YOUR TURN

5. Look up Credit Unions in the Yellow Pages. List the credit unions in your community. Call each of them and ask them to describe the common bond in their membership.

Government

AGENTS OF CHANGE

The Canadarm, built entirely in Canada, was designed by a team of engineers and scientists from both government and industry. It is used to move satellites and experimental packages in and out of the cargo bays of the U.S. space shuttles. Two small television sets are mounted on the arm's elbow and wrist to allow the operator (inside the orbiter) to see what is happening.

Both the federal and provincial governments provide money to new ventures that have the potential to create jobs, develop a new technology, or provide a domestic product to compete against a foreign product. This money may come in the form of a **grant**, a **guarantee**, or a loan. If the entrepreneur obtains a grant, it generally does not have to be paid back. Loans and loan guarantees do require a pay-back schedule.

A number of government agencies provide support in the form of money and advice for entrepreneurs. Some provide a **"matchmaking service"** — matching the investor with the entrepreneur. Some provide loan guarantees — providing collateral to the bank so the loan will be made. Others provide direct funding, and still others offer advice.

The government is often referred to as the lender of last resort because entrepreneurs who are unable to obtain funding from other institutions come to the government for assistance.

A detailed list of the services offered by both provincial and federal governments is included in the Appendix at the back of this text.

YOUR TURN

6. Contact your local Member of Parliament for both the provincial and federal government. Ask for information on the government agencies that support new business ventures.
7. Once you have obtained all the information, prepare a chart listing the agencies and the type of support each offers.

8. In small groups, list all the places in your community from which a loan might be obtained. Select three places from your list and interview a representative from that location. Ensure that the places selected are different from each other, that is, one bank, one credit union, and one government agency. Ask the following questions at each of the lending institutions:
   a) What types of loans do you provide?
   b) What are the advantages for an entrepreneur in borrowing from you?
   c) What types of collateral do you require?
   d) What information do you need on a loan application?
   e) How do you review a loan application?
   f) What criteria do you use to evaluate the loan applications?

Venture PROFILE

A woman's place is on the site

The Globe and Mail, "Report on Business"

One banker asked McLeod, "Why don't you open a boutique?"

"Why," the banker asked Heather McLeod in 1984, "don't you open a boutique?" A 37-year-old woman selling skirts and blouses was something the banker could understand. A woman who wanted to start a manufacturing business to produce plywood forms for the construction industry wasn't.

Plywood forms are a specialized product used by builders to hold poured concrete while it hardens, but McLeod knew first-hand that nobody was meeting the demand for good-quality forms in Nova Scotia. She had worked seven years, first as an accountant and then in sales, for a company that made plywood forms, and her customers were telling her they weren't happy with the workmanship of the product they were getting.

"I thought, 'There's a good market here. Why don't I do something about it? If I don't, people from the States are going to move a plant up here.'" With her background and knowledge, she was dumbfounded that bankers should tell her she was in the wrong business. They were also unhappy that she wasn't married at the time, which meant no second income to support the new business. But she was able to get a mortgage on her house. She also "sold everything that wasn't tied down," including her car and her children's savings bonds, and got grants from the federal and Nova Scotia governments. Finally, she had a bankroll of $150 000.

In 1985, Superior Forming Systems and Supplies went into production in the village of Debert, near Truro. McLeod backed the quality of her product with a lifetime guarantee, and contractors — many of whom had encouraged her to go into business — were quick to place orders. Now she is expanding into New England and Ontario. Sales this year will pass the $1-million mark and she's investing more money in manufacturing. The company has 10 employees, including her husband of three years, who is vice-president.

McLeod says she loves working at her own business. At the height of the summer construction season, she puts in a staggering 16 hours a day. "If you want to work 9 to 5, you won't be successful," she says. She encourages customers to drop in any time for a chat or to call her at home if there's a problem.

To survive in a new business, says McLeod, "You have to monitor your costs and not get in over your head. We could have used more expensive equipment than we had at first, but we made do until we could afford better." Now that she's a success, McLeod has a car again. It's a well-travelled Pony and it looks right at home on a Nova Scotia construction site. McLeod says she wouldn't buy a Mercedes even if she could afford it. "Our customers couldn't relate to it."

EXPLORING • PLYWOOD FORMS

1. What aspects of Heather McLeod's background and knowledge should have made her a good business loan risk?
2. Give reasons for why she had difficulty obtaining a loan.
3. What does McLeod forecast as sales for her company, Superior Forming Systems and Supplies, this year?
4. What advice does she offer to help new businesses survive?

The Necessary Numbers

As you can see, the entrepreneur has many financial decisions to make. The investor also has to make the decision about whether to invest in this venture or alternatively place the money in a different investment.

Chapter 10 discussed the importance of financial planning. More specifically, it explained the importance of preparing a personal budget, a cashflow forecast, and a personal balance sheet. The personal budget was used to determine the amount of income the venture would produce or would need to produce for the entrepreneur. The cashflow forecast revealed projected startup and operating expenses and anticipated revenue. The personal balance sheet assessed the entrepreneur's assets and liabilities and projected his or her net worth, information necessary in order to determine what additional financing might be needed.

Whether the entrepreneur uses equity financing or debt financing to raise the necessary startup and operating capital required, he or she must convince potential investors and financial institutions that the venture is sound and attractive. To do this, the entrepreneur must prepare both an **income forecast** and a **projected balance sheet**. These two documents will help prospective **creditors** or owners assess the risk of the investment and the size of the potential return. Risk assessment is most important to creditors as their return is limited to the interest which they can earn on the outstanding balance of the loan. They want to be assured that the risk that the venture cannot pay its debts is small. Owners are most interested in the potential benefits, for example, the possibility of receiving part of the profits from the venture in the form of dividends or yielding a capital gain as the value of the assets of the successful venture increases in value.

The Income Forecast

The income forecast estimates the financial results of the operation of the venture and helps to determine whether the company will have enough earnings to pay its debts. It forecasts what the total income and total costs of a venture will be for a specific period of time. It also estimates the amount of the profit or loss for the venture. The income forecast follows the same format as an **income statement.** The only difference is that the figures in the income forecast reflect what the entrepreneur thinks will happen in the future rather than what has happened in the past.

In Chapter 10, the Venture Profile of Jasso Persad was examined as she attempted to establish her house painting business. Jasso's first attempt at preparing a cashflow forecast is reproduced here.

Table 11.3 Jasso's Painting
Cashflow Forecast, April-September, 199_

CASH IN	*April*	*May*	*June*	*July*	*Aug.*	*Sept.*	*Total*
Estimated Sales of Goods or Services	$1200	$3640	$4900	$4900	$2900	$800	$18 340
Student Venture Capital Loans	$2500						$ 2500
Other (Specify)							
Total	$3700	$3640	$4900	$4900	$2900	$800	$20 840

CASH OUT							
Purchase of Equipment	$2050						$ 2050
Rental Expenses	$ 75	$ 75	$ 75	$ 75	$ 50	$ 25	$ 375
Labour Expenses	$ 200	$1600	$2400	$2400	$ 600	$150	$ 7350
Personal Drawings	$ 50	$ 200	$ 250	$ 250	$ 150	$100	$ 1000
Materials	$ 100	$ 200	$ 300	$ 300	$ 200	$100	$ 1200
Business Licences and Fees	$ 10						$ 10
Advertising	$ 150	$ 100	$ 100	$ 50			$ 400

	April	May	June	July	Aug.	Sept.	Total
Insurance	$725						$ 725
Office Expenses	$200	$ 50	$ 50	$ 50	$ 50		$ 400
Other (Gas and Truck Repairs)	$125	$ 100	$ 250	$ 200	$ 75	$ 50	$ 800
Loan Repayment (To be completed by September 30 of this year)			$ 500	$ 500	$ 700	$ 800	$ 2500
Total	$3685	$2325	$3925	$3825	$1825	$1225	$16 810

NET CASH: (Cash In - Cash Out)

Monthly Surplus	$ 15	$1315	$ 975	$1075	$1075		
Monthly Deficit						$ 425	
Cumulative (to date)	$ 15	$1330	$2305	$3380	$4455	$4030	

Source: Adapted from: Ontario Ministry of Skills Development, *Student Venture Capital Program*

This cashflow forecast may be used to determine Jasso's income forecast. Table 11.4 illustrates the form an income forecast takes and inserts the appropriate data from Jasso's Cashflow Forecast for the month of April.

Table 11.4 Jasso's Painting Income Forecast

Jasso's Painting Income Forecast
Month Ending April 30, 199_

Operating Income

Sales	$1200.00	
Cost of Goods Sold		
Inventory, April 1	$0.00	
Plus: Cost of Goods Purchased/Manufactured	0	
Total Value of Goods for Sale	0.00	
Less: Inventory, April 30	0	
Cost of Goods Sold		0.00
Gross Profit on Sales		$1200.00

Operating Expenses

Equipment	$2050.00	
Rent	75.00	
Labour	200.00	
Personal Drawings	50.00	
Materials	100.00	
Business Licence & Fees	10.00	
Advertising	150.00	
Insurance	725.00	
Office Expense.	200.00	
Other	125.00	
Total Operating Expenses		3685.00
Net Profit(Loss) from Operations		($2485.00)

Jasso's income forecast is projecting a loss for the month of April of $2485.00. The loss is due to the combination of high startup costs and low sales income. Note that the income forecast includes only earned income. Borrowed money does not appear. Nothing appears in the Cost of Goods Sold section of the income forecast because Jasso was selling a service. All her costs are therefore considered expenses. Ventures which either manufacture a good or those, such as retail stores, which trade goods would complete the Cost of Goods Sold section of the forecast. In the case of a manufacturing venture, all the costs, such as labour and production, which have gone directly into the production of the good would be listed. In the case of a retail venture, the cost of purchasing inventory from suppliers would be listed.

YOUR TURN

9. Using the data from Table 11.3, Jasso's Cashflow Forecast, prepare an income forecast for Jasso's venture:
   a) for the month of July
   b) for the six-month period from April to September
10. Assume that Jasso wished to diversify her venture and sell brass house numbers which she could install after finishing a paint job. Assume also that she could purchase the numbers from suppliers on an "as needed" basis at a cost of $2.00 each. Assume that over the six months she was able to sell and install 450 numbers for a price of $5.00 each. Prepare her new income forecast for the six-month period from April to September.

The Projected Balance Sheet

The projected balance sheet is a snapshot of the financial condition of a venture at a given time in the future.

The projected balance sheet forecasts what a venture will own and what it will owe on a given date. Even more important, it shows the estimated value of the owner's equity.

As with the personal balance sheet described in Chapter 10, a projected balance sheet is divided into two main sections: assets, which are listed on the left side of the sheet, and liabilities and owners' equity, which are listed on the right side. Assets must equal liabilities plus owners' equity. Owners' equity is what is left after the liabilities of a venture are deducted from its assets.

Jasso's projected balance sheet can also be derived from her cashflow forecast. Before examining her projected balance sheet, we make the following assumptions:

- The projected balance sheet will forecast how things will be on June 30.
- Jasso only receives payment in cash as she completes each job, so there are no accounts receivable.
- The value of her capital assets have not declined since they were purchased.
- She pays for everything in cash at the time of purchase so there are no accounts payable.

Her Projected Balance Sheet would then look like this:

Table 11.5 Jasso's Painting Projected Balance Sheet

Jasso's Painting
Projected Balance Sheet
June 30, 199_

Assets		*Liabilities*	
Cash	$2305	Loan Payable	$2000
Equipment	2050	Accounts Payable	000
Accounts Receivable	0	*Owner's Equity*	
		Owner's Investment	000
		Profit(Loss)	2355
Total		Total Liabilities	
Total Assets	$4355	and Owners' Equity	$4355

To verify this projected balance sheet, check Table 11.3, Jasso's Cashflow Forecast. The data for the projected balance sheet comes from specific sections of this cashflow forecast. The cash asset of $2305 is found in the Net Cash: Cumulative column for June. The Equipment Asset of $2050 comes from the Cash Out: Purchase of Equipment for April. The Liability: Loan Payable of $2000 comes from the Cash Out: Loan Repayment column which indicates that $500 of the $2500 loan has been repaid.

YOUR TURN

11. Using the data in Jasso's final cashflow forecast, prepare the projected balance sheet for Jasso's Painting for September 30, 199_.
12. It is unlikely that the equipment Jasso purchased would retain its full value. Capital assets depreciate over time and their value on the balance sheet must be reduced to reflect this. Assume the equipment purchased in April will depreciate in value by 50 per cent by the end of September. How would Jasso's projected balance sheet for September 30 look after this change?
13. Assume that Jasso decided to close the business and sell off all the assets. How much income will she receive in total since she started the venture in April?

How Will You Proceed?

Now that you have some knowledge of financial planning and forecasting, there is an additional decision that you must make.

A unique idea for a venture, that is, one that has never been tried before, will require that you start from scratch. On the other hand, an idea for a venture that has been tried before offers a choice. You can either start from scratch or you can find a business that already exists, purchase it, and turn it into what you have in mind.

Starting from Scratch

Starting a venture from scratch can be very exciting. You can start very small — even on a part-time basis. You can choose where and how you will start. You can contribute your personal savings to your venture. As you have learned from this text, building your venture from nothing requires you to make many decisions. Where will you locate your venture? Who will your customers be? How will you reach your customers? How do you ensure that your cashflow projections materialize? When you start from scratch, you are not going with a "tried and true" known quantity, so there is an element of risk for the prospective entrepreneur.

AGENTS OF CHANGE

There were no products on the market that reflected the modern consumer's desire to be environmentally responsible, without costing a fortune. That is, not until Loblaws introduced its new Green Program, a whole line of environmentally friendly products. Loblaws came up with a great marketing idea that has also helped our environment!

Buying an Existing Business or Franchise

Depending on the kind of venture you plan to undertake, you might want to consider the safer route of buying an existing business, one that is already operating. You can then work at turning it into the kind of venture you had originally dreamed of. In some cases, financing the purchase of an existing business can be arranged so that it is cheaper than starting one up from scratch. Buying a business that is already bringing in an income is a fairly safe way to start. Your customers and suppliers are already there. Your location, equipment, and process for delivery are also already established. Your cashflow starts immediately. Buying an existing business includes buying the reputation that the business has in the community. If it has many happy customers, they will become part of the "package". If, on the other hand, you inherit unhappy customers, you will have to work harder to win them back.

Customers are people.

You might not be able to purchase the kind of venture you would have started from scratch but you might, eventually, be able to turn an existing venture into your original idea.

Buying an existing business can also include the option of buying a franchise. Even though most franchisors do not allow you to change the operation of the franchise business, there are exceptions. The following Venture Profile is an interesting case in point.

Venture PROFILE

Three men and a café: from franchise to freedoms

By Brenda Spiering, *Financial Post*, "Moneywise"

The Café Coco cast, from left, Mario, Paul and Joseph Giorgio

Enter Café Coco in downtown Toronto's College Park shopping mall any weekday morning or lunch hour and you are bound to find a steady stream of customers. Behind the gleaming new countertops and display cases, laden with such tempting delights as strawberry glazed tarts, chocolate-covered croissants, and apple danishes, you are bound to find at least one of the three brothers who share equal ownership of the operation.

Hustling in their neat brown aprons to see that everyone is served as quickly as possible, Paul, Mario, and Joseph Giorgio can smile today knowing their restaurant is a success. But it wasn't always so. Paul and his twin, Mario, 27, and Joseph, 34, can remember only too well when they first opened the doors of the franchised café six years ago and the crowds failed to appear.

"Back then, we wondered if the business would last three months," recalls Paul. "Many weeks went by when we didn't take home a paycheque." But now, with monthly sales of between $40 000 and $45 000, such lean times are a thing of the past. The Giorgios have successfully navigated every franchisor's dream course — from indebted franchisee to profit-making independent business owner.

The brothers started off as entrepreneurs shortly after high school. They had brief careers in retail management, then bought a small grocery in a Toronto shopping mall. But business was slow, and they began to consider franchise opportunities. When Café Coco moved into the same mall, it seemed just the thing. They contacted head office.

For a $25 000 franchise fee, they were offered a proven business concept and their choice of prime downtown locations. Lured by promises of a high-volume business, the brothers signed the deal and selected newly renovated College Park for its downtown location and towering office complex filled with potential customers. An additional $55 000 investment ($25 000 financed by the franchisor and $30 000 by a bank loan) got them a turnkey operation.

But the European-style café, with its pink chairs, espresso, and rich desserts, failed to draw customers. "We might have given up if our family hadn't encouraged us," says Paul.

"Our parents, who immigrated to Canada from Italy, have always been hard workers and I guess it rubbed off on us. So we decided to give it our best shot."

When the Government of Ontario offices in the building put out a tender for coffee wagons, the Giorgios jumped at the chance. If customers wouldn't come to them, they'd go to the customers. Twice a day for three years, they loaded up their carts and headed upstairs. Pretty soon, those lining up at their coffee carts began lining up at their restaurant. And in order to lure more of the lunch crowd, they gradually introduced more substantial fare. Today, customers can choose from a wide range of sandwiches, salads, soup, even veal cutlets and shepherd's pie. Prices are reasonable: Sandwiches range from $2.30 for a cucumber, lettuce, and tomato croissant, to $4.50 for seafood salad on rye. Hot entrées run from $3.25 to $3.95. And the quality is excellent. "We know we couldn't compete with the other franchise in the building if we offered the same line," says Paul. "We had to be original, and to keep people coming back, our quality had to be exceptional." All baked goods are delivered fresh daily, and all fruits and vegetables are selected from local markets. "We could have relied on a dealer to deliver the produce, but then we'd have no guarantee of the quality, says Paul. "Instead, our parents handpick the fruits and vegetables for us each day and deliver them to the restaurant in the back of their car."

Family support, dedication to the business — each of the brothers puts in 50 to 70 hours a week — and willingness to diversify have given the Giorgios a good taste of success. When they got a phone call a few years ago asking if they could cater a business luncheon, they said "sure". From that on-the-spot decision has grown a busy sideline that now makes up 30 per cent of their business. A recent liquor licence, letting them serve beer and wine both in the café and on their outdoor patio, is attracting even more customers.

Best of all, their perseverance has brought them independence. While other Café Cocos have long since closed their doors, and their parent franchise company has recently gone out of business due to management difficulties, the Giorgios have negotiated an out-of-court settlement for full ownership. (They might change the cafe's name in future, but for now it's still Café Coco, and there have been no objections from former franchise management.) Since they are no longer required to submit a monthly 6 per cent royalty on gross sales to head office, profits are better than ever.

Each brother draws an annual salary of about $45 000, though they reinvest most of the profits back into the restaurant. And even with the freedom of operating under their own rules, Paul says he'd still advise business newcomers to consider buying a franchise. "They provided us with training, financial assistance, a professionally designed restaurant, and even the suppliers we needed to get started. For someone just setting out, I don't think there's any other way to go."

EXPLORING • CAFÉ COCO

1. Describe the changes the Giorgio brothers made to the original franchise they purchased.
2. Give reasons for the changes.
3. What benefits do they suggest come with the purchase of a franchise?
4. Was the business financed through equity or debt? How can you tell?

Making a Choice

The decision to start from scratch or to buy an existing business is a complex one. It is inappropriate to base it purely on personal preference or on the financial resources you have available, though these two factors are important to consider.

If you are convinced that you can predict a reasonable market niche for your product or service, starting a new venture from scratch may be your best route. For every kind of business venture there are only so many potential customers. Each new venture needs to be able to attract and keep a large enough number of these customers in order to survive. If the competition seems to have control of the market, you are probably best advised to buy an existing business and make changes slowly until it has become your own unique kind of venture — the one you dreamed of starting from scratch. On the other hand, if you can determine that the market is growing, or that some of the existing businesses are poorly organized, and if you see that you can deliver a noticeably better product or service at a competitive price, there might be room for your venture to start from scratch in the marketplace.

> Whatever kind of venture you plan to undertake, it is a good idea to study as many existing similar ventures as you can.

Learn as much as you can before you start your venture. Interview personnel involved in comparable ventures to the one you wish to establish. Find out how they got started, what they accomplished in the early stages, what problems they encountered. Volunteer to work with them for a period of time so that you can learn more about the venture before you undertake one of your own. The more you can learn before you start on your own, the better your chances of financial and personal success.

YOUR TURN

14. Use the Research Assistance Grid model from Chapter 6 to prepare a list of questions to help you decide whether to start from scratch or to buy an existing business.
15. Ask an established small business owner in your community to help you identify additional questions that should be asked.

POINTS TO REMEMBER

- Entrepreneurs can raise money for their ventures through equity or debt.
- Equity financing represents ownership in the venture and can come in the form of:
  -personal savings
  -investments from friends or family
  -partnership
  -incorporating and selling shares
  -venture capital
  -private placement
  -employees investing
- Debt financing represents a loan to the venture.
- Loans usually come from:
  -banks
  -credit unions
  -government
- Most lenders investigate the entrepreneur's 6 C's of credit: character, capital, collateral, capacity, circumstances, and coverage.
- Entrepreneurs should prepare income forecasts and a projected balance sheet to show potential investors.

- Before obtaining financing, entrepreneurs must decide whether to start the venture from scratch or to buy an existing business.

W·H·A·T H·A·V·E Y·O·U L·E·A·R·N·E·D·?

1. Why is the first loan or investment the most difficult for the entrepreneur to obtain?
2. In what way can the venture plan increase the possibilities of obtaining outside funding for the venture?
3. What are the advantages and disadvantages of using equity financing for a venture?
4. What role do venture capitalists usually want to have in exchange for their money? Why?
5. What are the benefits of having employees share in the ownership of the venture?
6. Why do some entrepreneurs prefer debt financing?
7. Describe the 6 C's of credit.
8. Differentiate between a line of credit, a term loan, and a mortgage.
9. What is the purpose of the income forecast? the projected balance sheet?
10. What are the advantages of starting a business from scratch rather than buying an existing business? What are the disadvantages?

V·E·N·T·U·R·I·N·G O·U·T

1. Consider which type of financing best suits your venture — equity or debt. Briefly assess the pros and cons of each in chart form and then write a short written conclusion.
2. If you are planning to obtain equity financing, who will you go to? If you are planning to obtain debt financing, who will you go to?
3. Review the information required for each type of financing. Write a proposal to include in the financial

analysis section of your venture plan to obtain the money you need for your venture.

4. Using the cashflow forecast you prepared at the end of Chapter 10, prepare an income forecast for your venture.
5. Prepare two projected balance sheets for a venture you are planning: one for the end of its first six months and the other for the end of its first year of operation.
6. After your financial analysis section is written, review it to ensure what you have written is what you want to say. Plan the oral presentation to accompany this section of your venture plan. Practise it on one of your classmates.

The MANAGEMENT spoke will describe sound management practices and illustrate how leadership, motivation, and effective communication are used to manage a successful venture.

CHAPTER 12

Driving a Venture

LEARNING OUTCOMES

By the end of this chapter, you should be able to:

- understand that managing a venture is as important to its success as creating it
- explain the causes of venture failure
- recognize the components of effective leadership and various leadership styles
- understand the concept of motivation and how to motivate employees
- apply the elements of communication in a variety of situations
- identify conflict and understand the various methods for dealing with it
- understand why the four main functions of management are important to the continued success of a venture

ENTREPRENEURIAL LANGUAGE

demise
under capitalization
task oriented
autocratic leaders
paternalistic leaders
democratic leaders
collegial leaders
laissez-faire leaders
Maslow's Hierarchy of Needs
self-actualization
body language
the turtle
the shark
the teddy bear
the fox
the owl
long-range objectives
short-range plans
organizational chart
pro-active control
computerized inventory control system
quality control program

Venture PROFILE

Service Companies: Focus or Falter

By William H. Davidow and Bro Uttal, *Harvard Business Review*

During the week, People Express had a huge surplus of empty seats.

Fuzzy or conflicting strategies make good customer service impossible. Look at People Express. In 1981, it focused tightly on budget travellers — students, backpackers, vacationers, and others willing to sacrifice convenient schedules and airport gates for low fares. Customers actually enjoyed the airline's widely advertised "no frills" service, which gave them the options of bringing their own food or paying extra for a snack in flight, of carrying their luggage or paying $3 a bag to check it, and of buying a ticket on board instead of in advance. In five years, People Express's fleet grew from 3 airplanes to 117, and its revenues soared from $38 million to nearly $1 billion.

But People had overexpanded. Every day, the airline had thousands of seats available, but its steady customers wanted to fly mainly on weekends and during the summer and other vacation times. The glut of empty seats produced a $3.7 million loss in 1984. So People scrambled to get more revenue from its fleet. It scheduled each plane for as many flights as possible and it grossly overbooked to compensate for customers who made reservations but didn't show up. The airline also went after business travellers, whose demand is heaviest Monday through Friday and nicely complements the weekend demand pattern of budget fliers. To attract executives, the airline pitched its luxurious first-class service complete with leather seats.

Nearly everything People Express had done to serve the budget-minded conflicted with this new strategy. Businesspeople intensely dislike inconvenient schedules and gates, paying extra for checked baggage and for meals, and waiting until the last minute to buy tickets. People's tight scheduling meant that many flights were late, and overbooking meant that it often turned away customers who had reserved seats. The carrier earned a new name, "People Distress".

Business travellers stayed away, and the airline racked up to $300 million net loss in 1986, when Texas Air took it over. If it had continued to focus tightly on budget fliers and had sold off or leased planes to cut capacity, People Express might still be around. But it broadened, and irrecoverably blurred, its original winning strategy.

EXPLORING • PEOPLE EXPRESS

1. What winning strategy was used by People Express?
2. Put on your black hat and point out the negative aspects of People Express.
3. Put on your yellow hat and point out the positive aspects of People Express.
4. Be the Judge. What went wrong?
5. As an entrepreneur, what would you have done differently if you were the owner of People Express?

Why Some Ventures Fail

AGENTS OF CHANGE

As our aeronautical technology increased, so did the suffering pilots experienced from the effects of increased gravity. Dr. Wilbur Rounding Franks spent years designing an anti-gravity suit to protect pilots from these powerful forces. Dr. Franks' invention kept pilot safety in pace with our other advancing technologies.

According to statistics compiled by various government offices across Canada, between 70 - 80 per cent of all business startups will fail before their fifth anniversary. If entrepreneurs take the time to prepare a well-researched venture plan, if they identify potential risks and do everything in their power to eliminate or minimize these risks, and if entrepreneurs seek out the advice and support of experts, why is it, then, that there are so many failures in the first five years?

In many respects this failure statistic is somewhat misleading. It includes a number of business ventures that have grown in size and, to take advantage of their success, have changed their name, incorporated under a new name, or moved to another location. Because they are no longer operating under the same name and address as the one under which they started, they are grouped into the list of "no longer existing" business ventures or "failures".

Some ventures are in business for just a short period of time. Their startup teams may never have intended to keep the ventures going five years after they started out. Rock'n flowers, for example, were put on the market to catch a fad. The entrepreneur who started this venture had no plan to stay in business any longer than the "rock'n flower" market would allow. The life expectancy of some ventures is only a few months or a couple of years. These businesses have not failed. They have accomplished their goals, reached their objectives, and then closed down. The entrepreneurs who start these types of ventures probably go on to start up other ones.

Figure 12.1 Is this kind of success a failure?

Real business failures are those that start out strongly and then, for some reason, seem to fall apart.

Studies of real business failures show that the overwhelming reasons for failure were poor management, lack of experience, and insecurity. In the case of People Express, poor management was responsible for the company expanding into the wrong market, overestimating the company's income, and underestimating its expenses. The company had to borrow in order to meet its cash needs, and the cost of that borrowing proved to be a severe drain on its cashflow. When business executives decided not to purchase People Express flights any longer, the company could no longer afford to stay in business. In other cases of failed business ventures, the reason for failure can be described as general inexperience and insecurity. A fear of failure can sometimes become a self-fulfilling prophecy. Entrepreneurs who let their feelings of insecurity or inexperience affect the quality or timeliness of their decisions can end up with weak or even incorrect decisions that could lead to the ultimate failure of the venture.

AGENTS OF CHANGE

Since women were not legally "persons", they were ineligible to study law. Clara Brett Martin, who had applied for admission to the Law Society of Upper Canada but was rejected because the Society restricted admission to "persons", eventually succeeded in having a law passed to correct that wrong. She turned her own disappointment into freedom for all Canadian women.

Recognizing the Danger Signals

Very few ventures will fail without showing some signs of potential danger long before their actual **demise**. Some entrepreneurs ignore or fail to look for these danger signals. Even if the danger signals are seen, some entrepreneurs still do not recognize the potential for failure. Being aware of the causes of failure can give an individual the insight needed to identify what is going wrong and fix it before it is too late.

Entrepreneurs need to monitor and recognize the changes in a business along with the trends identified in the industry so that they can anticipate the problems that might occur and plan to avoid or at least minimize the risk of failure.

Rapid Growth

Success brings its own kind of problems. An important element of control is lost when a venture grows too quickly. The entrepreneur in charge is so busy accommodating this growth by making room for expansion and hiring more people that no time is left to keep accurate and up-to-date records, to monitor the process of maintaining supplies, to keep the customers happy, or to bring in the accounts receivable needed to maintain the cashflow and prevent business failure.

Comfort Clothing Inc. is a perfect example of a company that grew too quickly. It produced clothing with velcro fastenings and wider openings to appeal to people with poor vision, limited dexterity, or motor control problems. In 1985, it projected a sales figure of over $1 million but an operating loss for the third year in a row. Failure was imminent if the cause of the problem was not discovered and rectified.

The entrepreneurs involved in managing this venture were inexperienced in keeping financial records. They used a very simplified system that could not adequately handle their increasing sales. As a result, the financial information needed to make important business decisions with respect to product pricing, purchasing and storing of supplies, hiring of extra help, and collecting cash receivables was not available. Fortunately for Comfort Clothing, the problem was caught in time. The company is now back on track after learning some very valuable lessons on how to manage a growing business.

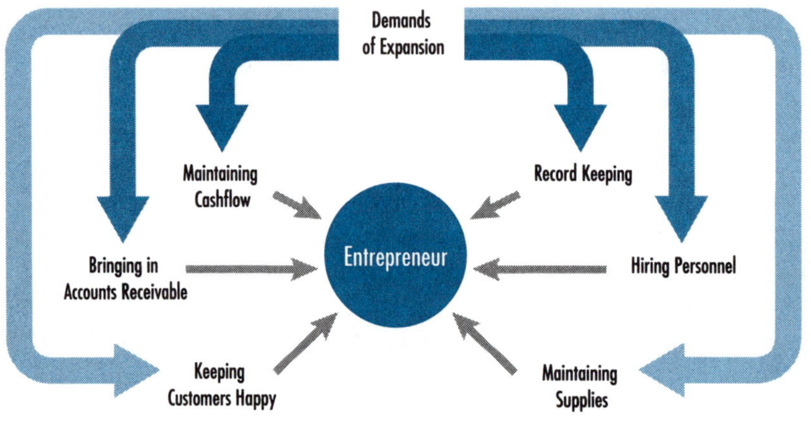

Figure 12.2 Rapid growth places many demands on the entrepreneur.

> **N**o business is unique. All require strong management, adequate cashflow, and a solid organization in order to survive.

Financial Mismanagement

Entrepreneurs are often able to raise enough money to start a venture, that is, to buy the equipment, rent or purchase a facility, and order the necessary inventory. However, many of them end up with insufficient funds to operate the business on a day-to-day basis. This is referred to as **under capitalization.**

If, for example, the venture is a retail business, customers will pay cash or use a credit card to cover most purchases. These cash receipts should provide the venture with an adequate and immediate cashflow fund that is sufficient to pay for the inventory needed to continue to operate the business.

> Inventories in retail businesses are expected to be paid for within thirty to sixty days of delivery.

If the venture is in the manufacturing or service industry, a larger amount of capital is required to operate the business because cashflow may take much longer to materialize. Without enough capital to cover the costs of inventory, production, and other operating expenses, the venture could go bankrupt even though sales are quite healthy.

If the venture is not-for-profit, income is often dependent upon contributions or government grants. For the venture to continue to operate and pay its expenses after startup, it will require sufficient startup capital to cover employee costs, space and utility charges, and any promotion or other operating costs incurred until a regular flow of income is assured.

Insufficient Profit Margins

Some entrepreneurs underestimate their expenses and underprice their product or service. Others do not allow for enough profit initially to cover price reductions that might have to be made later in the product's life cycle.

Overestimating Sales and Underestimating Break-Even Volume

Overly enthusiastic entrepreneurs who jump into a venture with unrealistically high sales expectations will find themselves in the potential failure group, as will those entrepreneurs who have not costed out their operations carefully. Break-even volume is not enough to stay in business. The break-even point must be considerably less than the volume of sales that is possible if the business is to remain profitable and functioning.

Poor Employer-Employee Relationships

Entrepreneurs who do not keep their employees involved in the progress of the company, committed to its goals and objectives, and satisfied with the reward system in place will find that employee-management problems take up a great deal of time and energy and ultimately affect the progress of the business.

Personal Stress and Time Management

Finally, entrepreneurs work long and hard to achieve their goals. They often suffer from a great deal of physical and emotional stress. Busy entrepreneurs are constantly trying to juggle their time between pursuing their ventures and finding time for their families, friends, and personal endeavours. If their home life is unhappy and relationships strained, their burden of business management may prove too stressful. If an entrepreneur's personal finances are used to start and run the venture until it brings in enough money to pay the entrepreneur's salary, personal financial commitments may be difficult to manage and this may also add to the entrepreneur's stress.

YOUR TURN

1. In small groups, using the experience of those in your group who have been employed in part-time or summer jobs, prepare a list of improvements you would suggest to the management.
2. Using case studies of business failures, prepare a list of the reasons for their failures.
3. Using what you learned in Chapter 5 about life cycles and timing, prepare a list of products and services that may soon be in jeopardy. For each product or service you list, include the reasons why you think each may soon be out of business.

Venture PROFILE

The entrepreneur: Pick yourself up and try once again

By Herve DeJordy, *Toronto Star*

Failure doesn't daunt true entrepreneurs.

I suffer from terminal entrepreneuritis. If you recognize some of my symptoms as your own...if you happen to be another independent, non-conformist, self-employed individual who is turned off by the prospect of a life-long 9-to-5 job with a pension at the end, then this article could be about you.

For example, you may not get paid for today simply because you woke up this morning and "just didn't feel like it today." Or maybe it's been one of those times when everything that could go wrong did, and you find yourself insolvent or bankrupt...again.

Countless people work part-time on their "full-time" jobs in order to devote more time to planning and dreaming how they're going to make a million. Maybe the million's important. Maybe it's not. One thing is certain, though. The independence it represents is everything.

Entrepreneuritis victims see opportunity all over the place. Those who are immune have a great deal of difficulty locating opportunity at all.

My first project — or, more honestly, my first failure — was back in 1980 when everybody was complaining how bad things were. I couldn't understand how anyone could have trouble finding a job, if that's what they really wanted.

Being in sales, I could have my pick of eight or more jobs on any given day. Could it be because some people were trying to fit their skills and experience only around what was available, instead of concentrating on what they truly wanted to do?

There was a wealth of knowledge available in many self-help books in the local bookstore. It was beyond me how anyone could miss. I finally figured it out: People were not aware this information existed. They simply weren't going into bookstores to find it.

What if, I wondered, these and other books were made available in high-profile areas where people would notice them? If they saw them, surely they would buy them.

The toughest part would be convincing independent retailers of such products as sporting goods, lighting fixtures, and waterbeds to not only carry my books, but also to display them prominently next to the cash register.

To my amazement, they all thought it was a great idea. I then spent several weeks tracking down publishers and distributors and setting up my own book stands. I was on my way to my first million! All I had to do now was wait for the re-orders.

So I waited...and waited...and waited. Sales were negligible. There was no stampede to buy my books. What I thought would be the most difficult part (selling the retailers) turned out to be the easiest part. The "sure thing" part never happened.

This experience was to be my first valuable lesson. Research your market first to find out who your customers are and why.

Half a year later, I started a regional type "people magazine". This time, I did my homework. I knew exactly who my readers and advertisers would be and why they would buy space in the magazine. Eighteen months later, however, I was $150 000 in debt and unable to raise the necessary capital I needed, because of a balance sheet which showed only liabilities.

This was my second important lesson. I learned that, "It always takes longer and costs more than you anticipate."

In the fall of 1984, I discovered that the home computer industry was bankrupt and needed my help. Sales of computers for home use were really soft and, I thought, anyone could see why. A computer to file recipes and birthdays was just too big an expenditure for the average home.

I reasoned that a home computer needed to be offered and demonstrated primarily for its educational benefits. People would be able to overcome their fear of the computer and better appreciate its benefits in the comfort of their own home.

My research of the market showed my customers were parents who cared about their children's education. I spent months revising a business plan and a detailed cost analysis for the project. We launched Home Education in March of 1985. Two months later, IBM discontinued the PCjr. Prices and margins [profits] plummeted.

My third lesson: "Timing and outside factors can blow you out of the water before you even get started."

There have been other projects and lessons since then and you've probably guessed that I'm not a business "genius". The only thing that keeps me going is entrepreneuritis.

I'm convinced there's a "corporate graveyard" out there somewhere just full of great videos that didn't work. The launch of pay-TV in Canada is a good example. There were five different stations, fully capitalized, having the best operations and marketing managers money could buy. After a couple of failures, a merger or two, and millions of dollars lost, only one channel remains.

Now I don't wish failure on anybody, but if the biggest players don't always make it, there just has to be hope and opportunity for smaller guys like me.

Entrepreneurs tend to learn more from their failures than their successes. It's a case of trying, failing, picking yourself up, dusting yourself off, and going at it again, this time smarter and wiser than before.

Ever notice how some individuals will fail once, twice, even three or more times without guilt, shame, or resentment toward the rest of the world? The impulse to create, to build, and to beat the odds just has to be an uncontrollable and incurable disease. I can see no other explanation, unless Confucius was right when he said, "For some, life is not the destination, but the journey."

EXPLORING • ENTREPRENEURITIS

1. What lesson did DeJordy learn from each of his failures?
2. In each instance, what do you think could have been done to prevent failure?
3. Most entrepreneurs do not even consider failure. Is this the case here? Explain.
4. Why do entrepreneurs learn more from their failures than they do from their successes?
5. What is meant by, "For some, life is not the destination, but the journey"? How does it apply to entrepreneurs?

Running the Venture

Figure 12.3 Entrepreneurs take responsibility for every step in their business lives.

According to DeJordy, entrepreneurs may fail once, twice, even three or more times without guilt, shame, or resentment. They say there is no such thing as failure. They claim their ventures "will experience a delayed success," or that they were "just off to a false start," or that they experienced "just a little setback." With each "setback", "false start", or whatever they choose to call it, they learn to do it just a little better next time. They learn a fundamental leadership, motivation, communication, or management technique and become better at directing their next venture to success. The experience of having failed before is usually an important asset for an entrepreneur starting out on a new venture. Successful entrepreneurs seldom repeat mistakes they made in the past.

YOUR TURN

4. Think of an experience you have had where you were in charge. Once you have the image of yourself in the role of an organizer, answer the following questions:
   a) Where did this experience take place?
   b) Did you initiate the experience?
   c) What exactly was your role?
   d) What changes did you make?
   e) What innovative things did you do?
   f) What risks did you take?
   g) In what way did you challenge others to do better than ever before?
   h) What did you do to sell others on the project?
   i) How did you help others feel strong and capable?
   j) What were your feelings at the beginning, during, and at the end of the project?
5. Share your answers with another student in your class. In what ways were your experiences similar and in what ways were they different?
6. In what way(s) was the experience entrepreneurial?

Leadership

Is it possible for an entrepreneur to be a leader?

Leaders have a vision. They are prepared for change and they see where change is leading. They are willing to experiment with new ideas, new methods, and new opportunities. Leaders are comfortable with an element of risk and have a strong desire to make things happen. Leaders depend on others to help them achieve success. They encourage collaboration and make others feel strong, capable, and committed to their vision.

Leadership is:

- motivating individuals or a group to work at achieving a specific goal
- inspiring people to consistently give their best
- earning the respect of others
- setting an example of honesty and fairness
- turning talent, effort, and creativity into results
- providing direction to others

Leadership is a challenging role for the entrepreneur. At times the entrepreneur has to be **task oriented** in order to ensure that employees meet designated deadlines and that customers receive their orders on time. At other times the entrepreneur has to motivate and inspire employees to work to attain the goals of the venture.

AGENTS OF CHANGE

Public awareness of industrial hazards was not very high. Ralph Nader, a prominent American consumer advocate, brought national attention to the problem and influenced legislation on it. He was greatly helped by students and volunteers called Nader's Raiders. Nader's reputation gave prominence to important safety issues and brought them to the public's attention.

Leadership Styles

There are a variety of theories about leadership styles. These styles seem to exist on a continuum between the type of leader who wants to get a job done and achieve a goal and the leader who is more concerned about the satisfaction of employees.

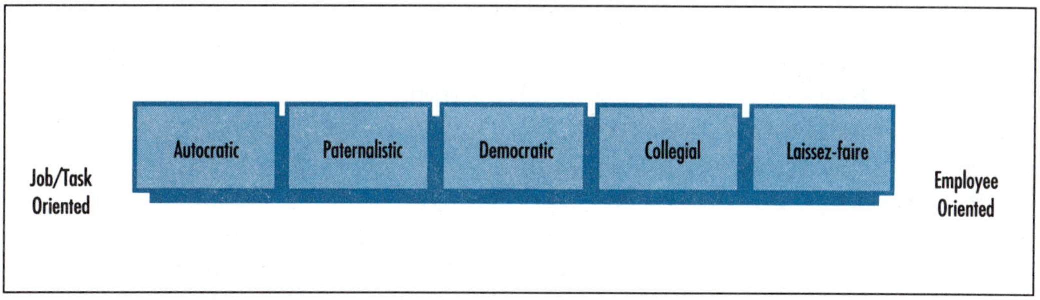

Figure 12.4 A Continuum of Leadership Styles

Autocratic leaders make all the decisions and command their employees to do exactly as they are told. Autocratic leaders lack confidence in their employees and are convinced that if they, the leaders, do not make all the decisions, nothing will be done correctly. Decisions are made quickly and efficiently with an autocratic leader but employees are not likely to feel involved or committed. Autocratic leaders are necessary in situations where employees are untrained, poorly prepared for the job, or uncommitted.

Paternalistic leaders also make all decisions but they take a more parental role in the way they "look after" their employees. Bonus incentives and warm family-like working conditions are put in place to improve employee attitudes and commitment. Paternalistic leadership is appropriate in situations where security or job retention is constantly in question.

Democratic leaders encourage employees to participate in the decision-making process. Authority for decisions is delegated to subordinates, and an atmosphere of trust is established. Democratic leadership works well in situations where everyone shares the same goals for the organization and where work assignments are not mechanical or routine.

Collegial leaders take democratic leadership one step closer to treating everyone as an equal. Team decision-making processes are used, and there is a high degree of loyalty and respect for what everyone brings to the managing team.

Laissez-faire leaders ignore the task or job specifics and concentrate on giving employees the freedom to determine what they should do and how they should do it.

It is important for leaders to recognize the needs of the people around them and to encourage them to pursue those needs and goals that are compatible with the needs and goals of the venture. Successful leaders reward their employees appropriately and demonstrate to them that the work they do is meaningful and worthwhile.

AGENTS OF CHANGE

Amelia Earhart was the first woman to fly solo across the Atlantic Ocean, as well as from Hawaii to San Francisco, and from Mexico City to New York City. Her career ended tragically when she crashed attempting to fly around the world. Her pioneering efforts paved the way for women in aviation.

Motivation

The leader who can identify the kind of reward that motivates an employee and then provide it will have an enthusiastic and committed work force. According to Abraham Maslow, a noted behavioural psychologist of the mid-1950s, people have five types of needs which exist in the form of a hierarchy. **Maslow's Hierarchy of Needs** is identified in Figure 12.5.

Figure 12.5 Maslow's Hierarchy of Needs

The most common needs that we as humans must satisfy are the basic physiological survival needs for food, clothing, and shelter. Maslow believed that it is necessary to satisfy these needs before one's attention can be focused on satisfying a need at a higher level. At the point when basic survival needs are satisfied, the need for safety and security becomes the main motivating force. Fortunately, most Canadians feel relatively safe and secure most of the time. Once basic survival and security needs are satisfied, people are motivated to find love and a sense of belonging, then self-respect, status, and the esteem and respect of others. At the peak of Maslow's hierarchy of needs is fulfillment and **self-actualization**. Self-actualization is the most difficult need to satisfy, partially because it can only be pursued after all the other needs have been fulfilled. Self-actualization occurs when an individual is able to live by the values which are most prized and pursue the goals which are most sought after. It is the freedom to live the life of choice and to experience fulfillment through making the best use of personal skills and abilities.

If a leader is aware of the level that each employee is at, an appropriate kind of motivation or reward can be selected to encourage the employee to reach up to a higher level of productivity.

Some people are motivated by a paycheque or other kind of financial remuneration. If employees are concerned about finding appropriate housing and sufficient food for their families, the only thing likely to motivate or satisfy them is money. A raise in pay will bring more affordable residences into the realm of possibility. This would satisfy the physiological and perhaps also the safety aspect of Maslow's hierarchy. If, on the other hand, most employees are already established in comfortable residences, in safe neighbourhoods, with all the conveniences their families desire, the motivating factor might be recognition in the form of an award like The Employee of the Month, or added responsibility on the job. This would satisfy the esteem aspect of the hierarchy. If individuals were asked to lead particular divisions of the company or research special projects crucial to the success of the business, the highest level, that of self-actualization, or self-fulfillment, might be satisfied. It is important to note that movement through the various levels may not always be in an upward direction. Sometimes individuals may encounter events in their lives, such as divorce or a house fire, which cause them to move down to a lower level.

YOUR TURN

7. In pairs, discuss the statement: Leaders are made, not born.
8. Describe a situation in which a leader should be more concerned with the actual work instead of with the person or persons doing it.
9. In small groups, discuss situations where each of the five leadership styles might be appropriate.
10. Prepare a list of rewards that would motivate individuals at each of the levels of Maslow's Hierarchy of Needs.
11. Prepare a list of the factors that motivate you to work harder.
12. In what ways does your teacher try to motivate the students in your class? Does the same method work for all students? How does your teacher know when to use which motivational tool?

13. Review the Bryan Adams profile in Chapter 2 (page 34) and the Bombardier profile in Chapter 3 (page 64). What leadership characteristics did each of these entrepreneurs display? In what ways were these two entrepreneurs able to motivate the people around them?

AGENTS OF CHANGE

Marshall McLuhan was concerned with the impact of media on culture. He argued that while the print culture (books, papers, etc.) locked each individual into his or her own consciousness, the electronic media had the opposite effect of creating a "global village". McLuhan's work changed the way we look at our world and how we relate to it.

Communication

Effective communication is very important to the smooth operation of any organization. People need to communicate with co-workers, supervisors, subordinates, and customers. People talk to each other about products and services, prices, distribution of goods, financial issues, and the future growth of the venture. Entrepreneur/managers need to articulate their visions for their ventures in such a way that employees will buy into the visions and adopt them as their own.

Figure 12.6 Effective communication nourishes the vision.

Written communication is used frequently in a business environment. People write memos to convey messages about important information related to the day-to-day operation of the venture. They write letters to customers and clients, and they may also prepare detailed reports and research papers.

Written material must be consistent with the message it means to provide. In oral communication, the speaker must be clear and unambiguous. Non-verbal communication, or **body language**, should be consistent with whatever point the speaker is trying to make. The tone of voice and intonation used are also important; they, too, convey a message.

Listening is also a vital part of communication. Information delivered clearly and completely is of little value if it is not listened to. Listening involves more than hearing; listening means understanding the meaning of what is being heard. Listening is a skill that can be practised and learned. Good listeners help the communicator by asking questions to clarify meaning and by using body language to acknowledge their understanding.

"I know you believe you understand what you think I said, but I am not sure you realize that what you heard is not what I meant."
Anonymous

When messages are transmitted from the speaker to the listener, the message is 7 per cent verbal, 38 per cent tone, and 55 per cent body language.

Table 12.1 Good Listeners and Bad Listeners

Good listeners....

1. look for information that can be used even if the subject is uninteresting.
2. concentrate on the content of the speaker's message.
3. hear the speaker out before evaluating the worth of what is being said.
4. listen for ideas.
5. adjust their notetaking to the speaker's method of delivery.
6. work at paying attention by making a conscious effort.
7. do not distract others or become distracted themselves.
8. welcome difficult, out of the ordinary presentations just for the experience of listening.
9. do not let the symbols of expression stand between themselves and understanding or learning.
10. use their ability to think faster than the speaker speaks to perform mental exercises such as:
    - anticipating the speaker's next point
    - mentally recapitulating every four or five minutes

Poor Listeners....

1. judge the subject uninteresting and write off the whole meeting as a loss before it starts.
2. criticize the speaker's method of delivery.
3. get over-stimulated on early points and fail to hear the entire description.
4. listen only for facts.
5. try to outline in logical fashion even when the speaker is basically disorganized.
6. fake attention.
7. tolerate or create distractions.
8. always avoid difficult or expository presentations and never develop experience.
9. let emotion-laden words throw them out of tune with the speaker.
10. waste the differential between speech speed and thought speed by wandering off on unrelated or related mental tangents.

YOUR TURN

14. Compare and contrast the special communication skills needed by an entrepreneur with those needed by an entrepreneur/manager. Prepare a list to reflect these skills. Compare your list with the lists made by other members of your class.
15. Which give more clues — visual or audio signals? Determine what the characters are saying on a television show with the sound turned off. Turn the sound back on, close your eyes, and determine what actions the characters are using just by listening to the lines they are speaking.
16. Reread the Venture Profile "Symbols that speak for those who can't" in Chapter 1 (page 6). In what ways did Shirley McNaughton use and improve communication? Why did she do this? How?
17. How many of the following listening skills do you practise? Make a list in your notebook of the ones that you practise and the ones that you do not.
    a) When I give instructions, I make sure my message is clearly understood.
    b) I listen to myself.
    c) I listen carefully even when I do not agree with the message.
    d) I ask questions when I am not clear what message the speaker is communicating.
    e) My body language shows that I am listening.

Conflict Resolution

Conflict occurs when individuals do not agree with each other. It poses a serious stumbling block to effective management. In order to understand the conflict, you must have an accurate perception of the issue and be able to communicate it clearly to others.

> Distortions in perception are often found to be at the root of conflict situations.

The ability to listen to both sides, to identify any distortions, to understand what the true problem or cause of conflict might be, and to use sensitive and effective communication skills is crucial when trying to resolve situations where conflict is interrupting the progress of work.

Five styles of managing conflict can be identified:

1. **The turtle** (withdrawing) Turtles withdraw into their shells to avoid conflicts. They give up their personal goals and relationships. They stay away from the issues over which the conflict is taking place and from the people they are in conflict with. Turtles believe it is hopeless to try to resolve conflicts. They feel helpless. They believe it is easier to withdraw from a conflict than to face it.

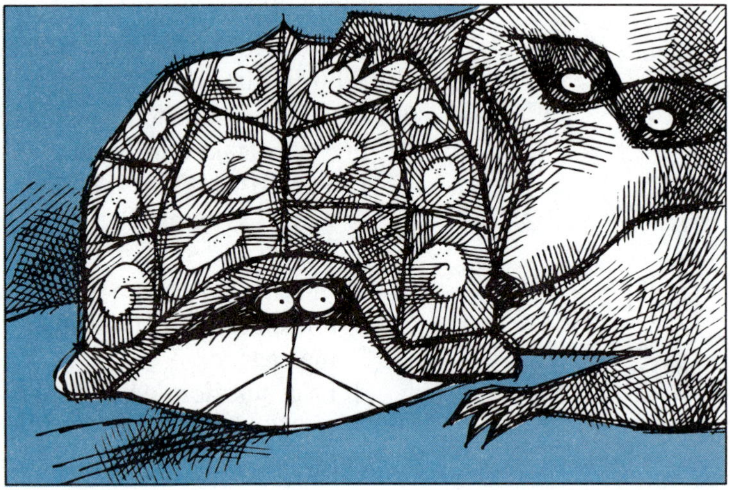

Figure 12.7 The turtle withdraws into its shell to avoid conflicts.

2. **The shark** (forcing) Sharks try to overpower opponents by forcing them to accept their solutions to conflicts. Their goals are highly important to them and relationships of minor importance. They seek to achieve their goals at all costs. They are not concerned with the needs of other people. They do not care if other people like or accept them. Sharks assume that conflicts are settled by one person winning and one person losing. They want to be the winners. Winning gives sharks a sense of pride and achievement. Losing gives them a sense of weakness, inadequacy, and failure. They try to win by attacking, overpowering, overwhelming, and intimidating other people.

AGENTS OF CHANGE

Does someone's snoring keep you awake? Peter Sandler has invented a pillow that he says stops sleepers from snoring. His Thera-P-Cushion Inc. sells more than 15 000 pillows a year. Large retail stores like Eatons, The Bay, Sears, and K-Mart are currently testing his pillow. He expects sales to "explode" in the next few years. A problem for many people became an opportunity for Peter.

Figure 12.8 The shark tries to force opponents to accept his or her solution to the conflict.

3. **The teddy bear** (smoothing) To teddy bears, relationships are of great importance, while their own goals are of little importance. Teddy bears want to be accepted and liked by other people. They think that conflict should be avoided in favour of harmony and believe that conflicts cannot be discussed without damaging relationships. They are afraid that if the conflict continues, someone will get hurt and that would ruin the relationship. They give up their goals to preserve the relationship.

Figure 12.9 The teddy bear tries to avoid conflict in favour of harmony.

4. **The fox** (compromising) Foxes are moderately concerned with their own goals and with their relationships with other people. Foxes seek a compromise. They give up part of their goals and persuade the other person in a conflict to give up part of his or her goal to find agreement for the common good. They seek a solution to conflicts where both sides gain something — the middle ground between two extreme positions.

Figure 12.10 The fox seeks a compromise between the two goals.

5. **The owl** (confronting) Owls highly value both their own goals and relationships. They view conflicts as problems to be solved and seek a solution that achieves both their own goals and the goals of the other person in the conflict. Owls see conflicts as improving relationships by reducing tension between two people. They try to begin discussion that identifies the conflict as a problem. By seeking solutions that satisfy both themselves and the other person, owls maintain the relationship. Owls are not satisfied until the tensions and negative feelings have been fully resolved.

Figure 12.11 Owls try to seek mutually beneficial solutions to conflict.

YOUR TURN

18. The proverbs listed below can be thought of as descriptions of some of the different strategies for resolving conflicts. Proverbs state traditional wisdom. These proverbs reflect traditional wisdom for resolving conflicts and relate to the five styles of managing conflict just discussed. Read each of the proverbs carefully. Using the scale given below, indicate how typical each proverb is of your actions in a conflict. Write your responses in your notebook.
    - 5 = very typical of the way I act in a conflict
    - 4 = frequently typical of the way I act in a conflict
    - 3 = sometimes typical of the way I act in a conflict
    - 2 = seldom typical of the way I act in a conflict
    - 1 = never typical of the way I act in a conflict

Your teacher will help you score your answers and will let you know whether you are most likely to use the turtle, shark, teddy bear, fox, or owl style when resolving conflicts.

1. It is easier to refrain than to retreat from a quarrel.
2. If you cannot make a person think as you do, make him or her do as you think.
3. Soft words win hard hearts.
4. You scratch my back, I'll scratch yours.
5. Come now and let us reason together.
6. When two quarrel, the person who keeps silent first is the most praiseworthy.
7. Might overcomes right.
8. Smooth words make smooth ways.
9. Better half a loaf than no bread at all.
10. Truth lies in knowledge, not in majority opinion.
11. He who fights and runs away lives to fight another day.
12. He hath conquered well that hath made his enemies flee.
13. Kill your enemies with kindness.
14. A fair exchange brings no quarrel.
15. No person has the final answer but every person has a piece to contribute.
16. Stay away from people who disagree with you.
17. Fields are won by those who believe in winning.
18. Kind words are worth much and cost little.
19. Tit for tat is fair play.
20. Only the person who is willing to give up his or her monopoly on truth can ever profit from the truths that others hold.
21. Avoid quarrelsome people as they will only make your life miserable.
22. A person who will not flee will make others flee.
23. Soft words ensure harmony.
24. One gift for another makes good friends.
25. Bring your conflicts into the open and face them directly; only then will the best solution be discovered.
26. The best way of handling conflicts is to avoid them.
27. Put your foot down where you mean to stand.
28. Gentleness will triumph over anger.
29. Getting part of what you want is better than not getting anything at all.
30. Frankness, honesty, and trust will move mountains.

31. There is nothing so important you have to fight for it.
32. There are two kinds of people in the world, the winners and the losers.
33. When one hits you with a stone, hit him or her with a piece of cotton.
34. When both people give in halfway, a fair settlement is achieved.
35. By digging and digging, the truth is discovered.

19. List five situations in which you have been in conflict with someone. What was the surrounding issue? Prepare a written description of how you resolve conflicts.

Venture PROFILE

What Nerve!

By Marcus Gill, *Success Magazine*

Hamilton shocked everyone when he made Tilton, a former cocktail waitress, his partner.

The date is February, 1984, and Sherman Hamilton is sitting in his favourite Denver jazz club, Spirits. Life has been better to this would-be entrepreneur.

Six months earlier, the feisty, independent Hamilton decided to test his entrepreneurial urges. After 12 years of being a loyal corporate player, he walked away from a well-paying job, sold his beloved Porsche Targa, and set out to chase his dream. He wanted to "be a master marketer," as he puts it — to build his own advertising and marketing agency.

But now he was nearly broke. At the age of 40, Hamilton, who had been divorced twice, couldn't even attract a business partner. The six people he'd approached wanted job security, not risk. Like so many corporate runaways before him, Hamilton was in danger of becoming just another entrepreneurial statistic.

Hamilton was on a date at Spirits, when he struck up a conversation with a bright and talkative cocktail waitress. Like Hamilton, she was a self-promoter with a sharp mind. She told him she was only a student, but did all the marketing for the club. That's when Hamilton was hit by an incredible notion. He wouldn't be like everyone else, he wouldn't follow the script. He would exploit all those things that made it "impossible" for him to succeed — most notably that he was a black man trying to break into mainstream business in a heavily white, conservative, economically depressed city like Denver. He would exploit the resources that were available to him and shrewdly use them to gain fame for himself and his agency.

At that very moment, Hamilton turned to Rebecca Tilton, the spunky 23-year-old white cocktail waitress, and asked her to come and work for his new advertising agency. A year later he made her his partner.

Ever since that day in 1984, nothing has been exactly normal at Hamilton Tilton Advertising Inc. The company has grown into one of the hottest agencies in Denver by following a business strategy that, at first glance, appears insane. For starters, Hamilton has all but ignored black market accounts — normally a death sentence for a black-owned agency. Last year, Hamilton Tilton did $8 million in billings with strictly general market clients, including the mammoth $3.5 million advertising and publicity account for the U.S. Department of Housing and Urban Development.

Then there's the matter of Hamilton's unusual staff. Most of his seventeen employees have no advertising experience and come from an offbeat mix of cultural, ethnic, and racial backgrounds. "My personal rainbow coalition," as Hamilton likes to call them. The agency will always be staffed with 50 per cent minorities because Hamilton believes blacks and Hispanics have been sold a bill of goods by their leaders in business. "It's okay for minorities to preach or teach or dunk a basketball," he says, "but to use your intellect makes you suspect."

Hamilton insists minorities need to believe in their right to succeed through ambition and hard work. "In Texas, my family used to live in a house with holes in the roof where the rain came through, and holes in the floor where the snakes came through. They used to say, 'The Lord will provide.' Why didn't anyone cut some wood and build a livable house? After all, Lincoln did it."

Today, the house that Hamilton built is a long way from that dilapidated shack where he grew up in Hemphill, Tex. Hamilton Tilton is headquartered in a 100-year-old Victorian-style mansion with winding hallways and a warren of small rooms. Six young women on the phones have replaced the ghosts in the attic. The usual corporate decor of padded partitions and fluorescent lights have given way to a large fireplace in the reception room, smoked glass windows, chandeliers, and thick chocolate carpeting. But even in these cozy quarters, Hamilton cultivates chaos.

It is Wednesday afternoon, and creative and account staff have assembled to discuss a newspaper ad for one of the agency's biggest clients, Public Service Company of Colorado (PSC), Denver's gas and utility company. Ideas are bouncing off the walls like boomerangs. Accounts executives are jumping up and down. Expletives are flying. At the back of the conference room, Hamilton smiles and props his big, tasseled loafers up on the table as he watches his staff.

Khadija Katherine Haynes, an outspoken black woman who supervises the Public Service Company account, holds up a drawing of two engineers standing next to a utility truck. The caption reads: "How Does a Company Like PSC Stay in Business for 64 Years? Service."

"That stinks," says Tilton, executive vice-president. Her red nails click against her tank watch. "The graphics don't connect with the message at all." Tilton rarely sits in on creative meetings, but when she does, she's ruthless.

"This must be 'slaughter Khadija week' or something," Haynes snaps back. She looks defensively at Hamilton. "What do you think Sherman?" she asks.

Heads swivel to the back of the room. Even in his wool pinstripe suit, Hamilton has the dimensions of a defensive lineman. To Hamilton, this is business at its purest. He relishes these meetings in which a new ad campaign is hammered and beaten until it begins to take on a professional sheen.

"Are we all madly in love with that '64 years' line?" he asks, ignoring Haynes's question. It's the voice of a leader provoking his staff on to higher results. And it works. Voices around the table ascend to screams again. The meeting churns on.

Hamilton has always known what his strengths were — that fact, perhaps more than anything else, has accounted for his success. When he met Tilton, he knew immediately that the two of them would make an ideal pair: They were complete opposites. "Sherman and Rebecca do seem like very odd sort of business partners," says Steve Volstad, manager of advertising and special projects for PSC. "But they complement each other perfectly." Hamilton brings the business in the door. Tilton services it. He's a leader, a strategist, and an actor. She's a marketing 101 manager: straightforward, precise, and practical.

As Harvard Business School's John P. Kotter writes in *The Leadership Factor*, "The process of controlling people and the process of motivating them can be very dissimilar." Hamilton knew he was a born leader, a master motivator. He could inspire his staff to believe in themselves and their ability to succeed long before they could recognize their own potential. Creating excitement is a big part of Hamilton's magic. He has sold clients on his vision of a $50 million agency even though it is still years away from being a reality. When it came to the nitty-gritty, day-to-day managing, however, Hamilton was perfectly happy to leave the job to Tilton.

Today, even without her $350 Anne Klein suits and her BMW, Tilton's no-nonsense manner intimidates people. She's highly demanding, even of Hamilton. "When he's pitching new business, he's a genius," she says. "But he's got absolutely no patience for rules or decorum."

Like other leaders, Hamilton enjoys the role of mentor. So, starting with Tilton, he set out to assemble a staff that he could shape in his image. Most of them had no advertising experience.

In return for Hamilton's belief in them, this odd group has repaid their leader with a respect and commitment bordering on the obsessive. Hamilton pushes, teases, and charms his staff into performing at their best. And they happily follow him — even if they do recognize his flaws, and sometimes because of them.

EXPLORING • HAMILTON TILTON ADVERTISING

1. Does Hamilton have a dream? What is it?
2. In what way does he articulate his dream to his staff?
3. What is unique about Hamilton in his role as entrepreneur?
4. In what ways does Hamilton "lead" his staff? Would you be comfortable in that kind of working environment?
5. What does Hamilton do to develop his followers into leaders?
6. What personal characteristics does Hamilton demonstrate in his role as leader?
7. Are these characteristics compatible with being an entrepreneur?

The Functions of Management

Entrepreneurs start ventures to initiate change. As soon as their ventures are started, there is a need for careful management so that they will achieve their goals. Entrepreneurs with creative energy, charismatic leadership, and a strong desire to achieve are not always the best people to manage a venture. Managers are required to plan, organize, direct and control all available resources, and facilitate the achievement of the organization's goals.

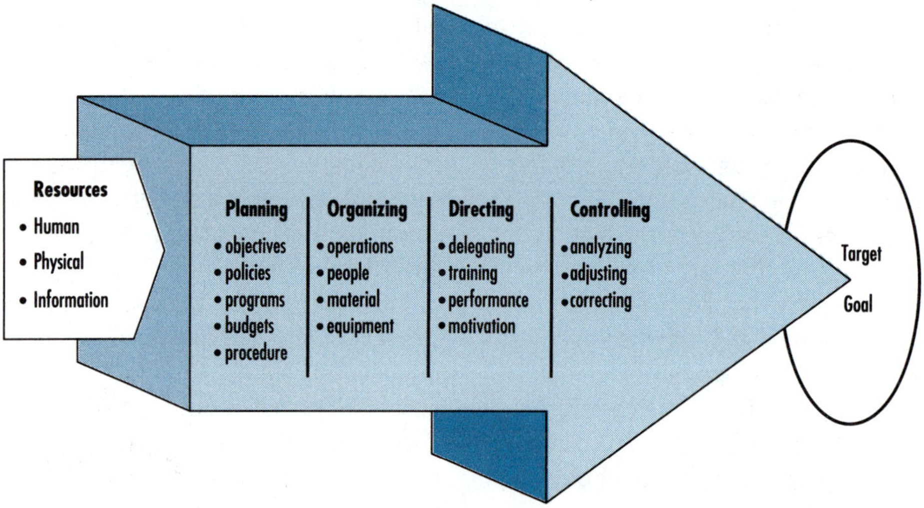

Figure 12.12 Managers must plan, organize, direct, and control an organization's resources aimed at achieving its target goal.

Planning

AGENTS OF CHANGE

Brian Orser's story is one of hard work and great sportsmanship. Anyone looking for a special achievement, a special goal, should look at how Brian worked to achieve his special magic. His years of determination and preparation helped him achieve his goal. His attitude has inspired many young Canadians.

Managing the operation of an existing venture requires careful planning.

Planning for an existing venture should be seen as the bridge between where the venture is and where it wants to be.

Managers need to look at the **long-range objectives** and goals of the venture and plan to get it there. Planning starts with the articulation of the venture's objectives, policies, programs, budgets, and procedures. It incorporates all aspects of the operation — from the purchasing of supplies to the production process, sales and service, and finance. Planning is important when a venture starts up. It is equally important as the venture begins to grow.

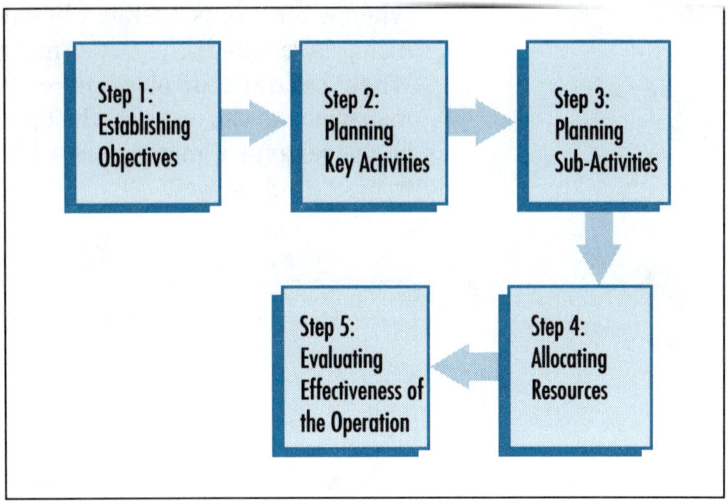

Figure 12.13 Planning Functions

Planning can be conducted on an informal basis or in a more formal way. Informal planning tends to be used when there is no well-defined company goal or when communication between those involved in managing the venture is minimal. Formal planning integrates **short-range plans** with long-range plans. If a long-range plan involves selling a particular product across Canada three years from now, immediate or short-range plans would have to be developed to include immediate smaller goals to establish a wider distribution network, train more personnel, and expand the manufacturing operation.

Computer software programs have made the process of planning much easier and more efficient. Spreadsheet software is being used by managers and employees alike to establish and manipulate the cost figures, sales forecasts, and operation budgets that form part of a company's planning process. Project management software enables managers to organize and manage each component of a special project, and to assign individual responsibilities and time lines, as well as available resources.

Organizing

When a venture is operated by one person, no special organizing is required. The owner/manager does everything alone. When a venture involves more than one person, it needs a manager who can organize the operation of the venture as well as the personnel, material, and equipment resources required to meet its objectives.

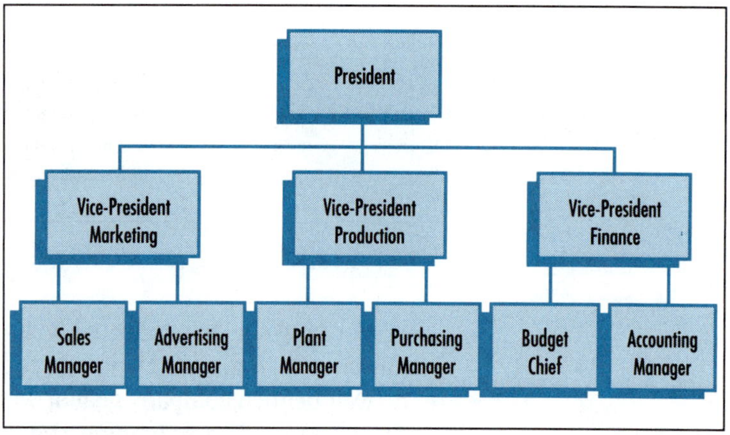

Figure 12.14 An Organizational Chart

As the venture grows in size, it is important to organize the people involved in the operation of the venture. An **organizational chart** is used to establish the hierarchy of management in an organization and to determine lines of communication.

Directing

Management is required to direct, lead, and motivate people to perform to the best of their abilities. Managers must also learn to delegate responsibilities for specific tasks, ensure that personnel performing these tasks are trained effectively, and encourage interpersonal communication at all levels. The leadership styles and communication processes covered earlier in this chapter are also important in the effective direction of personnel.

Controlling

The control function of management allows the manager to monitor all functions of the organization to ensure that plans are being implemented effectively.

> Effective control requires an analysis of what is happening in the business, and adjustments or corrections to keep the operation on target.

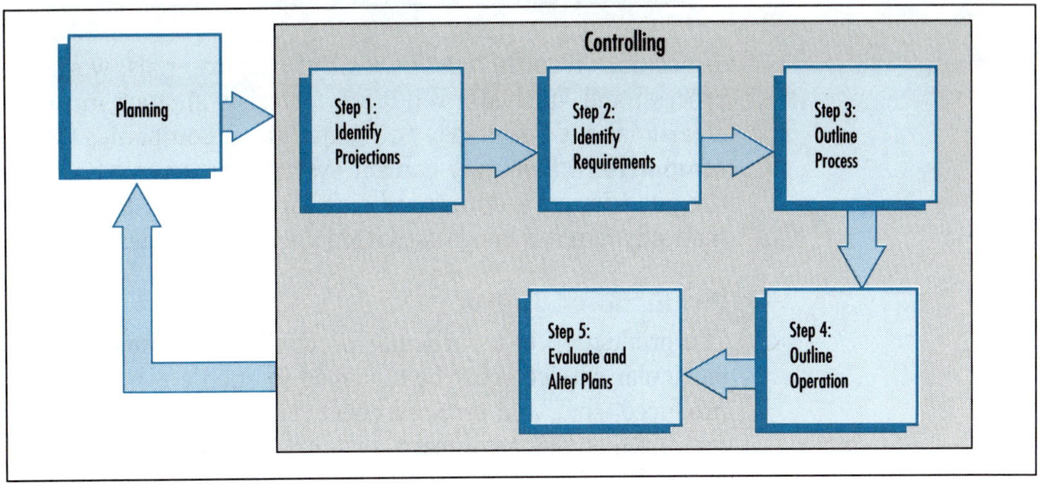

Figure 12.15 The Control Process

Controls cannot be implemented without careful forethought and analysis. Projected sales forecasts need to be used to determine how much should be produced, when it should be produced, what inventory is needed for production, what equipment and other facilities are required, and what processes should be used for production, sales, and distribution. People Express had to borrow money to meet its cash needs because those responsible for the control function did not alert management to the fact that projected sales forecasts were not being used to determine operation requirements. This borrowing put too heavy a burden on cashflow and led to the eventual collapse of the company.

Preventative or **pro-active control** requires that the organization establish and maintain a system or procedure for the handling of inventory, production, finance, and records management.

Inventory Control

Inventory systems must be established according to a carefully designed plan to ensure that the costs of ordering and storing materials are kept to a minimum.

> Inventories should be ready to use when needed and not left sitting on shelves or in warehouses waiting to be used.

Accurate records must be kept of raw materials, work-in-process, and finished inventories. Materials in stock must be clearly labelled and easy to locate. Many companies use a **computerized inventory control system** which records goods received using a computer software program and automatically removes goods used from the inventory files.

Production Controls

The production of a particular product or the provision of a particular service must be managed in such a way that it is produced, sold, and serviced effectively and efficiently. Every product made by a company, or every service provided, must be produced and delivered to meet a set of pre-determined company standards. A good **quality control program** will have:

- specifications and standards at the product design stage
- thorough inspection of all raw materials delivered to ensure that their quality meets the specifications of the product
- all work checked by an immediate supervisor, or fellow employee
- any product or service evaluated that does not meet the specifications for quality
- random inspection policies

AGENTS OF CHANGE

Walt Disney, disturbed by the growing strength of unions in the acting industry, was determined to show the world that great movies could be produced without employing unionized actors and actresses. Whether we agree with his motivation or not, his cartoon creations were instrumental in the development of an incredibly innovative animation industry.

Financial Controls

The importance of keeping accurate financial records cannot be overemphasized. If your customers are not paying their bills and you fail to keep accurate and up-to-date records, you will have no way of knowing that you are actually entitled to a larger amount of revenue. If you do not keep accurate records of all costs involved in the operation of your venture, you will have no way of knowing how much to charge for your product or service.

Records Management

Not only is it necessary to keep accurate and efficient records of financial matters, it is also important to keep up-to-date and accurate information on customer accounts, supplier information, and government rules and regulations. Like Comfort Clothing, companies that are growing very quickly need to ensure that they can maintain accurate and up-to-date information in order to make sound business and growth-related decisions.

YOUR TURN

20. There are two kinds of people — those who can make money and those who can save it. The first is more typical of the entrepreneur while the second reflects a skill of the manager. What kind of person are you? What makes you think so?
21. How successful do you think your venture will be if you are more the entrepreneur than the manager?
22. How successful do you think your venture will be if you are more the manager than the entrepreneur?
23. What aspect of good management do you see in the operation of your school or of a school club?

24. Visit a local retail or manufacturing business. Interview a representative of the business to determine what types of controls the company has put in place. Discuss strategies for inventory control, financial control, and records management control. If the business is involved in manufacturing, find out what production controls are in place.

P·O·I·N·T·S T·O R·E·M·E·M·B·E·R

- A venture has more chance of succeeding if it is well managed.
- Management involves the components of effective leadership, motivation, communication, and conflict resolution.
- Management includes the functions of planning, organizing, directing, and controlling.

W·H·A·T H·A·V·E Y·O·U L·E·A·R·N·E·D?

1. What two factors are considered the overwhelming causes for business failure?
2. What signs of failure would you look for in a company that is experiencing rapid growth?
3. Why is under capitalization an important factor in considering reasons for potential failure?
4. Why do most entrepreneurs experience a high degree of personal stress?
5. List six functions of leadership.
6. Identify each of the levels in Maslow's Hierarchy of needs.
7. Give three reasons why effective communication is important to the smooth operation of an organization.
8. List four strategies which can be used to reduce conflict.
9. What is the major purpose of the planning function?
10. Why is an organizational chart used in a company?
11. What is the role of the manager involved in the directing function?
12. List the four major areas involved in the controlling function.

V·E·N·T·U·R·I·N·G O·U·T

1. Identify your own leadership style and list the ways you plan to use it:
   a) as you start out on your venture
   b) as your venture grows
2. Describe how you will use the four main functions of management in your venture:
   a) as you start out
   b) as your venture grows

"First impressions count." THE VENTURE PLAN is your introduction to potential investors. Prepare a first-class plan and you will have a first-class introduction.

CHAPTER 13

Taking a Stand: Completing Your Venture Plan

LEARNING OUTCOMES

By the end of this chapter, you should be able to:

- identify the major sections of a venture plan
- identify and list the major potential risks involved with the venture
- write a draft venture plan
- proofread, edit, and prepare your venture plan for presentation

ENTREPRENEURIAL LANGUAGE

go/no-go decision
appendix
executive summary
table of contents
disclaimer
title page

Venture PROFILE

The Film Director

Canadian Business

Sandy Wilson, writer and director of the screenplay, *My American Cousin*

REALITY: "Most people don't realize that most of the work happens before you say 'action' and after you say 'cut,'" says Sandy Wilson, whose *My American Cousin* captured six Genie Awards in 1986. Filming took up only 25 days of the three years needed to make *Cousin*. During the first two years, Wilson developed the script while raising production money and two small children. Writing a screenplay is tough, but rounding up backers was "impossible," Wilson says — particularly since she "didn't even know what the word 'equity' meant." But she kept at it. "I talked to anyone who would talk to me — in bars, on airplanes. I even went to the Cayman Islands to talk to a friend's friend's brother-in-law," she laughs.

Eventually, in August, 1984, the $1.5-million financing package was ready and Wilson began the exhausting process of shooting. "On set, you're a shrink, a mother, a father, a boss — you're the works," she says. "At the end of the day's shoot, everyone else could go have a hot tub, but I'd go look at the rushes."

When it was over, Wilson went through "post-partum depression" as the crew went their separate ways and she went "back to being a Kitsilano housewife." And it was another full year — much of it spent in dark editing rooms — before the film was ready for release. "It's the same as being nine months pregnant and you think your baby's never going to be born."

Yet like a mother who quickly forgets the pain of childbirth, Wilson is eager to do it again. "I could always go back to being an usherette," says Wilson, "but directing gives me a bigger buzz."

AGENTS OF CHANGE

Have you read the story of Canada's most famous red-head, **Anne of Green Gables**? Lucy Maud Montgomery created this story and left us with a special picture of Prince Edward Island. People from around the world now read her story and travel thousands of kilometres to visit the place where it was created.

Failing to plan = planning to fail

EXPLORING • THE FILM DIRECTOR

1. How was the time spent getting ready to film?
2. How long did it take to do the actual filming?
3. What kind of activities occupied most of the planning period?
4. What similarities can you see between Sandy's film-making venture and the startup of a small business?

The Venture Planning Process

The Venture Profile you have just read may sound like a job description for a film maker. However, it also describes what entrepreneurs go through as they prepare to launch their successful ventures. Sandy sums it up well in her opening statement: "Most people don't realize that most of the work happens before you say 'action'..."

Before an entrepreneur says 'action', a comprehensive and carefully thought out venture plan must be developed. From information provided in Chapters 6 - 12, you have learned that the purpose of this very important overall plan is to:

- establish realistic goals
- assess the potential market
- identify the resources required
- describe how these resources will be used on a day-to-day basis
- project the costs involved and the revenues required for success

A venture plan should reflect the fact that all potential risks have been identified and strategies laid out to minimize them.

Preparing for a venture should not be a haphazard activity. A number of important steps should be incorporated into the planning process. These steps are diagrammed for you in Figure 13.1.

Figure 13.1 Important Steps in the Planning Process

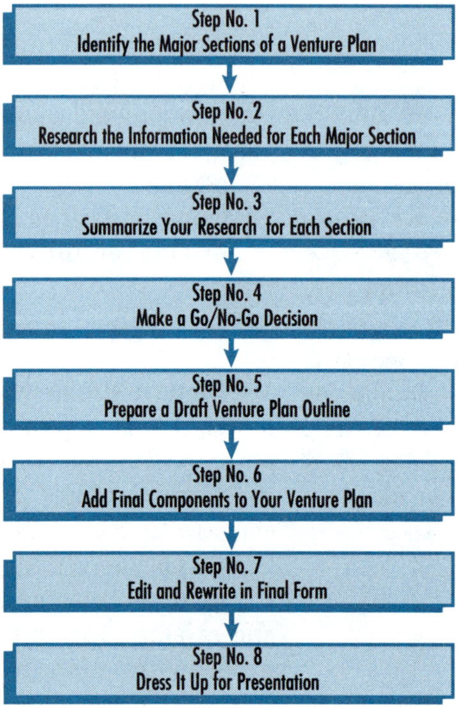

AGENTS OF CHANGE

Some people become agents of change by setting an example. Jeanne Sauvé worked her way from involvement with social causes to broadcaster and journalist, Member of Parliament, cabinet minister, and then the first woman Speaker of the House of Commons. She capped an amazing career with her appointment in 1984 as Canada's first female Governor-General. One woman helped changed the way we perceived the role of women.

The First Four Steps in the Venture Planning Process

If you review Figure 13.1, you will note that the initial four steps consist of the following tasks:

Identifying the Major Sections of a Venture Plan

You have already covered this step with your introduction to the venture plan in Chapter 6. Venture plans require a number of sections, including: The Description, Marketing Research, Resource Analysis, Operating Strategy, and Financial Strategy.

Researching the Information Needed for Each Major Section

You will have completed most of the research for your own venture plan in the Venturing Out sections at the end of Chapters 7, 8, 9, 10, and 11.

Summarizing Your Research for Each Section

After completing the research needed for each major section of a venture plan, it is important to organize and prepare a summary that can be used to make some major decisions.

Making a Go/No-Go Decision

> "Try? There is no try. There is only do or not do."
> *Yoda, in* The Empire Strikes Back

At this point in the planning process, it is necessary to review the research completed and make a decision to go ahead with the venture or to drop it entirely. The research summary prepared in Step No. 3 should help you put the whole venture in perspective. You will have defined a target market and confirmed an opportunity. You will have a good appreciation of all the human, financial, and facility resources you will need in order to undertake the venture. You will have determined a financial strategy for startup and continued operation. You will also have a clear picture of the cost of production as well as the revenue required for you to operate at a profit. This is the point at which you must make a **go/no-go decision.**

"Yes, I will proceed with the venture. " — Go!

Or, "I will not go ahead with this venture." — No-Go!

YOUR TURN

1. Using Table 6.2 (pages 172-73) as a guide, describe the purpose of each section of a venture plan.
2. Review the material you prepared in the Venturing Out sections at the end of Chapters 7, 8, 9, 10, and 11. Check each one for completeness and accuracy of information. Prepare each section for incorporation into your final venture plan. Redo anything you feel may not have been adequately researched or prepared in sufficient detail.
3. Based on the material prepared in Question 2, you now have enough information to decide whether your venture will be a go or a no-go. If you feel you can take your plan and turn your idea into a successful venture, make a go decision. If you think some part of it is too weak to succeed, go back to that part and make some revisions. Give reasons for your decision in either case and share these with the class.

Step No. 5: Preparing a Draft Venture Plan Outline

Entrepreneurs are often so enthusiastic about their ventures that they fail to realize what they do not know.

Lack of knowledge and experience can be sought from experts who offer advice to entrepreneurs. Jeanne Hryniuk, for example, sought the advice of the Canadian Executive Service Organization, a not-for-profit consulting firm. Hryniuk now owns and operates a convenience store in Patuanak, an Indian community in northern Saskatchewan. The volunteers from the Canadian Executive Service Organization have helped her organize her accounting records and write a venture plan. Jeanne is hoping the venture plan will help her obtain a government grant so she can move the business out of her home into a separate building and diversify her product line.

Figure 13.2 It is helpful to seek the advice of experts when preparing a venture plan.

No one should leap into the work of preparing a venture plan. It is useful to examine existing venture plans to identify what was stated and how it was stated. Examine these plans critically and note how they have presented information. If you require more direction on preparing your venture plan as well as some samples of actual plans, your local banks, accounting firms, and government agencies should be able to provide you with useful information.

Assessment of Risks

No venture plan should be prepared without a written assessment of potential risks. If your venture is to maintain a strong position in the marketplace, you must identify the problems or risks you might encounter and make plans to minimize or avoid them. Demonstrate that you are aware of potential problems in your venture, disclose and discuss all potential risks, and then identify the provisions you have made to minimize them. If you fail to do this, your credibility and your chances of success may be diminished. Again, consultants and specialists can assist you with this task.

AGENTS OF CHANGE

Business and government in Toronto always need documents translated from French into English. Louise Piller-Thay is bilingual and recognized that her skill could be used to start a translation business. Today, her firm translates more than two million words per year. Toronto's need translated into big business for Louise.

Risks are generally found in the following areas:

Competition	What will you do if your competition decides to cut its prices or offer improved service?
Sales	How will you minimize the effect of lower-than-projected sales figures?
Personnel	How will you respond to the possibility of one of your startup team members pulling out before the venture is financially underway? What will you do to compensate for an inexperienced management team or the lack of specially skilled employees?
Operational	How will you cover your losses incurred by shoplifting, liability to public, or property damage?
Financial	What will you do to overcome capital shortages or excessive bad debts?
Economic	How will you deal with downturns in the business cycle, increased taxes, and so on?

"Taking risks is like learning to ski. If you are not falling down, you are not learning."
William Smithberg, Chairman, Quaker Oats

The examples given above are only a few of the risks that entrepreneurs commonly have to face. Each venture, however, should expect to have its own special kinds of risks. Insurance can be purchased to minimize risks from such occurrences as theft, fire, or water damage. The negative aspect of a seasonal business can be offset by acquiring a different-season product line. Experienced people or the services of a professional consultant can be added to your startup team in order to compensate for inexperienced management.

AGENTS OF CHANGE

Susanna Moodie suffered through many long, hard years in Canada's early history. To ease her despair, she wrote stories and poetry about the loneliness of her backwoods life. Her writings have left us with a legacy of courage and survival in pioneer experiences and provided us with incredible insights into life in early Canada.

Preparing To Write

Make sure that all members of the startup team contribute to the development of the venture plan. All partners in the venture should be encouraged to provide ideas and to help write the content. A team effort is more likely to produce a plan that everyone can live with.

Before you begin, carefully consider what investors might want to see in your venture plan. They will be interested in how much money can be made on their investment. They will want to see written assurance that your financial projections are reasonable and based on careful market research studies. They will want to see that you have a clearly defined target market. They will want to be able to determine how much money they will make and when you will be able to pay them back what they have invested. They will want to see what the profit on their investment is likely to be and when it might be realized.

YOUR TURN

4. Contact your local Chamber of Commerce or someone in your community who is familiar with either writing or reading venture plans. Invite this person to speak to your class about the kind of information that should be included in a venture plan.
5. Identify and list who you will need to speak to to help you verify the information contained in each section of your venture plan.
6. Think through your particular venture and anticipate the risks or problems you might encounter. Discuss these risks in small groups and determine what you could do to eliminate or minimize each one.
7. Using the following headings, the information you prepared in the Venturing Out sections at the end of

Chapters 7, 8, 9, 10, and 11, and the research you completed earlier in this chapter, prepare the final draft outline for your venture plan:

- Description
- Market Analysis
- Resource Analysis
- Operating Strategy
- Financial Strategy

If you have a computer and a word-processing software package available, use them to create your venture plan.

8. Share your final draft outline with other student groups in your class. Ask them to help by checking that your content appears under the appropriate headings, that you have included all the information needed for a complete plan, and that you have presented your information in a logical and easy-to-follow manner.
9. When you are satisfied that this draft includes all the important pieces of information about your venture and that it is logical and well written, take it to a knowledgeable outside source such as a bank manager, someone connected with your local Chamber of Commerce, a business leader, a friend in a venture similar to the one you have in mind, or someone who acts as a consultant to entrepreneurs starting up or expanding their ventures. Many universities or community colleges have a consulting service run by their students under the direction of a faculty member. You might find a source of help at one of these institutions. Explain that your venture plan is in draft form and ask if you have covered everything required. Your source will probably be able to give you some advice on how to improve each section.
10. Rewrite your draft so that it reflects the advice given. If you have used a computer with word-processing software, this rewriting will be an easier process.

Venture
PROFILE

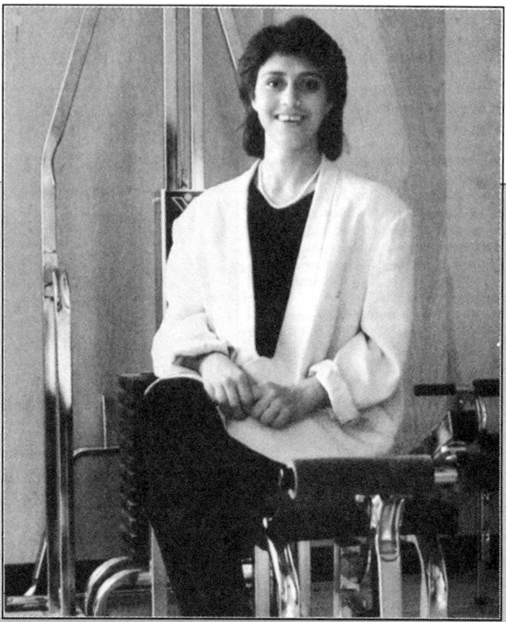

Brenda Cook: "If I'm going to work that long and hard, it had better be for my own account."

Strong Heart Sound Pocketbook

By Daniele Walker, *Your Money Magazine*

When Brenda Cook recounts her success story, people often tell her, "You must have had a plan from the beginning," or even, "You're very focused."

Indeed she is. Within months of earning her Bachelor of Physical Education degree from the University of Victoria, Cook went home to Regina and immediately created her own job as owner/employee of Fitwest Aerobics.

Today, she's not exactly rich, but she has developed three sideline businesses in addition to the still growing Fitwest club, and, at age 26, her financial net worth easily tops that of her fellow graduates now teaching high school Phys. Ed.

Nor has it been all business and no fun.

Along the way she took time to work out daily with some fellow rowers, a dedication which culminated in the gold medal, lightweight senior pairs division, in the Henley Cup. For Cook, reaching goals is fun.

In the summer, she's out in her rowing shell every morning. Year round, she's up at 5:45 a.m. for a cobweb-clearing run. That's when she does her planning: whom to hire, what to include in a new client's employee fitness plan, and what she should write in her quarterly client newsletter.

Designing employee fitness plans (for any size company that has an exercise space) is one of Cook's busiest sidelines. Once the main club was established — it has grown from 8 to 480 students — she methodically introduced related offshoots.

She now designs exercise clothes and oversees aerobics dance programs in two Regina health clubs on a contract basis.

Cook's temperament — "I tackle one goal at a time 'til it's through" — has helped a lot in business. It's not a bad formula in the public sector either, but she ruled out that path early on.

"I worked for a recreation department as part of my training. I decided that if I was going to work that long and that hard, it had better be for my own account."

The flip side of always knowing what she wants? A lot of frustration brought on by her inability to do it all herself. "It's very hard to delegate because you develop certain standards. I'd like everything to be done the way I'd do it."

To keep sanity, she follows the same regimen she prescribes for Regina's office workers: good nutrition and regular exercise — plus, in her case, a "very supportive partner."

She is working on her next goal — consolidating her classes in a single building to save travel time. Beyond that, she says, health club owners outside Regina are keeping a wary eye on her next move — "They'd hate to have me as competition."

EXPLORING • FITWEST AEROBICS

1. List the ventures which comprise Brenda Cook's major business and her three sidelines.
2. What evidence is there that she is a good planner?
3. What is Brenda's strategy for tackling goals?
4. What is her source of frustration?

AGENTS OF CHANGE

Although more and more people want to get some sort of physical workout, finding the time to run down to the local gym isn't always easy. Ann Rottenberg of Toronto will bring a fitness program or exercise class right to your home, pool, or corporate boardroom. Ann has left us with no more excuses not to get in shape!

Step No. 6: Adding the Final Components to Your Venture Plan

Your basic venture plan is now complete. All five sections have been written, revised, and reworked. The time has now come to finalize the schedule and create the additional written documents that add structure, support, and a sense of organization to the plan.

The Overall Schedule

Every aspect of the venture should follow an organized sequence and a specially laid-out timetable. Effective venture plans include an overall schedule that indicates the timing of each major activity. Schedules should lay out a step-by-step process for getting the venture started and running. A time line should be attached to this schedule so that the entrepreneur can keep on target, on time, and be aware of each next step.

Figure 13.3 Put a time line to your schedule.

Appendix

You will probably want to include a number of support documents to back up your statements. Breaking into the middle of your text material with such things as a copy of the form used to gather market information, or a copy of a special agreement, contract, or résumé of one of the startup members disrupts the reading flow and spoils the presentation of your venture plan. It is much better to include each support document as an **appendix** at the end of your venture plan. Each document can be numbered Appendix A, Appendix B, and so on.

Executive Summary

Whenever you write something that is more than three or four pages in length, it is a good idea to prepare a short summary of what your report contains. Depending upon the size of a particular venture, a venture plan could be anywhere from 10 to 50 pages long. The **executive summary** should be no more than one to two pages long and should include all of the information needed to help the reader see what is proposed, what is needed, what will be done, who will do it, and what it will cost.

AGENTS OF CHANGE

By the end of the 19th century, most Canadian men still did not believe women could participate equally in politics. Nellie McClung used her skills as a best-selling novelist and powerful public speaker to fight this belief she knew to be untrue. Nellie's confidence inspired thousands of women to fight for their rights as citizens of Canada.

An executive summary should be written after the rest of the report has been finished. It should include only the highlights of what is said in the report — only the more important statements. An executive summary should get right to the point. It will make the very first statement about a venture. It should be a good one.

Table of Contents

Once all the content of the venture plan is completed, it is a good idea to prepare a **table of contents** listing all the sections in the plan with the page numbers on which they may be found. This helps the potential investor or financial officer to find sections quickly and easily and also gives the desired impression of a good sense of organization.

Disclaimer

Information in a venture plan is considered to be confidential. As an entrepreneur, you will want to prevent unauthorized copying or distributing of your plan. A **disclaimer** statement, made at the beginning of a venture plan, can be used to prohibit copying and distribution. It can also protect you from challenges to your credibility or questions about the accuracy of the data you used. Although you may believe that the content of your venture plan is accurate, it may include unknown factual errors or erroneous forecasts and projections. Disclaimer statements are usually made at the start of your plan and printed on the title page.

Title Page

Finally, a **title page** should be prepared giving the name of the venture, the people proposing it, the date of transmittal, and a disclaimer.

YOUR TURN

11. List each major step of your proposed operation:
    - How you will develop your product or service.
    - How your venture will operate.
    - What selling procedures you will use.
    - How you will deliver your product or service.
    - What facilities will be required.
    - How the facilities will be set up.

12. Using a diagram, flowchart, or any other graphical presentation to show each major step, provide time lines and an overall schedule for each step.
13. Prepare all your support documents and number them Appendix A, Appendix B, and so on.
14. Prepare a table of contents for your venture plan.
15. Prepare a disclaimer for your venture plan.
16. Prepare a title page for your venture plan.

Step No. 7: Editing and Rewriting in Final Form

When your venture plan is finished and ready to present to a potential investor, banker, or advisor, you will want it to look professional and to represent as complete a picture of your proposed venture as possible.

Professionally prepared venture plans do not have to be extraordinarily long. In fact, they should be kept as short as possible without compromising the description of the venture and its potential. All key issues should be covered and every major step outlined. Only information that is unnecessary should be eliminated.

Ambiguous, vague, or unsupported statements should be avoided. They will only make you seem like a shallow or fuzzy thinker. An entrepreneur seeking additional funding to expand a particular venture should not claim in the venture plan, for example, that his or her markets are growing rapidly without concrete support for such a statement. Past, present, and future expectations of performance and market size should be identified.

Editing and rewriting take time and careful attention to details. There are a number of excellent reference books available to help you write using an effective style and correct language.

Careful editing will require that you read through your draft venture plan several times.

If you are using a computer with word-processing software that includes a spell check and thesaurus program, you will find this part of your work much easier.

Table 13.1 Proofreading and Editing Steps

1. *Read for content.*
   Does what you have said make sense? Is it complete?
2. *Read for style.*
   Have you used an effective writing style?
3. *Read for language usage.*
   Have you used jargon or too much technical language?
   Is it grammatically correct? Have you used punctuation correctly? Have you double checked?
4. *Read for spelling errors.*
   Are there any keying or spelling errors?
   Have you double checked?

When you have finished writing and editing your venture plan, have it reviewed and critiqued. No matter how good you and your team are, you will probably have overlooked some issues or treated a particular aspect of your venture inadequately. Good reviewers can point out such deficiencies and give you the benefit of an outside objective evaluation. They can act as a sounding board to help you develop alternative solutions to some of your venture's problems. They can also provide answers to some of the questions that investors might ask.

In some cases, you might want to take your plan to a lawyer to ensure that there are no misleading statements. One of the advantages of using word-processing software to prepare your venture plan is that it is never too much trouble to make the changes that will enhance the final product.

Step No. 8: Dressing It Up for Presentation

Appearance is often as important as content. The way a venture plan is presented will often influence the reader as much as the content. Using a computer with desktop publishing software to prepare your plan will allow you to develop an effective layout, select the most effective print style, and vary it for special effects. A computer will even facilitate the use of computer-designed graphics and illustrations to enhance the visual effect of your plan. Select a good quality paper for the final version of your plan. The first impression readers get will often determine the frame of mind they will adopt when reading through the venture plan.

> There is only one opportunity to make a first impression. Seize it!

Your venture plan should be logically organized:

- Title Page (including Disclaimer)
- Table of Contents
- Executive Summary
- Description
- Market Research
- Resource Analysis
- Operating Strategy
- Financial Strategy
- Appendix

Your plan should be neither too fancy nor too plain. Plenty of white space should be left on each page so that it is easy to read, attractive to look at, and convenient for the reader to make comments and references. Pages should be numbered and standard-sized white paper used. If you want a potential investor or advisor to take your plan home, it will have to fit into a regular-sized file folder, filing cabinet, and briefcase.

Your plan should be printed in black ink on one side of the page only. Colour may be used to highlight illustrations or charts, but other than that no unnecessary art work should be included. All graphs and illustrations should be labelled and numbered for easy reference. You should also indicate the source of any data used.

Formatting such things as cashflow projections that have a number of columns might be a difficult assignment. Sometimes large forms can be reduced to regular size through photocopying so that they will fit into the printed plan. If this is not possible, spread them out over a double page and fold to size.

Your finished venture plan should be put into an attractive binder or folder that will open easily and lay flat for reading.

Even though you have carefully edited your plan, before you assemble it into a folder, check once again for:

It's hard not to judge a book by its cover when the cover is the first thing you see.

- page numbers
- table and illustration numbers
- grammar, punctuation, and spelling

Figure 13.4 "How well did you read this before you sent it to me?"

Letter of Transmittal

The letter of transmittal is a letter that accompanies your plan when it is sent to a potential investor. It should explain:

- why you are sending him or her your venture plan
- why your proposed venture should be considered for financing
- what makes your venture unique

Letters of transmittal are more effective when they are simple, short, and honest. Two or three paragraphs are adequate. The first paragraph should introduce your proposed plan to the potential investor, briefly describing one or two of its unique features. The second paragraph should outline why your reader should be interested in your proposal. The third paragraph should outline what you want him or her to do after reading the proposal.

YOUR TURN

17. Using the proofreading and editing steps you have just learned, do a final edit of a classmate's venture plan.

18. Interview a banker, accountant, or consultant who has examined a number of venture plans. Ask him or her to discuss examples of some of the most and least visually attractive venture plans he or she has seen. Share this information with the class.
19. Prepare a draft letter of transmittal for your venture plan. Share this draft with a classmate and discuss how it might be improved.

AGENTS OF CHANGE

Most people know who David Suzuki is. He is admired as a working scientist, as a renowned geneticist, and as someone who can be counted on to speak out for the causes he holds dear. He is committed to the importance of science for the future of humanity and to helping humans understand that they are part of nature, not its masters. Not a new message, but one Dr. Suzuki delivers well and often hoping to change our perceptions.

Your venture plan will be a tool to help you achieve your goals. It will illustrate that you have thought through the venture carefully and considered all the problems and pitfalls that could interrupt the achievement of your goal. Your plan portrays you, the entrepreneur, in the driver's seat of a car. The car represents all the resources you need and have gathered ready for action. With your plan, your route map, in hand, you now have the responsibility of guiding the venture to success — driving the car to its destination.

Figure 13.5 Driving the Venture

POINTS TO REMEMBER

- It is important to carefully prepare what you will include in your venture plan before you start writing.
- The information you include should be carefully researched and written to satisfy the needs of the person or persons for whom the business plan is written.

- Potential risks should be identified and means included to either avoid or minimize them.
- Proofreading and editing are important steps in the completion of your venture plan.
- A venture plan needs to be professional and polished in appearance and content.

W·H·A·T H·A·V·E Y·O·U L·E·A·R·N·E·D·?

1. List the five major purposes of preparing a venture plan.
2. Name the eight steps involved in the planning process.
3. List the major sections of a venture plan.
4. Why is it important to include an assessment of potential risks?
5. Which additional components should be included in a venture plan?
6. List three strategies which can be used when editing and proofreading a venture plan.
7. What can you do to make your venture plan more attractive and easier to read?
8. Provide two suggestions for formatting large statements such as cashflow projections.

V·E·N·T·U·R·I·N·G O·U·T

1. Following the proofreading and editing steps outlined earlier and the final suggestions you received from a fellow classmate, prepare your venture plan for final copy.
2. Rewrite and prepare your plan for final presentation to a potential investor using desktop publishing software if this is available.
3. Prepare a letter of transmittal to accompany your venture plan when you send it to a potential investor.

"For every thing there is a season." Every venture passes through different seasons or phases and ends with a harvest. This chapter examines those phases and outlines what it will take to reap a sweet and bountiful harvest.

CHAPTER 14

To Life: Growing and Harvesting a Venture

LEARNING OUTCOMES

By the end of this chapter, you should be able to:

- understand the phases that a venture goes through
- describe the tasks that need to be completed in each phase
- recognize strategies which mature companies use to prevent decline
- explain different ways in which an entrepreneur may realize benefits from a venture
- distinguish between law and ethics
- specify a set of values you wish to use to guide you in your ventures and in your personal life

ENTREPRENEURIAL LANGUAGE

incubation phase
startup phase
growth phase
cost per unit
maturity phase
research and development
inventive task
innovative task
entrepreneurial task
managerial task
administrative task
bootleg
management buyout
code of ethics

Venture
PROFILE

Handing over the Oars of Power

Canadian Business

Entrepreneurs must learn to share responsibility and delegate when necessary.

Three years ago, Barry Russell was not only co-owner of Pola Graphics Ltd., but business manager, personnel director, and production coordinator as well. Being the more aggressive of the two partners, Russell had taken on the lion's share of the load. He grimaces at the memory: "Anytime there was a job that needed doing, I would take it on and carry it."

As a result, he found himself spending nights and weekends at the office. After years of such slogging, Russell was exhausted. Finally, his partner was inspired by a seminar on small-business management. He pointed out that Russell had fallen prey to one of the common pitfalls of entrepreneurship, the monkey-on-the back syndrome: he had taken on too much. The lights finally came on for Russell. "I told my partner, 'You're talking to a turkey, not a monkey'."

Russell's struggle with sharing responsibility is by no means unique. "The entrepreneurial personality is not conducive to delegation," says Oksana Exell, Vancouver regional director for the Canadian Federation of Independent Business. "Entrepreneurs by definition like to be in control — they take great pride in their independence and their gut sense of what's right — characteristics that make them poor team players and make them even poorer delegators."

Nevertheless, coming to grips with the necessity of letting others share the work load can result in substantial rewards. Studies have shown that a firm's performance increases significantly with the degree of delegation practised by its Chief Executive Officer. "It's difficult to be a two- or three-person operation in today's competitive market," asserts Ken Kirby, owner-manager of Kirby Floral Greens Inc., one of Vancouver's largest wholesale distributors of fresh flowers. By learning to share some of his work with his employees, Kirby has seen his firm grow over eight years to annual sales of about $5 million. "To grow and be successful — and not work 20 hours a day," he says, " you just have to learn to delegate."

EXPLORING • SHARING RESPONSIBILITY

1. What different types of jobs had Barry Russell taken on in his company?
2. What was the result?
3. Define the term "delegation" as it is used in this Venture Profile.
4. What are the advantages of delegation?
5. Why are entrepreneurs often not good delegators?

Phases in a Venture's Life Cycle

A venture is, in many ways, very similar to the good or service it produces. In Chapters 5 and 7, you learned that a product goes through stages in its life cycle. So does a venture. The problems Barry Russell faced are often encountered by entrepreneurs as their ventures move from the startup through the growth phase of operation.

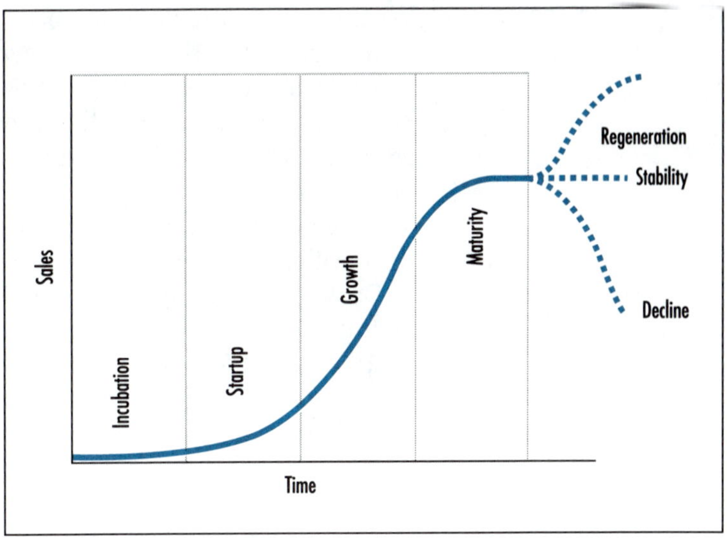

Figure 14.1 A Venture's Life Cycle

There may be a very long **incubation phase**. This text has focused on this period of preparation. It is during this phase that entrepreneurs develop and use their Explorer and Artist. They learn to become acute observers of human nature and circumstances. They see needs to satisfy. They learn to mix and combine what they observe in new ways. The result is a new idea. This development of the observant, creative aspect of the personality is matched by the development of the Judge who subjects everything to a careful analysis.

Typically, entrepreneurs tend to work alone or with only a few, highly trusted associates during the incubation stage.

"Some see things as they are and wonder why. Others dream of things as they might be and say 'why not?'"
Robert Kennedy

One reason why entrepreneurs work alone during the incubation stage is security. The fewer people who know about your idea, the better it can be. Many good ideas cannot be protected by patents or copyright. Even in cases where they are, patents and copyrights do not always offer sufficient protection.

Another reason for keeping the group involved with the incubation phase small is that necessity often demands it. Ventures at this stage have no income or assets to use as a source of capital. They do not even have a venture plan to convince others of the value of their idea. Costs must be kept down because there is little revenue to pay the bills. The Explorer, Artist, and Judge work together either as different facets of the entrepreneur or as a team of individuals to create a venture plan which becomes the basis for the second stage in the creation of a venture.

During the **startup phase**, the Warrior enters the picture and, using the venture plan, acquires all the resources the venture needs. The venture may even hire a few employees. These resources are then organized and the venture is born. Once born, the Warrior uses all the other creative roles to protect it and to help it grow. The Warrior acts as the parent of the fledgling venture; nurturing it, encouraging it, and seeing that it has all the resources it needs to grow strong. During the startup phase, sales are weak but increasing. The cost of producing each unit is high and the venture is probably operating at a loss. It is likely that there is little competition at this stage, and if this is the case, high production and operating costs can be passed on to the consumer in the form of higher prices.

AGENTS OF CHANGE

Sam Geraci took garlic, an everyday spice, and made a variety of spreads and juices from it. Derlea Products now employs ten people and its products are shipped all across Canada. Sam took an old product and found new ways to use it.

In the **growth phase**, the entrepreneur sees the venture grow in size and competence. It becomes able to co-operate and compete with other ventures. Success breeds confidence which results in more growth. During this phase, word spreads about the quality of its product or service, and demand for its output increases. The entrepreneur must be able to grow with the venture by incorporating and organizing the many resources the venture now needs. At this point, the entrepreneur needs to be able to step back from the creation and give up the details of day-to-day management to the people who have been hired. The entrepreneur is free to continue to put his or her other efforts into developing new ideas, products, and markets. It is during the growth phase that one sees the most rapid increase in sales. Profits increase because of a sharp increase in sales combined with a reduction in the **cost per unit** produced. With proper management and administration, the venture becomes more efficient as it grows. It may even be able to choose to lower its selling price because at lower prices, the quantity demanded tends to increase and this may result in greater sales revenues for the company.

Figure 14.2 "Growing a business is like raising a child." In what ways is an entrepreneur like a parent?

At some point, the larger profits of the growth phase will attract more competition. The period of growth ends. Nothing continues to grow forever. This does not necessarily mean the venture ceases to exist. It does mean that the venture has entered its fourth stage of development.

In the **maturity phase**, growing competition reduces prices and profit margins shrink. Demand may even decline slightly as needs are satisfied. Managing and running the venture efficiently on a day-to-day basis becomes most important if the venture is to survive. Once a venture has reached the maturity phase, it may develop in different directions. One possibility is that its sales, prices, and profits may stabilize and remain much the same from year to year.

Stability of earnings becomes the key objective of the venture.

Management may change the mix of products it offers. For example, a retail computer company may, during its growth phase, have placed its emphasis on selling hardware. In time, the market becomes saturated and sales decline. The computer retail company may shift its focus to selling other goods or services which are directly related to its product. These might include application or educational software or training courses and service contracts. Although these additional goods and services may originally have been part of the sales package, they now become of greater importance as they help the business to maintain a stable earnings flow.

A second possibility is that the firm can regenerate itself. It can continue to grow if its Explorer, Artist, and Judge can creatively and critically develop new goods and services to satisfy new needs. The venture can achieve this new growth by diversifying its product line by acquiring, for example, computer products from a wider variety of manufacturers. A firm may also diversify by producing new products which are not directly related to what it has been producing. It may also continue its growth by investing some of its profits in **research and development** to produce, for example, a more powerful computer, or it may buy or merge with another company and take over its product lines.

The third option, decline, will occur for those ventures which fail to stabilize their business by carving out a market niche. The sales and profits of such ventures fall, perhaps to the point where the firm will be driven out of business as competition becomes more intense.

YOUR TURN

1. In which phase of development would you place each of the following:
   a) Coca-Cola Ltd.
   b) a company which produces Fax machines
   c) a company which produces only cigarettes
   d) a company which produces VCRs
   e) General Motors?
2. Using your own research skills and personal contacts, list examples of ventures in your own community which you believe are at each phase of development. You may consult your local Chamber of Commerce or any financial or government lending institution for assistance. When you have chosen one example of a venture at each stage, share this information with a partner, giving reasons for your examples.
3. a) With the help of your classmates, generate a list of not-for-profit ventures in your community.
   b) Establish a list of criteria that you could use to describe each phase of the life cycle of a not-for-profit venture.
   c) Decide which phase each venture on your list is in.

AGENTS OF CHANGE

For years, blind people had no way to teach themselves to read braille. Seven volunteers with the Canadian National Institute for the Blind spent five years producing a textbook on how to transcribe braille. One group of volunteers helped another group help itself.

Development Tasks

As a venture develops from the incubation through the maturity phase, different tasks take on utmost importance. There are five development tasks which must be performed. The **inventive task** involves the creation of a new device or process by joining together previously unrelated elements in a new way. The **innovative task** consists of applying the new technology, process, or idea to satisfy an existing need. A great many inventions never make it past a file in the Patent Office because no one has been able to find practical uses for them. The inventive and innovative tasks are those which rely most heavily on the Explorer and the Artist. They are also the tasks which demand a great deal of attention during the incubation phase of a venture's life cycle.

The **entrepreneurial task** is the third task. It involves organizing previously unrelated resources to build a venture which can produce and market a good or service to satisfy a need. The new invention or innovation creates the opportunity to which the entrepreneur responds. The entrepreneurial task requires the addition of the Judge and the Warrior, for the entrepreneur must identify which creative ideas and innovations are going to address and satisfy the most needs and must recruit the resources to make the venture a success.

The fourth task in the creation of a successful venture is the **managerial task.** The manager directs the organization created by the entrepreneur by identifying day-to-day operating goals and the strategies needed to reach these goals.

Finally, there is the **administrative task**, which involves executing or carrying out the strategies identified by management in an efficient and effective way. The managerial and administrative tasks require a Warrior who can plan and coordinate the day-to-day operation of a venture.

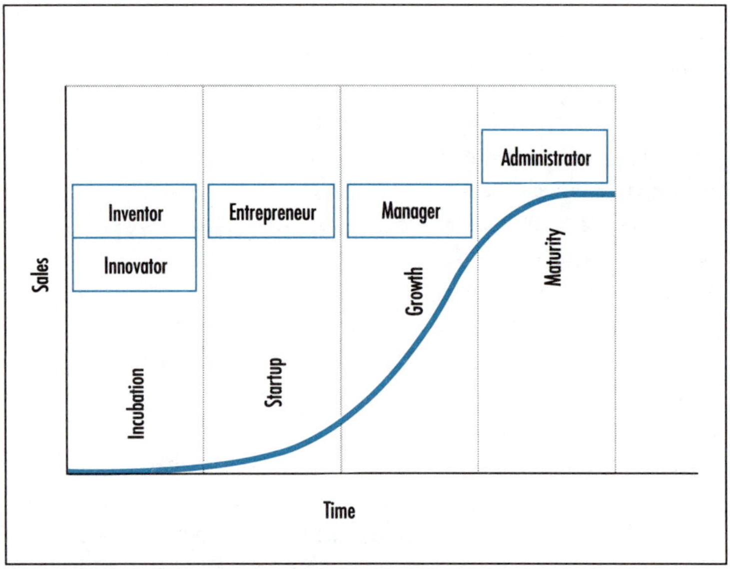

Figure 14.3 Development Tasks in the Venture's Life Cycle

Growing a Venture

The inventive, innovative, and entrepreneurial tasks will get a venture up and running and carry it through the incubation and startup phases. The managerial and administrative tasks are essential to the daily operation of the business and to pilot it through its growth phase to maturity. Each of these tasks requires different abilities and strengths. A venture needs different tasks performed at different times. It is rare to find all these abilities and strengths combined in one individual. As has been noted in earlier chapters, the entrepreneur is quite often not the inventor.

Entrepreneurs may have little interest in, or aptitude for, managing or administering a venture once it is past its startup phase. This can create problems for both the entrepreneur and the venture. Many a good startup has turned sour and many a venture has failed to grow because the entrepreneur could not perform, and would not learn, the managerial task. This was Barry Russell's problem in the Venture Profile which began this chapter. Ken Kirby's advice, to learn how to perform the managerial task of delegating work, would help save many an entrepreneur and many a venture from decline.

Growth is not simply the result of applying managerial and administrative skills. The entrepreneurial task still needs to be performed within the company during its growth phase. It is also possible for mature firms to maintain and promote an entrepreneurial thrust. The huge 3M Company, one of the most innovative companies, encourages its employees to **bootleg** — transfer without specific approval — up to 10 per cent of their time and resources from current production tasks and devote them to the development of new products. This idea has been so successful that 25 per cent of the company's sales in any given year come from products which did not even exist five years ago.

When Apple Inc. wanted to create a new type of powerful, user-friendly computer, Steven Jobs, the co-founder of Apple, created a separate and independent division within the larger company to attract and mobilize creative people. It produced the Macintosh computer. Northern Telecom, a Canadian firm which is a world leader in the communication industry, is an example of a venture which continues to grow creatively. Like other large companies which operate in a competitive market, it continually searches to find ways to accommodate the inventor, innovator, and entrepreneur within its business environment. Some large companies rely on smaller entrepreneurial firms to produce new ideas and technology. The large firm then purchases the new technology or, in some cases, the whole firm in order to acquire the use of the latest developments. Others invest some of their profits in research and development to revitalize growth. The major objective in either case is to identify new needs and develop new products or services to satisfy these needs.

YOUR TURN

4. Identify new goods or services which have been developed and produced for the first time during your lifetime. How has each contributed to your well-being?
5. Research the history of your own community or region and briefly describe any new goods or services which were first developed in your own area.
6. Identify existing ventures in your own area which are engaged in research and the development and production of a new good or service.

AGENTS OF CHANGE

For years and years, diabetes was a disease that baffled medical researchers and devastated those who suffered from it. When Canadians Sir Frederick Banting and Charles Best discovered insulin, diabetics around the world could finally lead relatively normal lives.

Venture PROFILE

Relentless Research the Key to Success

Toronto Star

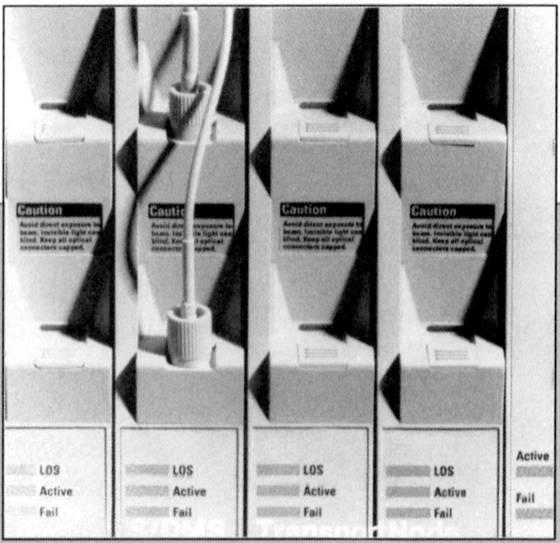

Northern Telecom's Fibre World Family

More information is being sent along telephone lines every year, with the spread of fax machines, bank cash machines, and other talk between computers.

Equipment suppliers like Northern Telecom are in a race to increase the speed and carrying capacity of phone networks, for these and a wide array of future needs.

They see movies being carried into homes on phone lines, more video conferences between businesspeople, and instant transmission to X-ray images from radiology rooms to doctors in distant offices.

Already Northern is participating in trials of a telephone conferencing system for X-rays within Ottawa Civic Hospital.

None of these new services would be possible without the carrying capacity of fibre-optic cables and the laser lights used to flash signals along the phone network.

Theoretically, the hairlike strands of glass that began replacing copper wire in telephone lines more than a decade ago have unlimited carrying capacity.

That potential has yet to be realized. But the pace of progress in applying miniature computer chip technology to switching and transmission equipment is head-spinning.

Today's generation of equipment from Northern sends four times more data per second than the last and five times more than equipment sold in the early 1980s.

A rival supplier introduced equipment in 1987 with double Northern's capacity. Another tripled the ante in 1988. But in October, 1989, Northern leapfrogged the competition again.

It said a new family of fibre-optic equipment would be four times faster than its old standard, with the potential to double again fairly readily within a couple of years.

A new Fibre World family of products will thus be capable of transmitting the equivalent of 32 256 conversations at a time along a single glass fibre strand.

By comparison, a pair of copper wires can carry not more than 24 conversations. Northern wants to do more than keep up. Robert Enos,vice-president of transmission and transport, says, "You always have to be six months ahead of the technology if you want to use it as an edge. If you don't invest in R&D, in three years you're irrelevant."

EXPLORING • NORTHERN TELECOM

1. Phone lines are carrying more information every year.
   a) The article mentions three examples. What are they?
   b) Explain how each of these examples improves our lives.
2. New technology in the communication field improves two aspects of the existing communications system. What are they?
3. What new ideas or technologies have made new developments possible?
4. The rate of change in this industry is staggering. Compared to ten years ago, Northern's new technology is capable of sending how much more information than it sent ten years ago? How is this expected to change within the next two years?
5. Compare the number of conversations which may be conducted at one time using the fibre-optic system with those which can be received by copper wire.
6. What, according to Robert Enos, is:
   a) the advantage, in terms of time, of having the best technology?
   b) the result of not investing in research and development?

Harvesting a Venture

The term "harvest" is an appropriate one, for harvesting a venture is like harvesting a crop. Harvesting implies that a seed has been planted and nurtured into growth by providing it with the water, nutrients, and sunlight it needs to mature. The entrepreneur's seed is the idea and opportunity on which the venture is based. The entrepreneur nurtures the growth of the idea into a venture by providing it with the resources it needs. Both the farmer and the entrepreneur have a long-term goal of creating something of real value. Neither have the "get-rich-quick" mentality of the promoter or rip-off artist. Once the crop has reached maturity, the farmer harvests it by cutting it down and selling it.

The entrepreneur creates a venture which does not have to be "cut down" to be harvested. There are other choices.

Financial Harvest

AGENTS OF CHANGE

Mary Pickford, a Canadian child actress, became the world's first movie star and one of the richest women in history. She made many films and won an Academy Award for her role as a small town southern woman in *Coquette*, her first "talkie" film.

Many entrepreneurs choose to stay with their ventures and grow with them by learning the skills of management and administration. They receive a financial harvest in the form of the income they draw from their ventures. Entrepreneurs can also realize a financial gain from their ventures by selling all or part of them. As a venture grows, the value of its assets increases. The entrepreneur, as partial or complete owner of the venture, is also the owner of the venture's assets which can be sold for a profit. The entrepreneur may sell his or her equity or share of the venture to existing partners or managers in the venture. This is referred to as a **management buyout**. The entrepreneur may also sell his or her venture and the new technology it produced to another larger company like Northern Telecom. Another choice is going public. This involves selling shares of ownership in the venture to the general public. Some of the proceeds of the sale of shares may be used to finance the further growth of a venture.

Financial reward is an important form of harvest from a venture. Profits are important to entrepreneurs. High profits signal that demand is great and more should be produced. They can also create a pool of capital to be used to expand production. Profits act as an incentive to those who undertake projects which involve some risk. They are also a measure of how effectively one entrepreneur is running his or her venture in comparison to another.

> The greatest profit should go to the entrepreneur who organizes production in the best, most efficient way.

Human Harvest

While profits are important to entrepreneurs, most successful entrepreneurs say that making a profit is not their main reason for starting new ventures. Many entrepreneurs, financially successful to the point of being multimillionaires, will continue to risk their wealth on one new venture after another. Why do they take the risk? This is a question concerning human behaviour. It strikes at the heart of the entrepreneurial process and at the hub of the Venture Creation Wheel. Entrepreneurship is, after all, fundamentally a human rather than a financial or technological process. All sorts of non-financial rewards exist, ranging from personal satisfaction to independence to self respect to increased family ties, if the venture is a family business. All of these rewards serve to motivate and satisfy the entrepreneur. Entrepreneurial endeavours provide a way for individuals to express themselves and to grow. In the process, the wider community, as well as the individual, may benefit greatly. More jobs and greater wealth are created. New goods and services are offered and more needs satisfied.

Three brief Venture Profiles are presented below. As you read each one, note the reasons why the entrepreneurs have chosen to do what they do.

Venture PROFILE

IGGY KANEFF
Kaneff Properties

Iggy Kaneff was born in 1926 in Bulgaria. He and his wife came to Canada in 1951 without a knowledge of either English or French. He planned to work in the construction field. His father had been a builder, and Iggy had had experience renovating houses in Austria.

He bought his first lot in Port Credit, a western suburb of Toronto, for $300 and built a small home for him and his wife. By 1955, he was acting as a contractor and building a dozen houses a year. When he first started building in Mississauga in the early 1950s, Mississauga was a suburb of Toronto with a population of only 7000. Now there are over 350 000 people living there, making it one of the 10 largest cities in Canada. His company grew with Mississauga. By 1985, he had built over 1500 houses and apartment buildings with a total of over 7000 units, along with numerous commercial buildings.

Why did he do it? He says it's his instincts. He is a dreamer who constantly wants to do better things and build better buildings. Among the better things he does is his charitable work on behalf of the mentally retarded. He also built a kindergarten in the Bulgarian village where he was born and fixed up the church in which he was christened. Although he doesn't live extravagantly and still chums with the same people he did when he was poor, he loves the system which combines freedom with the opportunity to "exercise your abilities".

Venture PROFILE

BARBARA RAE
Office Assistance

Barbara Rae joined Office Assistance, an organization which provides firms with secretarial help, one year after it had been founded in 1951. She worked her way up within the company and was appointed president in 1969. By this time, the Vancouver-based company had about $1 million in sales and employed 40 people full time, and about 300 to 400 part time.

Today there is a full-time staff of 125, about 3000 temporaries, and sales have reached $15 million a year, making Office Assistance the largest office-help placement firm in Western Canada. The firm grew so rapidly by opening branch offices. There are now six branches in Vancouver, three in Calgary, two in Edmonton, and two in Toronto.

Rae proclaims that as an entrepreneur she is proud that she has created so many jobs. She is even prouder of a profit-sharing plan which allows employees in each branch to share in the profits of the branch and receive shares in the company. Rae sold the company to Adia, a Swiss company, which is the second largest company handling temporary workers in the world. Shares which employees had bought for $250 were worth over $1000 each. Rae herself became a millionaire, but since the sale nothing much has changed. She still runs the company.

Office Assistance became the biggest in the West because of Rae's "own need to make things develop. I'm always growing and getting better with the business. It's always building, building, building. I'm never content with the status quo. There's almost nothing I can't do. I keep trying until I get it!"

Venture PROFILE

SERGE RACINE
Shermag

In 1977, Serge Racine and some partners organized Shermag, an enormously successful furniture manufacturing company. It began with a dozen employees. By the end of 1985, it had over 550 workers in six factories with sales of over $25 million. Shermag is the largest manufacturer of non-stuffed furniture in Quebec and the third largest in all of Canada. Racine has also moved successfully into the production of trucks. The University of Sherbrooke designed the truck, which is made of rust-free fibreglass guaranteed to stay fresh for 20 years.

To Serge Racine, success has been the result of a particular commitment and a philosophy which emphasizes doing ordinary things extraordinarily well. He insists there must be a love of hard work. There must also be social and intellectual integrity and complete honesty within the company and with customers.

The success of his business is seen by Racine as part of an awakening of entrepreneurship in Quebec, which he believes will save the province and even the country. He takes great delight in quoting a recent survey that one-third of all Quebecois trust businesspeople more than anyone else.

EXPLORING • MOTIVATION

1. For what reason(s) did each of the individuals in these Venture Profiles choose to be entrepreneurs?
2. Make a list of the things which seemed to contribute to their success.
3. What did each entrepreneur "harvest" from his or her venture?

Ethics, Integrity, and the Law

Several of the entrepreneurs in the last Venture Profiles mentioned the importance which certain values, such as hard work and honesty, play in entrepreneurial success.

Iggy Kaneff enjoyed his work because it was a challenge and it provided him with the resources to accomplish other community ventures unrelated to his work. Barbara Rae loves to create jobs and wealth for others as much as for herself. Serge Racine enjoys his work because it gives him the opportunity to do ordinary things extremely well and with the utmost integrity. There are, however, also entrepreneurs like J.R. Ewing of "Dallas" fame. J.R.'s life is run according to the profit motive and summarized by the results on the bottom line of an income statement. If it contributes to profit, it's good. If it doesn't, it's bad. Profits are not pursued as a means to an end; they become the end.

> "Winning isn't everything. It's the ONLY thing!!!"
> *Vince Lombardi (Football coach)*

What values should guide the action of entrepreneurs?

Figure 14.4 An entrepreneur's loss of profit should not affect his or her sense of integrity.

YOUR TURN

7. What would you do in each of the following cases? Select one of the four options given or devise your own response. Give two reasons for your choice. Do not discuss them with others.

a) Your venture is a small manufacturing firm in serious financial trouble. A large order of your product is ready to be delivered to a major customer when you discover the product is simply not right and will likely cause problems for the customer. What would you do?
   i) not ship the order at the risk of going bankrupt
   ii) tell the customer and offer to replace the products as needed if he or she pays for them now
   iii) ship the order and tell the customer you discovered the problem only after receiving and depositing his or her cheque
   iv) ship the order and say nothing

b) One of your suppliers tells you he or she can no longer supply you with an important raw material you need to produce your product. What would you do?
   i) try to persuade another supplier to fill your order, even though you know this will force another company which was counting on the product out of business
   ii) steal what you need from another source
   iii) offer a supplier a sizable "under the table" payoff to persuade him or her to meet your needs rather than someone else's
   iv) get it from another supplier by promising to buy much more from that supplier in the future than you have any intention of doing

c) You are trying to sell a computer package to a major prospective client. On her desk, you see two copies of a competitor's proposal and cost. Your client leaves the room to use the washroom, leaving your competitor's proposals less than an arm's length away. What would you do?
   i) nothing but await her return
   ii) sneak a quick peek at your competitor's proposal and costs
   iii) put one of the two copies in your briefcase
   iv) wait until your client returns and ask permission to see a copy

d) You are trying to prepare a cashflow analysis and have been working for days on it without the help of a computer spreadsheet which could speed the work up tremendously. Just as you finish, your boss wants new changes made quickly. A friend you know at another firm has a software program which would do the work for you. He has offered to make you a copy of the software. What do you do?

i) accept your friend's offer and make a copy at no charge
ii) continue on your own without the help of any program
iii) buy the software yourself and hope your company will pay you back in a month or two
iv) request an extension on the deadline for completion

8. After you have completed your answers, join with a group of your classmates and discuss what each of you would have done and why.

AGENTS OF CHANGE

Care of the elderly had always been an area in which physicians lacked basic training. Working out of the Royal College of Physicians and Surgeons of Canada, Dr. B. Lynn Beattie pioneered work to develop programs to better educate those who provide care to the elderly. Dr. Beattie's efforts improved the quality of life for others.

Laws and Ethics

The basic beliefs we share as a community are reflected in the laws we make. Obeying the law represents the minimum acceptable level of behaviour expected in a community. Is it enough to simply rely on the law as our guide though? If it is not expressly forbidden by law, it may be permissible, but does that make it right? The law itself is often a matter of interpretation. Should we look to the courts to decide for us how we should act?

Some professions have developed their own **code of ethics**. A code of ethics defines, usually in written form, the moral and professional duties which the members of the profession have to each other and to the public. Codes of ethics require a higher standard of behaviour than existing laws do. In fact, many professions write and enforce their own codes of ethics to be free of written laws. This gives the group or profession more control of itself and its members. Below are sections from the Code of Ethics of the Canadian Direct Marketing Association. It establishes guidelines (not laws) for sales and advertising.

Table 14.1 Sections from the Code of Ethics of the Canadian Direct Marketing Association

5.1 All offers must be clear and honest. They must not misrepresent a product, service, publication, solicitation or program and must not use misleading, partially true or exaggerated statement of techniques;

5.3 When price comparisons are used they must be factual, verifiable and not misleading;

5.5 All test or survey data referred to in an advertisement must be competent, reliable and must support the specific claim for which it is cited;

5.7 Testimonials and endorsements, when used, must be: a) authorized by the person quoted; b) genuine and related to the experience of the person giving it; and c) not taken out of context so as to distort the endorser's opinion or experience with the product or service.

5.8 Photography or artwork, when used, must accurately illustrate the actual product.

There is no Code of Ethics which guides the behaviour of entrepreneurs.

The behaviour of entrepreneurs is very important. Entrepreneurs run ventures. They are in positions of power, control, and leadership. They are frequently the bosses who direct the action of others. Often they have become entrepreneurs to escape the values imposed on them by some other job, some other boss.

If you damage your reputation, you're dead.

Some say entrepreneurs are ruled by the discipline of the marketplace which values and rewards honesty and fair dealing. Cheat your suppliers and you will not be able to get what you need to keep your venture going. Sell shoddy goods to your customers and eventually no one will buy your product. Word gets around!

Is virtue good because it is profitable? While this is certainly true in the long run, decisions must always be made in the short run, in the present. If the objective is to maximize profit, it may be difficult to accept the short-term pain of doing something that lowers immediate returns, or even results in losses, to ensure a long-term gain in the future. The profit motive is not an unerring guide to ethical conduct.

YOUR TURN

9. Upon what values is the Code of Ethics of the Canadian Direct Marketing Association based?
10. Find four examples of advertisements from any media which you think may not be in accordance with those set out in this Code.
11. Undertake some research to see if you can find other codes of ethics. What about teachers? or doctors? or lawyers?
12. Explain how entrepreneurs may be ruled by the discipline of the marketplace.

No matter what industry you're in, it's a small town.

Business Ethics and Personal Ethics

Are business ethics different from personal ethics? Should they be? Should we treat a competitor in the same way as we treat a friend, a neighbour, or a stranger in the street? These are difficult questions.

Ultimately, the entrepreneur is forced to rely on his or her own personal code of ethics. The individual with power and control must accept responsibility. The law will define the minimum acceptable. The rest depends on what the entrepreneur values in himself or herself and the chosen venture.

AGENTS OF CHANGE

Consumers, opposed to companies testing their products on animals, had no way of knowing which companies were doing this. Tita Zierer started sending out more than 50 000 cards, listing companies that don't test their products on animals. An ever-increasing number of consumers are now able to support those companies and protect a few more animals.

It is, after all, the entrepreneur who chooses the venture, not the venture that chooses the entrepreneur.

Entrepreneurs are agents of change in society. They are creators. Whenever something is created, something else is transformed. At the very least opportunities are given up. The values which entrepreneurs express through their ventures will have an important impact on society. They will affect us all. Hopefully, the benefits of the change entrepreneurs create are greater than the costs of that change.

Read the following article and answer the questions which follow it.

Outstanding ethical issues pose problems for all businesspeople

By Philip Mathias, *Financial Post*

The business community is going through two different ethical crises. The first is a collapse of ethics in some parts of that community. Bad business ethics are now damaging our health, our science, our capital markets, and the integrity of some of our politicians.

On balance, business ethics are no worse than the ethics of the rest of society, including Olympic athletes, politicians, and priests. But the poor public perception of business ethics gives rise to the second crisis — the business community no longer has an appropriate ethic for the times.

The old business ethic went like this: "Make as much money as you can for the shareholders, by resorting to any practice that is not forbidden by law. Rely on the marketplace to soften any corporate excesses and let the buyer beware."

A new business ethic is emerging. One that reflects a more human community in which each person takes creative responsibility for his or her actions. An ethic that expects business to seek a balance between aggressive profit-making, which is its right and its strength, and compassion toward a wide group of people: shareholders, customers, labour, and the public as a whole.

Let's look at some business practices that have raised ethical questions:

In the 1980s, 28 Canadian financial institution failed, or suffered severe difficulties. The Economic Council of Canada says half the companies failed because of "fraud and self-dealing by the owners."

Professional self-delusion is widespread in the kingdom of ethics. Consider the manufacture of bacon and ham, which are given a wonderful red colour by chemicals called nitrites, which cause cancer. Nitrites continue to be used because the meat industry has convinced itself, the government regulators, and the public, that they are needed to prevent another disease— botulism, which kills instantly, and is thus more dangerous than cancer.

The truth is that botulism almost never occurs in fresh meat. Cancer-causing chemicals are being employed to protect us from a risk that doesn't exist. I am convinced the ham and bacon people believe their own reasoning because it promotes what they subconsciously desire.

"Greed," somebody once said, "is not an essential part of capitalism." That would puzzle some people who have come into contact with the brokerage industry. The purpose of the stock market is to give entrepreneurs access to capital, and investors a chance to profit from the entrepreneurs' success. And what do the brokers sell? Far too many exotic products that are only generators of commission (for themselves).

Then there's the problem of stock scams. Small investors all over the world are being bled white through three or four North American exchanges, and the over-the-counter markets. The police have shelves of complaints about stock swindles, but can't act upon them because each investigation takes three or four years and they don't have the work force.

A unique subculture of ethical questions can be found in the banking industry. A few years ago, I investigated the destruction of dozens of small businesses by their banks. In each case, the bank loaned the small business money, became anxious, and demanded the money back — in some cases immediately. The small businessperson couldn't raise the funds that fast, was placed in receivership, and the business was destroyed. One victim had been a loyal customer for 30 years.

It is evident that a new business ethic is emerging. What is the authority behind the new ethic? Can we look to the churches as our ethical authority? They have a great deal to say about the way businesspeople behave. But church ethics are incomplete in the area of the environment, shareholders' rights, and many other questions. In any case the churches do not represent the Canadian public.

Can we turn to the law? The answer, again, is no. The law is always an incomplete embodiment of society's ethical concerns. At the moment, it's weak on monopolies and price-fixing, practices that are surely unethical.

Can we turn to market economics? Once again, the answer is no. The law of supply and demand says a business may charge any price the market will bear. But there are many people who are dismayed at the way that law sometimes works.

Business ethics have to spring from what society as a whole thinks at any time about what is the right way to behave. Society's sense of right and wrong is what is supposed to be embodied in the law, by our elected representatives. So a new business ethic would obey the law, and also anticipate good laws by keeping an ear on all society's concerns. Good ethics is the building of a solid, lasting enterprise, making useful products, on a well-founded base within the community. Good ethics is good business.

EXPLORING • BUSINESS ETHICS

1. What, according to the article, was "the old business ethic"?
2. How does the new emerging business ethic differ from the old?
3. Give four examples of unethical practices mentioned in the article.
4. Think of other examples of things which business does which you consider to be unethical.

5. The author mentions three traditional sources of ethics. What are they and why can we not look to them as the source or authority for the development of the new business ethic?
6. What, according to the author, will be the basis for the new business ethic?

Signs of Changing Times

Whether a new code of business ethics develops or not, the most important thing is that the values which guide and direct our actions, both business and personal, are self supporting and life sustaining. We are now learning that some of what has been done in the past in the name of profit has destroyed more than it has produced. Our wasteful use of our scarce resources and the growing environmental crises we face with polluted water and air are examples. However, there are also many positive signs as we enter the last decade of the century that a new ethic may be emerging.

Venture PROFILE

Saskatchewan's straw briquets are California-bound

By Steve Kruegber, *The Globe and Mail*

Biomass Industries straw briquets are virtually pollution free.

Kipling, Sask.

This tiny Saskatchewan farming community, situated three hours southeast of Regina, is an unlikely headquarters for a company with ambitions of becoming a major leisure-product exporter to the United States.

But Rick O'Sullivan, one of the two co-owners of Biomass Industries, says his business could well become a major exporter of straw barbecue briquets and fireplace logs within two years, thanks to stiff new environmental regulations in the lucrative California marketplace.

"We want to get into the U.S. market because there's a lot more potential in the southern areas, especially for the barbecue briquets," Mr. O'Sullivan said. "It's a year round market, and there's more money in briquets than in fireplace logs."

His optimism may be well placed. This spring, the Southern California Air Pollution Control District introduced stiff new regulations aimed at curbing air pollution in the Los Angeles basin. Among the new rules, which will be phased in over a five- to ten-year period, is a ban on the use of charcoal briquets.

"Our briquets are virtually pollution free," contended Mr. O'Sullivan. "There's less carbon monoxide, 97 per cent less sulphur, and no carbon at all. It's so clean that you can pick up the briquets in your hands and you don't get dirty."

The straw contains no chemicals or petroleum products, and doesn't give food any aftertaste of charcoal. The result is meat that has a sweeter and sharper taste than food cooked over coals or on gas barbecues.

The residue is different too. When the briquets are burned, they become potash, an efficient form of fertilizer that is in demand all over the world.

Mr. O'Sullivan and his partner Harley Ironside got the idea for Biomass while watching farmers in the Kipling area burn off surplus straw left behind after the fall harvest. Rather than simply burning the straw in the fields, the two men felt there should be some way to use it in manufacturing.

"We buy the straw from area farmers and bale it ourselves," said Mr. O'Sullivan, who works about 12 hours a day in the plant with his partner and two employees.

Biomass went into production last December, manufacturing fireplace logs for sale through convenience stores in the Regina area. The logs hit the market too late for an effective marketing campaign, but the product sold well enough that both Canada Safeway Ltd. of Calgary and Southland Corp. of Dallas, which operates 7-Eleven Stores, have signed deals to sell the logs next winter.

Next year, Biomass will try to work out a production and marketing plan with two other straw log manufacturers in Canada and five in the United States for a major move on the Southern California market.

"The people there know they've got a smog problem, " Mr. O'Sullivan said. "They want to do something, and we can prove to them that straw briquets in their barbecues are one thing they can do that will help make a difference."

EXPLORING • BIOMASS INDUSTRIES

1. Rick O'Sullivan and Harley Ironside saw an opportunity, came up with an idea, and organized resources to create a venture which satisfied those needs.
   a) What was the opportunity?
   b) What created that opportunity?
   c) What are the key resources in this venture?
   d) What needs are being satisfied?
2. In what ways does this venture reflect an ethic which is life supporting and self sustaining?
3. Why was this venture undertaken?

The Entrepreneurial Venture and Integrity

The ethics of the free market with its emphasis on profit making will always drive private enterprise. However, integrity and honesty have a strong and valuable role to play in venture creation. Moreover, ventures like Biomass, which are life sustaining and environmentally supportive, are on the increase.

"To thine own self be true,
And it must follow as the night the day,
Thou canst not then be false to any man."
Hamlet (Polonius to Laertes)

The greatest entrepreneurial ventures consist of creating something yourself and living the life you want for yourself. The harvest you receive from any venture you undertake will depend as much upon your personal values and your own code of ethics as it will upon entrepreneurial skill.

Whatever your venture, whether it is business or life itself, follow it with integrity. The *Concise Oxford Dictionary* defines integrity as wholeness and soundness. Make sure your venture is based on the things you value most. That way there can be no conflict between who you are and what you do.

P·O·I·N·T·S T·O R·E·M·E·M·B·E·R

- A venture goes through several phases of development: incubation, startup, growth, and maturity.
- Each phase requires a different development task: inventive, innovative, entrepreneurial, managerial, and administrative.

- A venture can avoid decline by investing money in research and development and by encouraging the entrepreneurial tendencies of its employees.
- An entrepreneur may harvest or gain returns from a venture in the form of income or by selling interest (shares) in the ownership.
- One's work may satisfy many more needs than simply the need for income.
- It is difficult to define a code of ethics for entrepreneurs.
- It is important that every entrepreneur define a personal code of ethics to use as a guide in his or her venture.
- One's entrepreneurial venture can be both a means to other ends and an end in itself.

W·H·A·T H·A·V·E Y·O·U L·E·A·R·N·E·D·?

1. Describe the characteristics of each of the four stages of development a successful venture will go through.
2. When a venture reaches maturity, it will follow one of three paths. Describe each of these paths.
3. Identify and describe the five development tasks associated with creating a successful venture.
4. Which development task(s) is/are associated with each stage of development?
5. The harvest the entrepreneur receives from a successful venture may take many forms. Describe at least four different forms.
6. What is a code of ethics?
7. What is the difference between the law and a code of ethics?
8. Comment on the relationship between personal and business ethics.
9. What must entrepreneurs rely on to guide the growth and development of their ventures? Explain your response.

V·E·N·T·U·R·I·N·G O·U·T

Write an essay about your future. Entitle it "To Life". In the essay, create the life you want. Write in the first person, present tense. Begin by describing what it is you value most in life. Open the letter you wrote to yourself as an activity in Chapter 2, page 44 (Your Turn, No. 4). Use it to help you get started. Since your life is a search for integrity, you must base the rest of the essay on the values you have identified. The essay must have the following sections:

a) the startup: from now to the age of 30
b) growth: from 30 to 50
c) maturity: from 50 to ....?

There is no stage of decline. At the very least, you have become a good manager and will be able to sustain maturity indefinitely. More than likely, you are truly entrepreneurial and will be able to constantly create and develop your life's venture to the end.

Appendix

This section contains a listing of the national and/or regional locations of government departments and agencies, as well as private organizations and associations that may be of assistance to you.

For many of the government offices listed below, the blue pages in your local telephone directory will list location and telephone numbers in your community.

INDUSTRY, SCIENCE AND TECHNOLOGY CANADA

Head Office:
235 Queen Street
Ottawa, ON
K1A 0H5 (613)995-5771

REGIONAL OFFICES

Newfoundland:
Parsons Building
90 O'Leary Avenue
P.O. Box 8950
St. John's, NF
A1B 3R9 (709)772-4884

Nova Scotia:
1496 Lower Water Street
P.O. Box 940 Station M
Halifax, NS
B3J 2V9 (902)426-2018

Prince Edward Island:
Confederation Court Mall
Suite 400
134 Kent Street
P.O. Box 1115
Charlottetown, PEI
C1A 7M8 (902)566-7400

New Brunswick:
770 Main Street
P.O. Box 1210
Moncton, NB
E1C 8P9 (506)857-6400

Québec:
Tour de la Bourse
800 Victoria Place
P.O. Box 247
Montréal, PQ
H4Z 1E8 (514)283-8185

Ontario:
1 Front Street West
East Building, 4th Floor
Toronto, ON
M5J 1A4 (416)973-5202

Manitoba:
330 Portage Avenue
Room 608
P.O. Box 981
Winnipeg, MB
R3C 2V2 (204)983-2300

Saskatchewan:
105 21st Street East
6th Floor
Saskatoon, SK
S7K 0B3 (306)975-4400

Alberta:
Canada Place
Room 540
700 Jasper Avenue
Edmonton, AB
T5J 4C3 (403)495-2944

British Columbia:
900-650 West Georgia Street
P.O. Box 11610
Vancouver, BC
V6B 5H8 (604)666-0434

Yukon:
108 Lambert Street
Suite 301
Whitehorse, Yukon
Y1A 1Z2 (403)668-4655

Northwest Territories:
Precambrian Building
10th Floor
Postal Bag 6100
Yellowknife, NWT
X1A 1C0 (403)920-8568

THE PATENT OFFICE

Consumer and Corporate Affairs Canada
Place du Portage, Tower 1
50 Victoria Street
Hull, PQ
K1A 0E1 (819)997-1936

FEDERAL BUSINESS DEVELOPMENT BANK

Head Office:
800 Victoria Square
Tour de la Bourse
C.P. 335
Montréal, PQ
H4Z 1L4 (514)283-5904

Ontario Regional Office:
777 Bay Street
29th Floor
Toronto, ON
M5G 2C8 (416)973-1144

Atlantic Regional Office:
Scotia Square
Cogshill Tower
Ste. 1400
P.O. Box 1656
Halifax, NS
B3J 2Z7 (902)426-7860

Prairie and Northern Regional Office:
155 Carlton Street
Suite 1200
Winnipeg, MB
R3C 3H8 (204)983-7811

British Columbia and Yukon Regional Office:
700-601 West Hastings Street
Vancouver, BC
V6B 5G9 (604)666-7800

Québec Regional Office:
Place Victoria, 800
Square Victoria
Bureau 4600, C.P. 190
Montréal, PQ
H4Z 1C8 (514)283-3657

PROVINCIAL GOVERNMENT CONTACTS

Newfoundland Department of Development
Atlantic Place
Water Street
P.O. Box 4750
St. John's, NF
A1C 5T7

Nova Scotia Department of Development
5151 George Street
P.O. Box 519
Halifax, NS
B3J 2R7

Prince Edward Island Department of Industry
West Royalty Industrial Park
P.O. Box 1510
Charlottetown, PEI
C1A 7N3

Manitoba Department of Industry, Trade and Tourism
155 Carlton Street
5th Floor
Winnipeg, MN
R3C 3H8

New Brunswick Department of Commerce and Development
P.O. Box 6000
Fredericton, NB
E3B 5H1

Saskatchewan Department of Tourism and Small Business
2103 11th Avenue
4th Floor
Regina, SK
S4P 3V7

Québec Ministère de l'Industrie et du Commerce
1 Place Ville Marie
23 étage
Montréal, PQ
H3B 3M6

Alberta Department of Economic Development and Trade
9940 106th Street
11th Floor
Edmonton, AB
T5K 2P6

Ontario Ministry of Industry, Trade and Technology
Hearst Block
Queen's Park
Toronto, ON
M7A 2E1

British Columbia Ministry of Economic Development
Robson Square
800 Hornby Street
Suite 315
Vancouver, BC
V6Z 2C5

ADDITIONAL SOURCES OF INFORMATION

In addition to the associations listed in this appendix, your local public library will have a variety of directories available for reference purposes. These directories deal with a wide range of different areas and can provide you with a great deal of useful information.

If the white pages of your telephone directory do not contain listings of the Associations identified below, you may want to write to them at the following addresses to ask for local information.

CANADIAN ASSOCIATION OF WOMEN EXECUTIVES AND ENTREPRENEURS
60 Dixon Avenue
Toronto, ON
M4L 1N6 (416)690-5142

CANADIAN CHAMBER OF COMMERCE
120 Adelaide Street West
Suite 2109
Toronto, ON
M5H 1T1 (416)868-6415

CANADIAN COUNCIL OF BETTER BUSINESS BUREAUS
2180 Steeles Avenue West
Suite 219
Concord, ON
L4K 2Z5 (416)669-1248

CANADIAN DIRECT MARKETING ASSOCIATION
201 Consumers Road
Suite 205
Willowdale, ON
M2J 4G8 (416)494-8585

CANADIAN FEDERATION OF INDEPENDENT BUSINESS
4141 Yonge Street
Suite 401
Willowdale, ON
M2P 2A6 (416)222-8022

CANADIAN FRANCHISERS' ASSOCIATION
88 University Avenue
Suite 607
Toronto, ON
M5J 1T6 (416)595-5005

Vancouver Chapter:
c/o Donna Lea Hawley
671-F Market Hill
Vancouver, BC
V5Z 4B5 (604)876-4486

Québec Chapter
c/o Ms Aline Lévesque
Bureau 1000
550 Ouest, Rue Sherbrooke
Montréal, PQ
H3A 1B9 (514)843-6355

CANADIAN INDUSTRIAL INNOVATIVE CENTRE
156 Columbia Street West
Waterloo, ON
N2L 3L3 (519)885-5870

CANADIAN SMALL BUSINESS INSTITUTE
1140 Bellamy Road North
Scarborough, ON
M1H 1H4 (416)439-6699

CANADIAN STANDARDS ASSOCIATION
178 Rexdale Boulevard
Rexdale, ON
M9M 1R3 (416)747-4000

JUNIOR ACHIEVEMENT OF CANADA
75 Brown's Line
Toronto, ON
M8W 3S2 (416)252-4602

Glossary

This glossary contains the key terms that appear in bold face type in the text, together with other terms useful to students of entrepreneurship. The definitions given here relate to how these terms are used in the context of entrepreneurship and, more specifically, to their usage within this text.

accounts payable. Amounts of money owed to suppliers by the company for goods and services purchased.

accounts receivable. Amounts of money owed to the company by customers for the purchase of goods or services.

administrative task. The task of carrying out identified strategies in an efficient and effective way.

advertising. A message carried by the media and paid for by the venture that communicates persuasive information about the venture's product or service.

agents of change. Entrepreneurs, so called because they are constantly challenging the status quo.

Agricultural Age. The historical time period, as described by Alvin Toffler, when most people gave up a nomadic hunting lifestyle to establish stable, permanent communities based on farming.

AIDA formula. A process used in advertising to gain the consumer's Attention, Interest, and Desire, and to stimulate the consumer into Action.

appendix. A section at the back of the venture plan that contains support documents.

Artist. The character role, as described by Roger von Oech, that experiments with new ideas.

assets. Anything owned by a business organization that can easily be turned into cash (e.g., accounts receivable, cash, and inventories).

attitude scale. A scale used to rate a consumer's attitude towards certain qualities of a product or service; the scale typically goes from 1 (poor) to 5 (excellent).

autocratic leaders. Employers who make all the decisions themselves, often without consulting anyone else.

behaviour patterns. A market segment based on behaviour patterns is one that consists of people who can be identified by when, where, and how often they shop, as well as by their media habits.

black hat. A mode of thinking, as described by Edward de Bono, that is logical and provides negative, objective, unemotional feedback.

blue hat. A mode of thinking, as described by Edward de Bono, that organizes and controls the other thinking modes and directs them into action.

body language. Non-verbal communication conveyed by body movements.

bootleg. To transfer resources without specific approval to entrepreneurial projects within the firm other than those for which the employer was originally hired.

brainstorming. A technique for exercising creativity that involves the generation of many new and unusual ideas; brainstorming is a group activity.

break-even point. The point at which total revenues equal total costs.

business. The production of goods and services for profit.

bylaws. Local laws of the municipal government.

Canada Pension Plan. A pension plan to which both employers and employees contribute.

Canada/U.S. Free Trade Agreement. An agreement designed to improve trade between Canada and the U.S. by eliminating tariffs and other barriers to trade.

capacity. One of the 6 C's of credit; the entrepreneur's ability to manage the venture effectively and efficiently.

capital. The funds that must be invested in a company in order to enable it to carry out its activities.
also One of the 6 C's of credit; the amount of money the entrepreneur has invested in the venture from his or her own savings.

capital gain. The profit acquired as a result of selling the venture, which reflects increases in the value of the owner's equity.

capital goods. Items such as buildings, furniture, and equipment installations which are owned by a business and used in the production process.

capital intensive. A method of production that relies more on machinery than on labour.

capitalist. A person who owns shares in a business venture.

cash in. The section of a cashflow forecast that keeps track of the flow of money that is actually received by the venture.

cash out. The section of a cashflow forecast that keeps track of all of a venture's expenses as they are paid.

cash poor. A venture is cash poor when its expenses are greater than its revenues.

cash rich. A venture is cash rich when its revenues are greater than its expenses.

cashflow. The amount of money that a business receives and the amount of money it pays over a specified period of time.

cashflow forecast. A prediction of the incoming cash through sales or other receipts alongside the outgoing cash to pay the company's bills.

causal research. A type of research designed to explain the relationship between a particular cause and its effect.

census. A survey conducted to determine the characteristics of the total population of a country.

centralization. The process by which control is centred in one spot.

cents-off merchandise. By using a special coupon, a customer can purchase a product or service at cents off (as specified on the coupon) the regular retail price.

chain. One of a group of retail outlets owned and operated by a central management.

character. One of the 6 C's of credit; honesty and reliability.

circumstances. One of the 6 C's of credit; the conditions (such as the competition, the state of the economy, the rate of inflation, and the nature of the product or service) that the lender considers when making a loan decision.

classic product. A product that does not enter the decline stage of the life cycle.

code of ethics. A statement (usually written) of the moral and professional duties that members of a specific profession have to each other and to the public.

collateral. One of the 6 C's of credit; the assets that can be offered as security for a loan.

collegial leaders. Employers who use a team decision-making process.

competition. A market in which rival sellers try to gain extra business at each other's expense.

computerized inventory control system. A system that records goods received and removes goods used from the inventory file using a computer software program.

concentration. The process of working on one area at a time.

consumption patterns. A market based on consumption patterns is one that consists of people who can be identified by their knowledge about, and loyalty to, particular products or brands.

convenience goods. Products that the consumer buys often, but is unwilling to spend much effort to find.

co-operative. A member-owned enterprise.

copyright. The exclusive legal right to reproduce, publish, and sell a piece of work.

corporate charter. The legal document that establishes a corporation or a limited company.

corporation. A form of business created by the legal process of incorporation, which gives the venture its own legal status separate from its owners. It may issue shares of ownership to raise capital. The liability of the owners is limited to the amount invested in the purchase of shares.
cost per unit. The amount of money needed to produce a single product.
cost-plus pricing. A pricing strategy in which the price is based on the cost, plus a markup.
coverage. One of the 6 C's of credit; insurance protection for the venture and the entrepreneur.
creative thinking skills. The skills required to generate new alternatives, possibilities, and ideas; a type of thinking often referred to as right-brain thinking and most closely associated with the role of the Explorer and the Artist and with the white and green thinking hats.
credit rating. The financial standing and reputation of a company, used to set the amount of money that the venture may borrow.
creditor. A person or institution that is owed money.
criteria. Standards, measures, or tests used to evaluate choices.
critical thinking skills. The skills required to analyze problems and evaluate proposed solutions; a type of thinking often referred to as left-brain thinking and most closely associated with the role of the Explorer, the Judge, and the Warrior and with the red, white, black, yellow, and blue thinking hats.
crown corporation. A corporation that is owned by the federal government but that operates independently.
culture. The combination of a people's beliefs, understandings, morals, values, customs, and habits which forms a distinct way of life.
customer profile. A description of the target customer for a specific product or service.
cyclical. A regular pattern of increases and decreases.
debt financing. The borrowing of money from a lending institution to start up a business; the money must be repaid with interest.
debt to equity ratio. The amount of debt compared to the amount of equity expressed as a ratio.
decline stage. The stage at which a product or service begins to lose sales and eventually becomes obsolete.
declining trend. A trend which is in a stage of decline or falling in magnitude.
demand. The combined desire, ability, and willingness of individuals to buy or use a product or service; the amounts of a good, a service, or a resource which will be purchased at different price levels.
demise. Decline; death.
democratic leaders. Employers who encourage employees to participate in the decision-making process.
demographic. A demographic market segment is one that describes a group of people of the same age, sex, marital status, family size, or who are in the same stage of the family life cycle.
depreciates. Lessens in value over a period of time.
depreciation. The decrease in value of equipment or facilities that has occurred since the original purchase (usually determined as an annual rate).
description. The first major section of a venture plan; an introduction containing general information without specific details.
disclaimer. A statement to the effect that while the writer believes everything within the venture plan to be correct, he or she cannot guarantee that it is.
dividend. The amount of profit paid out to a company's shareholders.
downsizing. Reducing the numbers of employees, the size of factory, or level of output.
economic resources. Those things that are used by producers to provide goods and services. Land, labour, and capital are examples of economic resources.
entrepreneur. A person who organizes resources to create a venture which satisfies needs.
entrepreneurial task. The task of organizing previously unrelated resources to build a venture that can produce and market a good or service to satisfy a need.
entrepreneurship. The perception of opportunities and the mobilization of resources to bring about change in new and innovative ways to achieve some benefit.
equity. Personal financial investment in a venture.
equity financing. A method of raising capital whereby shares of ownership in the venture are exchanged for a price.
European Common Market. An affiliation of European countries that operates as single market; there are no tariffs on products and services moving between the countries.

executive summary. A one- or two-page summary of a venture plan that states what is proposed, what is needed, what will be done, who will do it, and what it will cost.
expense goods. Goods that are consumed immediately during the process of production; expense goods include parts and supplies, hydro, telephone, and raw materials (also known as intermediate goods).
experimentation. A method of conducting marketing research that involves providing a small group of people with a product or service an entrepreneur is considering offering.
exploratory research. A type of research designed to define a problem more clearly or to obtain ideas for solutions.
Explorer. The character role, as described by Roger von Oech, that looks for new ideas, opportunities, and needs which are not being satisfied.
fact-finding stage. The gathering of data that confirms that the problem exists and that describes the nature of the problem.
fads. Products or services with a very short life cycle.
final user. The ultimate consumer of a product or service.
Finance Spoke. A spoke of the Venture Creation Wheel which deals with how to organize a financial strategy for a venture.
financial strategy. The fifth and final major section of a venture plan; a forecast of the financial needs and rewards of a venture.
fixed assets. Things owned by a company that are of a fairly permanent nature, such as real estate and equipment.
fixed costs. Costs, such as rent or interest on loans, that remain constant even though production increases or decreases.
follow the competition pricing. A pricing strategy in which the product or service is priced at the same level or slightly lower than the competition's.
forecast. A carefully calculated vision or perspective of the future.
fox. Used to describe a style of managing conflict that places the emphasis on seeking compromise.
franchise. A business operation that is licensed to sell a manufacturer's product or to provide a company's service in a given area; the franchisee pays a percentage of sales to the franchisor.
franchisee. The buyer (or licensor) in a franchise agreement.
franchisor. The seller in a franchise agreement.
fringe benefits. Compensation given to an employee in addition to salary; fringe benefits include such things as long-term disability and dental plans.
game plan. The blueprint for an entrepreneur's venture; the venture plan.
general partner. A partner with unlimited liability with respect to the debts and obligations of the partnership.
general partnership. An unincorporated partnership.
geographic. A geographic market segment is one that consists of people who live in regions of the country that could be defined by specific climate, or political or population boundaries.
global market. The market that exists throughout the world.
go/no-go decision. The decision to proceed or not with the startup of a venture after analyzing the research.
goal. A process or direction that one works towards.
good. A product produced by a firm for distribution to consumers.
grant. A sum of money given to a company by the federal or provincial government that does not have to be paid back.
green hat. A mode of thinking, as described by Edward de Bono, that creates new ideas, possibilities, and solutions.
gross margin. Sales minus the cost of goods sold.
gross sales. The total of cash and credit sales during a specific period of time.
growth phase. The period in which a venture expands and increases sales after the startup phase.
growth stage. The stage during which the demand for a product or service increases.
growth trend. A pattern of consumption or production which increases in size over time.
guarantee. Collateral provided on a loan by an investor or by the federal or provincial government.
harvesting strategy. A marketing strategy in which a business sharply reduces its expenses to increase its current profits.

homogeneous segment. A group of target customers who have common, identifiable characteristics.
human resources. The people involved in a venture; advisors, consultants, professional counsellors, financial backers, partners, startup teams and/or employees.
idea-finding stage. The second step in the problem-solving process; the generation of a variety of ideas on how to solve the problem.
Ideas Spoke. A spoke of the Venture Creation Wheel which generates and evaluates ideas for a venture.
in trust. One's personal assets are in trust when they are in the charge of another person or institution as a protection against personal liability.
income forecast. An estimate of the revenues earned by a venture.
income statement. A statement that shows the profit or loss of a company over a specified period of time; revenue minus expenses.
incubation phase. The period in a venture's life cycle when all the preparation and planning for a startup is completed.
Industrial Age. The historical time period, as described by Alvin Toffler, when people gave up a rural, farming way of life for an industrial, urban lifestyle.
Information Age. The time period, as described by Alvin Toffler, which we are now entering, during which there will be an increasingly rapid rate of change in our lifestyles and institutions brought about by new technologies and the explosion of knowledge.
innovation. The use of new ideas, materials, or technology to change either the goods or services produced or the manner in which they are produced or distributed.
innovative task. The task of applying a new technology, process, or idea to satisfy an existing need.
interest. A charge that a borrower is required to pay to the lender.
internal research. A type of research that is based upon a company's own, internal records regarding sales, products, customers, or complaints.
interpersonal skills. The skills required to communicate with, motivate, and encourage others.
intrapreneurship. Entrepreneurship within a large corporation.
introduction stage. The stage at which a product or service first appears in the market.
inventive task. The task of creating a new device or process by joining together previously unrelated elements in a new way.
inventors. People who generate new ideas, technologies, or goods and services.
inventory. Products that have been produced or purchased but are not yet sold, or expense (intermediate) goods that have been purchased but not yet used.
irregular. An up and down trend that does not follow a specific pattern.
joint venture. A venture undertaken by two or more parties.
Judge. The character role, as described by Roger von Oech, that evaluates choices to determine which one is best.
labour intensive. A method of production that uses more labour than capital.
laissez-faire leaders. Employers who ignore the task or job specifics and who leave employees free to decide what they will do and how they will do it.
lateral thinking. A flexible and creative thinking process; breaking away from standard solutions and solving problems in unique and different ways.
launch. The point at which a venture begins to operate.
lease. A contract to rent a property for a specified period of time.
left brain. The portion of the brain that is logical, analytical, and rational.
lending agencies. Institutions, such as banks, that lend money.
letters of patent. A legal document that gives the holder the right to exclude others from using, claiming, or selling the holder's invention within the country of patent for a specific number of years.
liabilities. All financial obligations of a business, including any creditor claims on the assets of a business.
life cycle. The four stages that a product or service goes through; introduction, growth, maturity, and decline.
lifestyle. A certain way of living that affects what people buy.
limited partner. A partner whose liability is limited to his or her investment in the venture.
limited partnership. A partnership in which the partners' liability is limited to their investment in the venture.

line of credit. An entrepreneur with a line of credit from a chartered bank can borrow extra money to a set limit.
linear. Constant change with little variation from one time period to another.
liquidity. The cash position of a company.
loan application. A written request to a lending agency made by a potential borrower for a specified amount of money.
logo. A graphic symbol that helps to identify a company.
long-range objectives. Ultimate goals.
loss-leader pricing. A pricing strategy in which products or services are priced at cost or less in order to attract customers who, it is hoped, will then buy other products or services.
"love money". Money that an entrepreneur's friends and family invest in the venture.
management buyout. The sale of an entrepreneur's equity or share of the venture to existing partners or managers in the venture.
Management Spoke. A spoke of the Venture Creation Wheel which deals with the details of how a venture will be run on a day-to-day basis after the startup phase.
managerial task. The job of directing the venture on a day-to-day basis.
market. The actual and potential buyers who create a demand for a product or service.
market analysis. The second major section of a venture plan; the process of analyzing and testing the needs of the market to determine whether or not an opportunity to meet those needs exists (also known as needs assessment).
market niche. A specific segment of the market.
market potential. The upper limit of expected sales of a particular product or service for the entire industry.
market-pulled entrepreneurship. Entrepreneurship that first identifies a problem or unsatisfied need and then develops an idea to resolve the problem or satisfy the need.
market segmentation. The categorization of individuals who share common characteristics into defined target markets.
market segments. Sections of the population with common needs that are defined by a number of common characteristics; namely, demographic, socioeconomic, geographic, psychographic, behaviour patterns, and consumption patterns.
market share. The percentage of total sales that a venture has.
marketing mix. The combination of the following marketing elements: product (or service), place (distribution), price, and promotion.
marketing research. A systematic and objective way of collecting, recording, and analyzing data that relates to a particular marketing issue or problem.
marketing strategy. A plan developed for the entire marketing process, from marketing research to advertising, promotion, packaging, distribution, sales, and service.
markup. A percentage of the cost of a product or service that is added to the cost when pricing the product or service.
Maslow's Hierarchy of Needs. A pyramid of needs described by Abraham Maslow; basic needs are at the bottom and self-actualization needs are at the top.
"matchmaking service". A service that matches the investor with the entrepreneur.
maturity phase. The period in a venture's life cycle in which competition is keen and profit margins shrink.
maturity stage. The stage at which the demand for a product or service levels off.
megashifts. Major trends, changes, or transformations.
milestone. A specific event that marks progress towards a goal.
mind mapping. A technique for exercising creativity that is used to chart the direction of one's thinking process.
mobilize. To use resources effectively.
monthly deficit. The amount of money by which expenses exceed revenues at the end of the month.
monthly surplus. The amount of money by which revenues exceed expenses at the end of a month.
mortgage. A loan made for the purchase of real estate.
need. Something that is essential to life.

needs assessment. The process of analyzing and testing the strength of the demand for a good or service to determine whether or not an opportunity to meet that demand exists (also known as market analysis).

net cash. The section of a cashflow forecast that records the balance of cashflow for a specified period; cash in minus cash out.

net profit. The amount of money that is left after all expenses have been deducted from a company's revenues.

net worth. The dollar value of a company's assets after all liabilities have been deducted from its assets.

network. A group of specialists, such as lawyers, accountants, and bankers, who are connected to one another by an entrepreneur who uses their skills to solve problems and create ventures.

new wave entrepreneur. An entrepreneur who looks for opportunities by carefully plotting trends or changes as we continue to move from the Industrial Age into the Information Age.

not-for-profit. An entrepreneurial venture whose goal is to break even financially while providing a special service or satisfying a specific need in society.

observation. A method of conducting marketing research that involves direct primary research.

operating expenses. The money needed to keep a venture going once it has successfully completed the startup phase.

operating strategy. The fourth major section of a venture plan which explains how the resources will be organized and used on a day-to-day basis.

Operations Spoke. A spoke of the Venture Creation Wheel which deals with organizing and using resources on a day-to-day basis.

Opportunities Spoke. A spoke of the Venture Creation Wheel which identifies entrepreneurial opportunities by noting the trends and changes in society that give rise to opportunities.

opportunity. A need, want, problem, or challenge that can potentially be satisfied by an entrepreneurial idea and venture.

opportunity cost. The loss of the benefits which could have been received from the next best option when a decision is made involving two or more options.

organizational chart. A graphic representation of the hierarchy of management in an organization.

owl. Used to describe a style of managing conflict which emphasizes confrontation.

Pacific Rim. The countries that border the Pacific Ocean.

partnership. An agreement between two or more parties to undertake a venture.

partnership agreement. A legal agreement between two or more people who jointly run a business.

patent. The legal right to ownership of an invention which prevents others from using the invention without compensation.

paternalistic leaders. Employers who make all the decisions themselves, confident that they know better than their employees what is in the employees' best interests.

payback period. The length of time that will be needed to accumulate enough revenue to return the cost of the initial investment.

penetration pricing. A pricing strategy in which a new product or service is priced considerably lower than the competition.

personal balance sheet. An itemized listing of an entrepreneur's assets and liabilities from which the entrepreneur's net worth can be calculated.

personal budget. An itemized listing of all of a person's living expenses, such as rent, food, and utilities.

personal drawings. A wage or salary paid to the entrepreneur by the venture.

personal financial leverage. An individual's ability to obtain a loan.

personal selling. Selling that is conducted on a person-to-person basis.

point-of-purchase display. A display of goods set up near the cash register to encourage impulse buying.

practical skills. The skills required to follow instructions and the knowledge of specific tools used in the entrepreneurial process.

prepaid expenses. Expenses that are paid for before they are used, such as insurance, fuel, and utilities.

price ceiling. The highest price a business can charge for a product or service and still attract customers.

price floor. The lowest price a business can charge for a product or service and still break even or make a profit.

price-takers. Ventures that price their products or services based on the existing market price.
pricing strategy. A method of determining the price for a product or service.
primary research. The technique of gathering data first-hand through such methods as personal observation, interviews, and questionnaires.
private placement. The investing of money by a small group of investors into a startup or growing business.
pro-active control. The establishment and maintenance of a system or procedure for handling inventory, production, finance, and records management; also called preventative control.
pro forma. Projecting the figures in a financial statement to indicate what the statement will look like at some point in the future after certain assumptions have been made.
problem-finding stage. The first stage in the problem-solving process; the identification and definition of the problem.
process oriented. A focus on the steps and human interaction required to make a decision-making process work effectively.
product- or service-driven entrepreneurship. Entrepreneurship that first develops an idea for a product or service, and then seeks out a marketing opportunity.
productivity. Output of goods and services; productivity is usually measured in terms of output per worker employed.
profile. Case study.
profit. The amount of money left after all expenses have been deducted from a company's revenues.
profit margin. The percentage of the final selling price that is greater than the cost of producing the good or service.
profit sharing. The process by which employees are given a certain percentage of a company's profits.
projected balance sheet. A projected financial statement that shows the company's assets, liabilities, and the amount of equity held by its shareholders.
prototype. The original version or model of something.
psychographic. A psychographic market segment consists of people with similar lifestyles or personality attributes.
psychological pricing. A pricing strategy that uses odd number amounts, leading the customer to believe that the item is less expensive than it actually is.
publicity. An unpaid message delivered by the media to the target market.
quality control program. A process for monitoring and controlling the quality of the product made or the service offered.
questionnaire. A list of questions used to conduct marketing research.
rate cards. Listings, printed by each of the media, that give the cost of advertising.
receipts. The revenue taken in from the selling of goods or services.
red hat. A mode of thinking, as described by Edward de Bono, which is based on emotions and feelings.
research and development. The process of investigating and instigating new directions for a company by, for example, developing a new or improved product.
Research Assistance Grid. A planning model that helps an entrepreneur identify the questions to ask before beginning a venture.
research instrument. A type of marketing research, such as a questionnaire, telephone survey, or personal interview.
resource analysis. The third major section of a venture plan which involves the identification and costing of the resources a venture needs in order to provide its good or service.
resources. The raw materials, supplies, capital equipment, factories, offices, labour, management and entrepreneurial skills that are used in producing a good or service.
Resources Spoke. A spoke of the Venture Creation Wheel which identifies, locates, and costs the resources needed for a successful venture.
retailer. A businessperson whose sales come primarily from retailing.
retailing. All of the activities involved in selling goods or services to consumers for their personal use.
return on investment. The income or profit that is earned on the capital which has been invested in a venture.
right brain. The portion of the brain that is creative, imaginative, emotional, and intuitive.

risk. The likelihood of undesirable, unforeseen, or uncontrollable events occurring.
sales forecast. An estimate of how much of a product or service will be sold during a specific period of time.
sales potential. An estimate of how much of a product or service an individual company would be able to sell over a given period of time.
sales prediction. A prediction of the expected actual sales volume for the next given period of time.
sales promotion. An activity directed at increasing sales and supporting advertising.
sample. A survey conducted with a small, representative group of the population.
secondary research. The techniques of analyzing and evaluating information which has been gathered by second-hand means, such as census data.
self-actualization. The ability to live by one's values and pursue one's goals freely; to be the best one can be.
Self Spoke. A spoke of the Venture Creation Wheel which focuses on analyzing the interests, strengths, and weaknesses of the entrepreneur at the hub or centre of the venture creation process.
service. The performance of an action that is useful to others.
share purchase. A means by which employees buy ownership in a business by buying shares.
shark. Used to describe a style of managing conflict that is typified by the use of force.
short listing. The process of choosing, from a number of possibilities, the ideas most likely to succeed.
short-range plans. A series of plans to attain small goals on the path to achieving long-range objectives.
silent partner. A partner who invests money in the partnership but is not actively involved in its management.
6 C's of credit. The six things a lender wants to know about an entrepreneur who is applying for a loan; character, capital, collateral, capacity, circumstances, and coverage.
6 P's of entrepreneurship. Profit, price, production, people, productivity, promotion; those elements that are considered and described in the operating strategy of the venture plan.
skimming. A pricing strategy in which a new product or service is given a high price because there is no competition.
small business. According to Statistics Canada monthly employment survey, a firm with 20 or fewer employees. According to the Ministry responsible for Small Business, a small business is any manufacturing firm with fewer than 100 employees, or a firm in any other sector with fewer than 50 employees. Using either definition, small businesses account for 80 to 90 per cent of all business in Canada.
socioeconomic. A socioeconomic market segment is one that consists of people with similar occupations, educational backgrounds, income, social class, or culture.
sole proprietorship. An unincorporated business venture that has only one owner.
solution-finding stage. The final stage in the problem-solving process; the evaluation of ideas generated and the choice of the best idea to solve the problem.
specialization. The concentration of resources on just one task.
specific research. A type of research designed to gather specific information related to a clearly defined problem.
stable situation. A trend which shows no tendency to either grow or decline.
standardization. A single, uniform way of doing things.
startup costs. All of the expenses that are required to open for business.
startup phase. The period in which a venture first begins to operate.
stepping stone. An objective that can be achieved within a relatively short period of time as one works towards one's goal.
stock option plans. A means by which employees buy into a business by buying stock.
strategic plan. A forward-looking plan that maps out the means to achieve longer-term goals and plans a response to potential problems and opportunities.
surveys. A method of conducting marketing research that involves questioning potential users.
suppliers. Businesses and individuals who supply the resources needed by the producer to produce a particular good or service.
synchronization. The performance of a process using routine procedures.
table of contents. A listing of all the sections of venture plan, with page numbers.
target customer. The consumers who, it is hoped, will buy a specific product or service.

target date. A specified date for achieving one's goals.
target market. A market consisting of the consumers who, it is hoped, will buy a specific product or service.
tariff. A duty or tax on imported products.
task oriented. An emphasis on completing a specific job.
tax deductible. An expense that can be deducted from income and thus reduces the amount of income tax payable.
teddy bear. Used to describe a style of conflict that is typified by smoothing things over.
term. The duration or time established between the date money is borrowed and the date when it is to be paid back in full.
term loan. A loan that must be paid back in specified payments within a specific period of time.
time-series forecast. A method of forecasting that involves plotting a trend from the past to the present on a chart, making comparisons to other trends, and projecting it into the future.
title page. The opening page of a venture plan, giving the name of the venture, the names of the people proposing it, the date of transmittal, and a disclaimer.
total cost. A venture's total expenditures.
total profit. Total revenue minus total cost.
total revenue. The total income a venture receives from all sources.
trademark. A brand or part of a brand that is given legal protection; it can be used only by the seller who obtains the trademark.
trends. General directions in the process of change.
turtle. Used to describe a style of managing conflict that is typified by withdrawing.
under capitalization. The situation a venture is in if it does not have sufficient capital for startup and day-to-day operation of the business.
Unemployment Insurance. A plan to which both employers and employees contribute that provides income for unemployed workers.
unsecured loans. Loans that are not backed by any security or collateral.
variable costs. Costs that change directly with the amounts produced.
vendor's permit. A licence to sell given to a retailer from the Ministry of Revenue.
venture capital. Money that is invested into a startup or growing business.
Venture Creation Model. A model that helps to explain the entrepreneurial process.
Venture Creation Wheel. The process of venture creation described in terms of a bicycle wheel.
venture plan. A comprehensive written plan that describes how the entrepreneur plans to accomplish the specific task of starting a venture.
ventures. Entrepreneurial undertakings which satisfy needs and which change the way we live.
visualizing. A technique for exercising creativity that involves seeing, in one's mind, different scenarios.
want. Something that is desirable, but not essential.
Warrior. The character, as described by Roger von Oech, that puts ideas into action.
white hat. A mode of thinking, as described by Edward de Bono, that is concerned with gathering facts, figures, and objective information.
wholesaling. All the activities involved in selling goods or services to those who are buying for the purpose of resale or business use.
window of opportunity. The part of the market into which a new product or service will fit; that length of time when an unmet need continues to exist.
word clustering. A technique for exercising creativity that involves the free association of ideas and words.
word of mouth. The spreading of a company's reputation by one person telling another about his or her experiences with that company.
Workers' Compensation. A plan to which both employers and employees contribute that provides income for workers injured in the course of their employment.
working capital. Current assets minus current liabilities.

Index